T0003426

I am deeply grateful to David for this book, a compendium of his decades of research in the realms of scientific, historical, and biblical disciplines as they surround the doctrine of Creationism. He presents an honest, searching and thoroughly referenced view of one of the most important, but frequently ignored aspects of the Christian faith—the biblical account of creation. This is a SERIOUS work. It is not light reading. But it is compelling. It changed my belief. No longer does intellectual honesty require my halfhearted attempt at framing some "reasonable" reconciliation of the Bible with evolution. What I found in David's work has undergirded my already committed faith in the Bible as the record of God's plan and offer of salvation, now including the Bible's account of Creation. Thank you, David! I highly recommend this book to anyone with an open mind to the truth.

—**Dean Flemming,** Pastor and Christian Counselor
Fountain of Life Church
Hannibal, NY

Never before have I read a book that makes our world get larger and smaller at the same time. David Burdick easily links ancient history with our current times while remaining committed to the authenticity of the world's greatest book, The Holy Bible, all in layman's terminology. Such an excellent read. Great work, David!

—**Dan Woodard,** Leadership Development Facilitator
Action International Ministries
Carstairs, Alberta, Canada

Chariots of the Fallen is a profoundly dense collection of scientific, historical, and biblical discussions and information shedding illumination on topics such as: the flood, Nephilim, carbon dating, dinosaurs, UFOs, evolution, Masonic activity, satanism, and the Space Force, to name a few. The theories we've long accepted as hard science have been trialed by author David Burdick, as he puts our acquired assumptions to the test against biblical fact and history. By exposing fault lines in our thinking, Burdick cracks open a whole new world of logic and discovery. *Chariots of the Fallen* is a brilliant and fascinating read, even for those who have only a cursory grasp of the topics and questions that concern our modern world and thinking. Burdick's sound reasoning and remarkable ability to explain the seemingly unexplainable will challenge your thinking and no doubt bring you to a deeper revelation of God's truths, if you let it. He who has ears to hear . . . let him hear.

—**Reverend Lori Blackburn,** Senior Pastor
Fulton Foursquare Church
Fulton, NY

If you follow Jesus, love, and live life for God, *Chariots of the Fallen* is essential reading. This is not a light read. In fact, it is a book to contemplate. At this time in world history, I seek knowledge from those who can explain using facts. What I was taught as a child was wrong and unfounded, and the lies were unearthed by David in this book. David Burdick is the great debater who has created a treasure map to the truth. There are so many in our society that follow blindly like sheep because they are afraid and/or indolent. Seek the truth, stand up, and walk in the truth as Jesus did for us, the truth that has been brilliantly written by David.

—**Paula Gerry**
Retired Nuclear Professional
Pocasset, MA

Each chapter brought new information and caused reflection on currently held knowledge and beliefs. My formal education leading to degrees in Nursing involved several biologic science courses. I may have been introduced to Darwin's Theory of Evolution in high school but if so, I do not remember. However, the theory was discussed in the science courses of the Nursing curriculum. As a young child, my mother and grandmother read to me from Genesis, and I accepted the story of creation. I believed that all things were possible through God. Hence came the conflict in my thinking. Creationists stress the intelligent, planned beginnings enacted by God. Darwin's theory is based on adaptation and natural selection from simple one-cell organisms of the ancient seas to the fish, birds, animals, and man. From the chaos came life. Though I resolved this conflict by attempting to blend creationism with evolution, I have always had lingering doubts. After reading Mr. Burdick's discussion on radiocarbon dating, the geologic column, and the theory of evolution, I now have information that rejects the theory of evolution and realize that the theory was flawed from the beginning. This is only one example of how this book has impacted my thinking, but there are numerous others. Anyone reading this book will be provided with information that will no doubt cause their own introspection and reflection.

—**Bruce Elliott**
RN-MS, Retired VA Nurse
Batavia, NY

Chariots of the Fallen is enlightened, inspired, and inspiring to the reader. We have always been God-fearing people that love Jesus and regularly practice our faith. Still, we learned something new with each and every chapter: the good, the bad, and the ugly. The Word of God was evident and indisputable. *Chariots of the Fallen* provides sound answers to what had previously only been accepted by faith. It was a great read and we highly recommend it to all who seek to know the truth of God, creation, and the history of mankind.

—**Michael and Candace Gilligan**
Heavy Metal Thunder Custom Cycles
Oak Island, NC

CHARIOTS

OF THE FALLEN

A Biblically Founded
and
Scientifically Supported
CREATIONIST'S SURVIVAL GUIDE

David V. Burdick

Chariots of the Fallen: A Biblically Founded and Scientifically Supported Creationist's Survival Guide

Copyright © 2023 by David V. Burdick

Published by Deep River Books
Sisters, Oregon
www.deepriverbooks.com

All rights reserved. No part of this book may be reproduced or transmitted in any form or by any means, electronic or mechanical, including photocopying and recording, or by any information storage and retrieval system, without permission in writing from the publisher.

All Scripture quotations, unless otherwise indicated, are taken from the New King James Version®. Copyright © 1982 by Thomas Nelson. Used by permission. All rights reserved.

Scriptures marked "KJV" are taken from The Holy Bible, King James Version (Public Domain).

ISBN – 13: 9781632695949
Library of Congress Control Number: 2023905734

Printed in the USA
Cover design by Joe Bailen, Contajus Designs

TABLE OF CONTENTS

FOREWORD

When I was initially approached about writing a foreword for David Burdick's newest book, *Chariots of the Fallen*, I did not know what to expect in the book itself. I have not had the privilege of meeting David, and I was informed that he was not a "trained theologian." I am pleased to say without a doubt, David is indeed a theologian. In his book, David explains the reason for his faith, the basis for his hope. This theme of faith and hope permeates every chapter and virtually every paragraph in the book.

David sees the world equally from two perspectives: scientific and biblical. For many years David has been employed as a corrective actions program engineer and performance improvement mentor at over twenty nuclear power plants throughout the United States. His education and scientific training have given him much experience in logical critical thinking. As a trained engineer, when faced with a problem or concern, David has the God-given ability to remove layer after layer of the already known and drill deeper into the unknown until he discovers the biblical and scientific truth of the matter.

David knows God. He is a Christian-thought leader and thought provoker. He challenges us to understand what we believe and why we believe it. Additionally, *Chariots of the Fallen* will challenge the preconceived ideas for both the evolutionist and the creationist.

Every page in *Chariots of the Fallen* has been gracefully interwoven with science and Scripture. He confidently and repeatedly lays out the evidence that science consistently aligns with God's written Word. David's scientific and analytical mind helps bring a coherent and spiritual understanding to the science versus the Bible debate.

David's book reminds me of a television series from the 1960s called *Dragnet*. In the series, when faced with a crime that needed to be solved, Sergeant Joe Friday (one of the main characters) interviewed various witnesses and reminded them that he was interested in one thing only: "The Facts." David deals with facts in his book: facts from the Word of God and facts from proven science. He is a man of deep logic and common sense. He has crafted his flow of thoughts in a very candid, honest, straightforward manner. He shows us how easy it is for science to be in harmony with the Word of God.

I wish to echo David's own words to underscore both truth and sincerity:

> The hope of this book is to reconcile some of the conflicts introduced by acceptance of worldly explanations to complicated issues that often undermine or contradict the underpinnings of our Christian beliefs. The intent is to kindle a fire, a desire to explore alternate solutions, and question provided truths.

I encourage believers and skeptics everywhere to allow David's book *Chariots of the Fallen* to challenge your thinking and preconceived ideas that you as a reader may have about the Bible, about science, and about the world we live in today. As a Christ-follower, consider allowing this book on biblical logic to be another stepping stone toward your spiritual growth and maturity.

Daniel W. Bowers, PhD, DMin (Theology)
St. Adolphe, Manitoba, Canada

ACKNOWLEDGMENTS

Thank you Holy Father in Heaven, God who is with me always. Thank you for all that you have done, all that you currently do, and all that you will do. Your grace is abundant. All glory and honor are yours, my God, my Lord, your Spirit.

Coming to the head of the class, to my lovely wife and partner of so many years, I want you to know that your acts of love have not gone unnoticed. Your acts of love are much appreciated and your acts of innocence are cherished. I will forever remember the time I asked you if you were looking for your locket as you began to search through a couple of drawers, and you turned and shushed me with your finger over your lips, like it was our little secret that you were looking for your locket. It was too cute and something that only I could love. Your occasional demonstrations of innocence remind me of what the world has lost. You humble me with your defiance. Two brain surgeries and a fall later, you are still the apple of my eye.

Near to the top of the list, I want to thank the many men and women of God who came together in this effort to bring glory to God in the highest. You have taken the time to read the draft manuscript, provided your thoughts, written my endorsements, and penned the foreword. My Lord has caused me to cross paths with many men and women of God and I am thankful for knowing each one of them, for enjoying their fellowship, and for their witness. Be of good cheer, my brothers and sisters. The Holy Spirit of God lives within us.

No less principal to the success of this work, I need to thank my friends and neighbors who have also read the manuscript and provided their thoughts. Your encouragement along the way has propelled this manuscript to the finish line. You were the fuel that fed the car from start to finish. Thank you for your gift of something so rare in this world—a positive word. It is my godly pleasure to know and love you.

Hardly last on a very short list, I want to thank the readers of this book. If you are reading this book, it was written for you. If it opens your eyes to the possibility of biblical truths, causes you to question what you have been taught, strengthens your belief in creation, or simply brings you closer to God, you have helped me to honor Him and I am well pleased to be a part of that. All glory and honor are yours, Almighty Father, forever and ever, amen.

Lastly, I want to thank my son, who had absolutely nothing to do with the writing of this book. I do, and I have for a long time, respected you as a trustworthy, upright, and honorable man. There are only a handful of people in this world that I know well enough that I can say that about them. Mike, you honor your mother each day and lessen my burden. Thank you.

**This book is dedicated
to my beloved**

Ann E. Burdick

With Christ - 01/14/2022

1

APPLES AND ORANGES: SEPARATING FACT FROM FICTION

Working as a corrective actions program engineer and performance improvement mentor at nearly twenty nuclear power plants throughout the United States over the course of the last thirty years, I have determined the cause of numerous unwanted events and equipment malfunctions and instituted countless corrective actions to prevent recurrence. One thing that became apparent in my years of working as a cause analyst is that fifty people can look at the same evidence and group of facts to come up with fifty different reasons for the same end result. It takes a good logic path to bring everyone to the same conclusion.

That said, I must confess that I am admittedly biased. I am a man of hope and faith. I believe that since being expelled from the garden of Eden, we have been born with an emptiness that can only be filled with the peace that comes from a relationship with God the Father through Jesus Christ the Son. I admit this now because my bias will become evident throughout this book. Half a glass of water will always be found half full to a man of hope and faith. To put it another way, all things being equal, I'll choose God.

One of the most valuable lessons I learned in college came in one of my advanced mathematics courses by a professor that I am sure had no idea how impacting his exercise would become. It was in a pre-calculus course. As the students took their seats, the professor began copying a complex numbers problem onto the blackboard and told the class to copy the problem into their notes as he solved it. The problem contained mathematical limits and imaginary numbers. The professor explained each step that he took to solve the problem, every term he simplified, and every cancellation he made. The professor even answered questions as he worked his way through the equation. After thirty minutes, the professor wrapped things up by circling one half of the equation, then circling the other half of the equation and drawing a line across the width of the blackboard, from one circle to the other, to show the class that he had proven without a shadow of a doubt that one (1) equals zero (0). The assignment was to finish copying his work into our notes and to find the error in his logic over the weekend.

As I recall, it was a very difficult problem to solve and only about half of the class was able to find the error in the professor's logic, but everyone who tried learned something. What I learned was that only slightly flawed logic can be used to convincingly tell whatever story you want. Never take it for granted that just because a person in authority tells you something that they are telling you the God-actual truth.

I have a favorite short story that effortlessly demonstrates the power of misdirection through flawed logic. It is the story of three ladies who decided to share a room at a prominent hotel in Anytown, USA. The desk clerk, a new employee, tells the ladies that the room costs thirty dollars a night. Each lady gives the desk clerk a fresh ten-dollar bill. The desk clerk then takes their money, checks them in, and gives them their keys. As the women are heading up to their room, the manager who had overheard the entire transaction explains to the desk clerk that he has overcharged the ladies because that particular room is only twenty-five dollars a night. The desk clerk apologizes for his mistake and immediately summons the bellhop. The desk clerk explains to the bellhop how he has mistakenly overcharged the three ladies, gives him the five dollars, and asks him to return it to the ladies with his apology. On his way up to their room, the bellhop begins to wonder how he will split five dollars evenly between three women. He decides that it will be just as easy to refund each of the ladies just one dollar and to put the remaining two dollars in his own pocket. After returning the three dollars, each of the ladies who had originally paid out ten dollars were now out only nine dollars. Three times nine dollars is twenty-seven dollars, plus the two dollars, now in the bellhop's pocket equals twenty-nine dollars. Where is the other dollar that makes up the original thirty dollars that was paid at the front desk?

The point being, it is easy to be misled when lines are drawn to support your logic that shouldn't be there. Once you are confident that the lines between the subsets of your equations are correct, that you are comparing apples to apples to make conclusions about apples, it is also just as important to ensure that the subsets of your equations are correct before drawing a circle around them to support your proof. The truth is oftentimes elusive in a world where we rewrite our own history, science replaces understanding with definition, and the Word of God is distorted by non-believers.

Before drawing a circle around a historical fact to support your argument, consider that history is often rewritten to support our current understanding or lost when society is forced to start over. China's first emperor completely altered the nation's history by demanding the destruction of all philosophy and literature that hailed from regions that he had conquered. In 206 BC, the Xianyang Palace and State Archives of Xianyang, in Xianyang, China were destroyed and the scholars were put to death. More recently, the 2015 post-war destruction of the Mosul public library in Iraq resulted in the burning and obliteration of the collective memory of an almost five-thousand-year-old civilization. Libraries have been purposely destroyed as a form of cultural cleansing for as long as man has kept records.

Before drawing a circle around science to support your proof, remember that science sometimes answers the how, but never answers the why. When contemplating the grand unification of nature's laws, theoretical physicist Stephen Hawking was quoted as saying, "Even if there is only one possible unified theory, it is just a set of rules and questions. What is it that breaths fire into the equations and makes the universe for them to describe? . . . a mathematical model cannot answer the questions of why there should be a universe for the model to describe."[1]

Even when using the Bible to support your thesis, before you hang your hat on Scripture, it is essential that you verify your source and ensure that your arguments are not taken out of context. If you believe that, "God helps those who help themselves," your faith is misplaced. These are the words of Ben Franklin, not God. Adam and Eve did not eat an apple in the garden of Eden (Genesis 3:5-6), not all the animals went into the ark two by two (Genesis 7:2-3), and the Ten Commandments are not described or listed as such anywhere in the Bible; rather, they are derived from a list of thirteen proclamations (Exodus 20:3-5, 7-10, 12-17).

Unlike carbon dating or evolution that are touted as exact science and absolute truth, this book will present theories, ideas, and concepts based on scientific principles and the biblical record. The hope of this book is to reconcile some of the conflicts introduced by acceptance of worldly explanations to complicated issues that often undermine or contradict the underpinnings of our Christian beliefs. The intent is to kindle a fire, a desire to explore alternate solutions, and question provided truths.

2

EAST MEETS WEST:
CIRCUMNAVIGATING A FLAT EARTH

To demonstrate how easily we can be misled by people in positions of authority with no factual basis or supporting evidence, I've chosen to begin the discussion with a concept that most of us should be able to agree on. The planet Earth is shaped like a ball and the church was misguided in their medieval declaration of the flat-Earth theory. People with only minimal exposure to planetary science concepts today recognize that the earth is round. To be more specific, the earth is spherical. From the first aerial circumnavigation of the planet in 1924, to the first "blue marble" photographs taken from the Lunar Orbiter 1 spacecraft in 1966, few can argue that science has not overwhelmingly proven this to be true.

If you are a part of my generation, you were no doubt taught in elementary school that Christopher Columbus was the first to conceive that the earth might be round. Everyone but Columbus believed that the earth was flat and, like a pea rolling off your plate, ships risked sailing over the edge of the earth. Though an enduring story, the concept of Christopher Columbus being the first to conceive of a spherical-shaped planet Earth is in fact a myth. The earliest documented mention of a spherical-shaped planet Earth is attributed to the ancient Greek philosopher Pythagoras and dates from around the sixth century BC when a spherical-shaped planet Earth was first contemplated in Greek philosophy. In the days of Christopher Columbus, more than two thousand years after the life of Pythagoras, the Catholic Church characterized the earth as a flat disc under an atmospheric dome.

The concept of a spherical-shaped planet Earth remained a matter of speculation for hundreds of years. Credit for proof of the earth's sphericity was achieved through Hellenistic astronomy and is most commonly attributed to Aristotle in the third century BC. The model of a spherical-shaped planet Earth was gradually adopted during Late Antiquity and the Middle Ages. A practical demonstration and final proof of the earth's sphericity was achieved when Ferdinand Magellan and Juan Sebastian Elcano sailed around the world (1519-1522). This was seventeen years after the purported discovery of America by Columbus.

Together, these facts provide confirmation that the flat-Earth theory and the round-Earth theory coexisted at the time Christopher Columbus was sailing to America. Unfortunately, what people thought and what people were allowed to openly discuss in 1492 were very different. Beginning in 1231, a group of institutions within the government of the Catholic Church established a judicial procedure and later an institution known as the Medieval or Roman Inquisition to combat heresy. The Catholic Church believed that God created the earth at the center of the universe and all other celestial bodies revolved around the earth. Additionally, they imagined a three-part world, with the heavens above, the flat earth in the middle, and the underworld below. To proclaim anything else was heresy.

To be accused of heretical depravity by the Inquisitors was a serious matter. Best known for his theories of the cosmos, Giordano Bruno (born Filippo Bruno in 1548), was an Italian Dominican friar, philosopher, mathematician, poet, and cosmological theorist. Bruno proposed that the stars were distant suns surrounded by their own planets. He even went so far as to suggest that these distant planets might foster life, a philosophical position known as cosmic pluralism. He was adamant that the universe is infinite and could have no celestial body at its center. In 1593, seventy years after Magellan's voyage and one hundred years after Columbus, Bruno was tried for heresy by the Roman Inquisition and charged with denial of several core Catholic doctrines. The Inquisition found him guilty and burned him at the stake in 1600. Historians debate the extent to which his heresy trial was in response to his astronomical views or other aspects of his theology. Either way, views of a spherical-shaped planet Earth were best kept to yourself during the Inquisition. Today, the trial of Giordano Bruno is considered a landmark case in the struggle for free thought and emerging sciences. The last execution sanctioned by the Inquisition did not take place until 1826.

A surviving letter from future Pope Pius II acknowledges knowing of up to 180 copies of the Vulgate (Gutenberg Bible) having been printed in 1455. Despite the invention of the printing press and modern movable type by Johannes Gutenberg in 1439, very few people had access to a Bible or the inclination to oppose the Catholic Church in 1492.

Notwithstanding, despite the multitudes of people who doubt that the words of the Torah and/or the Gospels are the inspired words of God, few argue that the books have not been around since the first days of the modern AD calendar. The age of the New Testament has been proven to the extent possible with carbon dating of the Dead Sea Scrolls. The Torah is calculated by genealogies to be nearly 1300 years older than the Gospels and was known to be studied by the rabbis, Pharisees, and Sadducees that were around at the time of Christ. The irony is that fifteenth- century families would have needed to have had a family Bible, seen that Bible as a legitimate historical record, and possessed an extensive understanding of English, Hebrew, and Greek for the flat-Earth theory to have been overturned any sooner than it was.

As Job explains it, God ". . . drew a circular horizon on the face of the waters, at the boundary of light and darkness" (Job 26:10 KJV). Solomon describes the creation of the earth as, God ". . . drew a circle (substitute sphere) on the face of the deep" (Proverbs 8:27 KJV) and the prophet Isaiah said, "It is He who sits above the circle (substitute sphere) of the earth, and its inhabitants are like grasshoppers, who stretches out the heavens like a curtain, and spreads them out like a tent to dwell in" (Isaiah 40:22 KJV).

To be clear, the English word "circle" is not the word actually spoken by Solomon or Isaiah in Proverbs 8:27 or Isaiah 40:22. Appearing in the Old Testament Hebrew Lexicon, the word (chuwg) is translated by the Strong's Hebrew Dictionary (Strong's Number 02329) to be circle, circuit, compass (BDB) vault (of the heavens). The word origin, "circular" (Strong's Number 02328) appears only once in the KJV Bible (Job 26:10) and clearly refers to the concept of an encompassing circuit or sphere.[2]

Interestingly enough, after drafting this chapter and soliciting a few friends for comment, it was brought to my attention that there is indeed a group of Christians who take the Bible very literally and, to this day, believe that the planet is flat. Their beliefs are not founded in science; rather, they are based on a literal interpretation of a few Bible verses where extreme distances and quadrants are described as the corners of the earth. Isaiah 11:12 says, "He will set up a banner for the nations, and will assemble the outcasts of Israel, and gather together the dispersed of Judah from the four corners (substitute extremities) of the earth," and Ezekiel 7:2 reads, "And you, son of man, thus says the Lord God to the land of Israel: 'An end! The end has come upon the four corners (substitute extremities) of the land.'" See also Revelation 7:1 which reads, "After these things I saw four angels standing at the four corners (substitute quadrants) of the earth, holding the four winds of the earth, that the wind should not blow on the earth, on the sea, or on any tree . . ." and Revelation 20:7-8 which reads, "Now when the thousand years have expired, Satan will be released from prison and will go out to deceive the nations which are in the four corners (substitute quadrants) of the earth, Gog and Magog, to gather them together to battle, whose number is as the sand of the sea."

The KJV Bible usage of the word "corner" in Isaiah 11:12 and Ezekiel 7:2 is translated from the Hebrew word (kanaph) and from the Greek word (gonia) in Revelation 7:1 and 20:7-8. Kanaph is translated in many ways; however, it generally means extremity and gonia literally means angles or divisions. It is customary to divide a map into quadrants as shown by the four directions. Certainly, if God had literally intended to refer to an actual corner, he would have used the Hebrew word (paioh) which means "geometric corner," (ziovyoh) which translates to "right angle" or "corner," or (krnouth) which refers to a "projected corner."

To take it just a bit further, I believe that, "the four corners of the earth" is a generalization used to describe the concept of far distances. To support this interpretation, I offer Jeremiah 9:25-26 where the prophet reports, ". . . all who are in the farthest corners, who dwell in the wilderness," and Jeremiah 25:23-26 where God refers to, ". . . all who are in the farthest corners, all the kings of Arabia . . . all the kings of Elam, and all the kings of Medes; all the kings of the north, far and near, one with another; and all the kingdoms of the world which are on the face of the earth." Consider that "the farthest corners" cannot be both "in the wilderness" and ". . . all the kingdoms of the world which are on the face of the earth" at the same time, unless it is a generalization used to describe the concept of extreme distances.

Lastly, for those who take each word of the Bible literally and allow for no consideration of alternative thought, I acknowledge that following creation and prior to the scientifically supported separation of land masses, the known earth was for all intents and purposes a single land mass that no doubt had four theoretical corners or extremes. "To Eber were born two sons: the name of one was Peleg, for in his days the earth was divided" (Genesis 10:25).

Wow, I seem to be tossing a lot of Bible quotes around like they are indisputable facts. Perhaps now would be an appropriate time to provide an argument for the use of the Bible as a historical record and to acknowledge what are admittedly the limitations of doing so. First, God does occasionally make generalizations and speak in symbols for concepts that the human mind might otherwise have difficulty understanding. These things are best taken on faith and can seldom be verified without physical evidence such as circumnavigating a spherical-shaped planet Earth or witnessing the fulfillment of prophesy. Consider the recapture of Jerusalem following the Six-Day War in 1967 (Zechariah 8:7-8; 520/518 BC), or the worldwide return of the Jews to Israel starting in the late 1900s (Isaiah 43:5-6; 701-681 BC). By the grace of God, those seeking to find truth in the Word of God will discover that numerous historical predictions of Christ's first coming have already come to pass. Consider Genesis 49:10, Isaiah 7:14, Isaiah 11:1-10, Jeremiah 23:5, and Micah 5:2.

To be honest, I chose to discuss the flat-Earth theory first because it seemed a good opportunity to introduce the KJV Bible as a historic record. There are admittedly many limitations to using the Bible as a historic record. Beginning with the calculations of Archbishop James Ussher who determined through genealogies that Adam and Eve were expelled from the garden of Eden in 4004 BC, most fix the date of the expulsion at approximately 6000 years ago. That said, the expulsion of Adam and Eve is the start of recorded history and not the beginning of the world. The Bible says very little about what happened outside of the garden of Eden prior to the expulsion and for the most part, its historical content is limited to Assyria and the surrounding lands of the ancient Near East. This is an important concept necessary to fully grasp before going into deeper concepts based on this premise. To fully embrace this concept may change your existing understanding of the Bible. Consider that although known to be populated at the time, the Bible makes no reference to what was taking place in North America, South America, Australia, Greenland, Japan, Ireland, Sweden, or Hawaii. Christianity was born in the ancient Near East and spread to the rest of the world from there. The Bible does however provide a basis for concluding that recorded history and time itself began with the expulsion.

To see the correlation between the expulsion and recorded time, we must first acknowledge that Adam and Eve were created to live forever. The basis for this conclusion is in Genesis 2:9, "And out of the ground made the Lord God to grow every tree that is pleasant to the sight, and good for food; the tree of life also in the midst of the garden," and Genesis 2:16-17, "And the Lord God commanded the man, saying, 'Of every tree of the garden you may freely eat; but of the tree of the knowledge of good and evil you shall not eat, for in the day that you eat of it you shall surely die.'" Being free to eat of the tree of life implies being created to live forever.

The basis for concluding that the biblical clock and recorded history started when Adam and Eve were cast out of the garden is in Genesis 2:17 (KJV), where God said, "But of the tree of the knowledge of good and evil, thou shalt not eat of it: for in the day that thou eatest thereof thou shalt surely die"; Genesis 5:5 (KJV), which tells us, "All the days Adam lived were nine hundred and thirty years"; and 2 Peter 3:8 (KJV), where we learn, "Be not ignorant of this one thing, that one day is with the Lord as a thousand years, and a thousand years is as one day." Being created to live forever, Adam only began to die when he ate of the tree of the knowledge of good and evil and was cast out of the garden. The Bible gives us no indication of how long Adam and Eve were in the garden before they were expelled. They could have lived for millennia in the garden before being cast out. As God said, Adam died that day—within a thousand years. This is where biblical time began, the first 930 years of biblical history. The age of Adam and other historical figures of the Old Testament will be explored later.

We know that man already existed outside of the garden because of Genesis 4:15-17 (KJV): "And the Lord set a mark upon Cain, lest any finding him should kill him. Then Cain went out from the presence of the Lord, and dwelt in the land of Nod, on the east of Eden. And Cain knew his wife: and she conceived and bore Enoch." From Genesis 4:1-2, we know that the only people that the Bible accounts for up to this point in time are Adam, Eve, Cain, and Abel. Who are the people who would find Cain and kill him? What is the existing land of Nod? Who is Cain's wife and where does she come from? The Bible is silent on these matters, as it is in all matters outside of the garden prior to the expulsion of Adam and Eve.

Now knowing some of the limitations of the Bible and having a basis for considering it as a historical record, we should examine the accuracy of the record to determine how much faith we can justify putting into it. To this day, archaeologists are continually uncovering previously unproven biblical sites and supporting artifacts. The Associates for Biblical Research announced "The Discovery of the Sin Cities of Sodom and Gomorrah."[3] When the archaeological, geographical, and epigraphic evidence is reviewed in detail, it is clear that the infamous cities of Sodom and Gomorrah have now been found. What is more, this evidence demonstrates that the Bible provides an accurate eyewitness account of events that occurred southeast of the Dead Sea over four thousand years ago. Across the site, archaeologists found evidence of a fiery destruction, layers of ash, and tumbled walls.

As recently as August of 2017, archaeologists announced that they have located the lost biblical city of Bethsaida-Julias which was the home of three of Jesus's apostles. The lost city of Julias, formally Bethsaida, was uncovered during excavations at el-Arai on the northern shore of the Sea of Galilee by archaeologists from the Kinneret Institute for Galilean Archaeology at Kinneret College, Israel and Nyack College in New York. Julias is believed to have been built around the year AD 30, on the ruins of Bethsaida. In the New Testament, Bethsaida is credited with being the home to Jesus's apostles Peter, Andrew, and Philip (John 1:44). The Gospel of Mark also recognizes Jesus as having healed a blind man at Bethsaida (Mark 8:22). Celebrated New Testament scholar, William Hendriksen believed that the miraculous feeding of the five thousand, also known as the "miracle of the five loaves and two fish" took place near Bethsaida-Julias (Luke 9:10). Archaeologists note that Saint Willibald, a German bishop who visited the Holy Land in the year AD 725, communicated that he visited a church at Bethsaida that was built over the remains of the houses of the apostles Peter and Andrew. It may well be that the current excavations have unearthed evidence for that church.

Sometimes a great discovery comes in the form of a single relic or stone tablet. The Pilate Stone is the name given to a damaged block of carved limestone (dating from 26–AD 36) that was uncovered in an archaeological site at Caesarea, on the Mediterranean coast in 1961. The tablet bears an inscription mentioning Pontius Pilate the procurator of Judea, and a structure built in honor of the Emperor Tiberius by Pilate. Prior to the discovery of the Pilate Stone, there had been much written to discredit the biblical narrative in regard to the existence of Pontius Pilate. The Pilate Stone clearly states that the structure was from "Pontius Pilate, Prefect of Judea" and verifies that he was a person that lived during the time of Jesus, exactly as written in the biblical narrative.

Few modern biblical archaeological discoveries have caused as much excitement as the Tel Dan inscription, a writing on a ninth-century BC stone slab that furnished the first historical reference to the Davidic dynasty and the biblical King David outside of the Bible. The Tel Dan inscription, or "House of David" inscription, was discovered in 1993 at the site of Tel Dan in northern Israel at an excavation directed by Israeli archaeologist Avraham Biran. Written and translated from Aramaic, the inscription commemorates the victory of an unnamed Aramean king over his two southern neighbors: the "king of Israel" and the "king of the House of David." It is believed to have been erected by the king of Aram, which is present-day Syria (2 Chronicles 22). What makes the Tel Dan inscription one of the most exciting biblical archaeological discoveries is its unprecedented reference to the "House of David," proving once and for all that the biblical King David was a genuine historical figure, not simply a literary creation by biblical editors. Perhaps equally as important, the Tel Dan inscription was created by one of Israel's fiercest enemies more than a century after David's death and still recognized David as the founder of the kingdom of Judah.

On occasion, new technology contradicts old science and proves once and for all that what was once considered irrefutable proof of a biblical inaccuracy is, in fact, proof that the biblical record is correct. A prime example of this is the availability of sufficient water to flood the entire earth. Prior to June of 2014 and contrary to Genesis 7:17-20, science was unbending in their declaration that even with the melting of the polar caps, there is not enough water on the planet to cover all the mountains of the earth.

In June of 2014, LiveScience.com posted an article written by Joseph Castro entitled, "Found! Hidden Ocean Locked Up Deep in Earth's Mantle."[4] New research shows that, "Deep within the Earth's rocky mantle lies oceans' worth of water locked up in a type of mineral called ringwoodite." Scientists have apparently, "long suspected that the mantle's so-called transition zone, which sits between the upper and lower mantle layers 255 to 410 miles below the Earth's surface, could contain water trapped in rare minerals. However, direct evidence for this water has been lacking, until now." To verify the presence of a water-rich ringwoodite reservoir in the transition zone, researchers analyzed seismic waves traveling through the mantle beneath the United States. What they discovered was that "downward flowing mantle material is melting as it crosses the boundary between the transition zone and the lower mantle layer." Brandon Schmandt, a seismologist at the University of New Mexico and coauthor of the referenced study published on June 12, 2014, in the Journal Science said, "If we are seeing this melting, then there has to be water in the transition zone."[5] Brandon went on to explain, "The transition zone can hold a lot of water, and could potentially have the same amount of H_2O [water] as all the world's oceans."

Surely, one of the greatest archaeological discoveries, if not the greatest archaeological discovery of the twentieth century was the discovery of the Dead Sea Scrolls in 1947 by a Bedouin goat herder named Juma in a cave overlooking the Dead Sea at Qumran. In the days following, and with the help of his cousins, Khalil and Muhammed, Juma removed what would come to be recognized as the greatest manuscript treasure ever found—the first seven manuscripts of the Dead Sea Scrolls. This was the discovery of a group of manuscripts which were a thousand years older than the then-oldest Hebrew texts of the Bible. Between 1949 and 1956, archaeologists and other Bedouin found an additional ten caves that yielded additional scrolls, as well as thousands of fragments of scrolls: the remnants of approximately eight hundred manuscripts dating from approximately 200 BC to AD 68.

Even older than the Dead Sea Scrolls are the silver scroll-shaped amulets that were discovered in 1979, in Chamber 25 of Cave 24 at Ketef Hinnom during excavations being supervised by Gabriel Barkay, professor of archaeology at Tel Aviv University. The two tiny silver scrolls were inscribed with portions of a well-known priestly blessing from the Book of Numbers and found in a rock-hewn burial chamber. Following their discovery, it took another three years to develop a process to unroll the scrolls without damaging them. The scrolls have since been dated to between the late seventh and early sixth century BC and are now known to contain what may be the oldest surviving texts from the Hebrew Bible.

As you decide how much faith you can justify putting into the Bible as a legitimate historical record, consider that other than the written language used in a particular manuscript, there is not one historical inconsistency between the KJV Bible and the over two-thousand-year-old Dead Sea Scrolls. One supports the other.

As it pertains to the content of this book, I intend to use the books of the New King James Bible, the King James Bible (KJV noted when used), and the Book of Enoch as factual historic records to support my arguments. Ignoring the biblical canon to this point, I am forced to bring it up now just briefly to justify using the Book of Enoch as an additional historic record. The term "canon" is used to describe the books that were determined to be divinely inspired. These canons were developed through debate and agreement on the part of the religious authorities of their respective faiths and denominations. These decisions were made by more learned men than myself and I have no intention of debating their validity here.

The Book of Enoch is referred to supportively in the writings of Irenaeus, Clement, Tertullian, Athenagoras, Tatian, Lactantius, Methodius, Minucius Felix, Commodianus, and Ambrose. Just as Enoch described his book as, "not for this generation, but for a remote one which is to come" (Enoch 1:1), the Book of Enoch has passed through several phases in its process of sequestration and reemergence. The Book of Enoch was in wide circulation until shortly after the ministry of Christ. Despite its evident popularity, having been viewed as one of the sacred Scriptures and being quoted in many other books, Jewish leadership decided rightly or wrongly upon a strict canon that eliminated the Book of Enoch and several other books. The discovery of the Dead Sea Scrolls has shown that prior to that decision, the Jews had been more willing to consider other writings as Scripture and they'd had a special interest in the Book of Enoch in particular. The discovery of the Falasha Jewish community of Ethiopia (1773), which had lost contact with the rest of the Jewish world before the birth of the Christian era, has borne this out; the Old Testament of these Jews still includes the Book of Enoch.

The fact that Enoch would say his book was not for his own generation makes complete sense when you consider that those living in Enoch's day heard the preaching of Enoch first hand. On the other hand, Enoch's words in written form, have become a kind of time capsule for a later generation which, by all indications, is this generation. The Book of Enoch was forbidden by the Council of Laodicea in the fourth century AD and later pushed into further obscurity by Augustine who was heavily influenced by Neoplatonic philosophy. Ultimately, the Book of Enoch was removed from the accumulated libraries of the churches of the Mediterranean world. Until the discovery of the Dead Sea Scrolls, only the isolated Ethiopian Jews and perhaps a handful of scholars were even aware that the Book of Enoch still existed. Enoch's book was hidden for a period of at least twelve hundred years.

Any doubts that the Ethiopic Enoch was the same as the one quoted in the New Testament were put to rest in the 1950s with the discovery of the Dead Sea Scrolls. Fragments from seven copies of Enoch in Aramaic were discovered, along with three copies in Greek. These fragments have since been used to authenticate the Ethiopic translation of Enoch. Unlike many books removed by canon that were written hundreds of years after the life of Christ, fragments from the Dead Sea Scrolls have dated copies of the Book of Enoch to two centuries before Christ. Also, unlike other removed books that were said to contradict portions of the

Bible, the Book of Enoch supports the Bible with additional detail to the Book of Genesis. Since the 1990s, the text of the Book of Enoch has been freely available on the internet and potentially available to people living anywhere on the planet. It would appear that against all the odds, Enoch's prophecy concerning the future ministry of his book is in the process of being realized.

The only long-term candle-bearers for the Book of Enoch were the Ethiopian Jews who brought it with them when they fled Israel's northern kingdom nearly 800 years before Christ. That makes the Book of Enoch verifiably over 2800 years old. The fact that the Book of Enoch was removed from the Torah through Jewish canon is not that significant when you consider how important Enoch was to God. Together with Elijah (2 Kings 2:11), Enoch was one of only two of God's prophets that He took directly to heaven from earth without passing through death (Genesis 5:24). Further evidence of the historical record contained in the Book of Enoch is detailed in Chapter 7.

At this point, I have provided you (the reader) with verifiable evidence that the Bible and the Book of Enoch are accurate historical records of man's existence in the ancient Near East. The body of proof presented is more than was ever provided when you were asked to believe that Columbus was the first to discover America. I offer the December 10, 2015, authentication of the Kensington Rune Stone, dated 1362, as proof that Columbus was not the first to discover America. The Kensington Rune Stone was discovered in the roots of a tree near the settlement of Kensington, Minnesota, by Olof Ohman in 1898. The inscription purports to be a recorded North American land claim left behind by Scandinavian explorers in 1362. On December 10, 2005, the Kensington Rune Stone was authenticated by Scott F. Wolter, geologist, principal petrographer in more than five thousand investigations, and President of American Petrographic Services.

Just as I believe that balance can only be found at a point between the extreme left and the extreme right, I believe that faith resides at a point between chance and extreme science. I believe that the Bible, and in particular, the KJV Bible and the Book of Enoch are accurate historical records of man's existence in the ancient Near East from the time of Adam and Eve's expulsion (approximately 4004 BC) to when the Gospels and the Acts of the Apostles were written (approximately AD 70). Based on fulfilled prophesies, the improbability of things foretold, and blind faith rewarded by answered prayer, I also believe that the Bible is the inspired Word of God. To ponder alternate solutions to those provided for many of life's greatest mysteries, I ask that non-believers suspend their disbelief just long enough to consider the possibilities.

— 3 —

WATER-WORLD:
LIVING UNDER A RAINBOW

In the last chapter, we learned about a hidden ocean of water locked up deep in the earth's mantle, in a mineral called ringwoodite. Even before the confirmation of the ringwoodite reservoir, the geological model of the earth's interior that children have been taught in elementary school (even to this day) has been proven to be profoundly incorrect with the drilling of the Kola Superdeep Borehole in northwestern Russia (1970-1992). Competing with the United States and seeking to discover the true makeup of the earth's crust, it took Russia two decades to drill the world's deepest man-made hole. After thirteen years, the Kola Superdeep Borehole reached a hard-stop at a depth of 12 km. In the following nine years, they were able to gain only another 262 meters for a final depth of 12.262 km, 7.6 miles. To put this into perspective, the deepest point in the ocean is only 11 km, 6.8 miles deep. Contrary to the geological model that tells us that the deeper we go into the earth's crust, the denser and less porous the rocks will become, rocks were found to be cracked and riddled with numerous pores that showed water solutions flowing freely for the entire twelve-kilometer hole depth. Scientists surmise that the water is created by extreme pressures that squeeze hydrogen and oxygen from rock crystals. Beyond twelve km, drilling the earth's crust was described as going from drilling rock to drilling a plastic slurry. Translated to English, the official Russian website for the Kola Superdeep Borehole says, "We pretty much knew and understood at once how little we still know about the structure of the planet."

With the surprising results of the Kola Superdeep Borehole and the discovery of the ringwoodite reservoir, let us assume for the moment that perhaps there is enough water on the planet to support a great flood that covered all the mountains of the earth (Genesis 7:20) when the fountains of the deep were broken up, and the windows of heaven were opened (Genesis 7:11). The obvious next question then becomes, if there was a great flood that covered the entire earth, where is all of the verifiable evidence? The answer is, there is more evidence to support a great flood than there is evidence to dispute it. The problem, of course, is that most of us wouldn't recognize the evidence if we stumbled over it. Not unlike the flawed geological model of the earth's interior, unsubstantiated theories have been provided as facts to support what would otherwise be impossible to explain without acceptance of the biblical record.

Originally appearing in a 1987 *New York Times* article entitled "Whale Fossils High in the Andes Show How Mountains Rose from Sea," Malcolm W. Browne documented an American Museum of Natural History–sponsored expedition to recover fossilized whale bones from a remote bluff, five thousand feet above sea level in the Andes Mountains. The discovery went relatively unnoticed because the location of the whale bones was attributed to plate tectonics and proof that the Andes rose from the sea floor, not breaking news supporting the existence of a biblical flood. We are told that the time it took for the fossils to rise from the ocean floor to their mountain deposit was relatively short in geological terms, fifteen to twenty million years. According to the leader of the expedition, Dr. Michael J. Novacek, "Nearly all of the fossils were embedded in surface rock and easy to pick up. . . . Best of all, despite weathering, many of the smallest fossils were remarkably intact and will be relatively easy to study." Identified fossils included both sea and land animals and the transition from oceanic to terrestrial environments was preserved in a smooth gradient. In addition to the whale bones, the expedition found species related to modern rodents, porcupines, rhinoceroses, and camels. Dr. Novacek was quoted as saying, "We found the oyster beds and sand dollars just beneath the lowest sediments containing land animals. At that point the water was shallow and receding rapidly—a time of transition from sea to land, as the land was thrust up by magma and the movement of tectonic plates."[6]

Whether the fossils are attributed to the receding waters from a rising land mass or the naturally receding waters of a great flood, it's worth noting that the evidence left behind would appear much the same. Plate tectonics may adequately account for the dead marine life, but it provides little explanation for the numerous dead land-dwelling mammals. As I consider plate tectonics, I recall the Kola Superdeep Borehole and how little we really know about the planet's interior. How do scientists know these things? How are they able to draw conclusions from something they've never witnessed and call it a fact? The theory of plate tectonics persists as the singular explanation for dry land deposits of marine fossil because it is a convenient alternative to the biblical record and it cannot be disproven any more than it can be proven. Consider the Lake Titicaca sea horses that are found only in the world's oceans and Lake Titicaca. Also located in the Andes, Lake Titicaca is the highest navigable fresh water lake in the world at an elevation of over 12,500 feet above sea level. Plate tectonics cannot account for the Lake Titicaca sea horses; only a flood of biblical proportion can account for the presence of these rare sea horses.

Surrounded by various myths and legends, Lake Titicaca has long been the source of much fascination. While the Incas, who are given credit for building Machu Picchu, believed that all civilization originated from Lake Titicaca, home to the sunken city of Wanaku that was submerged by a great flood, there is no doubt that the legend of lost Inca gold has been the impetus for the majority of exploration. It was, however, stories of both that drew French oceanographer Jacques Cousteau to explore Lake Titicaca in the 1960s. Unfortunately, Jacques Cousteau's only discovery was a bit of ancient pottery. It wasn't until nearly forty years later, in 2000, that the international scientific group Akakor Geographical Exploring launched the "Atahualpa 2000" expedition that ultimately discovered an underwater temple and ruins. The pre-Incan ruins are attributed to the indigenous Tiwanaku and include a terrace for crops and a 2600-foot-long wall. The holy temple measures 660 feet by 160 feet and was found by following a submerged road. The sunken city of Wanaku is still to be discovered.

Lake Titicaca is 120 miles long by 50 miles wide and 920 feet deep. The lake is fed by over two-dozen fresh water rivers, the largest being the Ramis River that drains about two-fifths of the Titicaca Basin; and yet, the water is brackish enough to support the Titicaca seahorse. Jacques Cousteau, who had imagined Titicaca to be teeming with fish, was surprised to find an actual scarcity of fish. These facts, combined with the discovery of submerged ruins in a lake located 12,500 feet above sea level, should provide sufficient contradiction to consider the possibility of a worldwide flood.

There is no limit to the number of fossilized marine life deposits that have been attributed to shifting plate tectonics. Shifting plate tectonics, separation of continents, and the raising of mountains from the sea floor are absolutely a fact of our planetary development. Likewise, the fact is that many of the sedimentary layers of fossilized marine life are so thick that it is simply inconceivable to consider that they could have been deposited by only four-hundred-plus days of biblical flood waters (Genesis 7:11, 8:13-14). The top 3000 feet of Mount Everest (26,000-29,000 feet) is made up of sedimentary rock packed with seashells and other ocean dwelling animals. Science tells us that these fossils are the remains of a 30- to 50-million-year-old collision between the Indian subcontinental plate and the Eurasian continental plate that pushed the floor of the ancient Tethys Sea to the top of the world's highest peak. I confess that there is probably no greater explanation for a 3000-foot layer of sedimentary marine life on the top of Mount Everest than the collision of tectonic plates. What I question is the when and how of plate tectonics.

Belief in the biblical record and a worldwide flood does not automatically rule out acceptance of plate tectonics; it simply puts it in a different perspective. Insight into plate tectonics and the early world after the great flood is found in one obscure and generally overlooked Bible passage. Genesis 10:25 tells us, "To Eber were born two sons: the name of one was Peleg, for in his days the earth was divided." Biblical scholars interpret this passage to describe a time when God supernaturally separated the continents one from another. The Bible says that Peleg, which means to divide, was born 100 years after the flood and lived for 239 years. The time frame for the continental split would therefore have been from 100 years after the flood (4200 years ago) until 339 years after the flood. The division is said to have taken place during his lifetime but doesn't say how long it took.

As a young boy, I fancied myself an amateur geologist and I had several dresser drawers full of rocks to prove it. I was probably seven or eight years old when I dug up a small piece of crumbly sandstone in the sandpit located through the woods and behind my father's house. The rock was made up of fossilized sea creatures and shell types that I had never seen before. It was a great discovery for a little boy and I thought about that rock for several days. Long before I had ever heard of plate tectonics, I had heard of Noah's ark. I looked out over the farmer's fields beyond the sandpit and imagined them being under thousands of feet of water. It was a wondrous time, not clouded by scientific explanation. I was in Silver Springs, New York, hundreds of miles from the Catskill Mountains and the Adirondacks and 450 miles inland from the Atlantic Ocean.

There is a reason that most people are not aware of the many scientific and geographic arguments that support the validity of a worldwide flood. Few Christians would dispute the fact that we live in an egocentric world that elevates man's intellect, evolution, and chance above God's intelligent design. Due to a culturally driven closed-mindedness and unwillingness to accept an opposing view, political correctness is used today as a weapon to discriminate against any thought that contradicts the accepted norm.

The many are controlled by the few, evil is masked as carbon dating, and acceptance of evolution abounds.

On sale in the Grand Canyon's bookstores for just a few months, the controversial *Grand Canyon: A Different View* quickly ruffled the feathers of multiple scientific organizations, whose presidents jointly signed a December 6, 2003 letter to the park's superintendent urging him to remove the book. On January 14, 2004, the news service WorldNetDaily.com (WND) reported that they had received over two thousand emails attempting to ban the non-evolutionist book from the Grand Canyon bookstores. On Wednesday, March 24, 2004, CNN reported that the National Park Service in Washington, DC was preparing to draft a letter telling Grand Canyon administrators the book makes claims that fall outside accepted science . . . so it likely won't be restocked. Meanwhile, the *Los Angeles Times* reported that a compromise was being contemplated: the book may be moved from the natural sciences section of the bookstore to an "inspirational" one (which would thus downplay the book's legitimate scientific message). The Grand Canyon bookstore that sparked this controversy ultimately won the right to stock the book when it was proven that the store location was founded by a group of nuns; however, I have to wonder how many similar complaints and lawsuits were lost and how many books disappeared to obscurity.

Grand Canyon: A Different View by Tom Vail is a collection of striking photographs and essays written by twenty-three well-known leaders within the creationist community. They reject the evolutionist view that the canyon was carved by the slow erosion of the Colorado River over millions of years; instead, these scholars present the case that the Grand Canyon was formed by a lot of water over a relatively short period of time. The majority of the book's contributors have doctorate degrees in science, and several of them have conducted serious geological research at the canyon. Ken Ham, one of the book's essayists and president of Answers in Genesis (AIG), argued, "Since the book shares the conclusion of most canyon geologists—whether creationist or evolutionist—that most of the canyon was created in a relatively short period of time, why then shouldn't its visitors be exposed to this view?"[7]

It is no secret that the evidence left behind by the birth of the Grand Canyon overwhelmingly supports creation by rapid flooding over gradual erosion. The top of the Grand Canyon is over four thousand feet higher than where the Colorado River enters the canyon, meaning that the river would have had to flow uphill for millions of years to carve out the canyon through erosion. Additionally, in contrast to other rivers, there is no delta, a place where washed-out mud was deposited. This alone makes the evolutionist's interpretation impossible. For a canyon which supposedly formed hundreds of millions of years ago through the gradual processes of erosion, there is amazingly little erosion on the rim. As a matter of fact, the sides of the Grand Canyon are in many cases straight up and down and the flat rim meets the wall of the canyon at close to 90 degrees. The sedimentary rocks exposed throughout the Grand Canyon are rich with marine fossils such as crinoids, brachiopods, and sponges. Hard to explain by any means other than a worldwide flood, Dr. Steven Austin, one of the contributors to *Grand Canyon: A Different View*, found billions of squid-like creatures (nautiloid fossils) catastrophically deposited in hundreds of kilometers of Grand Canyon limestone.

Further supporting creation of the Grand Canyon by rapid flooding and almost impossible to argue with is the presence of polystratic fossils. N.A. Rupke, a young geologist from the State University of Groningen in the Netherlands, first coined the term "polystrate." Polystrate means "many layers," and refers to fossils that cut through multiple sedimentary-rock layers. Henry Morris discussed polystratic fossils in his book *Biblical Cosmology and Modern Science*, where he first explained the process of stratification. Polystratic trees are fossilized, usually upright trees that extend through several layers of strata, often twenty to forty feet in height. There is no doubt that this type of fossil was formed relatively quickly; otherwise, the trees would have decomposed while waiting for strata to slowly accumulate around them.[8]

Even the footprints of now long-dead animals testify to the existence of a great flood. Analyzing eighty-two fossilized vertebrate trackways discovered in the Coconino Sandstone along the Hermit Trail in the Grand Canyon, Dr. Leonard R. Brand, Chairman, Department of Biology at Loma Linda University published his findings at the Geoscience Research Institute in 1978. He concluded that when the locomotion behavior of living amphibians is taken into account, the fossilized trackways imply that the animals must have been entirely under water (not swimming to the surface) and moving upslope (against the current) in an attempt to get out of the water. Furthermore, other trackways start or stop abruptly, with no sign that the animals' missing tracks were covered by some disturbance such as shifting sediments. It appears that these animals simply swam away from the sediment. This interpretation fits with the concept of a global flood, which overwhelmed even four-footed reptiles and amphibians that spent most of their time in the water.

Still pulling the string on evidence to support existence of a worldwide flood, archaeologists have unearthed numerous multi-structured sites in recent history that are believed to be thousands of years old, and at the same time, are found to be buried under sediments that geologists tell us would have taken millions of years to deposit.

Starting excavation in 1994, Gobekli Tepe was found to be an Early Neolithic site of enormous significance. Stanford University's Ian Hodder was quoted as saying, "Gobekli Tepe changes everything."[9] Furthermore, the German archaeologist responsible for the excavation, Klaus Schmidt, believes that Gobekli Tepe is most likely a temple from the biblical garden of Eden. To understand how a respected academic like Schmidt could make such a dizzying claim, we must first look at the evidence and basis for his claim. In the book of Genesis, it is indicated that Eden was west of Assyria. Gobekli Tepe is located west of Assyria. Likewise, biblical Eden is located by four rivers (Genesis 2:10-14), including the Tigris and the Euphrates. Gobekli Tepe lies between the Tigris and the Euphrates rivers. In ancient Assyrian texts and the book of Amos, there is mention of a "Beth Eden"—a house of Eden (Amos 1:5). This minor kingdom is found fifty miles from Gobekli Tepe. Isaiah 37:12 and 2 Kings 19:12 talk about the children of Eden which were in Talassar, a town in northern Syria, near Gobekli Tepe. When you put it all together, the evidence is persuasive. Gobekli Tepe has been interpreted as the oldest human-made place of worship yet discovered and is believed to be greater than ten thousand years old.

Erected within circular temple structures and featuring sixteen-foot-high monolithic pillars carved in relief, excavations have revealed that these structures likely cover the entire hillside and could number as many as twenty. The circular temple structures range from thirty to one hundred feet in diameter and are surrounded by rectangular stone walls about six feet tall. Many of the pillars are carved with elaborate animal figure reliefs. In addition to bulls, foxes, and cranes, representations of lions, ducks, scorpions, ants, spiders, and snakes appear on the pillars. Freestanding sculptures depicting the animals have also been found within the circles. According to mainstream science, ten thousand years ago the world was populated with only primitive hunter-gatherers. For the secular world, the idea that Early Neolithic hunter-gatherers built something like Gobekli Tepe is world changing.

Ignoring evolution and operating under the pre-supposition that man was created around six thousand years ago, the "surprise" of alternate and evolving perceptions to the genesis of mankind is no longer that big of a shocker. Dr. Elizabeth Mitchell (writer for AIG) voices this alternative: "Evolutionary anthropologists generally consider the 'hunter-gatherer' to represent the more 'primitive' condition of evolving humanity. But this view is false. Biblical history describes Adam's first 'job' to be tending the garden that God provided, and Adam's sons kept flocks and tilled the ground (Genesis 4:2–3). Genesis chapter 4 describes the establishment of a city, so we see that the hunter-gatherer lifestyle was not the original condition of mankind. Following the global Flood, farming resumed as Noah planted a vineyard (Genesis 9:20). We learn of a hunter named Nimrod (Genesis 10:9) about the time of the building of the Tower of Babel, and it is likely that once people dispersed from Babel the foraging/

hunting lifestyle became a necessary expedient for many. But such a life-style was not a symptom of evolutionary or intellectual inferiority."[10] Hunter-gatherer does not have to translate to "primitive" or "less intel-ligent." It is a lifestyle, oftentimes just a temporary one.

Confronted with the contradiction of a ten-thousand-year-old tem-ple being buried under sediments that would have taken millions of years to deposit, most archaeologists have surmised that these locations were intentionally buried by their inhabitants. In the case of Gobekli Tepe where the soil covering the temple is known to have come from as far away as forty miles, it becomes obvious that it would have taken more effort to bury the stone structures than to build them. The next ques-tion became, why would they go through all the effort? It would have been easier to destroy the stone structures than to bury them. The only remaining possible conclusion for the archaeologists was that they must have buried their temples in an attempt to save them (intact) to be discov-ered by future generations. The provided answers seem too contrived to be believable. Unlike the trained archaeologists, the same contradictions immediately drove my thoughts to conclude that Gobekli Tepe was most likely buried by a great flood.

Sand waves observed in rivers and locations on the ocean floor have now been produced in laboratory studies. Consequently, it has been dem-onstrated that sand wave height is directly related to the water depth. As the water depth increases so does the height of the sand waves which are produced. The heights of the sand waves are approximately one-fifth of the water depth. Science provides the means to calculate both the depth and the velocity of water necessary for transporting the quantity of sand through sand waves that would be required to make up the cross-beds of Coconino Sandstone in the Grand Canyon and portions of Utah. As it turns out, cross-bed layers of Coconino Sandstone have been found as thick as thirty feet. Cross-beds of that height imply sand waves of at least sixty feet high and a water depth of around three hundred feet. For water that deep to make and move sand waves as high as sixty feet, the minimum current velocity would need to be over three feet per second or two miles an hour. Beyond 3.75 miles per hour, velocity experimental and observational evidence has shown that only flat sand beds would be formed. Bearing all of this in mind, it doesn't seem that far of a stretch to consider that a biblical flood would have the means to bury Gobekli Tepe with sediments from forty miles away.

Finally, while searching for proof of a biblical flood, renowned underwater archaeologist Robert Ballard, finder of the *Titanic* and the *Bismarck*, again announced that he had found what he was looking for in December of 2012. Columbia University geologists William B.F. Ryan and Walter C. Pitman III theorized in an article from the Earth Institute at Columbia University that the Bosporus strait, which served as a natural dam between the Mediterranean and Black seas, broke open at the time of the great flood and caused salt water to flood the Black Sea with a force two hundred times stronger than Niagara Falls. Ballard and his team have since uncovered ancient shorelines four hundred feet below the surface of the Black Sea. Underwater robot scouts have discovered remnants of houses made of mud and wood, ceramic fragments, and tools made of polished stone. Most importantly, Ballard and his team discovered the shells of ancient freshwater mollusks along the underwater shoreline that carbon dating places at about 5000 BC, the same time as the biblical flood. To be completely fair, many creationists disagree with Ballard's findings. They believe that Ballard found proof of a flood that opened the Black Sea up to the Mediterranean Sea, just not a flood of biblical proportion. I fall somewhere in the middle and wonder why it can't be both.

Like Ballard, consider the evidence and assume for the moment that the biblical flood of Noah did take place just as the Bible said it did. What about Noah's ark and all the animals of the world? The dimensions of the ark are given in the Bible (Genesis 6:15-16) and the ark is simply not big enough to hold seven of each clean animal and two of each unclean animal (Genesis 7:2-3).

To answer this question, we need to remember and take into account that the historical content of the biblical record and Noah's ark are limited to Assyria and the surrounding lands of the ancient Near

East. As we discussed earlier in chapter 2, this concept may change your understanding of the Bible. Consider Genesis 7:23, "And every living substance was destroyed which was upon the face of the ground, both man, and cattle, and the creeping things, and the fowl of the heaven; and they were destroyed from the earth: and Noah only remained alive, and they that were with him in the ark." Perhaps "upon the face of the ground" should be interpreted, "not sustained in the ark" and "Noah only remained alive, and they that were with him in the ark" should be interpreted, "Only Noah and his family survived in an ark from the ancient Near East"—the only ark spoken of in the Bible. Pointed out in an article entitled "Theory Supporting the Biblical Account of the Great Flood" by James A. Marusek,[11] the magnitude and destruction of a great flood "would have left an indelible and permanent mark on the minds of any survivors. This story would have been told and retold, passing down from generation to generation. And so, it was. This story of the great flood is embedded in many cultures and beliefs." Dependent on factors like whether or not the great flood was attributed to God or whether or not the remembrances include the building of an ark, the estimated number of accounts range from 600 to 1200 throughout the world that have been carried down to this present day.

The Hawaiian Islands are home to many accounts of the great flood. One legend revolves around a man named Nuu, thirteen generations removed from the first man. The gods commanded Nuu to build an ark and carry on it his wife, three sons, and males and females of all breathing things. Waters came and covered the earth. They subsided to leave the ark on a mountain overlooking a beautiful valley. The gods entered the ark and told Nuu to go forth with all the life it carried. In gratitude for his deliverance, Nuu offered a sacrifice of pig, coconuts, and awa to the moon, which he thought was the god Kane. Kane descended on a rainbow to reproach Nuu for his mistake but left the rainbow as a perpetual sign of his forgiveness.[12]

The Hindu faith of India tells us that while offering oblations, a carp fell into the hands of Manu, the first human. The fish grew and cried to Manu to preserve it, and Manu moved it to progressively larger vessels, eventually moving it to the river Ganga and then to the ocean. When it filled the ocean, Manu recognized it as the god Janardana, or Brahma. It told Manu that the end of the *yuga* was approaching, and soon all would be covered with water. He was to preserve all creatures and plants aboard a ship which had been prepared. It said that a hundred years of drought and famine would begin this day, which would be followed by fires from the sun and from underground that would consume the earth and the ether, destroying this world, the gods, and the planets. Seven clouds from the steam of the fire would inundate the earth, and the three worlds would be reduced to one ocean. Manu's ship alone would remain, fastened by a rope to the great fish's horn. Having announced all this, the great being vanished. The deluge occurred as stated; Janardana appeared in the form of a horned fish, and the serpent Ananta came in the form of a rope. Manu, by contemplation, drew all creatures toward him and stowed them in the ship and, after making obeisance to Janardana, attached the ship to the fish's horn with the serpent-rope.[13]

The Islamic faith of the Arab nations teaches that Allah sent Noah to warn the people to serve none but Allah, but most of them would not listen. They challenged Noah to make good his threats and mocked him when, under Allah's inspiration, he built a ship. Allah told Noah not to speak to him on behalf of wrongdoers; they would be drowned. In time, water gushed from underground and fell from the sky. Noah loaded onto his ship pairs of all kinds, his household, and those few who believed. One of Noah's sons didn't believe and said he would seek safety in the mountains. He was among the drowned. The ship sailed amid great waves. Allah commanded the earth to swallow the water and the sky to clear, and the ship came to rest on Al-Judi. Noah complained to Allah for taking his son. Allah admonished that the son was an evildoer and not of Noah's household, and Noah prayed for forgiveness. Allah told Noah to go with blessings on him and on nations that will arise from those with him. [Koran 11:25-48].

The Buryats of eastern Siberia believe that the god Burkhan advised a man to build a great ship, and the man worked on it in the forest for many long days, keeping his intention secret from his wife by telling her he was chopping wood. The devil, Shitkur, told the wife that her husband was building a boat and that it would be ready soon. He further told her to refuse to board and, when her husband struck her in anger, to say, "Why do you strike me, Shitkur?" Because the woman followed this advice, the devil was able to accompany her when she boarded the boat. With the help of Burkhan, the man gathered specimens of all animals except Argalan-Zan, the prince of animals (some say it was a mammoth), which considered itself too large to drown. The flood destroyed all animals left on earth, including the prince of animals, whose bones can still be found. Once on the boat, the devil changed himself into a mouse and began gnawing holes in the hull, until Burkhan created a cat to catch it.[14]

The Hareskin people of Alaska tell the story of Kunyan, a wise man who foresaw the possibility of a great flood, and built a great raft, joining the logs with ropes made of roots. He told other people, but they laughed at him and said they'd climb trees in the event of a flood. Then came a great flood, with water gushing from all sides, rising higher than the trees and drowning all people but the wise man and his family on his raft. As he floated, he gathered pairs of all animals and birds he met with. The earth disappeared under the waters, and for a long time no one thought to look for it. Then the muskrat dove into the water looking for the bottom, but he couldn't find it. He dove a second time and smelled the earth but didn't reach it. Next, the beaver dove and he reappeared unconscious but holding a little mud. The wise man placed the mud on the water and breathed on it, making it grow. He continued breathing on it, making it larger and larger. He put a fox on the island, but it ran around the island in just a day. Six times the fox ran around the island; by the seventh time, the land was as large as it was before the flood, and the animals disembarked, followed by the wise man with his wife (who was also his sister) and son. They repopulated the land. But the flood waters were still too high, and to lower them, the bittern swallowed them all. Now there was too little water. Plover (Alaskan migratory birds), pretending sympathy at the bittern's swollen stomach, passed his claw over it, but suddenly scratched it. The waters flowed out into the rivers and lakes.[15]

The Masai of East Africa believe that Tumbainot, a righteous man, had a wife named Naipande and three sons, Oshomo, Bartimaro, and Barmao. When his brother Lengerni died, Tumbainot, according to custom, married the widow Nahaba-logunja, who bore him three more sons, but they argued about her refusal to give him a drink of milk in the evening, and she set up her own homestead. The world was heavily populated in those days, but the people were sinful and not mindful of God. However, they refrained from murder, until at last a man named Nambija hit another named Suage on the head. At this, God resolved to destroy mankind, except Tumbainot who found grace in his eyes. God commanded Tumbainot to build an ark of wood and enter it with his two wives, six sons and their wives, and animals of every sort. When they were all aboard and provisioned, God caused a great, long rain, which caused a flood, and all other men and beasts drowned. The ark drifted for a long time, and provisions began to run low. The rain finally stopped, and Tumbainot let loose a dove to ascertain the state of the flood. The dove returned tired, so Tumbainot knew it had found no place to rest. Several days later, he let loose a vulture, but first he attached an arrow to one of its tail feathers so that, if the bird landed, the arrow would hook on something and be lost. The vulture returned that evening without the arrow, so Tumbainot reasoned that it must have landed on carrion, and that the flood was receding. When the water ran away, the ark grounded on the steppe, and its occupants disembarked. Tumbainot saw four rainbows, one in each quarter of the sky, signifying that God's wrath was over.[16]

The Lithuanian people tell the story of a supreme god, Pramzimas, looking through his heavenly window and seeing nothing but war and injustice among mankind. He sent two giants, Wandu and Wejas (water and wind), to destroy earth. After twenty days and nights, little was left. Pramzimas looked to see the progress. He happened to be eating nuts at the time, and he threw down the shells. One happened to land on the peak of the tallest mountain, where some people and animals had sought refuge. Everybody climbed in and survived the flood floating in the nutshell. God's wrath abated; he ordered the wind and water to abate. The people dispersed, except for one elderly couple who stayed where they landed. To comfort them, God sent the rainbow and advised them to jump over the bones of the earth nine times. They did so, and nine other couples sprang up, from which the nine Lithuanian tribes descended.[17]

The Native American Skokomish tribe of Washington believe that the Great Spirit was angry with the wickedness of people and animals. The Great Spirit decided to rid the earth of all but the good animals, one good man, and his family. At the Great Spirit's direction, the man shot an arrow into a cloud, then another arrow into that arrow, and so on, making a rope of arrows from the cloud to the ground. The good animals and people climbed up. Bad animals and snakes started to climb up, but the man broke off the rope. Then the Great Spirit caused many days of rain, flooding up to the snow line of Takhoma (Mount Ranier). After all the bad people and animals were drowned, the Great Spirit stopped the rain, the waters slowly dropped, and the good people and animals climbed down. To this day there are no snakes on Takhoma.[18]

These are just a few of the accounts of a great flood that once covered the entire earth. Assuming that only a quarter of the estimated 1200 accounts of the great flood include some form of a boat or an ark to save the animals of the world, and assuming that only a quarter of those stories have any factual basis, that still leaves seventy-five arks to save the world's animals, a much more believable interpretation of the ark story than the one-ark version. Seven of each clean animal and two of each unclean animal might well fit into seventy-five arks.

The multiple-ark theory is presented as a possibility for consideration by those who are convinced that the number of animals said to have been housed in Noah's ark could not possibly have fit into the single ark described in Genesis. The theory is not intended to be presented as fact, but to cause you to think and ponder. When we go back to the actual

Word of God, which is much more specific than most of us care to admit, we discover that the Bible is not referring to every type, breed, and species of animal on the planet. The specific wording used in the Bible is kind (Genesis 6:20) which refers to the family. Consider that there are thirty-four species/breeds of dogs within the Canidae family (kind) that originated from wolves. Strict adherence to the Bible would then require only two wolves to be housed in the ark, not sixty-eight dogs. Generally, scientists believe that the planet is comprised of no more than 1400 kinds, and it is suspected the number may actually be closer to 1000. Either way, there would have been ample room in the single ark described in Genesis to house up to 1400 families of animals.

When you believe in the biblical record and what it tells us of a worldwide flood and the story of Noah, you must also acknowledge that the physical makeup of our planet has significantly changed post-great flood. Not the least of these changes was the birth of the rainbow and the fact that humans no longer live to be six and seven hundred years old. If you are a person of faith as I am, the reasons for these changes are easily explained; things are as they are because the God who spoke us into existence said so. "The Lord saw that the wickedness of man was great in the earth, and that every intent of the thoughts of his heart was only evil continually. And the Lord was sorry that he had made man on the earth, and he was grieved in his heart, the Lord said, 'My Spirit shall not strive with man forever, for he is indeed flesh; yet his days shall be one hundred and twenty years'" (Genesis 6:3). Following the great flood, God also said, "This is the sign of the covenant which I make between Me and you, and every living creature that is with you, for perpetual generations: I set My rainbow in the cloud, and it shall be for the sign of the covenant between Me and the earth. It shall be, when I bring a cloud over the earth, that the rainbow shall be seen in the cloud; and I will remember My covenant which is between Me and you and every living creature of all flesh" (Genesis 9:12-15). The scientific explanation for the birth of the rainbow and the fact that humans no longer live to be six and seven hundred years old requires a more in-depth look at the biblical record.

The fact that the first rainbow did not appear until after the waters of the great flood had receded tells us that at least one of the variables in the equations that define a rainbow changed; something was different. A rainbow is a meteorological phenomenon that is caused by reflection, refraction, and dispersion of light in water droplets resulting in a spectrum of light appearing in the sky. The first and most obvious change to the world was of course the introduction of rain. The biblical record tells us that in the day of the Lord, "God made the earth and the heavens, before any plant of the field was in the earth and before any herb of the field had grown. For the Lord God had not caused it to rain on the earth, and there was no man to till the ground; but a mist went up from the earth and watered the whole face of the ground (Genesis 2:4-6). Enoch goes on to tell us, "The spirit of dew has its abode in the extremities of heaven, in connection with the receptacle of rain; and its progress is in winter and in summer. The cloud produced by it, and the cloud of the mist, become united; one gives to the other; and when the spirit of rain is in motion from its receptacle, angels come, and opening its receptacle, bring it forth. When likewise, it is sprinkled over all the earth, it forms a union with every kind of water on the ground; for the waters remain on the ground, because they afford nourishment to the earth from the Most High, who is in heaven. Upon this account therefore, there is a regulation in the quantity of rain, which the angels receive" (Enoch 59:11-14).

Even in the absence of a pouring rain, mist produces water droplets suspended in the atmosphere; and yet, there was no rainbow. Looking closer at Enoch's words, we see that the mist came in the form of a cloud and water was transferred from one cloud to another. The implication is that there were many, many clouds, one touching another and close enough to the ground to release a mist that watered every living thing. Enoch tells us that ". . . in light and in darkness, in winter and in summer, the receptacle of mist is bright" (Enoch 59:11). In a time when the Lord God walked in the garden of Eden (Genesis 3:8) and men like Enoch (Genesis 5:22) and Noah (Genesis 6:9) walked with God, it is easy to imagine looking to the heavens and seeing a thick white blanket of backlit cumulus clouds, one connected to another. As seen today in the lighted moon, the safe reflected viewing of an eclipse, or the brief second that you may have accidentally looked directly at the sun, the light generated from the sun is both white and bright. The clouds would have also been white because the amount of rain in the clouds was regulated and shared. With so many clouds in the heavens that reached so near to the earth, only the brightest of stars, the sun, and the moon would have been visible through the cool white fluorescent backdrop that was the sky. This of course would have prevented the necessary direct sunlight from reaching water droplets and being dispersed to produce a rainbow (see also Genesis 1:6-7, 2 Peter 3:3-7, and Psalm 148:4).

Opening up the sky post-great flood did not come without great and detrimental consequences to the inhabitants of earth. Notwithstanding the occasional reminder to use a high sun protection factor (SPF) sunscreen when going to the beach, the damaging effects of the enormous nuclear fusion reactor that we call the sun are seldom discussed. Working in the nuclear power industry for over thirty years, I can tell you that there are only three ways to reduce the detrimental effects of radiation; they are time, distance, and shielding. Time refers to how long someone or something is exposed to the source of radiation. Unlike the earth's pre-flood inhabitants who spent the majority of their lives exposed to the elements, modern civilization typically affords people a house, a job, and a car that reduce their exposure to solar radiation. Distance has no merit in the equation whatsoever when you recognize that the sun remains the same distance from earth as it has always been: a constant at 92.46 million miles. Most interesting are the implied changes to shielding.

In a nuclear reactor, the moderator (the material in direct contact with the fuel bundles) is the first means of shielding and is most often water. Other reactor designs have employed other moderators like graphite, but time has shown that water is the safest and most effective moderator. When fast neutrons strike a hydrogen atom in the water, they slow down like a billiard ball striking another, over and over. The earth's pre-great flood inhabitants were afforded a nearly impenetrable level of shielding from solar radiation by a blanketed cloud cover, one cloud touching another, reached from the heavens to near the earth and all sharing water that would be released as mist. Although other factors are definitely involved, in my opinion, when you factor in the cumulative effects of genetic variations, cell mutations, benign tumors, cataracts, and multiple forms of cancer, direct and continuous exposure to solar radiation is by far the greatest reason that people no longer live to be six and seven hundred years old. Only the fish and other sea creatures remain shielded by the ocean's depths.

Probably the second most significant detrimental change would be the reduced oxygen levels introduced with the rainbow. What was once a higher concentration of oxygen produced by a worldwide foliage that was sustained under a canopy of clouds is now gone. Ancient rain forests have been devastated by deforestation, farmlands have been replaced by cities and parking lots, and the consumers of oxygen now outnumber the sources of oxygen. A Live Science contributor, Charles Q. Choi, concluded that, "the world's oxygen levels have decreased 0.7% over the last 800,000 years and, 'oxygen sinks—processes that removed oxygen from the air—were about 1.7 percent larger than oxygen sources during this time.'"[19]

The same scientists offered that there are two hypotheses to help explain the oxygen decline over the past million years. "The first is that global erosion rates may have increased over the past few to tens of millions of years due to, among other things, the growth of glaciers—glaciers grind rock, thereby increasing erosion rates." Previous research found that both pyrite and organic carbon can react with oxygen and remove it from the atmosphere [Infographic: *Earth's Atmosphere Top to Bottom* can be viewed at https://www.livescience.com/29572-earth-atmosphere-layers-atmospheric-pressure-infographic.html]. "Alternatively, when the ocean cools, as it has done over the past 15 million years, before fossil fuel burning, the solubility of oxygen in the ocean increases. That is, the oceans can store more oxygen at colder temperatures for a given concentration of oxygen in the atmosphere. Oxygen-dependent microbes in the ocean and in sediments can then become more active and consume this oxygen, leaving less of the element in the atmosphere."[20]

Currently under 21% oxygen, science tells us that our atmosphere was once nearer to 35% oxygen.[21] Science seems to agree that the oxygen level in our atmosphere is declining. What we disagree on is the time-frame that it has taken place in and the causes for the decline. What you believe will ultimately be up to you.

---- 4 ----

A LEVEL PLAYING FIELD:
CARBON BLASPHEMOUS
AND THE EVOLUTIONARY BUBBLE

Today I looked out and I saw that free thought was ridiculed by an overwhelming contingency of followers who, without question, believe every principle and concept imagined by self-appointed authorities and supported by the media. I likened my thoughts to what God must have thought before he confounded the language of his people at the Tower of Babel. "And the Lord said, 'Indeed the people *are* one and they all have one language, and this is what they begin to do; now nothing that they propose to do will be withheld from them'" (Genesis 11:6). The loudest voice prevails and the content of the message is never as important as who is delivering it or which greasy wheel supports it. Those who question what is touted as scientific fact are shunned and outcast. Independent of any rational thought or added value, a flashlight is no more welcomed in a dark cave full of smokers armed with lighters than an incubator is welcomed in an abortion clinic full of premature fetuses. Admittedly skeptical, I am comforted to find other educated minds who are not afraid to question accepted norms.

In the words of *Ancient Aliens* narrator Robert Clotworthy, "Science has built this house—it's called the Standard Model—and, unfortunately, this house has some big holes in its walls, and we hang paintings over them, basically, and we try to kind of paper those over. We want certainty, we want things to fit."[22] American author and owner of Adventures Unlimited Press, David Hatcher Childress, also known as the real-life Indiana Jones to his many fans, framed it this way, "Scientists are far too quick to put a period at the end of the sentence. They are looking at a giant jigsaw puzzle with only a few pieces that are there, but they are drawing huge conclusions without really seeing all the evidence, and this is a problem in trying to reconstruct our ancient history."[23] I contend that nothing new will ever be learned and no new theories will ever be put forth if we allow others to continually do all of the heavy lifting. Examine the facts. Draw your own conclusions. Recognize that not everything can be explained with our current level of understanding. Sometimes there are just not enough knowns to draw a conclusion, and we are left to theorize. This is where science gets blurry, when the facts and the theories are treated equally and become interchangeable.

As near as I can tell, despite risking the most significant consequence, man began to repeat the horrid mistakes of his more distant past in the early eighteenth century. He again let discovery and imagination feed his self-importance, where through his arrogance, he devised alternate universal theories that replaced God with self and chance. Science found theories to support theories and repeated them over and over until they were accepted as fact. What we are left with are three collaborating and unsubstantiated theories, each pillar equally sharing the load to support the provided scientific foundation of our world. The three pillars are more commonly and best known as radiocarbon dating, the geologic column, and evolution. The provided foundation propagates the wonders of man and effortlessly rejects the divine.

Radiocarbon dating (also known as carbon dating or carbon-14 dating) is a tool that is used to determine the age of an object containing organic material—material that was once alive. The process assumes that the carbon level of all living things is relatively equal to the carbon level of the environment that we live in. After living things die, they are no longer taking in or replenishing their carbon and it begins to decay at what is believed to be a known rate. This allows scientists to determine the age of dead organic material by measuring the current carbon level of that material. Knowing the rate of decay after death, they calculate how long it would have taken for carbon to decay to its current level from the level of the environment which is assumed to be a constant. In simplified terms, imagine a five-gallon plastic pail of water with a small pinhole leak in the bottom of the pail that allows water to drip from the bottom of the pail. If we put a cup below the pail to catch the drops of water escaping and keep track of the time required for those drops to fill the cup, we now have the tools to measure how long the pail has been dripping (organic material has been dead) at any point in time by measuring how much water (radiocarbon) remains in the pail. Time is the number of cups that have escaped from the initial five gallons of water multiplied by however long it took to fill the first cup. At a very basic level, radiocarbon dating is very similar.

Unfortunately, carbon decay is not linear so we have to add another factor into our example to account for exponential decay. To understand exponential decay, we need to replace our five-gallon plastic pail with a two-hundred-foot-tall, thirty-six-inch inside diameter pipe that is standing on end and capped off at the bottom. If we now fill that standpipe with water, have a similar pinhole leak in the bottom, and we measure our leak in seconds per gallon, what we find is that our seconds-per-gallon leak rate changes over time. This is because when we started, we had the weight of a two-hundred-foot-tall column of water pushing the water through the pinhole leak—water was spraying out of the pinhole like a high pressure fire hose. By the time the standpipe is nearly drained and only a few gallons of water are remaining, water may be dripping out of the pinhole so slowly that it might take hours to collect a cup of water. If it took ten days to deplete the two-hundred-foot-tall column of water to a hundred-foot-tall column of water, to cut the original force by one-half, you might assume that it would take only another five days to again cut the starting force by one half, leaving a fifty-foot tall column of water. In fact, it would be longer—it may be six or seven days because the force of the water pushing the water out of the pinhole leak decreases as the standpipe empties. This is exponential decay in its simplest form.

Exponential decay is, of course, still present in our five-gallon plastic pail, but because of the short time interval to drain the pail and the small amount of water, it would have little effect on the calculated time to empty the pail. To measure exponential decay in our standpipe, the time required to fill a one-gallon jug of water from the leak would have to measured continually, gallon after gallon, for eight to ten hours. That data would then be plotted on an X versus Y chart where the X (horizontal) axis would be characterized by equal intervals, each representing one gallon of water and the Y (vertical) axis would be characterized by equal intervals, each representing increasing time in seconds. Although the starting point is not important to the outcome, for our example, we will start with a full standpipe. As each gallon jug is filled, we need to identify the time required to fill that jug on the Y-axis, draw a horizontal line from that point across the chart and parallel to the X-axis. Next, we need to draw a vertical line, straight up from the first gallon marker on the X-axis. Where the two drawn lines intersect is our first data point. Gallon after gallon, we repeat the process, moving to the right until we have plotted eight to ten hours of data. For each gallon jug of water filled and documented along the X-axis, the magnitude of the Y-axis—time required to fill a gallon jug of water will increase over time, forming a curve, rather than a straight line. That curve can then be extrapolated to forecast when time equals infinity and water has ceased leaking. For those of you who are thinking ahead, other processes unaccounted for in the standpipe example are evaporation and condensation losses.

Once we have this information, we can come in at any point in time after the standpipe has been filled, measure the current level of water, convert it to gallons, and determine how many gallons of water have been drained (decayed) by subtracting the current level in gallons from the total number of gallons required to fill the empty standpipe. Locating the number of gallons drained on the X-axis of our X versus Y chart and finding the corresponding value on Y identifies how long the water has been draining (exponentially decaying) since the standpipe was last filled. In this manner, we are measuring the time required to achieve a defined level of exponential decay. We are demonstrating the exponential decay of 10,570 gallons of water over a period of thirty days. Now reflect on the exponential decay of radiocarbons as calculated in radiocarbon dating. The exponential decay of 0.0000765% (percentage explained later) of a given organic sample is used to extrapolate up to fifty thousand years into the past. Exponential decay becomes increasingly subject to error as we have less and less real data to extrapolate smaller and smaller quantities over millions and millions of years.

Now having a reasonable understanding of exponential decay, I would like to introduce a few specific values and scientific terms that will further facilitate a more in-depth understanding of radiocarbon dating. It is the decay of radiocarbons, a radioactive isotope of carbon that is used for radiocarbon dating. The method was developed in the late 1940s by Willard Libby, who received the Nobel Prize in Chemistry for his work in 1960. It is based on the fact that radiocarbon (14C) is constantly being created in our atmosphere by the interaction of cosmic rays with atmospheric nitrogen. Cosmic rays are atom fragments that rain down at the speed of light on the earth from outside of our solar system. Cosmic rays are, for the most part, atomic nuclei: the greatest portion of them being hydrogen nuclei, some being helium nuclei, and the rest, heavier elements. Although many of the low energy cosmic rays come from our Sun, the origins of the highest energy cosmic rays remain unknown. As we proceed with this conversation, we will find that there are many unknowns involved in the science of radiocarbon dating. Most scientists suspect the origins of high energy cosmic rays are related to supernovas (star explosions). The resulting radiocarbons combine with atmospheric oxygen to form radioactive carbon dioxide, which is incorporated into plants by photosynthesis; animals then acquire the radiocarbon by eating the plants. When the animals or plants die, they stop exchanging carbon with its environment, and from that point forward the amount of radiocarbon undergoes radioactive decay.

Measuring the amount of radiocarbon in a sample from a dead plant or animal such as a piece of wood or a fragment of bone provides information that can then be used to calculate when the animal or plant died. The older the sample is, the fewer radiocarbons there are to be detected, and because the half-life of Carbon-14 (the period of time after which half of a given sample will have decayed) is about 5,730 years, science tells us that the oldest dates that can be reliably measured by this process date to around 50,000 years ago. The decay of other radioactive elements with greater half-lives are utilized to look millions of years into our past.

Measurable and indisputable today is the fact that the earth's atmosphere is made up of 78% nitrogen (N), 21% oxygen (O), 0.06% carbon dioxide (CO_2), and an estimated 0.0000765% radioactive Carbon-14 (14C). Scientists calculate that approximately twenty-one pounds of 14C is created by the interaction of cosmic rays with atmospheric nitrogen each year. To give you an idea of how little 14C that is, it is 21 pounds spread out within a 100-mile-thick atmosphere, stretching around the entire circumference of the planet. If that were gold that was spread out evenly over the surface of the planet, it wouldn't even be worth looking for. The first tenet of the radiocarbon house of cards is that the 0.0000765% of Carbon-14 calculated to be in our atmosphere is treated as a constant in the equations used to calculate organic age through radiocarbon dating. To conclude that the level of 14C in our atmosphere is constant, we must also conclude that the rate at which unchanging cosmic rays produce 14C by interaction with constant atmospheric levels of nitrogen is equal to the rate at which 14C is consumed by all living organisms, regardless of the earth's population or levels of forestation.

Dr. Kent E. Hovind, Christian author and founder of Christian Science Evangelism compares the exchange of 14C to a garden hose filling a fifty-gallon rain barrel with holes in it. Assuming that the incoming water remains at a constant rate greater than the loss attributed to the leaks and that the leaks never get any bigger or smaller, the level of water in the barrel (14C) will eventually reach fifty gallons. In the provided scenario, cosmic rays are filling a fifty-gallon barrel of nitrogen to produce radiocarbons that are too large to leak out through the holes where the excess cosmic rays escape. Scientists have somehow calculated the period of time to reach equilibrium in our atmosphere (fill the fifty-gallon rain barrel) to be around thirty thousand years from when the cycle began. Flying in the face of creationists, science views thirty thousand years as insignificant in a world purported to be billions of years old. I am not a fan of this theory as it assumes that the size of our atmosphere (the fifty-gallon rain barrel) is also a constant. Our atmosphere can never get any thicker or any thinner. A large leap forward in cosmic ray science came in 2017, when the Pierre Auger Observatory studied the arrival trajectories of thirty thousand cosmic particles and concluded that there is a difference in how frequently these cosmic rays arrive, depending on where you look.[24] Oops, another constant in the equation found to be not necessarily so constant.

As we will discover later in this chapter, the levels of 14C in our atmosphere are also not constant—the basis of radiocarbon dating, a constant 0.0000765% of 14C in our atmosphere cannot be assumed to have always been the same. I contend that the level of radiocarbons in our atmosphere is made a constant in the equations used by science to calculate the radiocarbon decay of now deceased organic materials because it is the only way to obtain accurate results in the verifiable recent past. Based on those verifiable results, these same equations can then be used to extrapolate millions of years into our past. Consider the impacts of evaporation and condensation on our standpipe example. Let's assume that a cup of water was lost every day due to evaporation and condensation over the thirty days that it took to completely drain the standpipe. A similar error rate over the course of a million years would result in an error of 22,812,500 gallons, nearly twenty-three million gallons of water. Assume that number now to just be another factor in an equation that will be multiplied, squared, or divided and then subtracted from another

number, etc.; the error grows exponentially. Here is the kicker: evaporation and condensation are dependent on the environment and certainly
not a constant over the course of a million years.

Dr. Henry Morris is a leader in scientific research within the context
of biblical creation and the founder of the 1970 established Institute for
Creation Research (ICR). The mission of the ICR is to conduct scientific
research within the realms of origins and earth history and to educate
the public through any formal or informal means possible. The ICR was
one of three leading creation science organizations to sponsor the RATE
project. In 1997, a group of young-earth creationists met in San Diego,
California, to discuss the age of the earth. Their goal was to clarify the
chronology of earth history and search for a fundamental correction to
the usual assumptions of deep time. They were skeptical of the evolutionary timescale that dominates modern geology. These scientists reviewed
the assumptions and procedures used in estimating the ages of rock strata
and they recognized multiple weaknesses. The group identified themselves with the acronym RATE, which stands for Radioisotopes and the
Age of The Earth.[25]

Supported by the RATE project, the ICR was able to conclude that
with a short 5730-year half-life, no Carbon-14 atoms should exist in any
carbon older than 250,000 years. "Yet, it has proven impossible to find
any natural source of carbon below the Pleistocene (Ice Age) strata that
does not contain significant amounts of Carbon-14, even though such
strata are supposed to be billions of years old. Conventional Carbon-14
laboratories have been aware of this anomaly since the early 1980s, have
striven to eliminate it, and are unable to account for it. The world's best
such laboratory which learned during two decades of low 14C measurements how not to externally contaminate specimens, confirmed such
observations for coal samples and even for a dozen diamonds, which cannot be contaminated in situ with recent carbon. These constitute very
strong evidence that the earth is only thousands, not billions of years
old." Professor R.E. Taylor of the University of California concluded in
an *American Antiquity* article[26] that 14C has not yet reached a point of

equilibrium. Specifically, "Radiocarbon is forming 28-37% faster than it is decaying." Assuming that science is correct in their assertion that it would take 30,000 years for 14C to reach equilibrium in our atmosphere, it can only be concluded that if Professor Taylor is correct, the earth must be less than 30,000 years old.

If we know that the percentage of oxygen in our atmosphere was once considerably higher than it is today (closing remarks of chapter 3), we also know that something had to give. The only other element of sufficient quantity to adjust for a such a level change in oxygen is nitrogen. A 10% increase in oxygen (from 21% to 31%) would have to coincide with a 10% decrease in nitrogen (78% to 68%). We know this because there is simply not enough of any other element (0.06% CO_2 and 0.0000765% 14C) to be displaced of sufficient measure to compensate for such an increase in atmospheric oxygen. Decreased nitrogen means less nitrogen for cosmic rays to interact with, and assuming no change to the intensity of cosmic rays, the result would be less production of Carbon-14. This fact seems to elude the scientists who tell us that Carbon-14 levels in our atmosphere are and have been constant for billions of years.

Dr. Hovind points out in his video *Carbon Dating Flaws—Doesn't Carbon Dating Disprove the Bible?*[27] that, "If the earth once had a canopy of water above the atmosphere or a canopy of ice, . . . that would have blocked out a lot of radiation from the sun, which would have prevented most of the Carbon-14 from even forming. So animals that lived before the flood would have lived in a world with much less Carbon-14 to begin with, maybe none, but certainly less."[28] As the actual (versus projected) level of 14C at the time of death decreases, the inaccuracies of radiocarbon dating increase exponentially. If at the point of death, initial 14C levels of an animal were 1/16th the anticipated 0.0000765% and the animal's fossil were dug up after 5730 years, radiocarbon dating would tell us that the fossil had been through five half-lives and was 28,650 years old, when in fact, it had been through one half-life and was only 5730 years old.

Up until this point, we have discussed only conceptual errors in radiocarbon dating that would make a known or unknown sample appear to be older than it actually is. There are also factors affecting atmospheric 14C, both known and unknown that cause known samples to appear much younger than they actually are. The effects of atmospheric testing of nuclear weapons have been measured and known to increase the production of 14C concentration in atmospheric CO_2 since 1953. As reported by the United States Atomic Energy Commission in Health and Science Laboratory Report, *Carbon 14 Measurements in the Atmosphere—1953 to 1964*, "A C-14 sampling program has been conducted by the U.S. Air Force, U.S. Atomic Energy Commission and U.S. Weather Bureau since 1953 using balloons and aircraft. Whole air collections have been obtained from ground level to greater than 100,000 ft. Over 3,000 results of both total and bomb produced C-14 concentration in CO_2 are presented . . ." (April 1, 1965).[29]

The above referenced Health and Science Laboratory Report contains reams of data showing calculated excesses of 14C in terms of atoms per gram of air. Extraordinary steps were taken to ensure that samples were not contaminated during collection, and measuring techniques were shown to account for nearly everything, including correction for specific gravity. As a practical example of how atmospheric testing of nuclear weapons affects radiocarbon dating, author and host of the popular TV series *Ancient Aliens* Giorgio A. Tsoukalos took a small sample of redwood to Dr. John Southon, PhD, at the Earth Science Department's Carbon Cycle Research Lab, University of California in Irvine, California for radiocarbon dating in April of 2017. The redwood sample was known to have been subjected to nuclear testing in the 1950s, was tested twice, and found to be from 655 years in the future.[30]

The first atomic bomb was tested in the atmosphere on July 16, 1945 at Alamogordo, New Mexico. From the first nuclear test in 1945 until tests by Pakistan in 1998, there was never a period of more than twenty-two months with no nuclear testing. June of 1998 to October of 2006 was the longest period since before 1945 with no acknowledged nuclear testing. The scientific community tells us that increased levels of 14C due to nuclear testing do not affect radiocarbon dating because most samples tested were already long since dead and decaying by the time the first nuclear atmospheric test took place. The problems with this rebuttal are greater than just limiting radiocarbon dating to things dead before 1945. In the ancient city of Mohenjo-Daro, located to the west of the Indus River in the Larkana District of Sindh, Pakistan, vitrified sands turned to glass and melted brick walls testify to a destruction known only today to be created by a nuclear blast.

In his (1966) book *Riddles of Ancient History*, Alexander Gorbovsky, a Soviet munitions expert, seasoned scholar, and researcher reported the discovery of at least one human skeleton near Mohenjo-Daro with a level of radioactivity approximately fifty times greater than should be expected. Lord David William Davenport, a British Indian researcher, who spent twelve years studying ancient Hindu scripts and the destruction of Mohenjo-Daro, compares the radiation levels of the Gorbovsky skeleton to levels seen in post-war Nagasaki and Hiroshima. Reminiscent of the biblical description provided for the destruction of Sodom and Gomorrah, Davenport recounts a passage from the *Mahabharata* that he attributes to a pre-history nuclear blast at Mohenjo-Daro in his 1979 book, *Atomic Destruction in 2000 B.C.* ". . . white hot smoke that was a thousand times brighter than the sun rose in infinite brilliance and reduced the city to ashes. Water boiled . . . horses and war chariots were burned by the thousands . . . the corpses of the fallen were mutilated by the terrible heat so that they no longer looked like human beings . . ."[31] Davenport's theory of a four-thousand-year-old nuclear explosion was initially met with intense scientific interest. Nationally known expert American physicist William Sturm said, "The melting bricks at Mohenjo-Daro could not have been caused by a normal fire," while Professor Antonio Castellani, a space engineer in Rome, said, "It's possible that what happened at Mohenjo-Daro was not a natural phenomenon."[32] Ultimately, Davenport's discoveries and theories have been dismissed as pseudoscience because they contradict the basis for radiocarbon dating and do not align well with the geologic column or the evolutionary tree.

Compounding the problem, Mohenjo-Daro does not stand alone. First documented by Patrick A. Clayton in 1932, the world's largest deposit of sands turned to glass exists in the Western Desert of Egypt near the Libyan border, in an area known as the Great Sand Sea. There is so much glass in the area that it has a name and is referred to as Libyan Desert Glass (LDG). It is estimated that on a plain of about 6500 km², a mass of 1400 tons of LDG is distributed. Despite the fact that the chemical and physical characteristics are absolutely unique with no other comparable natural glass on earth, scientists rule out the possibility of a nuclear impact or airburst because they do not believe that a sufficient ground reservoir of pure silicon dioxide sands ever existed to be melted by such an event. Besides, they say, the desert did not exist in the Oligocene age. A search of the internet attests to the numerous studies, scientific papers, articles, and books that have been written about Libyan Desert Glass.[33] Despite all efforts, the origin of the LDG is up to now unsolved.

Flying in the face of a four-thousand-year-old nuclear blast, ruins of technologically advanced ancient civilizations, and advanced construction techniques that cannot be understood or recreated today, science maintains a huge ego that will not allow acknowledgment of the possibility of a now-extinct, once-smarter people. Any theory that suggests anything other than a singular and linear progression to where we are today contradicts the last hundred years of accumulated knowledge and is too humbling to accept. In a world where long-standing theory becomes fact, it is hard to step back and say, "We were wrong," or "I don't know." Rather, science demonstrates a tendency to try to force the unexplained into an existing box of adjustments or to discard it altogether.

In the spring of 1970, Marty and Rick Lagina retrieved a piece of timber from a depth of 150 feet in their search for a treasure known to have been buried (prior to 1795) on Oak Island, a 140-acre privately owned island on the south shore of Nova Scotia. The piece of timber was taken to the Earth Science Department of Brock University in St. Catharines,

Ontario, Canada for radiocarbon dating. The sample was tested and re-tested to ultimately reveal that it was from three thousand years in the future. Verifiably buried since before the purported first nuclear weapons test in 1945, the reason for a radiocarbon date from three thousand years in the future remains a mystery, but attests to the inaccuracies of an imperfect radiocarbon dating process.

Well known in the scientific community but not so often openly talked about is the fact that many, if not the majority, of dinosaur bones are found to be radioactive. It is a common practice in most museums to coat fossilized dinosaur bones of low reactivity with leaded paint to shield and protect visitors and staff. However, some dinosaur bones are so radioactive that museums can only safely display replicas. Dinosaur bones have a magnitude higher level of radioactivity when compared to most background sources. This fact is both known and exploited by paleontologists who use mobile scintillators with sensitive Geiger-Muller tubes to search out new dinosaur fossils.[34] Scientists attribute these radiation levels to a variety of radioactive elements in decay. Some are dangerously radioactive, while others are only mildly so. For example, radioactive dinosaur bones from the Morrison Formation are attributed to epigenetic uranium deposits in Colorado and Wyoming. Unfortunately, not all radioactive dinosaur bones are found near uranium deposits.

Perhaps grasping at straws, another scientific explanation for radioactive dinosaur bones is the possibility of an ancient gamma-ray burst. Scientists at NASA and the University of Kansas claim that gamma-ray bursts could have facilitated mass extinctions that would have significantly remodeled our atmosphere. A gamma-ray burst consists of a sudden explosion of a nearby star that may well have depleted half of the earth's atmospheric protective ozone layer. "A gamma-ray burst originating within 6000 light years from Earth would have a devastating effect on life," said Dr. Adrian Melott of the Department of Physics and Astronomy at the University of Kansas. "We don't know exactly when one came, but we're rather sure it did come—and left its mark. What's most surprising is that just a ten-second burst can cause years of devastating ozone damage."[35] For this discussion, the cause is not important. What is important is that the radioactivity of dinosaur bones exists. As shown above, exposure to radioactivity negatively impacts the results of radio-carbon dating.

Before we can have a minimal understanding of why some elements are radioactive and others are not, why some materials give off dangerous waves and particles and other do not, we will need an understanding of atomic structure and what holds atoms together to form the materials we see all around us. The structure of a single atom is much like the structure of our solar system. Similar to our sun and the orbiting planets, each atom contains a nucleus at its center that is held in place by orbiting electrons. As it relates to our solar system, planets are able to maintain their orbits because the centrifugal forces that push the planets toward deep space are equal to the attraction of masses between the planets and the sun. A general rule of thumb is that the bigger a planet is, the greater its mass and the greater the attraction of masses that must be overcome to reach steady-state orbit. This is why the smaller planets generally orbit closer to the sun. On an atomic level, attraction of masses is replaced by charged particles. The nucleus of an atom is comprised of neutrons that have no charge and protons that are positively charged. The orbiting electrons are negatively charged and it is the attraction between the negatively charged orbiting electrons and the positively charged nucleus that overcome the centrifugal forces pushing the electrons towards deep space and allowing for steady-state orbit to be sustained.

In our solar system, planets orbit the sun on a relatively flat plane that forms a disk around the sun. For the purposes of our discussion, imagine a similar solar system with only three planets of the same size and mass. With all forces being equally applied, all planets will form an orbit having an equal distance from the sun. Each taking an identical period of time to complete one revolution of orbital travel, no planet will collide with another planet. Now imagine two such solar systems, suspended side-by-side in space, one having three planets sharing a single orbital ring and one having four planets sharing a single orbital ring. If we view these two solar systems from above so that we are looking down at two orbiting rings of planets, each orbiting around a center nucleus that is their sun, we have a perfect model for demonstrating atomic bonding.

In our mind's eye, we need to move these two solar systems toward one another until the orbiting ring of each solar system just intersects. Assuming that the sun of each solar system is the nucleus of an atom and that each planet represents an electron, the result is an accurate depiction of two side-by-side atoms. As each electron passes through the point of orbital intersection, the negatively charged electron become equally attracted to the positively charged nucleus of each atom, now equally distanced from the electron. For that brief instant, the electron may transition from orbiting one atom to orbiting the other atom. This is known as *ionic bonding*. In some cases, the electron may transition back and forth between the two atoms, forming a figure-eight orbit. This is known as *covalent bonding*. Lastly, electrons are sometimes shared with all atoms in a given material. This is known as *metallic bonding*. These are the forces that hold all atoms together in everything that we see and touch. Although the single orbit, dual solar system model is a convenient tool for explaining atomic bonding, it should be noted that in fact, the model does not reflect how electrons really orbit around the nucleus of an atom. Electrons actually form multiple orbits at varying distances from the nucleus, are captured in holes, and travel at speeds that form a protective cocoon around the nucleus. Students are often asked to picture this cocoon as the outer shell of a ping-pong ball.

Another essential tenet of radiocarbon dating is radioactive decay. Not looking to lose any of my audience, I will try not to go any deeper into atomic theory than is absolutely necessary to gain an understanding of radioactive decay. As you are already aware, all atoms consist of electrons, neutrons, and protons. There are two things that are required to make an atom stable. Stable atoms must be electronically neutral, meaning that the number of orbiting electrons equals the number of protons in the nucleus and the number of protons and neutrons in the nucleus are equal. Stable atoms are at equilibrium and emit no radiation. Just as a tire rolling down a hill will eventually come to rest, those things in nature that are not stable are transitioning to become stable. It is in the process of atoms trying to become stable that radioactive decay occurs. Quantum theory tells us that it is impossible to predict when a particular atom will decay, regardless of how long the atom has existed. However, for a significant number of identical atoms, the overall decay rate can be expressed as a constant or a half-life. A half-life is the period of time after which half of a given sample will have decayed. The half-lives of radioactive atoms have a huge range, from nearly instantaneous to longer than the age of the universe.

Science can measure the process by which the nucleus of unstable atoms lose energy through emission of radiation, including alpha particles, beta particles, gamma rays, and conversion electrons. On the periodic table of elements, each element is listed in numerical order and thereby defined by atomic number. The atomic number is the equivalent to the total number of protons in the nucleus of a given atom of a particular element. Having 92 protons, uranium is listed as 92U. Also defined as U-238, the 238 represents the total number of protons and neutrons combined together in the nucleus of a uranium atom. U-238 is comprised of 92 electrons, 92 protons, and 146 neutrons. From what we have already learned, we know that U-238 is unstable and emitting radiation because the total number of neutrons is greater than the total number of protons in the nucleus.

Plotting measured values of radioactive decay over time for a given unstable element shows that the decay occurs at an exponentially decreasing rate. This is a proven fact that cannot be disputed. What I do have issue with is that these functions are extrapolated out to millions and billions of years. The extrapolated radioactive decay of U-238 predicts that U-238 will eventually decay to ^{82}Pb, Lead-207. After eighteen billion years, a given sample of U-238 will be 93.75% lead and only 6.25% uranium. How do we know that the exponential decay rate of U-238 remains constant for eighteen billion years? Who has been around to verify this or seen uranium turn to lead? How much real data was used to extrapolate eighteen billion years into the future? Remember that for our standpipe example, we took eight to ten hours of real data to predict something that took only thirty days to occur. As it relates to radiocarbon dating, the implication is that we could look at a piece of lead today and say with the same accuracy and certainty that eighteen billion years ago, that piece of lead was a piece of uranium.

As already explained, by definition, all plants, animals, and living things that eat plants and animals must contain a level of radiocarbon equal to the atmospheric level of 0.0000765% 14C. Once dead, radio-carbon is no longer replenished and begins to decay at a rate equal to the known half-life of radiocarbon. Carbon-14 has a 5730-year half-life, meaning that half of the radiocarbon present in a deceased organic sample will have decayed back to stable elements after 5730 years, leaving 0.00003835% 14C and half of that would again have decayed after another 5730 years, leaving 0.000019125% ^{14}C. Assuming that something has been dead for 57,300 years or 10 half-lives, only $1/1024^{th}$ of the original 0.0000765% ^{14}C or 0.00000007470703125% ^{14}C ($7.470703125 \times 10^{-8}$ ^{14}C) would remain. At some point, I have to question our ability to accurately measure something that small. When does the level of radioactive ^{14}C become too small to measure and what is the standard used to calibrate our measuring device?

To be fair to the scientific community, it is worth noting that there are other radioactive elements with greater half-lives than ^{14}C that are frequently used to make longer-range predictions. Potassium is one such radioactive element, having a purported 1.3-billion-year half-life. Potassium-argon (K-Ar) dating counts the half-lives of potassium as it slowly decays to argon. Potassium-argon dating was one of the methods used by James P. Dawson, Chief of Engineering and Operations for the Lunar and Earth Science Division at the Manned Spacecraft Center, NASA to determine the age of moon rocks.[36] Dawson confesses that he and other scientists were almost, "excommunicated from NASA" when they conclusively determined that the so-called Genesis rock (a composite rock containing multiple tiny glass spheres) could not be more than 20,000 years old. Pressured by NASA to date the moon rocks at four billion years or greater, Mr. Dawson argued, ". . . radiation counts are almost fictitious, because you don't know what was there to start with. They say, 'Well, when something is formed, like a rock formed, melted, from that point on, it decays.' Well, that's fine. But what do you do if every rock out there is a mixture? I mean, how many pure rocks do you have? Diamond. Okay."[37] Eventually, the Genesis rock was divided into six pieces and dated many, many times. Ages ranged from 2.5 billion to 4.6 billion years from the same sample (a 500% difference). These were the numbers that most closely aligned with the evolutionary and geological timescales and were the numbers published by NASA.

Whether 20,000 years or 4.6 billion years, I question the accuracy of any testing method that yields multiple ages with billions of years between them in a single sample. In a scientific report entitled "Potassium: Argon Agent of Iron Meteorites," L.A. Rancitelli and D.E. Fisher revealed at the 48th Annual Meeting of Planetary Science Abstracts that, "As much as 80% of the potassium in a small sample of an iron meteorite can be removed by distilled water in 4.5 hours."[38] If potassium is that easy to remove, how can anyone trust that a sample is uncompromised? Basalt from the 1959 eruption of Mt. Kilauea in Hawaii was recently potassium-argon dated and found to be 8.5 million years old.[39] The general rule of thumb appears to be that radioisotope dating of a sample of known age doesn't work and radioisotope dating of a sample of unknown age is assumed correct, regardless of the isotope. In 1971, a freshly killed seal was carbon dated as having died 1300 years ago.[40] Similarly, shells from living snails were carbon dated in 1984 and found to be 27,000 years old.[41]

The aforementioned James P. Dawson goes on to explain in the same oral history project, "There's a theory, and we were working on that back in the early eighties, that the speed of light decays. We have experimental measurements. It's all on our website. We have experimental measurements back to 1640 and it shows a definite decay in the value of the speed of light and to where now it's almost constant." Scientists have backed up and redone all of these experiments using the same equipment these people had back then, but don't understand why they don't get the same answers when the tests are performed today. "If the speed of light is decaying, that means that the time we measure for radiation also changes, because it's a function of the speed of light." Running through the calculations, James and his colleagues were able to show that the theory of light-speed decay yields a timescale that closely aligns with the biblical record. "The scientists are right; they're just using the wrong time scale as a function of what the solar time scale is." James and his colleagues published this theory, but nobody in the United States would pick it up. "If we had applied that back at the 'looney lab,' we would have probably got a completely different set of time frames. We know that the decay of the Earth's magnetic field indicates it's not more than 20,000 years old."

After years of seeking the truth, Dawson has concluded that, "There's all kinds of things that have the same decay. Everything on Earth that we've found, including the Scriptures, shows a decay curve, or expediential growth curve, like the population. So everything is going to that pattern." Dawson compares 2 Peter 3:8, ". . . one day is as a thousand years, and a thousand years as one day" to the top and bottom of the same expediential curve. "I think what he (God) was telling us is you've got the curve. . . . As a matter of fact, getting in and looking for truth, okay, you have to have good data, and the only thing I found that has perfect data is Scripture." Using the Scriptures as a valid data set and starting point, Dawson has been able to work backward with plate tectonics and 180,000 collected NASA planetary soil samples to reconstruct a single super continent. But when he did, ". . . It turns out that the Mideast or Israel is the center. Okay. That's exactly what he (God) said in Ezekiel, 'I put my people in the center of the earth.' So we got to looking at that, and it turns out that that's also the central point for the distribution of oil all over that hemisphere." Starting with the Scriptures, James and his colleagues have made many great discoveries; however, when ". . . great geologists come in and they say, 'Well, how'd you come up with this?' 'Well, it's right there in the Bible.' Out the door they go."

Much more detailed than discussed here, taking shifting poles, torques developed at right angles to planetary spin, and the theoretical center for the distribution of oil prior to accepted continental separation into account, Dawson was able to pinpoint a large reserve of oil near Arbuckle Mountain in Oklahoma. Combined with satellite imaging, Dawson's methods of plotting the world's oil distribution have resulted in an accuracy of 90%. When reading all of this, my mind couldn't help but jump to the next logical assertion. If the world's oil was distributed from a single point in the Mideast at the time of creation, is oil just oil and not the result of so many decaying dinosaurs? Was lead-206 simply created as lead-206 and not necessarily the result of decayed uranium-238? Was argon simply created as argon? With so many unknowns and so many proven discrepancies, a sane person with any kind of curiosity might ask, how has radiocarbon dating become an accepted science, taught as fact? Well, the world had a one-hundred-year-old established pseudoscience known as the geologic column to thank for that.

Unlike the unsubstantiated shot in the dark referred to as the geologic column or the imagined alternative to intelligent design known as evolution, radioisotope dating is a seriously flawed and imperfect science, but it is nevertheless a science with real principles behind it. As it relates to radioisotope dating, science has shot themselves in the foot and in so doing, broken the public trust. Rather than accepting what the science was telling them, they adjusted the science through alterations, tweaks, and exclusions until radioisotope dating supported the already accepted concepts of the geologic column and evolution. One truth became three lies.

The geologic column was first proposed by James Hutton in his *Theory of the Earth* in 1795. Hutton's theories were further developed by Charles Lyell and published in his 1830 work entitled *Principles of Geology*. The earth was divided up into several layers known as the Cenozoic, the Mesozoic, the Paleozoic, the Proterozoic, and the Archaeozoic layers. Each layer was then assigned what was considered a logical date and an index fossil. For the scientific community, this answered many unanswered questions and was almost instantaneously accepted as the most likely scenario. From that point forward and based solely on the geologic column, we have been taught that the earth is billions of years old. Shortly after returning from his fateful five-year voyage aboard the *HMS Beagle*, British naturalist Charles Darwin, admittedly heavily influenced by Sir Charles Lyell's *Principles of Geology*, began drafting *Origin of Species*. First published in 1859, *On the Origin of Species by Means of Natural Selection* supported the geologic column and introduced the world to the theory of evolution. Without reinventing history, rewriting over a hundred years of text books, and admitting a significant error in our understanding of the world, any new dating techniques would certainly have to align with the geologic column. And so, with a little tweaking, radiocarbon dating was born in 1949. In *American Journal of Science* article "Pragmatism versus Materialism in Stratigraphy," J.E. O'Rourke confirms that "Radiometric dating would not have been feasible if the geologic column had not been erected first."[42]

Similarly, I contend that acceptance of evolution could not exist without blind acceptance of the theoretical geologic column; for that matter, evolution could not exist without the supporting arguments of radioisotope dating. Nobody believes that kissing a frog will cause the frog to evolve into a prince, but if you throw in a few million years and tell people that a monkey will evolve into a man, the tendency is to consider the possibility. As a member of the common species that shares a common intellect, when I am exposed to a new theory that piques my interest, my first thoughts are to disprove it or rule it out with common logic or known facts. If that doesn't work, I tend to accept the possibility and look forward to future proofs. This seems to work most of the time, but falls apart when stronger contradicting beliefs and personal biases exist. Sadly, this is one of those cases. You cannot have a serious discussion about evolution without some mention of an opposing view and that includes intelligent design. Likewise, you cannot discuss Darwin, the father of evolution, without some mention of Darwin's self-admitted challenges imposed by the complexities of design evident in the human eye.

Charles Darwin admits that "to suppose that the eye with all its inimitable contrivances for adjusting the focus to different distances, for admitting different amounts of light, and for the correction of spherical and chromatic aberration, could have been formed by natural selection, seems, I freely confess, absurd in the highest degree." Unfortunately, in their efforts to discredit evolution, many creationists have used this quote out of context. They do themselves a great disservice in doing so because a deeper look at the entire quote shows that it in no way diminishes the assertions of evolution, and in fact, causes their argument to fall apart. Later in the same chapter of *On the Origin of Species*, Darwin goes on to explain how he believed the human eye evolved nevertheless and the absurdity he referred to was illusory, "When it was first said that the sun stood still and the world turned around, the common sense of mankind declared the doctrine false; but the old saying of Vox populi, vox Dei, as every philosopher knows, cannot be trusted in science. Reason tells me, that if numerous gradations from a simple and imperfect eye to one complex and perfect can be shown to exist, each grade being useful to its possessor, as is certainly the case; if further, the eye ever varies and the variations be inherited, as is likewise certainly the case and if such variations should be useful to any animal under changing conditions of life, then the difficulty of believing that a perfect and complex eye could be formed by natural selection, though insuperable by our imagination, should not be considered as subversive of the theory."[43]

Darwin was on a path of predetermined destination with no chance of turning back or reconsidering conclusions already set in stone. Nevertheless, modern scientific understanding of the complexities of the human eye have so far surpassed what was known 150 years ago that even Darwin might today question what he so freely attributed to natural selection. Science teacher, Tom Wagner directly challenges Darwin's explanation for the complexities of the human eye in "Darwin vs. the Eye."[44] Wagner tells us that modern ophthalmology (eye science) has discovered three almost imperceptible tiny eye movements. "These three, referred to as tremors, drifts, and saccadesí, are caused by minute contractions in the six muscles attached to the outside of each of your eyes. Every fraction of a second, they very slightly shift the position of your eyeball, automatically, without conscious effort on your part, making sight as you know it possible." Tremors are the tiniest and probably the most intriguing of these movements, continuously and rapidly wobbling your eyeball about its center in a circular fashion. "They cause the cornea and retina (front and back) of your eyes to move in circles with incredibly minute diameters of approximately 1/1000 (.001) of a millimeter, or .00004 inch." For a true understanding of how small these tremors are, Wagner suggests drawing a small circle on a piece of paper to represent a single tremor movement. Now put seventy of those circles side by side, each touching the other. If that row of circles could now be shrunken to a point capable of fitting on the width of a standard sheet of paper, one circle would represent the actual size of a single tremor movement. In Tom Wagner's words, "If you can do that, you will have a feel for the minuscule nature of the tremors along with some appreciation for the Creator who has demonstrated His capacity for designing such a thing."

Far from conclusive, these types of arguments may strengthen my beliefs, but they are not going to change any minds. Homology of vertebrate limbs is interesting, but still open to interpretation. Homology is the state of having the same or similar relation, relative position, or structure. Previously attributed to common design, Darwin was the first to attribute the striking similarities of the bone structures in the human hand, a whale's flipper, and a bird's wing to common descent. The truth is, bone structures by themselves tell us nothing. Homology of vertebrate limbs and the complexities of the human eye can be attributed to either. These facts are amazing, but they still leave me walking away asking, how does that prove or disprove the assertions of evolution? For that purpose, I need a bigger gun. Professor Jonathan Wells, PhD, Molecular and Cell Biology Senior Fellow, Center for Science & Culture, is an expert on biology science curriculum as it relates to Darwinian evolution. He has two PhDs, one in Molecular and Cell Biology from the University of California at Berkeley, and one in Religious Studies from Yale University. Often referred to as a scientific revolutionary, Dr. Wells is one of the nation's leading advocates for intelligent design, the theory that simply states that some features of life and the universe are better explained as the result of an intelligent agent than purely random, unguided processes. He has worked as a postdoctoral research biologist at the University of California at Berkeley, supervised a medical laboratory in Fairfield, California, and taught biology at California State University in Hayward.

In his book *Icons of Evolution: Science or Myth?*, Professor Wells argues that a number of the examples used to illustrate biology textbooks were "grossly exaggerated, distorted truth, or were patently false."[45] Wells believes that this shows that evolution conflicts with the evidence, and so (unsuccessfully) argued against its teaching in public education. The peppered moth is a prime example. The peppered moth is a famous icon of evolution that reportedly changed color during the industrial revolution because dark moths were better camouflaged on soot-darkened tree trunks and birds couldn't see them to eat them. The dark moths survived and the light moths were eaten. This is still used in many text books as a classic example of natural selection; when in fact, biologists discovered in the 1980s that peppered moths don't normally rest on tree trunks in the wild at all. And so (according to Professor Wells), "The text book pictures have all been staged and the story has serious flaws."[46]

Other famous icons of evolution are the Darwin finches, species of birds on the Galapagos Islands that are very similar except for the size and shapes of their beaks. Despite the differences in beaks most often being attributed to a common ancestor as a result of having to eat different foods on different islands, Dr. Wells is having no part of it. In his words, "The actual evidence shows us only that the beaks can change over a matter of years based on climate and diet, but the changes are temporary, they oscillate back and forth and they don't go anywhere. So, as evidence for the *Origin of Species*, Darwin's finches really don't work."[47] Minor changes within an existing species have never been controversial. Professor Wells points out that any beneficial mutations that might be used to support arguments in favor of evolution are extremely rare. Furthermore, they are biochemical in nature. For example, in antibiotic resistance, we know that mutations can lead to antibiotic resistance and then those bacteria can survive in the presence of say, streptomycin, where others could not. But the bacteria that survive are still the same species of bacteria. It's still tuberculosis, for example. So even the rare beneficial mutations we find do not really transform the organism.[48] The similarities and differences can cut either way, but what we are totally lacking is good evidence for Darwin's basic mechanism: common ancestry.

As defined by Professor Wells, Darwin's theory is that "all living things have descended from one or a few common ancestors, modified by unguided natural processes such as variation and selection."[49] He goes on to say, "Darwin called his *Origin of Species by Means of Natural Selection* 'one long argument,' but contrary to popular belief the argument was not based primarily on evidence. For instance, despite the title of his book Darwin had no evidence for the origin of species; nor did he offer any evidence for natural selection—only one or two imaginary illustrations. Instead, Darwin's book was primarily a theological argument against creation by design."[50] Minor changes within existing species are not the issue here. And yet, when Darwinists say, there is overwhelming evidence for Darwin's theory, what they talk about are minor changes within existing species. That's not the point at all. The point is the origin of new species by this same process. And no one has ever observed the origin of a new species through variation of selection; and they've tried. They've tried many times, but that key element in Darwin's theory, the origin of a new species, the title of his book has never happened."[51]

Further crumbling away the notion of common ancestry are recent scientific discoveries showing that many of the hominid species previously thought to have evolved from other earlier hominid species actually coexisted and interbred. In a study summarized in the *New York Times* science article "Ancestors of Modern Humans Interbred with Extinct Hominins" (March 17, 2016), Carl Zimmer reveals that a series of findings in recent years has conclusively shown ". . . the ancestors of modern humans once shared the planet with a surprising number of near relatives—lineages

like the Neanderthals and Denisovans that became extinct tens of thousands of years ago."[52] Zimmer quotes Carles Lalueza-Fox, a research
scientist at the Institute of Evolutionary Biology in Barcelona, Spain
(not involved in the study), as saying, "This is yet another genetic nail in
the coffin of our over-simplistic models of human evolution." The *New
York Post* Associated Press article "Neanderthal 'Love Child' Discovery
Shows Prehistoric Interbreeding" reveals that scientists have found ". . .
the remains of a prehistoric female whose mother was a Neanderthal and
whose father belonged to another extinct group of human relatives know
as Denisovans. The 90,000-year-old bone fragment found in southern
Siberia marks the first time a direct offspring of these two groups has
been discovered." The same article goes on to say, "Past genetic studies
have shown interbreeding between the two groups, as well as with our
own species, which left a trace in the DNA of today's people."[53]

Another icon of evolution is the four-winged fruit fly. Most fruit flies
have two wings, but on occasion, through a series of mutations, a fruit fly
develops a second set of wings. Very normal-looking, but in fact, there are
no muscles attached to the second set of wings and they are effectively
dead. The fly is a hopeless cripple. As Dr. Wells puts it, "This is not the
forerunner of a new race of insects, but an evolutionary dead end." In a
July 9, 2014 YouTube video entitled "Professor Exposes Impossibilities
of Evolution," Dr. Wells recalls in his own words, "I can take a fruit fly
embryo, and this has been done, in fact, and (the DNA) can be mutated
in every possible way . . . and there are only three possible outcomes, a
normal fruit fly, a defective fruit fly, or a dead fruit fly. That's it. You can't
even change the species, much less get a horse fly or a horse, or something
like that."[54]

Although creationists and evolutionists will disagree on when it took
place and how long it lasted, the fossil record clearly and unarguably demonstrates that most major animal phyla appeared suddenly in an event
known as the Cambrian explosion. This sudden appearance of a diverse
fossil record documents the emergence of modern metazoan divisions
of the kingdoms of living things. Prior to the Cambrian explosion, most

organisms were simple, composed of individual cells occasionally organized into colonies. Following the explosion, the rate of diversification accelerated, and the variety of life began to resemble that of today.

As it relates to the Cambrian explosion, Professor Wells believes, "There was an explosion of genetic information, very real and, I think, inexplicable on Darwinian terms. But there was also an explosion of information of another sort and that's the information that gets us body plans. The body plan as far as we know is not in the DNA. For example, we know that a lot of genes that play roles in development are very similar in fruit flies and humans; and yet, fruit flies and humans have totally different body plans. It turns out that those genes, the most impressive ones, the most dramatic ones, are active fairly late in embryo development, long after the body plan is established. So whatever is establishing the body plan, it's something else and there obviously had to be an explosion of body plans, as well as DNA information. Certainly, DNA is essential. You cannot get an animal without the proper DNA, but developmental biologists know that there is a lot more to the development than the DNA. We sometimes hear of the notion of a genetic program where the DNA is the blueprint for the organism. That's quite a common image, but in fact we know that there is a lot of information for development that is not in the DNA. So, properly speaking, the DNA is not the blueprint. It's more like a parts list. The DNA provides the body, the animal body with proteins and RNAs and other chemical constituents, but the DNA does not dictate the form of the animal, as far as we know."[55]

To better explain the concept of the body plan, Professor Wells compares it to the construction of a house. Again, in his words, "A house is a good analogy for the way DNA functions in the cell. The DNA, as I said, is like a parts list." Provided the same materials, you can build all kinds of structures. Ten contractors in ten different locations, each being provided identical lots of lumber, piping, wiring, nails, roofing, cement, and so on, would likely build ten different houses if asked to construct a home with no building plans. It's the same with the cell. "The DNA provides the building materials or the list of building materials, but then the cell

decides the floor plan. The floor plan is somewhere else ..." To be successful, things need to be done in a certain order. You can't build a roof before
a foundation or string the wires before the walls are framed. "The DNA
gives us the list of parts, but the rest, for the most part, certainly the floor
plan is somewhere else."[56]

Tirelessly searching for the elusive missing links and perhaps as a
result of the mounting evidence opposing common ancestry, esteemed
evolutionists have on occasion resorted to fraud in their desperate search
for validation. Found in a gravel pit in Sussex, England in 1912, the Pilt-
down man was considered by some to be the second most important fossil ever found, proving the existence of the evolution of man, at least until
forty-one years later when it was found to be a complete forgery. The
skull was found to be of modern age. The fragments had been chemically
stained to give the appearance of age, and the teeth had been intentionally
filed down![57] Found in southern Spain in 1982, the Orce man was for
a short period of time, touted as the oldest European fossilized human
remains ever found. One year after the discovery, officials were forced to
admit that the skull fragment was not human, but probably came from
a four-month-old donkey. Scientists had said that the skull belonged to
a seventeen-year-old man who lived 900,000 to 1.6 million years ago.
They even had drawings to represent what he would have looked like.[58]
More recently and perhaps the most notorious evolutionary fraud ever
committed occurred in China and was published in *National Geographic*
magazine. Dinosaur bones were put together with the bones of a newer
species of bird and Chinese paleontologists passed it off as a very important new evolutionary intermediate, Archaeoraptor Liaoningensis, in an
article entitled "Feathers for T-Rex" by Christopher P. Sloan.[59]

Those who have read this book to this point will not be at all surprised to know that I am an admitted creationist. I do not believe that I
am a descendant of a primate, or that fish once crawled out of the sea to
become land animals, or that evolution is anything more than adaptation
within a given species. As a creationist, I of course have a favorite proof
of creation—that proof for me is the coelacanth. By definition, any proof

of creation must also contradict evolution and as I see it, the coelacanth satisfies that definition.

Extensive fossil remains from the geologic column tell us that this sixty-six-million-year-old monster fish had a makeup so different from any other known fish that it can only be described as prehistoric. Defined as drift-hunters, this large two-meter-long predator had a body covered in scales that acted as armor. It had eight fins—two dorsal fins, two pectoral fins, two pelvis fins, one anal fin, and one three-lobed caudal fin. At the back of the skull, the coelacanth possessed a hinge, the intra-cranial joint, which allowed it to open its mouth extremely wide. The heart of the coelacanth was shaped differently from that of most modern fish; the heart's chambers were arranged in a straight tube. Today, the coelacanth is the most famous of all "living fossils" because it is the best-known example of a "Lazarus Taxon," that is, animals that were supposed to be long extinct (dead for sixty-six million years) and were unexpectedly found to be alive. Coelacanths were supposed to have become extinct in the Cretaceous period, along with the dinosaurs, but in 1938, a live specimen was caught in South Africa, nearly eighty years after Darwin's publication, *On the Origin of Species*.

Since 1938, more specimens have been seen and photographed. We now know that the eyes of the coelacanth are acclimatized to seeing in poor light by having rods that absorb mostly low wavelengths. The vision of coelacanths consists of a mainly blue-shifted color capacity and the coelacanth's auditory reception is mediated by its inner ear. They feed on smaller fish, including small sharks, and are usually found in deep, dark waters. With the discovery of a second coelacanth colony in the deep waters off the coast of Indonesia in 1999, there are now at least two known surviving coelacanth colonies. On Sunday, August 24, 2014, I watched a documentary of this discovery on television with eager anticipation. More closely related to lungfish, reptiles, and mammals than to the ray-finned fishes, coelacanths have commonly been considered by evolutionists to be a transitional species between fish and tetra pods (four-footed species). The vertebrate-to-land transition is considered to be one of the most important steps in evolutionary history. I was curious to see how this "transitional species" would be explained by evolutionists now that it has been found to still be alive and virtually unchanged since first being documented in the fossil record, sixty-six million years ago.

The answer was simple. The coelacanth is no longer a "transition species," but rather, a species critical to our understanding of the vertebrate-to-land transition. It was concluded that the closest living fish to the tetrapod (four-footed species) ancestor is now the lungfish, not the coelacanth. How can this be? The coelacanth has enamel-covered teeth and hand-like fins that connect directly to its backbone. Besides, the lungfish is already known to be alive today and according to the fossil record, has been for 380 million years. This seems erringly similar to the circular logic that was once used to convince all of Europe that the world was flat. I am from the generation before evolution was taught as a fact and reinforced by everything that we see and hear. To me, there is no greater proof of creation than the "transition species." Two fish that have existed for between 66 and 380 million years without change tell me that there really isn't that much going on with evolution.

As closely related as each leg of our scientific foundation is, it is not difficult to imagine that a single discovery might someday impact every leg of that foundation. After all, without the support of radiocarbon dating, the geologic column is nothing more than a list of scientific best guesses and without the geologic column, evolution has no place on a multi-thousand-year-old planet. A recent and accidental discovery by Professor Mary Schweitzer has done just that. Shattering the geologic column, her work has unintentionally contributed to the crumbling-away of the remaining two legs of our current scientific foundation.

On a *60 Minutes* broadcast, on December 26, 2010,[60] Lesley Stahl had no idea of the whirlwind that was about to ensue when she reported on how famed dinosaur hunter Jack Horner was shaking up the world of paleontology. Paleontologist Jack Horner was the inspiration for the 1993 classic film *Jurassic Park*, actually starred in *Jurassic Park* as paleontologist Alan Grant, and was the technical consultant on a host of *Jurassic Park* sequels. Most famous for discovering the first known dinosaur nesting ground, Horner has discovered more tyrannosaurus rex than any other person on the planet. His life's ambition is to genetically reconstruct a living dinosaur and with the help of his partner, recent B. rex laboratory discoveries have brought that dream closer to reality. His partner and fellow paleontologist, North Carolina University professor Mary Schweitzer, studies the internal makeup of ancient bones. To examine these, Professor Schweitzer must literally break bones apart and sometimes even dissolve the outer mineral layers in acid. As you can imagine, with the extreme rarity of recovered dinosaur bones, paleontologists were never standing in line to allow her the opportunity to destroy their hard-earned and recovered finds. It was the partnership of Jack Horner and Mary Schweitzer that made the least-known greatest discovery in modern history possible.

It all started in the year 2000 with a series of coincidences when paleontologist Bob Harmon, chief preparator at the Museum of the Rockies and a member of Jack Horner's team, discovered a T. rex skeleton near Hell Creek, Montana. In a remote cliff face and under fifty feet of rock, it took two years and three summers to fully recover the T. rex. By that time, the T. rex had been named B. rex in honor of the discoverer. Because of the remote location, the T. rex bones had to be transported by helicopter. Sadly, the T. rex femurs were too large to be air-lifted and had to be cut in half. The bone fragments that fell out during the cutting were shipped to Professor Schweitzer for examination. What happened next happened by mistake. Mary put some B. rex bone fragments in acid to dissolve away the outermost mineral layer, but the acid worked too fast and by the time she returned to her fragments, all the mineral had dissolved. Being a sixty-eight-million-year-old fossil, there should have been nothing left, but there was and it was elastic, like living tissue. According to Schweitzer, it looked like the tissue that she would expect to find with modern bone. Not believing what she had found, Professor Schweitzer and her technician repeated the process again and again. In sample after sample, there appeared to be what looked like flexible and transparent blood vessels and intact cells. What Mary found inside dinosaur bones posed a radical challenge to existing science that dictates that organic material cannot survive even a million years, let alone sixty-eight million.

Finally, Schweitzer mustered the courage to take her findings to her partner and after additional testing, Mary, Jack, and their team published their findings in a series of papers and the *Journal of Science* and were promptly attacked. Critics said that their samples might have been contaminated or that the proposed blood vessels were actually something called bacterial biofilms, a type of slime that mimics real blood vessels. However, the results were indisputable. As demonstrated on *60 Minutes*, Mary was able to reproduce her findings with an even older eighty-million-year-old, well-preserved duck-billed hadrosaurid. After dissolving the minerals away, the microscope showed that blood vessels were again clearly evident. Over and over, the results were the same. Mary published her new results in 2009 and while some of her critics were swayed, the controversy still rages. The stakes are high and scientists who believe ask, if blood vessels can survive eighty million years, what about DNA?

Once serious labs began publishing scientific papers declaring the discovery of dinosaur soft tissue, it didn't take long for creationists to also decalcify dinosaur bones and subject the resulting soft tissue to radiocarbon dating. This had never been done before. The age of dinosaur bones had always been determined by the geologic column and verified by potassium-argon dating. With a half-life of 5730 years and admittedly, no ability to measure anything beyond 50,000 years, it made no sense to radiocarbon date bones that were purported to be millions of years old. It was the discovery of dinosaur soft tissue that made it all possible. What they found were measurable levels of ^{14}C. The geologic column, evolution, and science itself tell us that the presence of ^{14}C in dinosaur soft tissue is impossible. Then again, the geologic column, evolution, and potassium-argon dating tells us that dinosaur soft tissue shouldn't exist. If a ball of ^{14}C the size of our planet existed and was never replenished, the laws of carbon decay tell us that the entire planet-sized ball of ^{14}C would have decayed within a million years.

The presence of ^{14}C implies that the dinosaur bones are thousands of years old, not millions. Creationists soon published their own discoveries and the whirlwind began. The first to discover dinosaur soft tissue, Jack Horner and Mary Schweitzer immediately rejected the notion that dinosaur bones could be anything other than millions of years old. Instead, they attempted to discredit the results by attributing the presence of ^{14}C to contamination. Eleven universities, including Harvard, have since verified the presence of ^{14}C and that the soft tissue being found inside the dinosaur bones is, in fact, original biological material from the dinosaur. Any possibility of ^{14}C contamination is now well beyond even consideration. Jack Horner and Mary Schweitzer ignored the radiocarbon results and instead, struggled for excuses to explain how dinosaur soft tissue might have survived for millions of years. Bob Enyart of Real Science Radio in Denver, Colorado offered Horner a $30,000 grant to allow him to have a soft tissue sample from B. rex radiocarbon dated. Horner declined. Paleontologists began publishing scientific papers proclaiming proof that dinosaurs are thousands of years old, only to find themselves unemployed. One such scientist to lose his job was creationist Mark Armitage. According to Mark Armitage, no soft tissue could survive for even ten thousand years, let alone eighty million years in the presence of insects, microbes, rodents, plants, and fungal bodies.

By the time of this writing, fifty-plus articles in scientific journals have documented fourteen bio-organic materials in dinosaur bones that testify to the fact that they cannot be millions of years old. They include: blood vessels, red blood cells, hemoglobin, bone cells, ovalbumin, kinetin, unmineralized bone, collagen, limited DNA, skin pigments, FEX proteins, histones, keratin, and elastin. Dr. Mary Schweitzer has published nine studies in *Science* that "challenge traditional notions of what a fossil is: a stone replica of the original bone."[61] Schweitzer is now quoted as saying, "If that 'stone' includes proteins from a living animal, I don't know what the definition is anymore . . ."[62] Without the millions of years of cover provided by the geologic column, arguments supporting evolutionary conclusions become nearly impossible to digest. Gradual transitions that supposedly took place over millions of years must now be accepted as radical changes taking place over hundreds and thousands of years. If that were so, it would seem that we might see changes within a lifetime or a few generations.

Common sense and logic cry out to even the most hardened supporters of Darwinism. Unproven theories cannot stand in the face of contradicting facts of such mammoth proportion. The fact is that after nearly two centuries of intense research, the paleontological evidence for evolutionary theory is not only rare, but highly questionable. If evolution had really happened, the evidence would be in great abundance and incontestable. The museums would be overflowing with fossils clearly documenting the transitions between the various biological groups. Yet there are none. Moreover, there is no indication that the situation will change in the future. Those very few fossils that are claimed to show some kind of evolutionary link such as the bone fragments of the Pleistocene ape called Homo habilis are very far from conclusive.

There you have it: the three-legged stool. The geologic column, radio-isotope dating, and the common ancestry of evolution testify to a 4.6-million-year-old planet. Each leg helps to support the others and holds up a platform that is constructed with hollow legs and cannot be trusted. If we can no longer assume that dinosaurs are millions of years old, the geologic column falls away, and the three-legged stool becomes a two-legged stool. Likewise, without the millions of years of cover provided by the geologic column, gradual changes become rapid changes and the common ancestry of evolution disintegrates. The two-legged stool becomes a one-legged stool and sitting requires continual adjustment. The point being, a one-legged stool cannot stand alone. Soon enough, the arguments and excuses are greater than the facts. If and when this is recognized, the remaining faulty leg that is radioisotope dating collapses. Without radioisotope dating, the geologic column, and evolution, the world is again open to interpretation and miraculously seems to align with the biblical historic record. A level playing field is established.

When you consider that world-impacting decisions with potentially life-ending consequences are routinely based on the assumptions of theories and pseudo-sciences, identified inconsistencies to scientific interpretations should be just as important to the atheist as they are to the creationist. There are real-life consequences when science promotes theories as fact.

In June of 2019, I read an article entitled "Deep Borehole Nuclear Waste Disposal Just Got a Whole Lot More Likely."[63] Deep borehole nuclear waste disposal is a strategy put forth by Deep Isolation, a start-up company from Berkeley that seeks to dispose of nuclear waste at a much lower cost than existing strategies. Elizabeth Muller, CEO of Deep Isolation, noted, "Bechtel was the first major industry player that understood the significance of what Deep Isolation is doing. They appreciate the importance of innovation and urgency in solving the nuclear waste problem."[64] Worldwide, with an estimated 450,000 metric tons of nuclear waste awaiting disposal, I agree that finding a means to safely dispose of the world's nuclear waste is paramount, but I do not agree with risking the lives of future generations for lack of a real-world solution. Fully onboard, James Taylor, general manager of Bechtel's environmental business line, added, "Deep geologic disposal is the scientific consensus for permanently removing and disposing used nuclear fuel and high-level waste from their current locations around the world."[65] The article goes on to claim that deep borehole disposal of nuclear waste is not just theoretical, but a proven technology. "As geologists, we know how many millions of years it takes for anything to get up from that depth in the Earth's crust, especially in tight rock formations like shale."[66] That's when my ears perked up. You don't know how many millions of years it takes for anything to get up from that depth. Deep Isolation and Bechtel are asking the world to gamble the lives of future generations on a theoretical, seventeenth-century unproven shot in the dark known as the geologic column. This is why it is important to find out for yourself what is fact and what is theory.

5

OUR STAGGERED PAST:
THE DINOSAURS THAT TIME REMEMBERS

By now you may be wondering where the author is trying to take you. What point is he trying to make? Does he disagree with all that civilization has learned about their development and existence? Is his intention to disprove the tenets of modern science? I assure you that nothing could be further from the truth. I believe that it is only through the discoveries of modern science that I can open my eyes and yours.

At an early age, I made a hard decision, a decision that would inescapably impact the greater portion of my life. I chose to seek the truth of God, to find a basis for blind faith. I acknowledged that the cost of my search might be the comfort provided by my faith. The foundation of my inner soul might well crumble beneath my feet. It was a scary thought and I stepped gingerly at first. I feared offending God; or worse yet, discovering he wasn't there. As an altar boy at a time in life when most young minds would typically refine their lifelong beliefs, I wondered if the hypocrisy and self-justification of my mother's church existed in all organized religion. More importantly, I wondered if the ever-present Holy Spirit was confined to a specific religion? Fifty plus years later, I have found much of what I sought and much is based on an independent interpretation of modern archeological finds and scientific discoveries. My findings and conclusions are what I wish to share. To maintain any possibility that the reader might consider or even embrace any of the extreme, bizarre, and far-fetched concepts that I now consider facts, I must first provide an overview of the modern archeological finds and scientific discoveries that those conclusions were made upon.

In the previous chapter, I attempted to tear down the artificial barriers that would prevent you from believing the concepts that I will put forth in this chapter. I provided my arguments for why we should not blindly accept theories of the geologic column, evolution, and carbon dating as hard science. In this chapter, I will discuss the infrequently covered archaeological finds and scientific discoveries that have convinced me that dinosaurs are thousands of years old, and not millions of years old. I will create another building block to show that the Bible may contain a more accurate account of our existence than our so-called history books.

Giving credence to the likelihood of an accurate biblical historic record, a favorite non-biblical proverb comes to mind. That proverb is that the devil will show you ten truths to convince you of one lie. As it relates to dinosaurs, I think the one lie is that the geologic column shows us that dinosaur bones are millions of years old. To suppose that dinosaurs roamed the earth only a few thousand years ago, you must first suspend your belief in such baseless and contradicting theories (chapter 4). We as a people like to believe that we have been on a linear path that has brought us to where we are today, but facts indicate that our journey may not have been as linear as evolution and the supporting geologic column would have us believe. Archaeological evidence shows that advanced societies perhaps even greater than today have existed in our past and inexplicably faded to obscurity. Unmatched technologies have been born and lost.

Time erodes everything, but stone stands the test of time. Located in the Beqaa valley of Baalbek, Lebanon, proof of ancient technology is unmistakable in the quarried megalithic foundation stones under the Temple of Jupiter. The German Archaeological Institute estimates that one of these foundation stones weighs nearly 2.5 million pounds. Even today, only a handful of the world's most monstrous cranes would be capable of lifting such a stone; and yet, we are told that these foundation stones were laid between 7,000 and 12,000 years ago. Lasting nearly forever, stone remnants of previous advanced civilizations and lost technologies are by no means rare. Weighing several tens of tons, the interlocking finely cut andesite building blocks of the temple complex of Puma Punku in Bolivia fit together like identical puzzle pieces, forming load-bearing joints without the use of mortar. The precision with which the angles of these interlocking blocks have been crafted to create flush joints is indicative of an advanced and thorough understanding of descriptive geometry. Not even a piece of paper can be passed between these stones. They represent a highly sophisticated knowledge of stone-cutting techniques that cannot be matched with the limitations of today's technology. And yet, archeologists tell us that these blocks were created by a civilization that flourished between AD 300 and AD 1000, had no form of written language, and was ignorant of the existence of the wheel.

Just as impressive, but rarer, are the metallic leftovers of ancient civilizations and technologies that have not yet completely corroded away. Dated between 70 BC and AD 50, the Antikythera mechanism was discovered in 1901 by a sponge diver in a shipwreck off the coast of the Greek island of Antikythera. This mechanism was recently proven through X-rays, research, and reconstruction to be the world's first known computer. Accounting for the elliptical orbit of the moon and the cyclic variations of that orbit, multiple interlocking brass gears with prime numbers of teeth and variable speed rotations have been shown to accurately predict the location of the planets and the exact hour of future solar and lunar eclipses. Following the fall of the Roman Empire and the decline of Greek civilization, knowledge of rudimentary interacting gear works was not reintroduced to Europe until the thirteenth century when the Arab Moors integrated through Spain. Simple by today's standards, the gear-driven clock would not be invented for another hundred years when clocks suddenly began appearing in Europe during the Renaissance of the fourteenth century. To put this in perspective, a precise astrological computer existed 1400 years before man was able to measure time independent of the shadow of the sun.

Another often overlooked contradicting artifact of linear history is the iron pillar of Delhi. Originally erected and dedicated to the Hindu deity lord Vishnu in the third or fourth century AD, the twenty-three-foot-tall iron pillar of Delhi stands in the Qutb complex at Mehrauli in Delhi, India. Outside and exposed to the elements, the iron pillar of Delhi remained rust-free for well over 1500 years. Only recently beginning to show signs of weathering, numerous high-definition photographs document that the current rust has been over 1500 years in the making. Material scientists have concluded that the corrosive resistance resulted from an even layer of crystalline iron hydrogen phosphate hydrate forming on the high-phosphorus-content iron, which has served until just recently to protect the pillar from the effects of weather. The rust-resistant composition of the metal testifies to the skills achieved by ancient Indian ironsmiths in the extraction of impurities and the processing of iron, a process that has not since been duplicated.

These mysterious discoveries of previous lost and often never duplicated technologies can only be explained with the accepted recognition of gaps in our historical record. Even following the birth of written language, our planet's documented record contains many holes and inconsistencies. The world has been reset and the historical record stopped and restarted many times. Although it is important to recognize how these gaping holes in the human story open doors for the inquisitive to ponder theories of universal acceptance, it is just as important to recognize how much has been lost and left open to speculation. The reasons for these stops and starts are many and varied. They include, but are not limited to: asteroid impacts, the great flood, the fall of the Tower of Babel (2200 BC), the Dark Ages (AD 400–1000), the black death (1347–1353), the Mini Ice Age (1646–1715), nuclear destruction (1945), genocide, cultural cleansing, and natural disasters.

The mile-wide Meteor Crater (also known as the Barringer Crater) in the northern desert of Arizona is just one of many examples throughout the world that show us that our planet is and has been scarred with the craters and pockmarks of celestial impacts since inception. Small by comparison to other known examples, the meteorite that created the Barringer Crater is estimated to have had an impact of 150 times greater than the 20-kiloton nuclear blast that destroyed Hiroshima in August of 1945. Regardless of any preconceived beliefs of how, when, or even if the dinosaurs went extinct sixty million years ago, six thousand years ago, or six hundred years ago, it is evident that life on earth and history itself have been significantly changed by celestial impacts since time began. The impact of the massive asteroid that created the 105-mile-wide Chicxulub Crater in the Yucatan Peninsula of Mexico no doubt caused mega-tsunamis, earthquakes, and volcanic eruptions around the world. Estimated to have been the equivalent of a one-billion-kiloton explosion, the impact of the Chicxulub Asteroid was certainly big enough to cause mass extinctions and to change the world forever. More recently, a small icy comet or stony asteroid disintegrated in an airburst explosion over the Siberian Stony Tunguska River in Krasnoyarsk Krai, Russia, in 1908. The explosion occurred in an area so remote that Russian scientists were unable to reach the site until 1927. What they found was that every tree had been leveled in over 770 square miles of forest. Had a similar airburst explosion occurred over a populated area, the concussion alone could have erased an entire tribe from Northern Siberia and the world.

Biblical stories of Noah, the great flood, and the Tower of Babel tell us of breaks in history where the discoveries, folklore, stories, and beliefs of many were left in the hands of a very few. Even more responsible for these lapses in the historical record are the commands of God for the taking of the Promised Land. Speaking for God, Moses told the Israelites, "These *are* the statutes and judgments which you shall be careful to observe in the land which the Lord God of your fathers is giving you to possess, all the days that you live on the earth. You shall utterly destroy all the places where the nations which you shall dispossess served their gods, on the high mountains and on the hills and under every green tree. And you shall destroy their altars, break their *sacred* pillars, and burn their wooden images with fire; you shall cut down the carved images of their gods and destroy their names from that place" (Deuteronomy 12:1-3).

Beginning with the utter destruction of the Canaanites under Moses (Numbers 21:1-2) and continuing with the fall of Jericho under Joshua (Joshua 6:20-21), entire civilizations have been intentionally stricken from the record in the name of God throughout history. "And they utterly destroyed all that was in the city, both man and woman, young and old, ox and sheep and donkey, with the edge of the sword" (Joshua 6:21). Over and over, entire populations were erased from the face of earth. "The Israelites returned to Ai and struck it with the edge of the sword. So it was *that* all who fell that day, both men and women, *were* twelve thousand— all the people of Ai. For Joshua did not draw back his hand, with which he stretched out the spear, until he had utterly destroyed all the inhabitants of Ai" (Joshua 8:24-26). "Joshua took Makkedah, and struck it and its king with the edge of the sword. He utterly destroyed them—all the people who *were* in it. He let none remain" (Joshua 10:28). Burning the city of Hazor, Joshua ". . . struck all the people who *were* in it with the edge of the sword, utterly destroying *them*. There was none left breathing" (Joshua 11:11). "So, Joshua conquered all the land: the mountain country and the South and the lowland and the wilderness slopes, and all their kings; he left none remaining, but utterly destroyed all that breathed, as the Lord God of Israel had commanded. And Joshua conquered them from Kadesh Barnea as far as Gaza, and all the country of Goshen, even as far as Gibeon. All these kings and their land Joshua took at one time, because the Lord God of Israel fought for Israel" (Joshua 10:40-42).

Compounding the immeasurable world losses incurred from expunged populations are periods of human survival where records were simply not kept. Despite history revealing that Europe was home to some of the most advanced civilizations in the world—the Minoans, the Greeks, and the Romans—out of nowhere, the advancement of Europe suddenly stopped dead in its tracks. For centuries, society regressed, people became hand-to-mouth hunter-gatherers, existing technologies vanished, and recorded history all but disappeared. It was the Dark

Ages. Known as one of the least progressive eras that mankind has ever endured, the Dark Ages is defined as the period of time that took place in Europe between the decline of the Roman Empire and the Renaissance of the fourteenth century. Economic growth was virtually non-existent for over a millennium, living standards fell into decline, and the average mortality rate dropped to near thirty. Continual rains resulted in constant famines and streets were littered with sewage. Set back centuries, poor sanitation and limited education led to what can only be defined as primitive subsistence. There are many reasons why this sudden regression occurred, but historians believe political instability to be the most influential. In the absence of the Roman Empire, western Europe became politically fragmented, leading to constant wars and invasions. Established trade routes and public infrastructures crumbled. Poor sanitation meant that plagues were a regular occurrence. The black death wiped out an estimated twenty million people across Europe. Those who didn't die from the plague died from famine.

In a Europe consisting mostly of illiterate people scrambling around, looking for food, and trying to hide from the plague, it comes as no surprise that few Dark Age records exist. With the exception of European monasteries, whose monks laboriously copied ancient texts in their efforts to preserve them, few historical events or technological advances were documented. In terms of historical events, much is lost in regard to the European exploration of the Americas. The famous fifteenth-century Vinland map purportedly shows a detailed map of the North American coastline at a time before it was even known to exist. We know for certain that the Vikings reached Newfoundland on their travels across the Atlantic Ocean, but what we don't know is, how far did they actually travel in their exploration? Some evidence suggests that the Vikings traveled as far west as Minnesota, but thanks to the Dark Ages, there are no written records to support related land claims. The rise and fall of leaders have also been poorly documented. Al-Hakim Bi-Amr Allah was the ruler of Egypt and much of North Africa during the early eleventh century, but according to history, one day he just up and disappeared. Then there are the mysteries surrounding famous artifacts. For example, does the shroud of Turin trace back to Christ, what was the recipe for Greek fire, and what exactly was the purpose of the Voynich Manuscript?

With minimal education and few people maintaining an ability to read or write, the resulting lack of skills has been greatly responsible for the loss of classical knowledge from centuries past. The writings of our greatest thinkers, scientists and philosophers were replaced by spirits and superstitions. To the detriment of a formerly advanced society, hard-lined beliefs replaced rational thought. Not intended as an attack on religion, this view was espoused by devout individuals such as the Tuscan scholar, Petrarch, who described the non-Christian Greek and Roman eras as a light compared to the darkness and gloom of the Dark Ages. While the classical civilization sought to understand the natural world, investigating such fields as biology, physics, and meteorology, Dark Age society believed that demons cause disease, that licking leprosy wounds would cure them, and that bloodletting was a sound idea. Unfounded beliefs replaced achievements and records from one of the most desperate of times in history simply vanished.

Just as Europe's population began recovering from the Dark Ages, Mother Nature followed up with the Little Ice Age. At the dawn of the fourteenth century, sometime around 1300, an unseasonable chill began to descend on the warm world of the Middle Ages. With brutal swiftness, over the course of only a decade, global temperature dropped dramatically. Birds fell dead out of the sky and millions perished as the cold triggered a chain reaction across civilization. Teofilo F. Ruiz, a professor of Medieval History at UCLA writes, "In 1315, from the Euro Mountains, deep in the heart of what is European Russia today, all the way to Ireland, the weather changed dramatically for the worse."[67] From Norway to New Zealand, glaciers began their rapid advance. The New York Harbor froze for five weeks, allowing people to walk from Manhattan to Statin Island. Eskimos sailed their kayaks as far south as Scotland and two feet of snow fell on New England in June and July, during a season so cold that it was remembered in both America and Europe as "The Year without a Summer." In England, the Thames River froze frequently, inspiring a carnival-like tradition called the Frost Fair. Merchants and merry-makers set up food stores and sideshows on the ice. The first was celebrated in 1607 and the last in 1814.

With estimates as high as 4° colder than today, Peter B. Demenocal, PhD, Professor of Earth Sciences, Columbia University believes that the Little Ice Age cooling was only 2-3° less than the average temperatures of today. It was a time of extreme volatility, of unpredictable climate shifts, rather than a constant cold. Brian Fagan, PhD, writes "Mixed up with no logic or cycle to them, changes in weather could not be predicted."[68] Lloyd D. Keigwin, Jr., PhD, of the Woods Hole Oceanographic Institution says, "It was a modest change compared to the things we see in the geologic record, but we know from historical accounts that it didn't take much to disrupt society."[69] Throughout Europe, fertile farmlands became waterlogged mud pits. Just as the crops were planted, it started to rain. "And it rained and it rained and it rained and many of the crops planted on marginal lands were simply washed away due to soil erosion."[70] Once again, many could do little more than survive, and recorded discoveries, folklores, stories, and beliefs suffered.

Climatologists believe that the Little Ice Age was not an isolated event, but part of a recurring cycle and a blueprint to our future. Scientists at the Kharkiv National University in the Ukraine recently identified a comet which struck the earth sometime around AD 536-540. This comet which exploded in the upper atmosphere smothered our planet in ash and dust, causing a previously unknown medieval-style nuclear winter in the process. Again and again, uncontrollable forces seem to wipe the human slate clean. Leaders rise and fall with a whimper and volumes of history, medical, and technological advances are lost. Surely the absence of linearity in man's historical record ought to be some indication that we may have missed a few things. We are reminded over and over that we are not the ruler of the universe, though we often think we are.

Adding to the devastating effects of nature and fate are the self-imposed genocidal crimes of man against man. Time and time again, mankind has attempted to eliminate difference and alternate thought through extermination. According to the US Holocaust Memorial Museum, up to seventeen million people were killed during the Holocaust of World War II. Six million of these were Jews—approximately two-thirds of all the Jews living in Europe at the time. Despite world outrage and a United Nations decree to never let this happen again, crimes of genocide continue to this day. In 1994, the world stood by and did nothing as Hutu extremists who controlled Rwanda murdered an estimated 800,000 innocent civilian Tutsis in the worst episode of genocide since World War II. Man does not need God or Mother Nature to destroy recorded discoveries, folklores, stories, and beliefs; he has proven himself capable of doing that himself. So much has been lost to the world; and yet, we believe that we still have all the answers.

Following the Iraq War and taking full advantage of the vacuum created by the official withdrawal of US forces, the Islamic State began an unrestrained campaign against the history and heritage of the Arab people, the destruction of the artifacts of ancient Mesopotamia. Islamic State militants utterly destroyed the now bulldozed city of Nimrud, an ancient Assyrian city that thrived between 1350 BC and 610 BC. Claiming that shrines and statues are "false idols," the Islamic State of Iraq and Syria (ISIS) destroyed the artifacts at the Mosul Museum, the second largest museum in Iraq in 2015. Irina Bokova, the Director-General of the United Nations Educational, Scientific and Cultural Organization (UNESCO) told Oksana Boyko in *Worlds Apart* that, "The persecution of people based on their ethnicity and the deprivation of their intangible heritage has become part of the human tragedy in the Middle East."[71] Recognized as financially advantageous to future acts of terrorism, looting antiquities for profit now goes hand-in-hand with the destruction of idols. Following an unimaginable month of torture, in August of 2015, Dr. Khaled al-Asaad, an eighty-two-year-old custodian and retired antiquities chief in Palmyra, Syria, was beheaded by the jihadists. He was tortured in a failed attempt to force him reveal the locations of hidden artifacts intended to be looted for profit.

As I said in the beginning, the reasons for history and the record of mankind itself to reset, stop, and restart are many and varied. Much has been lost or never recorded. It is in the nature of man to want to understand, to put reason where there is none, to string existing facts together to tell the story that fills the gaps and plugs the holes. These are the questions that great philosophers, theologians, and mathematicians ponder. The unknown is the birthplace of knowledge and theory. All is well until we believe our arguments at the expense of truth. I am reminded of the pains endured by Einstein in the birthing of his theory of relativity. Albert Einstein's 1915 predicted effects of gravity on light were met with much skepticism because they contradicted Sir Isaac Newton's 1687 formulated and accepted mechanics model. According to reports in *The New York Times*, the scientific community was fighting Einstein's theory head-on and enthusiastically. It took three years, until May 29, 1919, before a clear sky, a full solar eclipse, developing photographic technology, and the known location of a star behind the sun proved that light could bend and $E=MC^2$ became fact. Before May of 1919, everything known about gravity was imagined and theory. It is society's responsibility to ensure that science does not present theory as fact and that new discoveries that contradict existing theory are not suppressed at the expense of truth.

Evolution holds that dinosaurs evolved some 220 million years ago and died about 65 million years ago from any of a number of extinction events. But the Bible teaches that all land animals, including dinosaurs, were created on the sixth day, just thousands of years ago, and that they were all named by Adam just before God handed them over, charging Adam and Eve to take dominion over his creation. Then about 4,400 years ago, the entire world was deluged by Noah's flood and many dinosaurs, along with billions of other creatures, were wiped out. Accepting that much of our record has been lost to gaps in recorded history and suspending an unfounded belief in the theoretical geologic column, a closer look at the evidence suggests that the biblical account of dinosaurs may actually be correct. They may be thousands of years old rather than millions of years old. The evidence supporting this thesis is greater than the evidence disputing it.

The fossil record is filled with giant creatures and plants. We know this because all over the earth, there are billions of dead things buried in rock layers laid down by water. When we look at the dinosaur fossil record, we see that they were buried furiously, rapidly, and simultaneously, often-times, found fleeing in groups. The Hilda mega-bonebed in Alberta, Canada, was first described in the scientific literature in 2010.[72] Thousands of centrosaurus were catastrophically buried over an entire square mile. In China, thousands of different kinds of dinosaurs were simultaneously buried in a single 980-foot ravine. There are hundreds of dinosaur bone beds all over the world, including the United States where the Morrison Formation covers thirteen states and 700,000 square miles. Thousands of torn-apart dinosaurs are buried here in hundreds of mass graves. Many are found in the classic death pose with their necks arched back, choking as they died. More often than not, modern museum signage concedes that they died in a watery catastrophe. Some dinosaurs are even found mummified with tree leaves, flowers, ferns, shrubs, and algae still in their stomachs. Dinosaurs are even found buried with marine creatures. Isn't a global flood the best explanation for this? There is also a notable absence of dinosaur ancestors and transitions. Even the sign at the Chicago Field Museum admits that there have been zero transitions between dinosaur kinds. The sign shows question marks regarding where they came from. It's almost like someone just put each basic kind on earth, right at the same time.

Job, chapter forty, describes a majestic creature using the name "behe-moth," which means "colossal beast." In context, Job and his friends just finished over thirty chapters of dialog trying to explain God and why he would allow Job to suffer such hardships. Then God shows up in a whirlwind, tells Job to brace himself like a man, and says that he will be the one asking the questions now. For the next four chapters, God asks Job seventy-seven rhetorical questions, all having to do with creation. After explaining to Job that he is the master designer of space and earth,

God describes thirteen of his created animals such as the ostrich, horse, and deer. Then God caps off the discussion by telling Job about his two grandest creations: the behemoth and the leviathan. God calls the behemoth the first of all his ways, meaning the first in rank, the chief, the most supreme of his creative works. In context, God is saying to Job, sit down, brace yourself, and now I will tell you of the chief of all my works, the biggest, most amazing land creature I ever made. When we scan through all land-dwelling creatures, both living and extinct, the first in rank, the most colossal, or the chief, is clearly the sauropod dinosaur. Comparing God's word that the behemoth is the grandest creature he ever made with the fact that the sauropod is the largest land creature ever found, we find a substantial clue to the behemoth's identity.

The largest sauropod found to date was over 120 feet long; that's ten freeway lanes across. These massive reptiles were expertly designed with weight-bearing systems from head to toe that allowed their 200,000-pound body to propel itself. To make lifting their heads even possible, the neck vertebrae of the sauropods were filled with air. In fact, Dr. Mathew John Wedel, Associate Professor at the Western University Health Sciences Department of Anatomy in California, was granted an international award for discovering many of the secrets behind their unprecedented mobility. Their bones were pneumatic. Dr. Wedel notes that sauropods were wonders of biological engineering and that efficiency of design is especially evident in their vertebrae. The bones that make up their backbones were found to be increasingly lighter as he looked higher up their spinal column; they were filled with air, some up to 90%. CT scans revealed not marrow, but a honeycomb pattern inside the dinosaur's back and neck bones. Matt's work showed that the bigger the dinosaurs got, the more air they had in their vertebrae.

While this may solve the puzzle of how these gigantic creatures could lift and move their massive heads and necks, it doesn't solve the challenge of how the sauropods could possibly inhale enough oxygen through their tiny nostrils which were only about twice the size of those on a living horse. Perhaps they thrived better in a world before Noah's flood when oxygen levels were likely higher. Many unique dinosaur features indicate the existence of a completely different pre-rainbow, pre-flood world. The long necks and tails of the sauropods resembled living suspension bridges. For this creature to eat, breathe, and move its long neck, a series of over twelve neck vertebrae had to be interlocking and twistable. They had to have anchoring points in just the right places for muscles and ligaments to connect in such a way to prevent the neck from pinching veins and nerves and to brace the trachea and esophagus.

God describes the behemoth's strength in his hips and says that his power is in his stomach muscles. Again, we have a strong clue that the behemoth was the sauropod dinosaur because while many animals have strong hips and stomach muscles, none were as strong as the sauropod. The muscle structure required around the hips and stomach that were necessary for the sauropod to move, walk, turn, and eat would be incredible. In fact, for some sauropods, like the diplodocus, the highest point of its core body was the hips, and its whole body balanced on the hips, front to back. The diplodocus was able to rear up on its back legs and balance on its tail like a tripod, making use of its hips to support not just the back half of its body, but the front half as well. This required enormous strength in the hip and stomach muscles, lifting tons of its own body mass into the air. Below the hips was an incredible weight distribution system that went from massive femurs (in some cases eight feet long) to dual shin bones, and then to five toes.

The behemoth's tail also closely matches the sauropod's tail. God says that the behemoth moves his tail like a cedar tree and the sinews of his thighs are tightly knit. Paleontologists have learned from the muscle attachment locations on the sauropod's bones that the tightly knit structure of their thighs and hips actually made their tail swing from side to side with each step, much as a cedar tree does when it sways in the wind. Tail-drag marks are only rarely found behind sauropod footprints, indicating that their tails were raised while they walked. It's difficult to think of a creature that fits this biblical description better than the sauropod dinosaur.

God describes the sauropod's bones like beams of bronze. Most Bible versions translate this phrase as tubes of bronze, conduits of bronze, or pipes of brass, which conveys both strength and being hollow like a channel or a tube. This matches the fact that sauropods have the largest leg bone of any animal and they are, in fact, just like tubes of metal, having a hard outer casing and spongy marrow on the inside. Then God says, its ribs are like bars of iron. Unlike much of sauropod's skeleton that was spongy and filled with air for weight savings, its ribs were fully ossified. They were made out of solid bone. Again, we have a perfect match.

God even describes the behemoth's habitat. He lies under the lotus trees, in a covert of reeds and marsh. The lotus trees cover him with their shade; the willows by the brook surround him. This was a creature that lived in a lush tropical environment and had to be near lots of green food. Large sauropods are estimated to have eaten as much as a half a ton of vegetation each day and they likely had to eat all day long to consume it. Further emphasizing this fact, God tells Job that the greatest creature he ever created ate grass like an ox. Contrary to evolution that holds that grasses didn't evolve until millions of years after dinosaurs had gone extinct, in 2005 researchers in India found grass in sauropod coprolites. Open-minded paleobotanists have surmised that this fact alone may cause a re-write in our understanding of how dinosaurs evolved.[73]

Next, God says that indeed the river may rage, yet he is not disturbed; he is confident, though the Jordan gushes into his mouth. Why would God point out that this animal can stand in a rushing river? Lots of animals can do this, depending on the size of the rushing river. The Jordan River remains the largest river in Palestine and yet today, flows at a rate estimated to be only 15% of what it was in the not-so-distant past. In the winter, this river would be incredibly difficult to cross. It would take a very sizable animal to stand undisturbed in this rushing current and even more, let the current gush into its mouth. Some of the larger sauropods stood over twenty feet at the shoulders and weighed over seventy tons. Creatures of this size and mass could certainly withstand a raging river better than any others.

God says that only behemoth's Creator can approach him, that he cannot be captured by humans when he is on watch, and that no one can use barbs to pierce his nose. With a head that reached over forty feet high, the sauropod could also see people coming from far away. Its massive tail made him unapproachable. Based on what we know from fossils, some sauropods could cover a 200-foot circle with deadly force, using their tails which could be over fifty feet long and weigh over thirteen thousand pounds. Recent studies have shown that some sauropods could probably create sonic booms with their tails, just like a whip. It's not by chance that God says to Job that the behemoth can only be approached by his Creator. Even with all this evidence, some say that the behemoth was just a mythical creature, but why would God say that the behemoth was chief of all his creation after describing thirteen real and still living animals in the same passage? Why go to all the trouble of describing the behemoth as a grass-eating animal that lies peacefully in the shadow of the river plants along with his physical description, diet, and habitat, all of which happen to fit a known creature, a sauropod dinosaur?

God next calls to the attention of Job the leviathan (Job 41). God tells Job that the leviathan has a thick scaly armor that is impervious to human attack and should be feared. "Can you fill his skin with harpoons, or his head with fishing spears? Lay your hand on him; Remember the battle—Never do it again! Indeed, any hope of overcoming him is false; Shall not one be overwhelmed at the sight of him? No one is fierce that he would dare stir him up.... Though the sword reaches him, it cannot avail; Nor does the spear, dart, or javelin. He regards iron as straw, And bronze as rotten wood. The arrow cannot make him flee; Slingshots become like stubble to him. Darts are regarded as straw; He laughs at the threat of javelins" (Job 41:7-10, 26-29). God goes on to tell Job that the leviathan is not only a beautifully designed creation of self-defense, but also a formidable combatant with unique offensive skills. "His sneezings flash forth light, and his eyes are like the eyelids of the morning. Out of his mouth go burning lights; Sparks of fire shoot out. Smoke goes out of his nostrils, as from a boiling pot and burning rushes. His breath kindles coals, and a flame goes out of his mouth" (Job 41:18-21).

Consistent with the many stories from antiquity of fire-breathing dragons, creationists theorize that whatever the creature, the leviathan must have had glands to produce flammable chemicals and a spark of sorts to ignite the composition. Look no further than the combined chemical interaction of the bombardier beetle to know that such a thing can and does exist in creation. The bombardier beetle has a complex chemical factory that produces reactive chemicals: hydrogen peroxide and hydroquinone, held inert until they are squirted into a combustion chamber where an activating enzyme then causes an enormous, almost instantaneous increase in heat and pressure that explodes out of two twin cannons that are located to the rear of the beetle. Benzoquinone is ejected in a superheated pulsating jet that can be activated up to thirty times consecutively at a speed that is five times faster than any other spraying insect. The point being, if God could do this with a one-inch beetle that is indigenous to the temperate climate zones around the world, imagine what he could do with a twenty- or thirty-ton leviathan.

Assuming for a moment that the Bible is correct and that the existence of dinosaurs a few thousand years ago has somehow mysteriously been lost to the annals of documented history, surely some substantiating proof must still exist. Certainly, all evidence that contradicts scientifically embraced concepts of evolution and the geologic column could not have been suppressed or destroyed? Surprisingly, evidence of more recent living dinosaurs does exist, but you have to open your eyes and look for what may not be meant to be found, what is sparsely publicized. You have to open your mind to concepts that are contrary to what you were taught in school. Consider gravity. Prior to substantiating proof of Einstein's theory of relativity in 1919, the world had a completely different understanding of gravity. Remember, theories of evolution and the geologic column have never been proven.

A well-known old science book, *The Historia Animalium* by Paul S. Taylor, claims that dragons were still not extinct in the 1500s, but the animals were extremely rare and relatively small by then. After the flood, lifespans decreased and dragons became much smaller. This was precipitated by a tremendous change to the climate and ecology of the earth. According to the *Historia Animalium*, dinosaurs eventually went extinct in Europe because of overhunting. Having trouble adapting to a harsher world after the great flood, man pushed them into extinction. Now the dominant and most aggressive creature on earth, man has caused many animals to go extinct by overhunting. In the early 1800s (prior to Darwin), Indian arrowheads were often reported found mixed together with iguanodon, duck-billed dinosaur, ichthyosaur, and plesiosaur fossils. With teamwork and poison-tipped weapons, man can kill the largest of animals. Even Carl Sagan concedes in his book, *The Dragons of Eden*, that, "the pervasiveness of dragon myths in the folk legends of many cultures is probably no accident. . . . It is a worldwide phenomenon." Sagan believed that all these legends of dragons sounded almost exclusively like known dinosaurs and struggled unsuccessfully to explain them from an evolutionary point of view, ". . . in the dreams of humans; the dragons can be heard, hissing and rasping, and the dinosaurs thunder still."[74]

Dragons are everywhere in China; in their legends, festivals, astrology, art, names, and idioms. Depictions of dragons have been found in the tile artwork adorning the Ishtar Gate to the ancient city of Babylon in Mesopotamia, on a thousand-plus-year-old vase from Bolivia, the wood carvings of St. David's Cathedral in Wales, and in the Latin *Book of Hours* (c. AD 1450) which is illuminated by the Master of Jean Chevrot and currently housed at the Morgan Library & Museum. In an ancient Roman mosaic from the second century AD, two long-neck dragons are shown fighting or playing on the banks of the Mediterranean Sea. The joint structure of their legs, the layout of their bodies, and the lengths of their necks are an uncanny, very accurate depiction of a sarcoptic reptile known as the Tanystropheus. How in the world did the Romans know that? Were they just lucky in their guessing or maybe, the *Historia Animalium* is true?

Further evidence of man's unexplained knowledge of dinosaur anatomy is found in northern Cambodia, at one of the largest temple complexes in the world, Angkor Wat. Here, among the intricate stone carvings that adorn the walls of the sacred site, researchers have been fascinated by numerous images of animals that supposedly roamed the region where the temple was built. But one depicting what appears to be a dinosaur has archaeologists and scholars scratching their heads. There is a temple called Ta Prohm and it has a series of medallions that are carved into its surface, and one medallion in particular has attracted attention because it looks just like a stegosaurus. Some have cited this as an example of a dinosaur that lived into historical times. It is a stegosaurus carved in relief, not as a skeleton, but it is a stegosaurus with its skin and muscle as if someone saw it while it was alive. So how is it possible that the artist was able to carve something like this? What could explain the ancient builders of Angkor Wat having such a sophisticated knowledge of dinosaur anatomy? Could it be that their knowledge came firsthand, the result of actual interaction?

Bunyip is a name given by the Australian Aborigines to a big reptilian swamp monster that lived as late as the middle of the 1800s. When white settlers moved to that area, one of them found a huge, fresh, unfossilized leg bone. He asked the Aborigines, what on earth kind of monstrous animal lives in your swamp that could possibly have such a massive bone? The Aborigines replied that it must be the bone of the Bunyip or swamp monster. The G. Long Advertising Newspaper was intrigued by the story and decided that they wanted to know what this creature looked like. So they interviewed Australian Aborigine eyewitnesses, gathered all the details, and put together a detailed composite sketch of the Bunyip. The sketch was published in the paper in 1845. It was and is a museum-quality depiction of a known type of dinosaur, a duck-billed dinosaur called a hadrosaurus. It is accurate in the minutest detail. The amazing thing is that it is not a dead fossil; the Aborigines knew it as a living, walking, breathing creature. Yet this particular type of dinosaur had not been discovered until thirteen years after the publication of the composite sketch. Finally, someone found it in the fossil record and reported on it. It was previously unknown to science, but the Aborigines knew it as a living, breathing Bunyip. The creatures survived the flood and lived with man for a time. They were growing increasingly extinct, but apparently were still there in Australia as late as the mid-1800s.

Seemingly obvious to even the most avid critic of the Bible, the Nazca Indians not only coexisted with dinosaurs, but interacted with them in their day-to-day lives. The Nazca Indian Culture of South America is distinguished by having dinosaur motifs found often in their tapestry and pottery recovered from their ancient tombs. Centuries ago, in the days of the Spanish conquistadors in South America, the Spanish occupying the ancient Inca Empire kept a history of the Incas called *The Chronical of the Incas*. In there they have a passage mentioning that the Incas were fond of etching pictures on rounded river stones and then burying the etched stones ritualistically in their tombs. They said that most of the pictures were understandable, but that some of them were of strange monstrous reptilian dragon-like creatures that the Spanish were not familiar with. It was graphically illustrated and described by the Spanish centuries ago— centuries before the middle of the nineteenth century when dinosaurs were rediscovered as fossils. That's interesting because archaeologists would predict that if the Spanish were correct, that when we find and excavate Inca tombs, we would find these etched stones, and indeed we have found them, literally by the tens of thousands. And between twenty to thirty percent of them have etchings on them that look like unambiguous depictions of known types of dinosaurs. So unambiguous that the evolutionist's response was to call the depictions a fraud.

Ancient Incas could not possibly have known what dinosaurs looked like. However, according to the Bible, they could have because they survived the flood and they perhaps only recently disappeared and went extinct. Accusations of fraud are simply ridiculous. If you are going to perpetrate a fraud, you create one or two forgeries, not thousands of copies and then bury them in ancient Inca graves that are hard to find. But how in the world did the Spanish accurately report the existence of the river stones centuries before dinosaurs were rediscovered in the fossil record? If in fact these stones were forgeries, the sheer number of them discovered to date would have required an artist to carve one thousand of them a year, every year for fifty years.

Founder of the Cabrera Scientific Museum in Ica, Peru, Dr. Javier Cabrera, a qualified archaeologist and anthropologist, was also an MD and founder of the largest teaching medical hospital in Peru. Dr. Cabrera, a very respected academic, was not a creationist—he was an evolutionist. Yet he said that his archaeological findings forced him to concede that Darwin was wrong about one thing: he was wrong about assuming that dinosaurs went extinct millions of years ago. He believed this aspect of evolution to be false because, ". . . the ancient Incas were obviously intimately acquainted with known types of dinosaurs." Over 50,000 Inca burial stones have been found in Peru since 1961. Dr. Cabrera began his research in 1966. He excavated multiple Inca tombs at a time when it was legal to excavate them and keep the artifacts. To this day, Cabrera's acquired collection of Inca andesite burial stones is the largest collection of pre-Columbian artifacts of this type in any private collection or museum in the world. He has since passed away, but the Cabrera Museum is operated by surviving family members and remains open.

One stone in Dr. Cabrera's collection shows an ancient Inca riding elephant style on a three-horned, armored, plated triceratops dinosaur. This artifact recovered from a tomb fifteen centuries old shows dermal frills along the backbone of the triceratops. The world did not know that dinosaurs had this anatomical feature until the 1990s. They are made out of a skin-type of material that usually rots and is not preserved in the fossil record. In the 1990s, archeologists uncovered some of the best-preserved dinosaur remains ever found. From these remains, it was recognized that several sauropod and triceratops-type dinosaurs had that dermal backbone anatomical feature. Following the discovery of the hoard of well-preserved dinosaur remains in the 1990s, the British Broadcasting Company (BBC) came out with a special entitled "Walking with Dinosaurs," in which they trumpeted how proud they were to have the most anatomically correct depiction of dinosaur anatomy in world history. Dr. Kindell begs to differ. It appears that the ancient Incas had a better representation many centuries ago because they knew something that we didn't know. They had eyewitness accounts, not just dead bones and fossils to look at. Apparently, this type of dinosaur could be domesticated like an elephant as a beast of burden. As evidenced by the existence of thousands of river stone depictions of Inca warriors defending themselves and/or being killed by various other dinosaur types, all dinosaurs were obviously not able to be domesticated.

Also in Dr. Cabrera's collection, and even more significant, are the findings of many clay baked figurines—three-dimensionally depicted dinosaurs. These are extremely significant because baked clay can be dated by an entirely independent dating method from Carbon-14 testing. Carbon-14 is well known to give spurious dates even on artifacts of known dates in antiquity. Thermoluminescence testing is based on the luminosity index: energy trapped in the crystals in the clay. It is pumped in, so to speak, when they fire-heat the clay so you can tell how long it has been since the time of fire-heating by how much energy has leaked out of the crystal. The thermoluminescence testing method correlates closely with known dates of antiquity. When the baked figurines were found, the evolutionists chose to use this very accurate and accepted method of testing to prove that the dinosaur figurines were recently manufactured. However, thermoluminescence testing showed that the dinosaur figurines were many centuries old. There are many examples of these baked clay figurines in Dr. Cabrera's museum, many of them showing men and dinosaurs interacting. This includes riding triceratops dinosaurs, taking baby dinosaurs from their mother, feeding adult dinosaurs, hunting dinosaurs, and defending themselves from dinosaur attacks. The Inca people did not know that it was not politically correct to live with dinosaurs. They just portrayed life as they knew it and these creatures were normal to them and their life as they depicted it.

Centuries-old clay figurines of dinosaurs were not only discovered in Peru, but also in Mexico. In 1945, Waldemar Julsrud, a German immigrant riding a horse along an irrigation ditch on the side of El Toro Mountain, saw that a small landslide had revealed baked clay figurines sticking out of the soil and he began to excavate them. Decades of excavation have now been done and tens of thousands of these clay figurines have since been recovered. Many of them show known types of dinosaurs. Not only that, but thermoluminescence dating has shown them to be more than twice as old as the similar clay dinosaur figurines found in Peru. Some archeologists have identified the clay figurines with the preclassical Chupicuaro culture that existed between 800 BC and AD 200. Particularly interesting about these figurines is that the sauropod dinosaurs are depicted maneuvering in a manner that science did not believe was possible until the end of the twentieth century. Computerized analysis of sauropod anatomy has now confirmed that the great bone structure and muscle strength contained in the loins of the sauropod made it possible for it to stand and balance like a tripod on its tail and hind legs. Apparently the Acambaro Indians knew this not by computer analysis and animation, but by firsthand knowledge and eyewitness accounts.

The Acambaro depictions of the iguanodon dinosaur were better than modern man had until the latter part of the twentieth century. Sir Richard Owen first tried to reconstruct the iguanodon on four legs with a drooping tail and a horn at the end of his nose before realizing that they did not have a horned nose, rather, they had spiked thumbs as defensive weapons on their two front arms, walking on two legs with their tail dragging. Finally, by the late twentieth century we realized that they walked with their tail straight out, just as depicted in the clay figurines. Again, the ancient Chupicuaro culture appeared to have better knowledge of dinosaurs than modern man. These two-thousand-year-old clay dinosaur figurines are very well documented in Dr. Don Patton's DVDs, *Creation Evidence from South America and Mystery of Acambaro*.[75] The majority of the figurines are today housed in the Fr. Bernardo Padilla Museum in the city of Chupicuaro, approximately eight kilometers north of Acambaro.

Additional evidence of human interaction with dinosaurs is found in ancient cave paintings and petroglyphs. Just a few years ago at Natural

Bridges National Monument in Utah, creationists finally located a petroglyph long rumored to be discovered years earlier by evolutionists who would not confirm its existence and intentionally kept its location secret. It is the depiction of a auropod-type reptile believed to be an apatosaurus next to an Anasazi Indian warrior. We know that this is not a modern creation because it is thickly covered with a reddish chemical compound known as desert varnish that takes centuries to slowly build up on the surface of desert rocks. It easily dates back more than a thousand years, to a time when the climate was better and the Anasazi culture, as well as apparently some dinosaurs, was still thriving in what today is a very austere environment.

Geologist Dr. Don Patton of Dallas, Texas, heard about an ancient Indian petroglyph in Colorado, just across the Utah border, and went to photograph it. The petroglyph is referred to by the locals as the triceratops petroglyph because it has three horns, an armored plate behind its neck, and a triceratops-looking mouth. Evolutionists say no. The ancient Native Americans never saw a triceratops. They were just trying to draw a goat. However, just above the triceratops and much smaller is an actual petroglyph of a goat, showing that the Native Americans actually knew what a goat looked like and it didn't look like a triceratops. For those who care to look, similar proofs of the coexistence of dinosaurs and man exist all over the world. An ancient cave painting from Zimbabwe depicts what appears to be a tenontosaurus. A pictograph found in the Amazon rainforest illustrates nine warriors surrounding a sauropod—one with a raised spear in what appears to be a war party that dates back to the time of Job. Humans obviously saw these creatures alive if they were attempting to hunt them.[76]

Might ancient depictions of dinosaurs really be proof that humans and dinosaurs did at one time coexist? According to science, the notion is not only incredible, but downright impossible, even when confronted with indisputable evidence in the form of fossilized footprints of a dinosaur side by side with that of a human being. Dinosaur Valley State Park in Glen Rose, Texas, is famous for its dinosaur tracks. Less publicized or known is the fact that human tracks have also been found there, not only in the same formation, but on the same bedding plane and, in some cases, overlapping dinosaur tracks. Sauropod tracks were first found by local resident Charlie Moss and others in the 1930s, who reportedly mistook them for ancient mammoth or mastodon tracks. In 1938 they were officially identified by paleontologist Roland T. Bird of the American Museum of Natural History in New York, who formed a local work team under the WPA program to chisel out a long series of the tracks, most of which were later mounted behind a sauropod skeleton at the American Museum. In the process of extracting the sauropod tracks, Bird reported finding what appeared to be human footprints alongside dinosaur tracks in the same layer of riverbed limestone. According to mainstream scientists, the evidence was inconclusive at best.

In 1969, Stan Taylor began excavation of what would later become known as the Taylor Trail, a series of fourteen sequential human footprints on the same platform with at least 134 dinosaur tracks. At first, only the two tracks first believed identified by Roland Bird could be seen in the Paluxy riverbed. By following the trail back under the river bank, seven more very human-like tracks were exposed between 1969 and 1972. The process involved removing tons of limestone overburden, effectively eliminating the possibility that the tracks were carved. Subsequent excavation has extended the trail to a total of fourteen tracks in a consistent right-left pattern. The entire sequence can be seen through the water, even though a thin layer of mud obscures the details. A trail of three-toed dinosaur tracks can also be seen crossing at an angle of approximately thirty degrees. The drought of 1999 revealed the entire trail in dramatic detail. Many spectacular photographs were taken and can be found on the internet today. The evidence is indisputable. Tracks in mud do not last long. To be preserved, they must be solidified rapidly, within days. Once the material hardens, the tracks are preserved and footprints will no longer leave an impression. Furthermore, exposed tracks weather rapidly. Therefore, we know the next layer was deposited immediately and rapidly.

The human tracks within the Taylor Trail are consistently 11.5 inches in length and alternate between rights and lefts. They are among and, in this case, within dinosaur tracks. One of the most spectacular fossilized footprints in the sequence (-3B) is a right human footprint of compelling detail that is almost completely within a dinosaur footprint. The outline of the dinosaur track, then the outline of where the human stepped partially into the dinosaur track, clearly shows the detail of the owner's toes. Fortunately, photographs of these extraordinary footprints were taken prior to their discovery being released to the public. This particular footprint (-3B) was one of three tracks featured at the 1989 Dayton, TN creation conference, but was destroyed the next day. On August 12, 1989, Dr. Don Patton spoke at the creation conference in Dayton, TN. He presented compelling evidence that both human and dinosaur tracks were present at the Taylor Trail. Two well-known evolutionists were present, and at least one was noticeably disturbed by this presentation. Both flew to Dallas the next morning and went immediately to the Paluxy River. It is reliably reported that they were in the river that afternoon, chipping away with an iron bar. Before and after photographs are available on the internet for those who look. More prevalent are stories claiming that, "The Mystery of The Puluxy Footprints Has Finally Been Solved." The Puluxy footprints are referred to as a mystery because they contradict the doctrine of mainstream science. For myself and other like-minded promoters of free thought, there was never a mystery; a human footprint is a human footprint. For a prominent evolutionist to spend three days defacing footprints with an iron bar, there obviously must have been contradicting evidence worth hiding.

Also photographed in 1988, another interesting human footprint in the Taylor Trail (+5) is superimposed on the heel of a twenty-five-inch dinosaur track. Individual toes can be discerned in seven of the fourteen tracks. Such detail is unexpected. In Mary Leakey's Laetoli tracks, one great toe can be distinguished but no individual small toes can be seen. Left-right distinctions can be made in twelve of the fourteen tracks. Two are simply oblong shapes. The average distance between the tracks is 2.6

feet. If the individual's proportions were average, a height of six foot four would be indicated. For such an individual, an average distance between steps of 2.6 feet is completely normal. At 3B (a standing track) he appears to stop. The heel of the next print is not as far ahead as the toes of 3B. From that point they begin to lengthen, indicating increasing speed. The greatest distance is between the last prints. With momentum increasing, the longer distances between these tracks is appropriate. When the tracks are dry it is easy for a person of average height to stride from footprint to footprint as has been demonstrated on a number of occasions.

Other dinosaur-human fossilized tracks found in the Puluxy riverbed and its tributaries since the Taylor Trail was uncovered include The McFall Trail, The Ryals Track, The Morris Track, and The Burdick Track. Fossilized human footprints have additionally been located in Permian Strata of the mountains of New Mexico, purported to be formed by man at a time even before the dinosaurs (The New Mexico Track). Paraphrasing Don Patton, occasionally, one can observe strange things in nature—things that serendipitously resemble other things. You may see a man in the moon or the profile of an old man in a mountain. A cloud may resemble an elephant. This is not unusual. However, a sequence of such things defies credibility. One simply cannot believe that a sequence of clouds resembling fourteen elephants holding each other's tails could occur naturally, even if some of them are not perfect. If objective people see four old men in the mountain that resemble presidents, they will not believe the scene was produced naturally by erosion. These readily understood examples illustrate the strength of a sequence in terms of evidence. It eliminates the idea of accidental resemblance by natural, unintelligent processes from the sphere of rational discussion. Fourteen tracks in a consistent right-left pattern, consistent in length, including several amazingly detailed tracks with all five toes, instep, and clearly defined heel, demonstrate conclusively that these tracks are not the product of natural erosion.[77]

Contrary to evolution and current scientific understanding, fossilized human remains have on occasion been found in the same strata and location as fossilized dinosaur remains. Not unlike the arrowheads found with fossilized dinosaurs, numerous verifiably ancient depictions of human and dinosaur interactions, and the indisputable tracks of the Paluxy River platform, reports of fossilized human remains being found with fossilized dinosaur remains are met with anger and shaming. The world's immediate response to anything that contradicts current scientific explanation is rejection, dismissal, and discrediting. As evidenced by creationist Mark Armitage, former employee of the California State University at Northridge (chapter 4), many careers have been ruined and/or negatively impacted by announcement of controversial findings. Such known and repeated responses serve only to discourage further exploration and discovery. They hide a greater truth. For science to acknowledge any fact that contradicts a prize theory masked as truth, science must first admit that their wavering theory may be saturated with serious flaws that prevent it from being plausible. After all, a theory is only a theory until proven, and indisputable facts are indisputable.

Often used by creationists as an argument for humans coexisting with dinosaurs, the Moab Man (also called Malachite Man) refers to several human skeletons found when bulldozing an old mine where the rock dates to the early Cretaceous period. According to the geologic column, these skeletons and later excavated dinosaurs were 140 million years old. The original discovery of two human skeletons was made in 1971 by Lin Ottinger in the Keystone Azurite Mine near Moab, Utah. When scientists found out that human fossils had been found in the same layer of the Morrison formation as dinosaur fossils, they quickly concluded that the humans must have fallen down a crevasse at some time in the recent past that allowed their bodies to later be discovered with the dinosaurs. Adding further credence to their crevasse explanation, scientific examination of the Moab Man skeletons later concluded that they were unfossilized remains that were "accurately" carbon dated to between 210 and 1450 years old.[78] Undaunted, in the 1980s, creationist Carl Baugh purchased a Moab Man skeleton from Ottinger and began displaying it in the Creation Evidence Museum in Glen Rose, Texas, as evidence that humans lived at the same time as dinosaurs.

Indistinguishable from modern humans, history reveals that in the late 1700s many human skeletons were excavated from a limestone formation that dated as Miocene, or about twenty-five-million years old. The limestone formation was located just offshore of Guadeloupe, in the West Indies. "One of the quarried specimens, ensconced in a 2-ton slab, was shipped to the British Museum where It arrived in 1812 and was placed on public display. But with the ascendance of Darwinism, the fossil skeleton was quietly spirited away to the basement."[79] This discovery has been well documented in scientific literature.

I cannot say with any certainty whether or not human fossils have ever been found together in the same strata with dinosaur fossils. However, what I can say is that I believe it to be highly unlikely, but very possible. I say this not because they didn't coexist, but because of the difficulty in forming a fossil and the rarity of dinosaur fossils. Dead animals lying on the side of the road do not fossilize. In order for something to become a fossil, it must be buried rapidly in just the right place. "Consider as an example all the bison that were killed and left to decompose on the Great Plains of the United States. . . . By the end of the 19th century, the bison population in America had been reduced from millions to approximately 500 (Jones, n.d.). What happened to the millions of carcasses? They are not scattered all along the Great Plains today. Why? Because their flesh and bones were scavenged by insects, worms, birds, and other animals. The smallest portions were digested by fungi, bacteria, and enzymatic degradation until the buffalo remains disappeared. Even oxygen plays a role in the breakdown . . ."[80]

More recently, in the winter after the great Yellowstone fires of 1988, thousands of elks perished from extreme cold and lack of food. Late the following spring, their carcasses were strewn everywhere. Yet, only a few years later, bones from the great elk kill are virtually non-existent.[81] In the 2004 tsunami that happened in South East Asia, no remains of nearly 43,000 victims were ever found. It is extremely rare for things once living to fossilize. Indicative of a worldwide flood, 95% of the world's fossils are marine organisms such as corals and shellfish. From the remaining 5%, 95% are algae and plants. Drilling down even further, 95% of the remaining 0.25% are the invertebrates and insects. The remaining 0.0125% are the vertebrates and mostly fish. In fact, 95% of the land vertebrate fossils consist of one bone.[82] The point being, dinosaurs and humans form a very small percentage of the world's fossil record. Even rarer than the possibility of a human and a dinosaur being captured together in the same rapid burial that caused them both to fossilize together would be the possibility of someone searching in just the right place to find them. It's not likely, but it could happen.

When looking at the entirety of what is actually known about humans and dinosaurs, evidence seems to point to some inconsistencies in what science has told us is truth. Either dinosaurs are considerably younger than science has told us or mankind is considerably older. Never proven to be wrong in my eyes, I prefer to land somewhere in the middle and accept the biblical perspective. Coexistence seems to be the only logical solution that takes all the facts into account. "So God created great sea creatures and every living thing that moves, with which the waters abounded, according to their kind, and every winged bird according to its kind. And God saw that *it was* good. . . . So the evening and the morning were the fifth day. . . . And God made the beast of the earth according to its kind, cattle according to its kind, and everything that creeps on the earth according to its kind. And God saw that *it was* good. . . . So God created man in His *own* image; in the image of God He created him; male and female He created them. . . . Then God saw everything that He had made, and indeed *it was* very good. So the evening and the morning were the sixth day" (Genesis 1:21, 23, 25, 27, 31).

Assuming that all living creatures were made on the fifth and sixth days of creation and that dinosaurs were brought onto the ark or arks (perhaps as juveniles), it seems a small leap to conclude that dinosaurs likely suffered the same reaction as humans to post-flood changes in the environment, atmosphere, and exposure to the sun (chapter 3). After all, as documented in this chapter, *The Historia Animalium* claims that although extremely rare and relatively small by the fifteenth century, dragons still remained into the 1500s. The author believed that after the flood, the lifespans of dragons decreased and they became much smaller. Combining shorter lifespans with a recognition that modern reptiles continue to grow in size for the entirety of their lives, some have concluded that today's reptiles are yesterday's dinosaurs. They simply do not live long enough to reach the size of their ancestors. I understand the need to fill in the gaps and read between the lines when searching for the truth, but I caution against it without supporting facts. After all, this is how evolution was first conceived. Did dinosaurs still roam the earth as recently as a few thousand years ago? Absolutely! Yes! Did dinosaurs coexist with man? Absolutely! Yes! Are today's reptiles the descendants of yesterday's dinosaurs? Possibly, but it hasn't yet been proven one way or the other.

6

MIRACLES CAN HAPPEN:
THE SEAS PARTED AND TIME STOOD STILL

An opportunity is never lost by the secular media to trumpet as fact the latest scientific findings that confidently promote the evolutionary worldview of history in a continuous and uniform framework and timescale. There is a scientific explanation for nearly everything, including radioactive dinosaur bones, whales in the Andes Mountains, human footprints alongside dinosaur tracks, the Grand Canyon, and even the miracles of Exodus. Nevertheless, the provided answers are found lacking when applied to a time when man barely had the wheel. For example, how could God, through Moses, have so precisely predicted the time and place of so many miracles if those events had not been by his decree? Other such examples include water from the rock at Horeb (Exodus 17:6), the parting of the Red Sea (Exodus 14:16), and the sun standing still in the sky (Joshua 10:12-13). Science may attempt to explain these things with current knowledge, but what science will never explain is how anyone in antiquity would know when and where these events would occur. Miracles didn't just happen, they happened at God's command.

Television has provided us with documentaries on the National Geographic, Discovery, and History channels that explain how the miracles of Exodus could have occurred through natural processes that would not necessarily have required the hand of God. To the non-believer, these documentaries simply provide confirmation of non-belief. To the believer, these same documentaries tell us how God may have brought these events to bear, all the time following the same scientific principles that he himself put into place. My favorite of these is a documentary by National Geographic entitled *Exodus Revealed*. Starting with the burning bush and ending with the parting of the Red Sea, *Exodus Revealed* offers multiple scenarios of how events may have unfolded to result in each of the miracles of Exodus. As I interpret them, at least one of the provided scenarios for each miracle satisfies the details of the account as told in the Bible.

Sometimes the best answers are also the simplest ones. As Cambridge University physicist and professor Colin J. Humphries points out in *Exodus Revealed*, if the burning bush was not consumed by the fire that engulfed it (Exodus 3:2), the fire must have been fueled by a secondary source. Recognizing that the Arabian coast along the Gulf of Aqaba is abundant in natural gas, Professor Humphries surmised that the fire may have been fueled by a natural gas leak, likely ignited by lightning. If the burning bush were an acacia bush, also common to the area, it would turn to charcoal long before it would breakdown or appear to be consumed. Using a backyard barbeque, a tank of natural gas, and an acacia bush, Professor Humphries was able to demonstrate how a burning acacia bush maintains its form, appearing unconsumed while turning to charcoal.

The ten plagues of Exodus began with Egypt's rivers and streams turning to blood and the simultaneous killing of Egypt's fish (Exodus 7:17-21). For years, believers have ascribed Egypt's blood waters to a phenomenon known as the red tide, a profusion of microscopic algae responsible for the killing of millions of fish. Collectively, the microscopic algae turn the waters blood red in color. Red tides occur around the globe to this day; however, as medical epidemiologist Dr. John Marr points out in *Exodus Revealed*, there is a problem with accrediting Egypt's blood waters to the red tide. The microscopic algae that form a red tide are typically associated with salt water. The blood waters of Egypt remained a mystery until 1995 when a billion fish were found dead in the Neuse River, a coastal freshwater river in North Carolina, which turned blood red. Labeled the cell from hell, the culprit was eventually determined to be a deadly micro-organism known as pfiesteria. Certainly, if this happened in North Carolina in 1995, it could happen in Egypt 3000 years ago.

The blood-red waters of the Nile were followed by the coming of the frogs. "Behold, I will smite all your territory with frogs. So, the river shall bring forth frogs abundantly, which shall go up and come into your house, into your bedroom, on your bed, into your houses and your servants, on your people, into your ovens, and into your kneading bowls. And the frogs shall come up on you, on your people, and on all your servants" (Exodus 8:2-4). It doesn't take much imagination to recognize why the frogs would want to leave the Nile River once it was polluted with disease-spreading micro-organisms and millions of dead and decomposing fish. Early research on pfiesteria has resulted in the hypothesis that it acts as an ambush predator, utilizing a hit and run feeding strategy by first releasing a toxin that paralyzes the respiratory systems of susceptible fish, thus causing death by suffocation. It then survives by consuming the cast-off and decomposing tissue of its dead prey. If this is true, the frogs may have left the water simply to continue breathing. Exposed to whatever killed the fish and separated from their food source, whether they left the river or not, the frogs were on a course to their own inevitable death. "So, the Lord did according to the word of Moses. And the frogs died out of the houses, out of the courtyards, and out of the fields. They gathered them together in heaps, and the land stank" (Exodus 8:13-14).

Then came the lice. "Aaron stretched out his hand with his rod and struck the dust of the earth, and it became lice on man and beast. All the dust of the land became lice throughout all the land of Egypt" (Exodus 8:17). As University of Wyoming entomologist, Professor Jeffrey A. Lockwood points out in *Exodus Revealed*, interpretation of the biblical record needs to consider the meaning of words at the time they were spoken. There is no one species of lice that feeds on both man and beast. In ancient Hebrew and Aramaic languages, lice refer to any tiny blood-sucking insect. Professor Lockwood believes that the most likely suspect is the biting midge (Culicoides, Diptera), a tiny insect that attacks both man and beast with a sword-like tongue that draws a pool of blood which it then feeds on. Insect outbreaks seem a natural progression to heaps of dead frogs that were propagating hordes of insects that were no longer able to be eaten by the dead frogs.

Then came the flies. Moses told Pharaoh, "Thus says the Lord: Let My people go that they may serve Me. Or else, if you will not let My people go, behold, I will send swarms of flies on you and your servants, on your people and into your houses. The houses of the Egyptians shall be full of swarms of flies, and also the ground on which they stand. And in that day, I will set apart the land of Goshen, in which My people dwell, that no swarms of flies shall be there, in order that you may know that I am the Lord in the midst of the land" (Exodus 8:20-22). Professor Lockwood was able to show through covering stable flies and houseflies in different colored powders that the biting stable fly is significantly more aggressive than the housefly and the most likely candidate for spreading the bacteria responsible for the later plague of boils. There were no swarms of flies in Goshen because the heaps of dead frogs were with the Egyptians, not in Goshen. Again, insect outbreaks seem a natural progression to heaps of dead frogs that were breeding hordes of insects, no longer able to be eaten by frogs.

Comparing the life cycles of the biting midge to the stable fly, it becomes apparent that the outbreak of biting midges had to come before the outbreak of stable flies. Both life cycles start with the laying of an egg. The biting midge's egg takes two to seven days to hatch and enter the larval stage while to the stable fly's egg that takes four to thirty days to hatch and enter the larval stage. The biting midge is in the larval stage for a minimum of two weeks before it transitions to the pupal stage as compared to the stable fly which is in the larval stage for a minimum of thirty days before transitioning to the pupal stage. Lastly, it takes two or three days for the biting midge to emerge from the pupal stage as an adult and four to seven days for the stable fly to emerge from the pupal stage as an adult. Life cycles considered, it takes a minimum of eighteen days to develop a swarm of biting midges and a minimum of thirty-eight days to develop a swarm of stable flies. The biting midges (lice) had to come first.

After the outbreak of flies came the pestilence of livestock. "Then the Lord said to Moses, "Go in to Pharaoh and tell him, 'Thus says the Lord God of the Hebrews: "Let My people go, that they may serve Me. For if you refuse to let them go, and still hold them, behold, the hand of the Lord will be on your cattle in the field, on the horses, on the donkeys, on the camels, on the oxen, and on the sheep—a very severe pestilence. And the Lord will make a difference between the livestock of Israel and the livestock of Egypt. So, nothing shall die of all that belongs to the children of Israel.'" Then the Lord appointed a set time saying, 'Tomorrow the Lord will do this thing in the land.' So, the Lord did this thing on the next day, and the livestock of Egypt died; but of the livestock of the children of Israel, not one died. Then Pharaoh sent, and indeed, not even one of the livestock of the Israelites was dead" (Exodus 9:1-7, KJV). As Professor Lockwood points out in *Exodus Revealed*, the pestilence of the livestock is most likely attributed directly to the outbreak of lice. The biting midge is a known carrier of many animal diseases, including blue tongue and African horse sickness. There was no disease in livestock in Goshen because there was no outbreak of biting midges there. The heaps of dead frogs were with the Egyptians, not in Goshen.

After the pestilence of livestock came the plague of boils. "So, the Lord said to Moses and Aaron, 'Take for yourselves handfuls of ashes from a furnace, and let Moses scatter it toward the heavens in the sight of Pharaoh. And it will become fine dust in all the land of Egypt, and it will cause boils that break out in sores on man and beast throughout all the land of Egypt.' Then they took ashes from the furnace and stood before Pharaoh, and Moses scattered them toward heaven. And they caused boils that break out in sores on man and beast" (Exodus 9:8-10).

As I picture Moses and Aaron scattering handfuls of furnace ash over their heads and toward the heavens, I imagine that they must have been covered in the ash as it fell back to earth and all over themselves. As opposed to being the actual cause for boils to break out on the Egyptians and their remaining beasts, I believe that it may have been the ash that caused Moses and Aaron to be the only two people in Egypt that didn't suffer boils. Wood ash is rich in a multitude of minerals, such as sodium, calcium, iron, potassium, magnesium, phosphorous, cobalt, manganese, zinc, and copper. As practiced by many modern-day survivalists, wood ash can very effectively be used as a natural bug repellent, for making soap from lye water, as tooth paste, and to wash dishes. Handmade soap has for years been recognized as an effective agent against hygiene related illnesses. Professor Lockwood believes that the boils were caused by the stable flies that are very capable of spreading bacteria. The boils, of course, came after the pestilence of livestock because swarms of stable flies emerged after emergence of the biting midge (lice).

Then came the crop-destroying hail and fire from heaven. As God commanded, ". . . Moses stretched out his rod toward heaven; and the Lord sent thunder and hail, and fire darted to the ground. And the Lord rained hail on the land of Egypt. So, there was hail, and fire mingled with the hail" (Exodus 9:23-24). If you are alive today and reading this book, you no doubt have access to the internet and numerous cellphone videos of damaging hailstorms that pummeled the shatter-proof glass of automobiles where people sought refuge. If you have been around long enough, you may have even experienced such a hailstorm. Worldwide, hailstones the size of golf balls have been captured on film destroying property, breaking windows and denting the metal roofs and hoods of cars. The crop-destroying capabilities of hail are without question. What is not so commonly recognized is a weather phenomenon known as dry lighting. Dry lightning occurs when rain clouds form so high in the atmosphere that falling rain evaporates before it hits the ground. Unlike the more commonly recognized rolling thunderstorm, dry lightning causes the fields and trees to remain dry and unprotected from lightning strikes. Dry lightning is responsible for starting the greater part of the seasonal forest fires that yearly plague the dry forests of the western United States. When nature simultaneously combines hail with dry lightning, the resulting storms have the potential to become the crop-destroying hail and fire described in Exodus. On Thursday, May 22, 2008, a rare combination hailstorm with dry lightning produced hailstones the size of softballs and lightning-induced fires in Wakeeny, Kansas that were captured on film by storm chasers. The storms were accompanied by high winds and tornados that further fanned the flames of a lightning-induced transformer and field fire. People who were caught in the storm referred to it as earth-ending and biblical.

Not unheard of in a world now known to have experienced locust outbreaks in every continent except Antarctica, God chose to deliver locusts to Egypt in the eighth plague of Exodus. "Then the Lord said to Moses, 'Stretch out your hand over the land of Egypt for the locusts, that they may come upon the land of Egypt, and eat every herb of the land—all that the hail has left.' So, Moses stretched out his rod over the land of Egypt, and the Lord brought an east wind on the land all that day and all that night. When it was morning, the east wind brought the locusts. And the locusts went up over all the land of Egypt and rested on the territory of Egypt. They were very severe; previously there had been no such locusts as they, nor shall there be such after them" (Exodus 10:12-14). Considering the largest recorded locust outbreak in history and the fact that God declared there shall be no larger outbreak than the one that plagued Egypt, I cannot imagine the fear that must have gripped the Egyptians, seeing so many locusts for the first time. First observed in Nebraska, the 1875 swarm of locusts that devastated the western agricultural production of the United States was measured at 100 miles wide by 1800 miles long and a mile and a half high. The swarm was so thick that it blocked the sun for five days as it passed. The population was estimated at 3.5 trillion locusts, each locust weighing half an ounce, being three inches long, and consuming its own body weight each day.

The miracle of the locusts is not that they came, but that they came upon God's command when he said they would. Just as the poisoned waters caused the invasion of frogs that resulted in the insect plagues that brought the death of the livestock and boils to the Egyptians, the plague of locusts may well have set the stage for the ninth and tenth plagues of Exodus. "Then the Lord said to Moses, 'Stretch out your hand toward heaven, that there may be darkness over the land of Egypt, darkness which may be felt.' So, Moses stretched out his hand toward heaven, and there was thick darkness in all the land of Egypt three days. They did not see one another; nor did anyone rise from his place for three days. But all the children of Israel had light in their dwellings" (Exodus 10:21-23). The National Geographic documentary *Exodus Revealed* speculates that it was a terrible sandstorm that blocked the sun. Others have theorized that it was likely an eruption of the nearby Santorini volcano that blocked the sun. I prefer to believe that it was the exiting swarm of locusts that blocked the sun for three days. This seems entirely possible when you consider that the smaller documented swarm of 1875 was able to block the sun for five days. God turned the locusts around and sent them back from the direction they came. "And the Lord turned a very strong west wind, which took the locusts away and blew them into the Red Sea. There remained not one locust in all the territory of Egypt" (Exodus 10:19).

To many, the last plague of Egypt is the most mysterious. How could God or even chance have possibly selected only the firstborn to be taken? And it came to pass, ". . . at midnight the Lord struck all the firstborn in the land of Egypt, from the firstborn of Pharaoh who sat on his throne to the firstborn of the captive who was in the dungeon, all the firstborn of the livestock. So, Pharaoh rose in the night, he, all his servants, and all the Egyptians; and there was a great cry in Egypt, for there was not a house where there was not one dead" (Exodus 12:29-30). In *Exodus Revealed*, Professor Martin J. Blaser, MD, epidemiologist and microbiologist at New York University, attributes the death of the firstborn to the bubonic plague. Professor Blaser believes that the Jews were spared by Jewish dietary laws and ancient traditions that required the granaries to be cleaned out every spring—eliminating rats and the source of plague-carrying fleas. I have trouble with this explanation because it still does not address the firstborn. More significantly, any biblical scholar worth their weight in salt would give little credence to Jewish dietary laws and ancient traditions that likely didn't exist until after the Exodus, the tablets of the law, and the widely accepted later writing of the Torah by Moses.

I have heard many theories on how God brought about the death of the firstborn, but only one that had the sound of truth. God does not leave anything to chance. If he speaks it, it will happen. As explained in *Exodus Revealed*, medical epidemiologist Doctor John Marr believes that God used a long-established Egyptian custom to cause the Egyptians to unknowingly poison their firstborn. It was their custom to feed the firstborn first with a double portion so that the family lineage would be protected from starvation in times of famine. Recall that the locust had just eaten "every herb of the land—all that the hail has left." By this time, the only remaining food in Egypt was the hail saturated, moldy, and likely toxic grain stored in the darkness of the granaries built by Joseph some four hundred years earlier. The mold would have grown on the top of the grain first; the grain taken to feed the firstborn. "So, he gathered up all the food of the seven years which were in the land of Egypt and laid up the food in the cities; he laid up in every city the food of the fields which surrounded them. Joseph gathered very much grain, as the sand of the sea, until he stopped counting, for it was immeasurable" (Genesis 41:48-49).

Then Pharaoh called for Moses and Aaron by night and said, "Rise, go out from among my people, both you and the children of Israel. And go, serve the Lord as you have said. Also take your flocks and your herds, as you have said, and be gone; and bless me also" (Exodus 12:31-32). And when the children of Israel had departed Egypt by way of the Red Sea, "... the Lord hardened the heart of Pharaoh king of Egypt, and he pursued the children of Israel; and the children of Israel went out in boldness. So, the Egyptians pursued them, all the horses and chariots of Pharaoh, his horsemen and his army, and overtook them camping by the sea" (Exodus 14:8-9). As God had planned, it was here that he parted the Red Sea and gained honor over Pharaoh, and over all his army. And Moses said, "Do not be afraid. Stand still, and see the salvation of the Lord, which He will accomplish for you today. For the Egyptians whom you see today, you shall see again no more forever. The Lord will fight for you, and you shall hold your peace" (Exodus 14:13-14). "Then Moses stretched out his hand over the sea; and the Lord caused the sea to go *back* by a strong east wind all that night, and made the sea into dry *land,* and the waters were divided. So, the children of Israel went into the midst of the sea on the dry *ground,* and the waters *were* a wall to them on their right hand and on their left" (Exodus 14:21-22).

For years, the parting of the Red Sea has caused many of the faithful among the scientific community to struggle for a believable explanation. So much so that many scholars have resorted to an unproven typo to explain what their minds cannot comprehend. As if to place limits on God's ability, scholars tell us that the crossing must have taken place in the much shallower Reed Sea. I, for one, place no limits on God's abilities and believe that the crossing took place in the Red Sea, just as the Bible said it did.

In *Exodus Revealed*, Professor Floyd W. McCoy, geo-archaeologist from the University of Hawaii, presents what is known as the big tsunami to explain the parting of the Red Sea. Professor McCoy theorized that a big tsunami would allow the Jews to cross the Red Sea in the trough of a tsunami wave, when the water is drawn down and before the crest brings it back in. However, it would take a huge event such as an earthquake or an asteroid to create sufficient time between the trough and the crest of the wave to allow all the Jews of Egypt to cross the Red Sea. Professor McCoy attributes the source of the big tsunami to the Santorini eruption. A well-studied eruption, Santorini is estimated to have erupted with a force of 24,000 megatons, creating a forty- to fifty-mile-high plume, and pyroclastic flows of volcanic ash and debris that flowed down the slopes of the mountain and into the ocean, causing the big tsunami. Computer models show that a Santorini tsunami would have headed directly toward the Nile Delta. Professor McCoy however also openly admits that a Santorini induced big tsunami is a long shot, because science dates the eruption of Santorini ((1600-1630 BC) at nearly 200 years before the Exodus (1450 BC). I disagree with Professor McCoy's conclusion. Knowing what I know about the accuracy of radiocarbon dating and mankind's ability to accurately document the distant past, this less than 5% error in the date of something that occurred nearly 3600 years ago seems inconsequential.

Volcanologist Stephen J. O'Meara of Volcano Watch International suggests that an eruption in an underwater volcano in the African Rift System formed a volcanic land bridge in the Gulf of Aqaba that gave way when the Egyptians followed the Jews into the Red Sea. All these theories are interesting, but none of them follow the biblical account. Specifically, the Bible tells us that the waters of the Red Sea formed a wall to the right and left of the Jews as they walked on dry land (Exodus 14:22).

The most compelling site for the crossing of the Israelites is the site once marked by identical Phoenician columns found on either side of the Red Sea. The western pillar was initially found lying in the water with eroded inscriptions that could no longer be read. Believed placed by Solomon to be a memorial to the Israelites' crossing, Isaiah 19:19 tells us, "In that day there will be an altar to the Lord in the heart of Egypt, and a monument to the Lord at its border." The name of the place where the pillar was found is called Nuweiba, or Nuwayba, short for Nusaybah al Muzayyinah which means "waters of Moses opening." A similar pillar was discovered on the Saudi side of the crossing by explorer Ron Wyatt in 1978. The Arabian pillar was found still standing with Hebrew inscriptions still legible on the leeward side of the column. They read, "This monument is erected by King Solomon in honor of Yahweh in commemoration of the crossing of the Red Sea." The column on the West (Egyptian) side is still present today in Nuweiba where it has been moved across the road and stood up in a cement base. The column to the east (Arabian) side has since been removed and possibly placed in a museum. Between the two Phoenician columns and under the Red Sea is a natural land bridge that forms the proposed site of the Israeli crossing. An underwater land bridge, approximately eighteen kilometers (11.2 miles) long, cuts northeast from the Sinai Peninsula across the Strait of Tiran. The land bridge is between sixty and eighty meters (197 to 262 feet) below sea level.

Building a model of the Red Sea within a large aquarium, from gravel-sized river stones, Professor Collin J. Humphreys, a physicist at Cambridge University, fashioned a six-inch-wide underwater bridge about an inch and a half below water, in a nine-inch-deep body of water. Then, with an electric leaf blower, Professor Humphreys was able to apply a source of constant wind parallel to the underwater bridge that exposed the top of the river stones, forming a miniature land bridge across the width of the aquarium with a wall of water on both sides of the bridge. For me, this scenario most closely follows the biblical record. "So, the children of Israel went into the midst of the sea on the dry *ground*, and the waters *were* a wall to them on their right hand and on their left" (Exodus 14:22). "Your right hand, O Lord, has become glorious in power; Your right hand, O Lord, has dashed the enemy in pieces. And in the greatness of Your excellence, You have overthrown those who rose against You; You sent forth Your wrath; It consumed them like stubble. And with the blast of Your nostrils the waters were gathered together; The floods stood upright like a heap; The depths congealed in the heart of the sea" (Exodus 15:6-8).

When I contemplate any of God's many wondrous miracles, I realize that even if the rocks were to cry out (Luke 19:40), whatever God brings to bear may or may not follow the existing scientific principles that he himself enacted. God has put into place natural laws that he ordained during the week of creation and continues to sustain (Genesis 1:14-15, 8:22; Colossians 1:16-17; Hebrews 1:3). However, God is not bound by the laws that he has upheld since creation; he transcends them and gives them their force. God may allow wonders to occur through natural processes and often works miracles which can be scientifically explained, but he also works in supernatural ways to bring about marvels that cannot be explained. God deflects the fired bullet from its intended target, removes the inoperable terminal cancer, and restores life where there was none. I acknowledge that I have only just begun to understand what is possible with a God in whom all things are possible.

To me, there is no greater act to show that God is God than for him to cause the sun to stand still in the sky for the entire course of a day. Surely, only he who created time can cause it to stop for twelve hours. God no doubt leveraged several extraordinary and unique circumstances to cause the sun to stand still at Joshua's command. "There has been no day like that, before it or after it, that the Lord heeded the voice of a man; for the Lord fought for Israel" (Joshua 10:14). Perhaps because science does not believe in the supernatural acts of God or perhaps because pride forbids science from acknowledging what it does not understand, whatever the reason, science tells us that the sun cannot stand still; it is an impossibility and never happened. I am intrigued by what can only be attributed to God and I want to dig deeper. As I search for understanding and truth, I wonder if answers exist in earthly terms that can be understood.

I am only a man and no man can say with any certainty how God has caused anything to take place, but I can take what is known and gather the facts together in a logical fashion to form a possibility of what in God's creation might have caused the sun to stand still. It starts by recognizing that at least three scenarios exist that would make it appear that the sun was standing still. First, we must recognize that the sun is actually standing still in relation to the planets that orbit around it—a fact that may or may not have been known at that time. The sun only appears to be moving in the sky because of the earth's rotation on its axis between its true north and south poles. Independent of the earth's orbit around the sun, the sun would of course appear to be standing still in the sky if the earth's rotation on its axis were to suddenly stop. The sun would also appear to be standing still if the earth stopped orbiting around the sun and spinning on its axis concurrently, essentially becoming motionless in space. Lastly, the sun would appear to be standing still if while the earth continued rotating on its axis, the sun began orbiting the earth in the same direction as the earth's rotation and perpendicular to the earth's poles. This seems the least likely scenario because the sun is 94.41 million miles from earth and the sun would have to travel at an unimaginable ($2\pi r/24hrs$) 24.72 million miles per hour, the speed necessary to travel a 593-million-mile orbit in twenty-four hours.

Before we examine these scenarios, let's consider a simple model. This is admittedly a very simplified model intended to show the relationship between attraction of masses and the centrifugal forces of orbiting bodies. The model does not and is not intended to account for the more complex variations of forces that result in the actual elliptical orbit of the earth around the sun. Imagine yourself standing on an X painted in the center of a large parking lot, holding one end of a very strong ten-foot-long rubber band. Having a baseball secured to the other end of the rubber band and remaining on the X, you begin spinning the baseball around in a circle, over your head until the rubber band becomes fully extended. In this model, you would represent the sun, the baseball would represent the earth, the rubber band would represent the forces imposed by attraction of masses, and the spinning ball would represent the centrifugal force of the earth's orbit. At a constant rate of spin, the baseball would remain at a constant distance from you just as the earth remains at a constant distance from the sun (model only). The centrifugal force imposed by the rotation equals the force imposed by attraction of masses. Attraction of masses is defined by Newton's law (of gravitation) which states that any two particles having respective masses, separated by a certain distance attract each other with a force directly proportional to the square of the distance between the masses.

Now, imagine if a short friend were to position themselves with a wooden box under the rubber band while you spun it around over their head, somewhere near the middle of the distance between you and the baseball. What would happen if your friend then stood on the wooden box and slowly raised a razor-sharp blade that ever so slowly cut the rubber band as it spun around over their head? The baseball would soon fly off into space as the centrifugal force of the baseball exceeded the attraction of masses and the strength of the now damaged rubber band. The rubber band would break and you would no doubt get snapped with its remnant. This simplified model demonstrates the loss of attraction of masses.

Now, imagine if your same shorter friend sat a small wooden box directly behind you that he or she then stood on as they reached up with both hands and grabbed your spinning arm that was whipping the ball around over their head. The elasticity of the rubber band would immediately overwhelm the centrifugal force of the spinning baseball and momentum would cause the baseball to continue spinning in ever decreasing orbits as it grew closer and closer. Slowed only by earth's gravity and the friction of our atmosphere, the baseball would probably strike you somewhere in the shins two or three revolutions later. As it is in outer space, without gravity and the friction of our atmosphere, the baseball would return to your hand. This simplified model demonstrates the loss of the centrifugal force created by the ball's rotation. Now, consider the scenario where the earth suddenly stops orbiting the sun and spinning on its axis, becoming motionless in space. Similar to the baseball returning to your hand, the centrifugal force created by the earth's orbit around the sun would be lost, attraction of masses would take over and the earth would be hurled into a collision course with the sun.

Consider the already discarded scenario where the sun orbits the earth. The sun would instantly accelerate from zero to 24.72 million miles per hour and our planetary system would immediately begin destroying itself. In actuality, while the sun is always standing still in relation to the planets that orbit around it, the planetary systems that make up the Milky Way galaxy are consistently moving through our expanding universe at greater than 2.2 million miles per hour. In the proposed scenario, the sun would begin traveling in and out of multiple existing planetary orbits as it started circling the earth—it would grow closer to some planets and further away from others. Each time the sun grew closer to a planet it would consume it as the attraction of masses exceeded the centrifugal force of the planetary orbit. Conversely, each time the sun grew further away from a planet, the centrifugal force of the planet's orbit would exceed the planet's attraction to the sun and the planet would be thrown into the fringes of space.

Without re-writing the existing laws of physics, the most likely remaining scenario for the sun to appear to be standing still in the sky would be for the earth's rotation on its axis to stop as the planet continued to orbit the sun, maintaining the centrifugal force of the earth's orbit and the attraction of masses in equilibrium. Can this happen? Can the earth stop rotation on its axis without a shifting of the poles, devastating tsunamis, earthquakes, and volcanic eruptions? Before we answer these questions, it is important to recognize that science and the Bible both tell us that the earth's crust floats atop of the mantle. If this were not the case, how would the continents have separated from a single land mass as we were told they did in elementary school? To Eber were born two sons: the name of one was Peleg, for in his days the earth was divided (Genesis 10:25). As shown in the above model, it is not necessary for the earth to rotate on its axis to maintain the centrifugal force of planetary orbit and attraction of masses. Even if the baseball were spinning like a top at the end of the outstretched rubber band, it would not have changed the results of any of the scenarios modeled above.

Charles H. Hapgood, PhD, Professor of Medieval and Modern History at Harvard University, proposed a theory in his 1958 book entitled, *Earth's Shifting Crust*. He explained that rather than individual continents slowly moving over long periods of time, the earth's crust would, on occasion, suddenly shift within a short period of time. Hapgood believed that this last happened around 9600 BC, with the entire crust shifting nearly fifteen degrees. His theory never went into detail to explain how these shifts occurred, but neither did the rival theory, so for a period of time they were both equally likely. Further credence was given to Hapgood's theory when Albert Einstein penned the foreword for *Earth's Shifting Crust*, writing, "I frequently receive communications from people who wish to consult me concerning their unpublished ideas. It goes without saying that these ideas are very seldom possessed of scientific validity. The very first communication, however, that I received from Mr. Hapgood electrified me. . . ."[83] Albert Einstein supported Professor Hapgood's ideas and corresponded with him frequently. In one letter, Einstein wrote, "I find your arguments very impressive and have the impression that your hypothesis is correct. One can hardly doubt that significant shifts of the crust have taken place repeatedly and within a short time."[84]

Professor Hapgood makes it clear in his later 1966 published, *Maps of Ancient Sea Kings* that he supported Arlington Mallery's belief that a portion of the early fifteenth-century Piri Reis map was a depiction of the area of Antarctica known as Queen Maud Land. The map depicts an ice-free Antarctica, complete with a detailed shoreline, trees, mountain ranges, and rivers. The map was made over three hundred years before the first documented sighting of Antarctica, four hundred years before twentieth-century technology was able to verify the details depicted below the ice. The Piri Reis map and the Oronteus Finaeus map were instrumental in forming Professor Hapgood's belief that the earth's crust had shifted sometime around 9600 BC. The 1531 Oronteus Finaeus map portrays the entire ice-free continent of Antarctica, accounts for the curvature of the earth, and demonstrates a vantage point some eighty miles above the earth. Aside from the obvious details that are no longer visible through the ice, the only difference between the Oronteus Finaeus map and a modern map of Antarctica is the location of the south pole. From the Piri Reis map, Hapgood concluded that a warmer ice-free Antarctica once existed some fifteen to thirty degrees further north. He believed that the Piri Reis map, the Oronteus Finaeus map and others were based on ancient maps derived from ice-age originals that had been created by an advanced civilization thousands of years earlier.

Nevertheless, a geologic revolution took place in the 1960s. The verification of tectonic plate movement shifted Professor Hapgood's theory of sudden crust shifts from the forefront to the realm of pseudo-science. Then in 1995, economist Graham Hancock proposed a new idea that combined tectonic plate movement with sudden crust shifts in his book *Fingerprints of the Gods* to form Earth Crust Displacement (ECD) theory. Hancock's theory acknowledged gradual tectonic plate movement, but also allowed for the occasional sudden and rapid shift of the earth's crust. This is where my beliefs on crust displacement fall. Unfortunately, science has written off both Hapgood and Hancock. Science tells us that it is important to critically analyze what is being said and by whom. Hapgood was a historian, not a geologist, and Hancock was a writer with no credentials in cartography, archaeology, or geology. To that I say, Benjamin Franklin and Thomas Edison were, for the most part, homeschooled, George Eastman and Andrew Carnegie dropped out of high school, and Albert Einstein started as a patent clerk.

I believe that God may have caused it to appear that the sun stood still in the sky at Joshua's command by maintaining the earth's orbit around the sun, maintaining the earth's rotation around its axis, and allowing the crust to shift atop the planet's rotating mantle. To explain how God may have caused this to happen, I will combine Hapgood's theory of Earth's Shifting Crust with Hancock's theory of Earth Crust Displacement with some new and previously unexplored concepts to form what I call Earth's Floating Crust (EFC) theory. Before I can explain the basis behind this theory, we will first have to examine a few known facts about plate tectonic movement and draw a couple of conclusions.

Continental plates rest in the lithosphere that floats above the asthenosphere. The heavy and dense, but thinner oceanic plates dive under the thicker, but lighter continental plates where they again melt and turn into magma. As hard rock forms in the magma, it expands and moves upward where it cools and moves sideways, oozing out to form new ocean floor at mid-ocean ridges and sinking down again, at subduction zones where the ocean floor slides under the continental crust, sinks back into the mantle and starts the cycle over again. It is an endless cycle where new ocean floors are continually created at a rate relatively equal to their consumption. The plates are constantly moving at a rate similar to the growth of our fingernails. Only when adjoining plates are lodged together long enough for sufficient pressure to cause them to break free and jump ahead, resulting in an earthquake or a tsunami, do we even take notice that they are there. Creation and destruction of the tectonic plates takes place in the mantle, above a liquid core that consists of 89% molten iron and 6% molten nickel. It is the heat of the liquid core that both melts and fuels the creation of the new oceanic floors. The earth's liquid core is the remnant of a molten planet of volcanic slurry that has now cooled to the point of equilibrium. Our liquid core is maintained by many forces, not the least of which are the attraction between the sun and the earth, the pulling of our planetary orbit, and the pressure created by the weight of the solid layers above it.

Scientists believe that previous continental shifts can be reconstructed with great accuracy. Without question, science can now precisely measure continental movements using satellites. Indeed, continental drifts are significant enough to mean that GPS locations have to be recalibrated to account for them. Every country has a geodetic datum it uses for precise mapping. Since 1994, Australia has used a geodetic datum called GDA94 that moves with the continent as it drifts. The continent of Australia is the fastest moving continent, drifting some 7 centimeters (about 2.75 inches) per year. Since 1994, Australia has drifted approximately 1.8 meters NE; that is nearly 6 feet in less than 25 years. By comparison, the Americas move about 2.54 centimeters further away from Europe and Africa each year (about 1 inch). The point being, it is a proven fact that not all continents drift at the same rate. It is therefore logical to conclude that varying rates of continental drift are a result of some as yet unknown and undefined factors that if manipulated, could increase or decrease rates of continental drift.

Knowing that it is easier to push a child's Radio Flyer wagon up a steep hill than it is to push a full-size Buick up the same hill, one might assume that the size of a continent would be a factor affecting the rate of continental drift, but it is not. Independent of size, the ratio of applied forces to opposing forces of continental drift are distributed over an entire continent, equally holding each continent in their relative position on the globe. Further supporting the sustainability of the earth's continental structure and independent of movement through continental drift, redistribution of landmasses occurred before God caused the sun to stand still in the sky and has not been known to have reoccurred since the initial breaking up of the firmament, when the continents of today were formed. The relative size of each continental plate is assumed to have been constant since Genesis.

Similar to the speed of a race car being affected by the force applied to the brake, rate of continental drift is affected by opposing forces encountered at subduction zones when the ocean floors are pushed under continental plates. Recorded in earth's recent history, uneven surfaces and varying degrees of hardness have on occasion caused tectonic plate drift to grind to a halt along the opposing subduction zone. Just as a drag racer applies the accelerator to build opposing forces before releasing the drag-brake, when a continental plate grinds to a halt, opposing forces immediately begin building until the resulting pressures are sufficient to overcome blockages and cause the halted plate to suddenly jump ahead, triggering earthquakes and tsunamis. These are known forces and processes that God would have to overcome if the entire earth's crust were to suddenly stop planetary rotation and float atop the mantle, causing the sun to stand still in the sky. Tectonic plate movement (drift) at all subduction zones would be required to cease.

Lastly and most importantly, consider the frictional forces that hold the earth's crust in place as it rotates with the planet atop the mantle. If we think of the bottom of the earth's crust as the underside of a very coarse sheet of sandpaper and the molten slurry of the mantle as an aggregate rich mixture of not fully hardened cement, it is easy to imagine gravity pushing the grit of the coarse sandpaper into the floating aggregate of the unhardened cement. In this way, the crust grips and rotates with the mantle. This factor, the frictional bond between the crust and mantle is what I believe God may have manipulated to cause the sun to appear to be standing still in the sky for the course of a day.

Just as the baseball held firm at the end of the extended rubber band demonstrates that the centrifugal forces of our simulated orbit are maintained equal to the pulling forces of the rubber band, so do the centrifugal forces of the earth's rotation around its axis push the mantle out from the liquid core, toward the outer fringes of the earth's surface. Similar to the few soaked and floating cheerios that might be seen circling the edge of a half-full bowl of milk when stirred with a spoon, medical technicians and chemists routinely use a centrifuge in this manner to separate the elements of a given sample by density. More complex than can be explained with this simplified model, gravity, attraction of orbiting masses, and the centrifugal forces imposed by the earth's rotation around its axis all work together to maintain the earth's spherical shape around its liquid core.

If the earth's rotation around its core were to suddenly stop, the forces of planetary orbit are such that the spherical shape of our planet and liquid core would begin to elongate, much like the shape of an egg. Remaining forces would seek a new equilibrium and our planet would begin collapsing in upon itself. To simulate this self-destructive and catastrophic planetary failure, simply replace the ridged baseball in the above demonstration with a round water balloon. The balloon itself would represent the earth's crust and the water within the balloon would represent the earth's liquid core. The faster the water balloon is spun around over your head, the more distorted the balloon becomes, until it bursts. This is why I believe the only possible scenario that maintains the integrity of our planet and the scientific principles that God put into place is for the crust to float freely above the mantle while maintaining the earth's orbit around the sun and the earth's rotation on its axis. Such a scenario would cause the sun to appear to be standing still in the sky. To accomplish such a thing, God would only have to overcome the frictional bond between the crust and mantle.

During normal tectonic plate movement, the oceanic crust sits atop the oceanic plates that together float above the asthenosphere and together are pushed under the lithosphere by growing ocean floors, into the asthenosphere where they again melt and turn into magma. The continental plates sit atop the lithosphere that also floats above the asthenosphere. Technically speaking, it is the bond between the oceanic plates and the asthenosphere and the bond between the lithosphere and the asthenosphere that was earlier characterized by the analogy of coarse sandpaper riding atop an aggregate rich and not yet hardened slurry of cement. If this bond were to suddenly be removed and the coefficient of friction between the oceanic plates/lithosphere and the asthenosphere were to go to zero, the earth's crust would begin to float freely above the mantle.

Only a slight breeze would be required to cause the rotation of the crust to spin from east to west as the mantle continued to spin from west to east and the sun stood still in the sky. Similar to our moon, rotation of the earth's crust (from east to west) at a speed equal to and opposite the planet's natural rotation (from west to east), one complete revolution every twenty-four hours, would place the earth in a synchronous orbit with the sun. One side of the planet would remain in continuous light as the sun stood still in the sky.

The argument is now boiled down to one question. How could the coefficient of friction between the tectonic plates and the asthenosphere suddenly go to zero? I can think of only one possibility. As discussed in chapter two, when the sinking oceanic plates begin to melt back into magma, water trapped in ringwoodite is released. Now consider a fact proven daily in our nation's operating pressurized water reactors (PWRs) and nuclear submarines: water released under extreme pressures and temperatures has the potential to flash to superheated steam that simultaneously expands in volume. To give you an idea of how much regular steam expands the volume of water, one cubic inch of water translates to one cubic foot of steam at atmospheric pressure and 212°F. This is equivalent to increasing the initial volume by 1728 times (12x12x12). As the pressure and/or temperature increases, so does the expansion of water to steam. Imagine the potential, the pressures, and temperatures in the asthenosphere, miles below the earth's surface, where rocks are melted and magma is created.

Recalling PWR theory for just a moment, water is intentionally kept from flashing to steam in the primary cooling system of a pressurized water reactor by balancing the ratio between pressure and heat. It is a fine balance, but necessary to avoid the problems that would be introduced by a steam bubble. This balance is no doubt also maintained by nature in the asthenosphere where the ringwoodite is known to be released as water. Now imagine if all the ringwoodite were made available at one time and the balance between heat and pressure were only slightly manipulated in the asthenosphere. A reservoir of water equal to or greater than the volume of all the earth's oceans would instantly flash to superheated steam and be expanded in volume by greater than 1728 times. Certainly, the result would be more steam than necessary to take the coefficient of friction between the tectonic plates and the asthenosphere to zero. The earth's crust would float above the mantle on a bed of steam. This premise seems entirely possible when we consider, "If just one percent of the weight of mantle rock located in the transition zone is H_2O, that would be equivalent to nearly three times the amount of water in our oceans."[85]

Causing our planet's crust to stand still in relation to the asthenosphere would also cause the planet's oceans to stop rotation. This would, no doubt, break the tidal lock between our moon and our oceans, possibly resulting in other unknown consequences. This, of course, is all conjecture and hypothesis, well beyond what we are taught in school or read in the Bible. What we do know is that gravity would be unaffected and the sun would appear to be standing still in the sky. If this is hard to imagine, imagine yourself standing on the moon that is already in synchronous orbit with the earth. The earth appears at the same point in the sky from the moon that continually rotates to keep the same recognizable face always looking at the earth, just as the sun would appear at the same point in the sky from an earth's crust as it maintained a (simulated) synchronous orbit with the sun, all the time maintaining normal rotation about its axis and orbit around the sun. Right now, the Earth's Floating Crust (EFC) theory is nothing more than speculation on my part, something I supposed when researching the topic. Science regrettably does not have the knowledge or data to support the EFC theory any more than it has the knowledge or data to support evolution. The point of sharing these thoughts and concepts is to paint a picture of what is possible. In God the Creator who spoke life into existence, all things are possible!

If the possibility of the crust shifting above the mantle seems farfetched, consider that it just happened again (on a much smaller scale). History has repeated itself in your lifetime. On March 11, 2011, a magnitude 9.0 earthquake struck off the coast of Japan and unleashed a devastating tsunami that engulfed entire towns. As reported by the US

Geological Survey (USGS) and documented on a map provided by the GSI (Geospatial Information Authority), when the tremors had subsided and the waters receded, the entire main island of Japan had moved by eight feet (2.4 meters) and shifted the earth on its axis. Reports from the National Institute of Geophysics and Volcanology in Italy estimated that the March 11, 2011 quake shifted the planet on its axis by nearly four inches (ten centimeters). Science would have us believe that the scenarios presented here are impossible, but the continents did separate, Japan did move, and the moon is in synchronous orbit with the earth. The odds of the moon randomly being a distance and diameter as seen from the earth that exactly matches the distance and diameter of the sun as seen from the earth are beyond measure, and yet it is proven every time we have a solar eclipse.

Taking it just a step further, it is only a small leap to conclude that those same building blocks were manipulated on October 13, 1917 in Fatima, Portugal, to bring about the Miracle of the Sun where for ten minutes, tens of thousands of people witnessed the sun zigzagging back and forth in the sky. From photographs taken that day, it was estimated that between fifty and one hundred thousand people were in attendance. They came to see the miracle that was foretold by three shepherd children and promised by Our Lady of Fatima. The event was declared to be of "supernatural character" in 1930, an "approved apparition" in 1940, and an "approved miracle" in 2017 by the Catholic Church. And yet, because science could not explain how the sun could dart around the sky, they concluded that it never happened. To that, I say, despite reasonable logic shouting the impossibility of something contrary to the laws of known science, if for a moment, we are able to stifle those arguments and entertain the concept that all things are possible through God, how much more could we understand and how wondrous would our world be?

$-7-$

THE NEPHILIM:
LAND OF THE GIANTS

So far, we've talked about theory, scientific fact, and the blurry line that sometimes exists between the two, but what we haven't discussed is how falsehoods become truths and facts are distorted through disinformation. Acknowledging the recently called out and yet to be acknowledged biases of our news agencies and the presidential addition of "fake news" to our daily vocabulary, I can think of no more contemporary example of disinformation than the recently surfaced and instantly viral video of Nancy Pelosi. The Majority Speaker explains a political tactic that she refers to as "the wrap-up smear": "You demonize. . . . You smear somebody with falsehoods and all the rest, and then you merchandise it."[86] Often attributed to anonymous but reliable sources, the press then reports on the smear and we say, "See, it's reported in the press that this, this, and this. . . . Now I am going to merchandise the press report on the smear that we made. It's a tactic." To be fair, I am sure that similar tactics are employed by all political parties; somebody just happened to catch a Democrat admitting to it on tape.

As discussed in chapter four, new discoveries and theories are routinely dismissed as pseudoscience because they contradict the basis for radiocarbon dating and do not align with the geologic column or support the evolutionary tree. These views are often reinforced through disinformation and the promotion of falsehoods. Identical reasoning justifies the silencing of Goliaths within our midst. The intentional century-long acquisition and coverup of extraordinarily large human bones and full skeletons by the Smithsonian has altered the archeological record and rewritten history. *The Giant Skeleton* tells the story of two men traveling from Mesa Rica, New Mexico to El Cuervo, Mexico to purchase the unearthed bones of a giant skeleton for resale to the Smithsonian. In the January 27, 1902 issue of the *Albuquerque Daily Citizen*, Don Gregorio and Marcelino Martinez theorized that "The Smithsonian people would be proud of a giant of the dimensions of this one." One leg is "eight feet in length."[87] Once prominently displayed, skeletons of giants began to disappear shortly after the acceptance of evolution. Prior to the early 1900s, accounts of unearthed giants were numerous and heavily reported. The common thread was always the Smithsonian where the bones were typically donated or sold, never to be heard of or seen again. In the words of Vine Deloria, a Native American author and professor of law, "The great interloper of ancient burial grounds, the nineteenth-century Smithsonian Institution, created a one-way portal, through which uncounted bones have been spirited. This door and the contents of its vault are virtually sealed off. . . . Among these bones may lay answers not even sought . . . concerning the deep past."[88]

In Jim Vieira and Hugh Newman's book *Giants on Record: America's Hidden History, Secrets in the Mounds and the Smithsonian Files*, there is well-documented evidence of the Smithsonian coverup of giants in North America. "Over a 200-year period, thousands of newspaper reports, town and county histories, letters, photos, diaries, and scientific journals have documented the existence of an ancient race of giants in North America. Extremely tall skeletons ranging from seven feet up to a staggering eighteen feet tall have been reportedly uncovered in prehistoric mounds, burial chambers, caves, geometric earthworks, and ancient battlefields. Strange anatomic anomalies such as double rows of teeth, horned skulls, massive jaws that fit over a modern face, and elongated skulls have also been reported. Many of these discoveries were sent to the Smithsonian Institution in Washington DC, seemingly never to be heard about again. The Smithsonian's own records describe at least seventeen giant skeletons in annual reports. This book examines a possible coverup initiated by Smithsonian scientists starting in the late 1800s."[89]

As I collected old newspaper articles of giant remains to be used as reference material, I ran across an article entitled "Smithsonian Admits to Destruction of Thousands of Giant Human Skeletons in Early 1900s."[90] Reading the article, I learned that just around the corner, in 2020 the Smithsonian Museum would be forced to release documentation of the intentional destruction of thousands of giant human bones. The article said that, "The public release of these documents will help archaeologists and historians to reevaluate current theories about human evolution . . ." I was aware of rumored lawsuits against the Smithsonian and not at all surprised to hear of a final judgment against the Smithsonian. I eagerly anticipated the release of this damning information. Sadly, I soon discovered that the article was bogus, just more fake news, more disinformation. The process works too perfectly. If and when the Smithsonian is ever forced to admit to any coverup or destruction of bones, everyone will recall that this article was found to be false and nobody will believe it.

Everybody remembers Doug Bower and Dave Chorley of Hampshire, England who confessed in 1991 to making England's crop circles with nothing more than a board and a length of rope. Nobody questions the enormous and complex mathematical crop designs of today that are created on nearly every continent, appear in moments, physically elongate the nodes of plant stems, leave crops undamaged, and reappear sometime later in the harvested ground or subsequent crops. Once a cover story is established to distract the curious from the uncomfortable or unknown, that lie then becomes the truth when it is substantiated by witnesses, reported in the news and digested. Intellectually lazy and eager to accept provided answers to complicated issues, we allow ourselves to be misdirected by misinformation. Why challenge the unknown or dig any deeper when the provided answers have already been given to us on a silver platter?

The archive of published stories detailing the discovery of early American giants are endless. On July 11, 1919, the *Coconino Sun* of Phoenix began the story of "A Giant Skeleton Eighteen Feet Tall" with the declaration, "'If the report that the fossilized skeleton of a giant eighteen feet tall has been found near Seymour, Tex., is true, it is the most important ethnological discovery ever made in the world,' remarked Dr. J. E. Pearce, professor of anthropology of the University of Texas." The *Sun* article explained, "The skeleton is in possession of W. J. McKinney, Houston, Tex., oil prospector, who found it, and has been seen by a number of people who vouch for the truth of the size of the relic of a heretofore unknown race. Mr. McKinney, while making an excavation on the narrow watershed between the Brazos and Wichita rivers, came upon the fossilized skeleton near the surface.'I estimate that this man weighed from two thousand to twenty-five hundred pounds. . . . The skull is six times the size of that of an ordinary man.'" Ever a looming presence, the same article goes on to admit, "It is possible that the bones of the giant will be donated to the Smithsonian Institution which, under the direction of Dr. J. Walter Fewkes, is now conducting anthropological research work in Texas."[91]

Fed by the Industrial Revolution, the conquest and modernization of the Americas transformed this country with the excavation for new railways, foundations, farmlands, and waterways from coast to coast. The overturned soil, gravel pits, fields, and backyards exposed American settlers to a previously unknown and undocumented history of earlier civilizations. Among the unearthed artifacts and relics were the bones of thousands of giants. Copied from the pocket almanac of the late Judge Atlee, *The New York Times* published "Two Very Tall Skeletons" on August 10, 1880. The story said in part that, "On the 24th of May, 1798, being at Hanover (York County, Penn.,) in company with Chief Justice McKean, Judge Bryan, Mr. Burd, and others, on our way to Franklin, and taking a view of the town, in company with Mr. McAllister, and several other respectable inhabitants, we went to Mr. Neese's tan-yard, where we were shown a place near currying-house from whence (in digging to sink a tan-vat) some years ago were taken two skeletons of human bodies. They lay close beside each other and measured about 11 feet 3 inches in length; the bones were entire, but on being taken up and exposed to the air they presently crumbled and fell to pieces." Stories of unearthed gargantuan human remains just kept piling up.

Although not all giants were discovered through the intentional excavation of the Americas, many were. On Christmas of 1868, *The New York Times* reprinted the earlier "Reported Discovery of a Huge Skeleton" from the December 18 *Sank Rapids* (MN) *Sentinel*. The publication stated that, "Day before yesterday, while the quarrymen employed by the Sank Rapids Water Power Company were engaged in quarrying rock for the dam which is being erected across the Mississippi, at this place, found embedded in the solid granite rock the remains of a human being of gigantic status. . . . The remains were found embedded in the sand, which had evidently been placed in the quadrangular grave which had been dug out of the solid rock to receive the last remains of this antediluvian giant. The grave was twelve feet in depth, and is today at least two feet below the present level of the river. The remains are completely petrified, and of gigantic dimensions. The head is massive, measures thirty-one and one-half inches in circumference. . . . The femur measures twenty-six and a quarter inches, and the Fibula twenty-five and a half, while the body is equally long in proportion. From the crown of the head to the sole of the foot, the length is ten feet nine and a half inches. . . . The giant must have weighed at least 900 pounds."

It is important to note that unlike the tall and lanky Robert Pershing Wadlow that Ringling Brothers promoted as the tallest person in recorded history, who grew to a height of eight feet, eleven inches, suffered from a weakened immune system, had hyperplasia of the pituitary gland, and died from an unrecognized infection attributed to the rubbing of his leg braces at the age of twenty-two, the giants of old are believed to have had extremely long and healthy lives. Their height was not caused by hyperplasia of the pituitary gland and their proportions were massive. On December 25, 1845, the *Evansville Journal* of Indiana published the story of a skeleton that was found in Williamson county, about sixty feet below the surface of the earth, embedded in a stratum of hard clay. "The bones are said to be in a perfect state of preservation, and weigh in aggregate 1500 pounds. All the large and characteristic bones are entire, and the skull, arms, and thigh bones, knee pans, shoulder sockets and collar bones, remove all doubts, and the animal to whom they belonged has been decided to belong to the genus Homo. This gentleman when he walked the earth, was about 18 feet high and when clothed in flesh must have weighed not less than 3000 pounds. The bones of the thigh and leg measure 6 ft., 6 inches; his skull is said to be about two-thirds the size of a floor barrel and capable of holding in its cavities near two bushels. He must have had a goodly quantity of brains, and if intellect be in proportion to the size of the brain, he must have possessed extraordinary intellectual powers. . . . The jaw teeth weigh from 3-½ to 6 pounds."

Prior to the widespread acceptance of evolution over intelligent design, predominately Christian nations were challenged by few opposing views. Giants were sought out and unearthed worldwide. In an October 7, 1905 article entitled "Giants of the Past," the *Coeur d'Alene Press* of France recalled that, "The past was more prolific in the production of giants than the present. In 1830 one of these giants, who was exhibited at Rouen, was ten feet high, and the giant Galabra, brought from Arabia to Rome in the time of Claudius Caesar, was the same height. Pannum, who lived in the time of Eugene II, was eleven and one-half feet in height. The Chevalier Scrog in his journey to the peak Tenerife found in one of the caverns of that mountain the head of a giant who had sixty teeth and who was not less than fifteen feet high. The giant Paragus, slain by Orlando, the nephew of Charlemagne, according to reports, was twenty-eight feet high. In 1814 near St. Gernad was found the tomb of the giant Isolent, who was not less than thirty feet high. In 1500 near Rouen was found a skeleton whose head held a bushel of corn and which was nineteen feet in height. In 1623 near the castle in Dauphine a tomb was found thirty feet long, sixteen feet wide and eight feet high on which were cut . . . the words 'Kentolochus Rex.' The skeleton was found entire and measured twenty-five and one-fourth feet high, ten feet across the shoulders and five feet from the breastbone to the back." Further validation of the giants of France can be found in an excerpt from the *London Globe* entitled "A Race of Giants in Old Gaul" that was published in *The New York Times* on October 3, 1892.[92]

As verified through published eyewitness accounts, and the repeated stories of legends and folklore, there are very few places on this planet where giants haven't been found. Near Palermo, Sicily, in 1516, was found the skeleton of a giant thirty feet high and in 1559 another forty-four feet high . . ." ("Giants of the Past," the *Coeur d'Alene Press*, October 7, 1905). "At the current location of Glastonbury Abbey in the 1190s, a great oak coffin was discovered by the monks sixteen feet below the surface between two small pyramids. A controversial object was also found, at only eight feet below the surface. The infamous lead cross had this carved on it in Latin, 'Here lies interred the famous King Author on the Isle of Avalon.' This became a sensation, and some say a hoax. However, the skeleton that was excavated was said to be close to 9 feet tall. Giraldus Cambrensis, a respected historian personally examined the bones and the grave about four years after the discovery and pronounced it a genuine find. In 1278, in the presence of King Edward I and Queen Eleanor, the remains were transferred to inside the Abbey. Then, in 1962-63, after doing some additional excavations at the grave site, Dr. Raleigh Radford, an archeologist, 'confirmed that a prominent personage had indeed been buried there at the period in question.'"[93]

On April 3, 1914, the *Evening Star* of London reported that a ten-foot giant had just been recovered in Ireland. In the story "Giant Skeleton Found," the *Evening Star* reported that, "According to a dispatch published here today, the skeleton of a person who had been apparently ten feet in height has been found at Dysart, County Louth, Ireland. The skeleton was unearthed together with that of two others supposed to have been buried in prehistoric times. The three bodies had been interred in separate graves, all incased with stones. The skull of the giant measured eighteen inches from the crown of the head to the chin."

Without question, stories and documented accounts of giants and giant bones being found on the island of Crete outnumber the stories and accounts from anywhere else in the world. Greek mythology keeps these stories alive to this day. The Greeks tell us that the offspring of giants were known as Titans. They were said to come from the East and were considered the offspring of Caelus and Terra. Together, the mythological gods, Neptune and his brother Jupiter, also known as Zeus, remain connected to the legends of Crete. Neptune and Zeus battled against the Titans and were known as destroyers of giants. Crete was once known as Arcadia. The Greek historian Herodotus wrote of another historian, Eustathius who had said that Arcadia was once called Gigantis, "The Land of Giants." Several of the world's most influential writers throughout history have verified these accounts. Among the great writers who have verified the existence of giants on Crete were Diodorus Siculus, Pliny, Strabo, Plutarch, and Plato.

History has shown that stories of myths and legends are most often based on some underlying truth. Stories of Greek mythology are no different. Proving that Crete may indeed have been the land of the giants, the largest human bones ever recovered were found on the island of Crete. During the Cretan War (205-200 BC), skeletal remains of a recovered Cretan giant were first officially measured. The giant had a measured length of thirty-three cubits, which equates to nearly forty-two feet. Nearly a century later, philosopher and poet, Philodemus of Gadara reported on another giant found on the island of Crete that was forty-eight cubits in length, which equates to an astonishing seventy-two feet. First-century philosopher and Roman author, navy and army commander Pliny the Elder (AD 23-79), who authored *The Encyclopedic Naturalis Historia*, otherwise known as *The Book of Natural History*, spoke about a mountain on the island of Crete that had been overturned by an earthquake and uncovered the bones of a massive giant. Second-century Greek writer under Roman Emperor Hadrian,

Phlegon of Tralles documents the discovery of several giant skeletons on the island of Crete. In the *Geography of Strabo*, Phlegon of Tralles writes that giants were discovered in a city founded by the biblical Corinthians who previously resided on Crete. Franciscan and world traveler Cristoforo Buondelmonti (AD 1386-1430) wrote about a Cretan city named Sarandopolis that was formerly inhabited by giants, and where the modern jurisdiction of Setia derived its name. Reports of giants previously inhabiting the island of Crete have existed since time immemorial and persist to this day.

While the rest of the world may have already had an established history of giants, the giants of the Americas were newly discovered and abundant in the late eighteenth/early nineteenth centuries. As reported in the February 25, 1904 *Taney County Republican*, "Workman engaged in digging gravel at Winnemucca, NV, the other day uncovered at a depth of about 12 feet a lot of bones, part of the skeleton of a gigantic human being. Dr. Samuels examined them and pronounced them to be bones of a man who must have been nearly 11 feet in height." First picked up by the *Fort Worth Daily Gazette* on August 15, 1883, later covered by the *Democratic Northwest* of Ohio on August 23, 1883, and finally published in the Baltimore *Sun* on September 26, 1883, all three papers recalled the account of a twelve-foot giant, exposed by rain erosion in Barnard Missouri on August 14, 1883. The Baltimore *Sun* entitled their article "Must Have Been Goliath" and reported, "A farmer named John W. Hannon found the bones protruding from the bank of a ravine that has been cut by the action of the rains during the past years. Mr. Hannon worked several days in unearthing the skeleton, which proved to be a human being whose height was twelve feet. The head through the temples was twelve inches. From the lower part of the skull at the back to the top was fifteen inches and the circumference forty inches. The ribs were nearly four feet long and three and a fourth inches wide. The thigh bones were thirty inches long, and the entire foot eighteen inches in length. . . . Some of the bones crumbled on exposure to the air, but many good specimens were preserved and are now on exhibition at Barnard. Medical men are much interested." "Must Have Been Goliath" was also printed in the Rhode Island *Providence Evening Press* on September 13, 1883.

As reported in *The New York Times* article "Giant Skeletons Found" on February 11, 1902, "Los Angeles, Cal., Feb. 10. – Owning to the discovery of the remains of a race of giants in Guadalupe, NM., antiquarians and archaeologists are preparing an expedition further to explore that region. This determination is based on the excitement that exists among the people of a scope of country near Mesa Rico, about 200 miles southeast of Los Vegas, where an old burial ground has been discovered that has yielded skeletons of enormous size. Luciana Quintana, on whose ranch the ancient burial plot is located, discovered two stones that bore curious inscriptions, and beneath these were found in shallow excavations the bones of a frame that could not have been less than 12 feet in length. The men who opened the grave say the forearm was 4 feet long and that in a well-preserved jaw, the lower teeth ranged from the size of a hickory nut to that of the largest walnut in size. The chest of the being is reported as having a circumference of seven feet. Quintana, who has uncovered many other burial places, expresses the opinion that perhaps thousands of skeletons of a race of giants long extinct will be found. This supposition is based on the traditions handed down from the early Spanish invasion that have detailed knowledge of the existence of a race of giants that inhabited the plains of what now is Eastern New Mexico. Indian legends and carvings also in the same area indicate the existence of such a race."

As I paged my way through the huge library of giant skeletal finds, I discovered that most serious and intentional archaeological efforts to seek out giants concentrated on the excavation of burial mounds. As I read on, the reasoning behind this curiosity became apparent. The excavation of burial mounds typically came with funding and more often than not, resulted in the unearthing of valuable artifacts. Even more importantly, they routinely yielded giants of not more than seven foot six inches in height. The importance of routinely finding very tall Native Americans may not at first seem significant, until you recognize the value of disinformation. A credentialed expert (with a purpose) can easily and repeatedly explain away the existence of a very tall Native American. It is not so easy to justify the existence a fourteen-foot Goliath.

On April 2, 1903, the *Warren Sheaf* of Minnesota published a story entitled "Tall Men Are Freaks" and informed its readers that, "Prof. Cunningham, who has been appointed to succeed and serve under his old teacher, Sir William Turner, in the chair of anatomy in the University of Edinburgh ... has shown that the mental characteristics of giants ... good nature, sloth and poor intelligence—are those shown by the victims of a rare disease of overgrowth called acromegaly. This is due to the enlargement of an appendage of the brain, and Prof. Cunningham has personally examined every giant skeleton in the British and continental museums, and found that the little cavity in the skull corresponding to this part of the brain is enlarged in all of them." Well, there you have it. As long as exploration can be counted on to not threaten or overturn existing science, the search to verify pre-existing conclusions is more easily funded and undertaken than the search for truth. I don't know if Professor Cunningham noticed, but giants generally also have enlarged thumbs, bigger big toes, and huge eye sockets. I wonder what it all means.

First told in *The New York Times* on November 20, 1883, and later published in *The Daily Bulletin* on May 22, 1884, "A Pre-Historic City" tells the story of Professor P. W. Norris, Assistant US Ethnologist, who had been excavating Indian burial mounds in the recently discovered ruins of an ancient city in the Kanacoha valley, near Charleston, West Virginia. The story reported that found, "... lying horizontally on its back was a giant skeleton, 7 feet and six inches long, and measuring 19 inches throughout [sic] under the arms. On each wrist were large copper bracelets, four of which had been enclosed in cloth or dressed skin. Under the skull was a stone lance-head. There was a copper gorget upon the breast with two holes in it. The gorget, which was 4 inches square, is regarded as having been a badge of authority. In the right hand was a hematite iron hatchet having a 4-inch blade. In the left hand were several lance heads, 6 inches in length, of flint manufacture." Similar relics were seldom recovered with the remains of giants not so interred. Professor Norris unearthed fifty-six burial mounds in the Kanacoha valley, each yielding a half-dozen or so skeletons. First published in the *East Oregonian* on August 10, 1912, and later reported in the *San Juan Islander* on August 23, 1912, William Altmann, Assistant Curator of the Golden Gate Park Memorial found a seven-foot, four-inch giant while "... excavating an old Indian burial mound in the nursery of Thomas S. Dunne. . . . The giant skeleton was found ten feet from the surface, and around it was a large number of mortars and pestles, charm stones and obsidian arrow heads." The number of recovered relics was untold.

Repeatedly reporting conjecture as fact, *The New York Times* first released the story of scientists who had unearthed relics of Indians reported to be seven hundred years old on November 14, 1916. The story was republished in *The Wellsboro Gazette* of Pennsylvania on September 21, 1916 as "Giant's Bones in Mound." The story reported, "Professor A. B. Skinner of the American Indian Museum, Professor W. K. Morehead of Phillips Andover Academy, and Dr. George Donohue, Pennsylvania State Historian, who have been conducting research along the valley of the Susquehanna, have uncovered an Indian mound at Tioga Point, on the upper portion of Queen Esther's Flats, on what is known as the Murry farm, a short distance from Sayre, Penn., which promises rich additions to Indian lore." Heard again and again, repeated oratories sound like fact. Less opinionated and closer to the truth, on October 3, 1916, *The Bemidji Daily Pioneer* of Minnesota announced that the "Bones of an Ancient Person Unearthed Near Spooner; May Have Been a Giant." The article announced that, "An enlightening contribution to historical data concerning the early mound builders of the Rainy Lake region has been made in the finding of a skeleton of a prehistoric being near Spooner. The skeleton was found on a caved in bank of clay off the Rainy river. It is well preserved and is thought to be that of a woman. . . . Physicians who have examined the skeleton declare that it represented a type of early prehistoric persons who were seven feet or more and who possessed an especially large lower jaw." What I find notable about this article is that it doesn't jump to the conclusion that the remains were that of an American Indian simply because they were found in an ancient burial mound.

In an April 25, 2016, *Ancient Origins* web article entitled "Ancient Race of White Giants Described in Native Legends from Many Tribes," Tera Macisaac of *Epoch Times* writes, "Several Native American tribes have passed down legends of a race of white giants . . ."[94] Tera recalls that, "Chief Rolling Thunder of the Comanches, a tribe from the Great Plains, gave the following account of an ancient race of white giants in 1857: 'Innumerable moons ago, a race of white men, 10 feet high, and far more rich and powerful than any white people now living, here inhabited a large range of country, extending from the rising to the setting sun. Their fortifications crowned the summits of the mountains, protecting their populous cities situated in the intervening valleys. They excelled every other nation which was flourished, either before or since, in all manner of cunning handcraft—were brave and warlike—ruling over the land they had wrested from its ancient possessors with a high and haughty hand. Compared with them the palefaces of the present day were pygmies, in both art and arms . . .' The chief explained that when this race forgot justice and mercy and became too proud, the Great Spirit wiped it out and all that was left of their society were the mounds still visible on the table-lands." This account was documented by Dr. Donald "Panther" Yates, a researcher and author of several books, including, *Lovelock Cave: A Tale of Giants or A Giant Tale of Fiction.*

In the same *Ancient Origins* web article, Tera goes on to share Navajo and Choctaw legends of white giants. She recalls that in addition to documenting Chief Rolling Thunder of the Comanches, Dr. Yates also wrote about the Starnake people of Navajo legend, describing them as, "A regal race of white giants endowed with mining technology who dominated the West, enslaving lesser tribes, and had strongholds all through the Americas. They were either extinguished or 'went back to the heavens.'" Tera tells us that, "Horatio Bardwell Cushman wrote in his 1899 book, *History of the Choctaw, Chickasaw, and Natchez Indians* that, 'The tradition of the Choctaws . . . Told of a race of giants that

once inhabited the now State of Tennessee, and with whom their ancestors fought when they arrived in Mississippi in their migration from
the west. . . . Their tradition states the Nahullo (race of giants) was of
wonderful stature.' The Nahullo were said to be cannibals whom the
Choctaw killed whenever the opportunity arose." Searching for additional legends of giants in Native American folklore and culture, I came
across a June 1, 2016 article on the web-based *Phoenix Enigma* that was
written by the site's founder, Cory Daniel and simply titled "Giants."[95]
Cory's research shows that the Hopi Indians speak ". . . of Giants in the
days before the great flood. These stories read nearly identical to the
Bible if one allows for local flavor. According to the Hopi, there were
giants on the earth in those days and they were cannibalistic. Many of
them had bred with the humans as well as infecting them with their
DNA, these offspring were warlike and caused much destruction in
the world. A Kachina Massawu came down from the stars and after
entrusting the uncorrupted of the Hopi to the ant people underground,
he proceeded to flood the earth and rid it of these giants and monsters."

   In an excerpt from William R. Cody's (a.k.a. Buffalo Bill Cody's)
autobiography, Cory Daniel shares a story of an encounter with the Pawnee in which Buffalo Bill recalled, "While we were in the sandhills, scout-
ing in the Niobrara country, the Pawnee Indians brought into camp some
very large bones, one of which the surgeon on the expedition pronounced
to be the thigh bone of a human being. The Indians said the bones were
those of a race of people who long ago lived in that country. They said
these people were three times the size of a man of the present day, that
they were so swift and strong that they could run by the side of a buffalo,
and, taking the animal in one arm, could tear off a leg and eat it as they
ran (Colonel Wm. F. Cody, 1920)." Cory's research found that the Pawnee
believed that the giants denied the existence of the Great Spirit, so the
Great Spirit ". . . caused a great rainstorm to come, and the water kept rising higher and higher so that it drove these proud, and conceited giants
from the low ground to the hills, and thence to the mountains, but at last
even the mountain tops were submerged and then those mammoth men

were all drowned. After the flood had subsided, the Great Spirit came to the conclusion that he had made man too large and powerful, and that he would, therefore, correct the mistake by creating a race of men of smaller size and strength. This is the reason, say the Indians, that modern men are small and not like the giants of old. They claim that this story is a matter of Indian history, which has been handed down among them from time immemorial."

The *Phoenix Enigma* article explains how the Paiute Indians are forever connected to the giants of the Lovelock Cave. Cory recalls that, "This story was first written down by Sarah Winnemucca Hopkins, the daughter of a Paiute Chief in her book titled, *Life Among the Paiutes: Their Wrongs and Claims*." Although appearing in print for the first time in her book, this recollection was already an old story to the Paiute people. "Sara Hopkins relays the not so ancient story of a race of red-haired giants who roamed the area that is now Nevada." These giants were unfriendly and cannibalistic. Cory tells us, "These giants were known as Si-Ti-Cah, which translates to Tule-eaters. Tule being a reed-like plant which they fashioned into boats in order to escape the Paiute. These boats were used to sail across the great lake that once covered much of the area that is now Nevada. The Paiute tribes, growing weary of being eaten . . . decided to put their differences aside to hunt down and eradicate this race of giants. They hunted them all over what is now Nevada and the surrounding area, killing them as they found them. The last of these giants were driven into a cave and fire was set at the entrance. Those giants who attempted to flee were shot and killed with arrows and the rest died of smoke inhalation." Collapsed and now inhabited by bats and guano, the Lovelock Cave was successfully excavated for giant remains in 1912 and 1924.

In setting up an outline for this chapter, my intentions were to limit discussions of American giants to the legends of the Native American tribes. However, that was before I discovered a link between the giants of the indigenous people of Peru and the giants of the American Paiute.[96] Tera Macisaac points out that, "In 1553, Pedro Cieza de Leon wrote in

Chronicle of Peru about legendary giants described to him by the Manta indigenous people: "There are, however, reports concerning giants in Peru, who landed on the coast at the point of Santa Elena.'" The natives shared the following traditions, which had been received from their ancestors from very remote times, "There arrived on the coast, in boats made of reeds, as big as large ships, a party of men of such size that, from the knee downward, their height was as great as the entire height of an ordinary man, though he might be of good stature. Their limbs were all in proportion to the deformed size of their bodies, and it was a monstrous thing to see their heads, with hair reaching to their shoulders. Their eyes were as large as small plates." What I find fascinating about this oral tradition is that the American giants were fleeing the Paiute Indians in reed boats and the Peruvian giants were arriving by reed boats. Perhaps only a coincidence, this happenstance seemed worth mentioning. Pedro de Leon went on to explain in *Chronicles of Peru* that ". . . the sexual habits of the giants were revolting to the Natives and heaven eventually wiped out the giants because of those habits."[97]

Although not directly tied to any particular Native American tribe, another story that is worth repeating is the well documented and more recent story of Queho. In the words of Cory Daniel, "The story of Queho is a fascinating tale that comes to us from the Las Vegas area. . . . Queho spent the bulk of his life living in the canyons just south of present-day Las Vegas as a wanted man. He reportedly murdered several people in different encounters, presumably dry gulching them for their supplies. One sheriff's posse once spent four months in the desert attempting to track him down but failed. His remains were found in a shallow cave just south of the Hoover Dam area by local workers during the construction. . . . The remains were positively identified as belonging to Queho as the skull contained two rows of teeth, which Queho was known to have had. There are many eyewitness accounts to his life, people who had met him, and even one story of a man who sat with him and shared a sandwich one afternoon. He reported Queho as being a great figure of a man and quite decent in manner. He reported that Queho didn't speak but made grunting noises and gestures instead and even attempted to share a dead rodent with him."

Reported stories of giants were so common in the early nineteenth century that news outlets often forgot to report on the most noteworthy aspect of the story, the height of the unearthed monsters. The *Evening Star* of Washington DC published a short story called "Find Giant Skeleton" on August 21, 1921, that reported, "While excavating for a building in the rear of the Morrison property here yesterday, William A. Liller, contractor, unearthed parts of a giant skeleton. The find was under a flat stone that weighed about a half ton." On August 23, 1892, the *Pittsburg Dispatch* published "Two Giant Human Skeletons Found," in which they reported, "Workmen, while digging a ditch from the new shovel works to the river at Aliquippa today unearthed the remains of two skeletons. They are of gigantic size." On September 7, 1904, *The New York Times* released "Find Giant Indian's Bones," that explained, "While a gang of men in the employ of the New York and Harlem Railroad were taking sand from an immense mound near Purdy's Station today to fill in an excavation, they unearthed several skeletons of unusual size. The bones are believed to be those of Indians who once lived in this vicinity and belonged to a tribe that was led by the great Chief Teekus." On September 11, 1891, the *Dodge City Times* announced, "Further investigation of the Sweeny mounds near Carthage, Ill., resulted in unearthing hundreds of human skeletons of giant proportions." These four stories have more than the obvious in common. The reader has no idea if these colossal behemoths were six-foot-eleven-inches tall or eleven-foot-six-inches tall. Inches are important and I can only assume that if similar stories were not so commonplace, relevant statistics like the height of a giant would not only have been reported, but it would have made it to the headline.

For a more recent, twenty-first-century accounting of giants, I refer to the Solomon Islands. If it were not for the marriage of a Solomon Islander to an Australian helicopter pilot turned author, Marius Boirayon, the world would have no idea that the Solomon Islands are ideal for modern-day research of giants. The Solomon Islands is a sovereign state in Oceania, east of Papua New Guinea, consisting of nearly one thousand islands. First discovered by the Spanish in 1568 and believed to have been inhabited by the Melanesians for thousands of years, giants have remained an integral part of the island's culture for as long as native residents can remember. At the time of this writing, Marius Boirayon, author of *Solomon Island Mysteries*, is drafting a second book with Mark A. Hall, entitled *True Giants: Is Gigantopithecus Still Alive?* Now a Solomon Islander by marriage, Marius has observed firsthand that the native residents see nothing special about their ancestral stories and personal encounters with giants. To them, it is just a fact of life, something they grew up with. By fate or by chance, it seems appropriate that the Solomon Islands' national logo is "The Place That Time Forgot."

Because of the World War II Battle of Guadalcanal (1942-1943), Guadalcanal is the most recognizable of the Solomon Islands. The residents believe that today, there are literally hundreds, if not thousands of giants currently living inside the huge tropical rainforest jungles and mountain range cave systems of Guadalcanal. While the giants were by all accounts quiet during the first major offensive of the Allied forces against the Empire of Japan, the giants of Guadalcanal were not so docile during the initial invasion and occupation by Japan. As the Japanese soldiers traversed the island's thick rainforests, they reported encountering giants that ranged from ten to fifteen feet in height. They had long brown or reddish hair, flat noses, wide mouths, and prominent brows. All of the creatures had immense arms and typically brandished crude weapons such as clubs or bones. The Japanese soldiers characterized their encounters with these monsters as very aggressive. The beasts were described as crashing through the foliage to ravage small squads of soldiers. They often snapped apart trees and branches to display their power and not even bullets would intimidate them. The soldiers had difficulty sleeping at night due to the threatening noises coming from these behemoths. As the Allied forces arrived and began to liberate the island from the Japanese occupation, the giants inexplicably retreated back to the tropical rainforest and mountain range cave systems. This was believed to be because the giants are territorial and as forewarned by the island residents, the Allied forces knew enough to stay clear of giant trails and territories.

The stories of the giants of Guadalcanal continue to this day. In 1998, Gold Ridge Mining was putting in a road that bordered areas known to be claimed by the giants when one of the pins securing a ten-ton blade to the front of a bulldozer broke. The decision was made to remove the blade, leave it behind, and take the bulldozer back to the yard. It was getting near dark and the plan was to return the following morning with the needed parts to secure the blade. When the crew returned the next morning, the blade was nowhere to be found. Seeing giant footprints near the point where the bulldozer had turned around and headed back to the yard, the crew began searching for the missing blade. The ten-ton blade was eventually found one hundred meters away on the side of a hill where, rather than being dragged or carried away, the crew believed that the giants had thrown it. After completing construction of that same road, the National Minister and the Guadalcanal Minister decided to take a 4WD Toyota to a proposed mine site to do some surveying. Nearly there, they ran into some rain and their vehicle slipped off the road where it became stuck in the mud. After making some effort to get back up onto the road, they decided to leave their vehicle and walk back to the last village that they had passed on the way in to get some men to help pull them out. Returning with some thirty-odd men, the ministers rounded the corner where they expected to find their abandoned vehicle and there the ministers and the men witnessed two fifteen-foot-tall giants, one in the front and one in the back, setting their 4WD Toyota back up onto the road. Everyone screamed and scattered. Returning some thirty minutes later, the ministers found their 4WD Toyota unharmed, back up on the road and ready to go.

Marius Boirayon writes of one giant in particular, Luti Mikode, who is famously responsible for negotiating an agreement with the giants to stop eating islanders. Despite reaching this agreement over a century ago, Luti is still believed to be alive to this day and is considered the "Chief of the Giants" because the treaty is still in effect. Island folklore says that prior to this agreement, island children were captured along the shore-line, penned up, and raised like pigs for food. Stories are passed down from generation to generation of giants that once stormed villages and tore off human limbs to be eaten uncooked and on the spot. To this day, many residents of Guadalcanal offer unblemished white pigs with beetle-nut-lime, ground from snail shells as a sacrifice to the giants. I take these accounts of cannibalism with a grain of salt. Recorded history tells us that when the Solomon Islands were first discovered in 1568, the islanders themselves were cannibals. Perhaps accusing the giants helps the island-ers to come to terms with their own savagery. Occasional survivors can testify to the fact that giants are known to forcibly take women from their villages to be their wives. One such survivor, Mango, was released after twenty-five years, survived into her fifties, and died in 2007/2008. What I find so fascinating about these recollections is that the sightings and encounters are published and broadcast with no fanfare, awe, or amaze-ment. It's all just so matter of fact.

The Solomon Islander woman who married Marius Boirayon came from an island named Choiseul, a 185-mile-long by 50-mile-wide island that remains, for the most part, conspicuously uninhabited in the center territories that are said to be inhabited by giants. Only recently explored by researchers and archaeologists, the center regions of Choiseul have been shown to be a warehouse of giant skeletal remains. Not yet exca-vated, the site is reported to have numerous giant bones scattered about, unburied, and above the ground. A nearby village to where Marius's wife hailed from is said to retain an eight-foot femur bone as the center sup-port post to a village hut. The preponderance of evidence combined with the number of reported sightings make the possibility of present-day giants on the Solomon Islands a likelihood that is hard to ignore.

As even the casual reader of the Bible would already know, Scrip-ture recounts numerous encounters between giants and the clans and tribes of the ancient Near East, including David's killing of Goliath. If science hadn't already attempted to cover up, distort, and negate the fact that giants once shared this planet, I would likely be compelled to argue against offered scientific explanation. However, there are no scientific interpretations to argue against, not even an acknowledgment. Despite mountains of evidence indicating that giants once lived in our midst, only a few verses of the Bible and the Book of Enoch provide any explanation of where they came from. The Bible tells us that the introduction of giants, the corruption of man, the corruption of the planet, and the resulting great flood can all be traced back to the sins of fallen angels. "Now it came to pass, when men began to multiply on the face of the earth, and daughters were born to them, that the sons of God saw the daughters of men, that they were beautiful; and they took wives for themselves of all whom they chose. And the Lord said, 'My Spirit shall not strive with man forever, for he is indeed flesh; yet his days shall be one hundred and twenty years.' There were giants on the earth in those days, and also afterward, when the sons of God came in to the daughters of men and they bore children to them. Those were the mighty men who were of old, men of renown. Then the Lord saw that the wickedness of man was great in the earth, and that every intent of the thoughts of his heart was only evil continually. And the Lord was sorry that He had made man on the earth, and He was grieved in His heart. So, the Lord said, 'I will destroy man whom I have created from the face of the earth, both man and beast, creeping thing and birds of the air, for I am sorry that I have made them'" (Genesis 6:1-7).

While Enoch had already ascended to heaven and was no longer on earth for the onset of the great flood, the great-grandfather of Noah did witness the corruption of man by fallen angels (runaway Watchers) and the Book of Enoch begins where Genesis 6 leaves off. "And it came to pass, when the sons of men had increased, that in those days there were born to them fair and beautiful daughters. And the Angels, the sons of Heaven, saw them and desired them. And they said to one another: Come, let us choose for ourselves wives, from the children of men, and let us beget, for ourselves, children. And Semyaza, who was their leader, said to them: I fear that you may not wish this deed to be done and that I alone will pay for this great sin. And they all answered him, and said: Let us all swear an oath, and bind one another with curses, so not to alter this plan, but to carry out this plan effectively. Then they all swore together and all bound one another with curses to it. And they were, in all, two hundred and they came down on Ardis, which is the summit of Mount Hermon. And they called the mountain Hermon because on it they swore and bound one another with curses. And these are the names of their leaders: Semyaza, who was their leader, Urakiba, Ramiel, Kokabiel, Tamiel, Ramiel, Daniel, Ezeqiel, Baraqiel, Asael, Armaros, Ananel, Zaqiel, Samsiel, Satael, Turiel, Yomiel, Araziel. These are the leaders of the two hundred Angels and of all the others with them" (Enoch 6:1-8).

And the fallen angels ". . . took wives for themselves and everyone chose for himself one each. And they began to go into them and were promiscuous with them. And they taught them charms and spells, and they showed them the cutting of roots and trees. And they became pregnant and bore large giants. And their height was three thousand cubits. These devoured all the toil of men; until men were unable to sustain them. And the giants turned against them in order to devour men. And they began to sin against birds, and against animals, and against reptiles, and against fish, and they devoured one another's flesh, and drank the blood from it. Then the Earth complained about the lawless ones. And Azazel taught men to make swords, and daggers, and shields, and breastplates. And he showed them the things after these, and the art of making them; bracelets, and ornaments, and the art of making up the eyes, and of beautifying the eyelids, and the most precious stones, and all kinds of colored dyes. And the world was changed. And there was great impiety, and much fornication, and they went astray, and all their ways became corrupt" (Enoch 7:1-8:2).

And the angels of heaven saw the mass of blood that was being shed on the earth and all the iniquity that was being done on the earth and Michael, Gabriel, Suriel, and Uriel said to one another: "Let the devastated Earth cry out with the sound of their cries, up to the Gate of Heaven. And now to you, Oh Holy Ones of Heaven, the souls of men complain, saying: Bring our complaint before the Most High.

And they said to their Lord, the King: Lord of Lords, God of Gods, King of Kings! Your glorious throne endures for all the generations of the world, and blessed and praised! You have made everything, and power over everything is yours. And everything is uncovered, and open, in front of you, and you see everything, and there is nothing that can be hidden from you. See then what Azazel has done; how he has taught all iniquity on the earth and revealed the eternal secrets that are made in Heaven. And Semyaza has made known spells, he to whom you gave authority to rule over those who are with him. And they went into the daughters of men together, lay with those women, became unclean, and revealed to them these sins. And the women bore giants, and thereby the whole Earth has been filled with blood and iniquity. And now behold the souls which have died cry out and complain unto the Gate of Heaven, and their lament has ascended, and they cannot go out in the face of the iniquity which is being committed on the earth. And you know everything, before it happens, and you know this, and what concerns each of them. But you say nothing to us. What ought we to do with them, about this? And then the Most High, the Great and Holy One, spoke and sent Arsyalalyur to the son of Lamech, and said to him: Say to him in my name; hide yourself! And reveal to him the end, which is coming, because the whole earth will be destroyed. A deluge is about to come on all the earth; and all that is in it will be destroyed" (Enoch 9:2-10:2).

Critics and non-believers may rightfully ask, if God decreed that the world and the majority of his creation be destroyed by flood to wash away the corruption introduced by fallen angels fornicating with the daughters of men and giving birth to giants, what could possibly account for the existence of post-flood giants? Many have speculated that fallen angels must have returned and again fornicated with the daughters of men. I do not personally ascribe to this theory as it seems highly unlikely. If it were so severe that ". . . it repented the Lord that He had made man on earth" (Genesis 6:6), it would seem significant enough to at least mention if the fallen angels again corrupted man in the 99% of the Bible that takes place after the great flood; and yet, no mention is made. It seems a far more likely scenario that along with Noah and his family, some portion of the corrupted DNA of man also survived the flood. Perhaps some descendants of giants made it onto one or more of the multiple arks postulated in chapter three. Consider that even today, children are occasionally born to shorter parents that are as sizable as the previously unearthed giants of American burial mounds. Towering over his parents, retired seven-foot, six-inch Chinese Houston Rockets basketball player Yao Ming was born to an already extremely tall six-foot, seven-inch Chinese father and six-foot, three-inch Chinese mother. Also, taller than his parents, retired seven-foot, seven-inch Sudanese Washington Bullets and Philadelphia 76ers basketball player Manute Bol was born to a six-foot, eight-inch father and a six-foot, ten-inch mother. To an admittedly untrained eye, it appears that the DNA woodpile of man likely retains some semblance of a big-and-tall gene.

Whether the result of corrupted human DNA or further post-flood interbreeding with fallen angels, the inevitable existence of post-flood giants is predicted by the Book of Enoch. As the messenger of God, Enoch condemns the children of the Watchers, "Why have you left the High, Holy and Eternal Heaven, and lain with women, and become unclean with the daughters of men, and taken wives for yourselves, and done as the sons of the earth, and begotten giant sons? And you were spiritual, Holy, living an eternal life, but you became unclean upon the women, and begot children through the blood of flesh, and lusted after the blood of men, and produced flesh and blood, as they do, who die and are destroyed. And for this reason, I give men wives; so that they might sow seed in them, and so that children might be born by them, so that deeds might be done on the Earth. But you, formerly, were spiritual, living an eternal, immortal life, for all the generations of the world. For this reason, I did not arrange wives for you; because the dwelling of the spiritual ones is in Heaven. And now, the giants who were born from body and flesh will be called Evil Spirits on the Earth, and on the Earth will be their dwelling" (Enoch 15:3-8).

Just as Chief Rolling Thunder of the Comanches spoke of a time in North America when ". . . a race of white men, 10 feet high, and far more rich and powerful than any white people now living, here inhabited a large range of country, extending from the rising to the setting sun," the Israelites testified to a time of many giants in the Promised Land when as directed by the Lord, Moses sent representatives of each of the tribes of Israel to search out Canaan, the land that God had given them. "And they returned from searching of the land after forty days. And they went and came to Moses, and to Aaron, and to all the congregation of the children of Israel, unto the wilderness of Paran, to Kadesh; and brought back word unto them, and unto all the congregation, and shewed them the fruit of the land. And they told him, and said, we came unto the land whither thou sentest us, and surely it floweth with milk and honey; and this is the fruit of it. Nevertheless, the people be strong that dwell in the land, and the cities are walled, and very great: and moreover, we saw the children of Anak there. The Amalekites dwell in the land of the south: and the Hittites, and the Jebusites, and the Amorites, dwell in the mountains: and the Canaanites dwell by the sea, and by the coast of Jordan. And Caleb stilled the people before Moses, and said, let us go up at once, and possess it; for we are well able to overcome it. But the men that went up with him said, we be not able to go up against the people; for they are stronger than we. And they brought up an evil report of the land which they had searched unto the children of Israel, saying, the land, through which we have gone to search it, is a land that eateth up the inhabitants thereof; and all the people that we saw in it are men of a great stature. And there we saw the giants, the sons of Anak, which come of the giants: and we were in our own sight as grasshoppers, and so we were in their sight" (Numbers 13:25-33 KJV).

Still in the original five books of the Torah, we next hear of post-flood giants in Deuteronomy when the Lord tells Moses to pass over the lands of the Moabites and the children of Ammon because they were given for a possession onto the children of Lot. "And the Lord said unto me, Distress not the Moabites, neither contend with them in battle: for I will not give thee of their land for a possession; because I have given Ar unto the children of Lot for a possession. The Emims dwelt therein in times past, a people great, and many, and tall, as the Anakims; Which also were accounted giants, as the Anakims; but the Moabites called them Emims" (Deuteronomy 2:9-11 KJV). "That the Lord spake unto me, saying, thou art to pass over through Ar, the coast of Moab, this day: And when thou comest nigh over against the children of Ammon, distress them not, nor meddle with them: for I will not give thee of the land of the children of Ammon any possession; because I have given it unto the children of Lot for a possession. That also was accounted a land of giants: giants dwelt therein in old time; and the Ammonites call them Zamzummims" (Deuteronomy 2:17-20 KJV).

The book of Deuteronomy further tells us that the Lord delivered Og, the king of Bashan and the last remnant of the land of giants into the hands of the Israelites. Moses recalled, "Then we turned, and went up the way to Bashan: and Og the king of Bashan came out against us, he and all his people, to battle at Edrei. And the Lord said unto me, fear him not: for I will deliver him, and all his people, and his land, into thy hand; and thou shalt do unto him as thou didst unto Sihon, king of the Amorites, which dwelt at Heshbon" (Deuteronomy 3:1-2 KJV). "And we utterly destroyed them, as we did unto Sihon king of Heshbon, utterly destroying the men, women, and children, of every city. But all the cattle, and the spoil of the cities, we took for a prey to ourselves. And we took at that time out of the hand of the two kings of the Amorites the land that was on this side Jordan, from the river of Arnon unto mount Hermon; Which Hermon the Sidonians call Sirion; and the Amorites call it Shenir; All the cities of the plain, and all Gilead, and all Bashan, unto Salchah and Edrei, cities of the kingdom of Og in Bashan. For only Og king of Bashan remained of the remnant of giants; behold his bedstead was a bedstead of iron; is it not in Rabbath of the children of Ammon? Nine cubits was the length thereof, and four cubits the breadth of it, after the cubit of a man. And this land, which we possessed at that time, from Aroer, which is by the river Arnon, and half mount Gilead, and the cities thereof, gave I unto the

Reubenites and to the Gadites. And the rest of Gilead, and all Bashan, being the kingdom of Og, gave I unto the half tribe of Manasseh; all the region of Argob, with all Bashan, which was called the land of giants" (Deuteronomy 3:6-13 KJV).

Reference to post-flood giants next appears in the Old Testament when Joshua was stricken in years and the Lord decreed that the lands which the children of Israel were yet to conquer should be divided by lot and given to the tribes of Israel as an inheritance. "Now therefore divide this land for an inheritance unto the nine tribes, and the half tribe of Manasseh, With whom the Reubenites and the Gadites have received their inheritance, which Moses gave them, beyond Jordan eastward, even as Moses the servant of the Lord gave them; From Aroer, that is upon the bank of the river Arnon, and the city that is in the midst of the river, and all the plain of Medeba unto Dibon; And all the cities of Sihon king of the Amorites, which reigned in Heshbon, unto the border of the children of Ammon; And Gilead, and the border of the Geshurites and Maachathites, and all mount Hermon, and all Bashan unto Salcah; All the kingdom of Og in Bashan, which reigned in Ashtaroth and in Edrei, who remained of the remnant of the giants: for these did Moses smite, and cast them out" (Joshua 13:7-12 KJV). "This then was the lot of the tribe of the children of Judah by their families; even to the border of Edom the wilderness of Zin southward was the uttermost part of the south coast. And the border went up by the valley of the son of Hinnom unto the south side of the Jebusite; the same is Jerusalem: and the border went up to the top of the mountain that lieth before the valley of Hinnom westward, which is at the end of the valley of the giants northward" (Joshua 15:1, 15:8 KJV). "And the children of Joseph spoke unto Joshua, saying, why hast thou given me but one lot and one portion to inherit, seeing I am a great people, forasmuch as the Lord hath blessed me hitherto? And Joshua answered them, if thou be a great people, then get thee up to the wood country, and cut down for thyself there in the land of the Perizzites and of the giants, if mount Ephraim be too narrow for thee" (Joshua 17:14-15 KJV). "And the lot of the tribe of the children of Benjamin came up according to their families: and the coast of their lot came forth between the children of Judah and the children of Joseph. And the border came down to the end of the mountain that lieth before the valley of the son of Hinnom, and which is in the valley of the giants on the north, and descended to the valley of Hinnom, to the side of Jebusi on the south . . ." (Joshua 18:11, 18:16 KJV).

Occurring several generations after Noah and the flood, at a time when the children of Israel already numbered in the hundreds of thousands, David's killing of Goliath is documented in the first book of Samuel. "Now the Philistines gathered together their armies to battle, and were gathered together at Shochoh, which belongeth to Judah, and pitched between Shochoh and Azekah, in Ephesdammim. And Saul and the men of Israel were gathered together, and pitched by the valley of Elah, and set the battle in array against the Philistines. And the Philistines stood on a mountain on the one side, and Israel stood on a mountain on the other side: and there was a valley between them. And there went out a champion out of the camp of the Philistines, named Goliath, of Gath, whose height was six cubits and a span. And he had a helmet of brass upon his head, and he was armed with a coat of mail; and the weight of the coat was five thousand shekels of brass. And he had greaves of brass upon his legs, and a target of brass between his shoulders. And the staff of his spear was like a weaver's beam; and his spear's head weighed six hundred shekels of iron: and one bearing a shield went before him. And he stood and cried unto the armies of Israel, and said unto them, why are ye come out to set your battle in array? am not I a Philistine, and ye servants to Saul? choose you a man for you, and let him come down to me. If he be able to fight with me, and to kill me, then will we be your servants: but if I prevail against him, and kill him, then shall ye be our servants, and serve us" (1 Samuel 17:1-9 KJV).

"And Jesse said unto David his son, take now for thy brethren an ephah of this parched corn, and these ten loaves, and run to the camp of thy brethren; And carry these ten cheeses unto the captain of their thousand, and look how thy brethren fare, and take their pledge. Now Saul, and they, and all the men of Israel, were in the valley of Elah, fighting with the Philistines. And David rose up early in the morning, and left the sheep with a keeper, and took, and went, as Jesse had commanded him; and he came to the trench, as the host was going forth to the fight, and shouted for the battle. For Israel and the Philistines had put the battle in array, army against army. And David left his carriage in the hand of the keeper of the carriage, and ran into the army, and came and saluted his brethren. And as he talked with them, behold, there came up the champion, the Philistine of Gath, Goliath by name, out of the armies of the Philistines, and spoke according to the same words: and David heard them. And all the men of Israel, when they saw the man, fled from him, and were sore afraid. And the men of Israel said, have ye seen this man that is come up? surely to defy Israel is he come up: and it shall be, that the man who kil-leth him, the king will enrich him with great riches, and will give him his daughter, and make his father's house free in Israel. And David spoke to the men that stood by him, saying, what shall be done to the man that kil-leth this Philistine, and taketh away the reproach from Israel? for who is this uncircumcised Philistine, that he should defy the armies of the living God?" (1 Samuel 17:17-26 KJV).

"And David said to Saul, Let no man's heart fail because of him; thy servant will go and fight with this Philistine. And Saul said to David, thou art not able to go against this Philistine to fight with him: for thou art but a youth, and he a man of war from his youth. And David said unto Saul, thy servant kept his father's sheep, and there came a lion, and a bear, and took a lamb out of the flock: And I went out after him, and smote him, and delivered it out of his mouth: and when he arose against me, I caught him by his beard, and smote him, and slew him. Thy servant slew both the lion and the bear: and this uncircumcised Philistine shall be as one of them, seeing he hath defied the armies of the living God. David said moreover, The Lord that delivered me out of the paw of the lion, and out of the paw of the bear, he will deliver me out of the hand of this Philistine. And Saul said unto David, Go, and the Lord be with thee. And Saul armed David with his armor, and he put a helmet of brass upon his head; also, he armed him with a coat of mail. And David girded his sword upon his armor, and he assayed to go; for he had not proved it. And David said unto Saul, I cannot go with these; for I have not proved them. And David put them off him" (1 Samuel 17:32-39 KJV).

"And he took his staff in his hand, and chose him five smooth stones out of the brook, and put them in a shepherd's bag which he had, even in a scrip; and his sling was in his hand: and he drew near to the Philistine. And the Philistine came on and drew near unto David; and the man that bare the shield went before him. And when the Philistine looked about, and saw David, he disdained him: for he was but a youth, and ruddy, and of a fair countenance. And the Philistine said unto David, Am I a dog, that thou comest to me with staves? And the Philistine cursed David by his gods. And the Philistine said to David, come to me, and I will give thy flesh unto the fowls of the air, and to the beasts of the field. Then said David to the Philistine, thou comest to me with a sword, and with a spear, and with a shield: but I come to thee in the name of the Lord of hosts, the God of the armies of Israel, whom thou hast defied. This day will the Lord deliver thee into mine hand; and I will smite thee, and take thine head from thee; and I will give the carcasses of the host of the Philistines this day unto the fowls of the air, and to the wild beasts of the earth; that all the earth may know that there is a God in Israel. And all this assembly shall know that the Lord saveth not with sword and spear: for the battle is the Lord's, and he will give you into our hands. And it came to pass, when the Philistine arose, and came, and drew nigh to meet David, that David hastened, and ran toward the army to meet the Philistine. And David put his hand in his bag, and took thence a stone, and slang it, and smote the Philistine in his forehead, that the stone sunk into his forehead; and he fell upon his face to the earth. So, David prevailed over the Philistine with a sling and with a stone, and smote the Philistine, and slew him; but there was no sword in the hand of David" (1 Samuel 17:40-50 KJV).

Several years after David killed Goliath and following his last battle with the Philistines, four additional slain giants are called out in the second book of Samuel. "Moreover, the Philistines had yet war again with

Israel; and David went down, and his servants with him, and fought against the Philistines: and David waxed faint. And Ishbibenob, which was of the sons of the giant, the weight of whose spear weighed three hundred shekels of brass in weight, he being girded with a new sword, thought to have slain David. But Abishai the son of Zeruiah succoured him, and smote the Philistine, and killed him. Then the men of David sware unto him, saying, thou shalt go no more out with us to battle, that thou quench not the light of Israel. And it came to pass after this, that there was again a battle with the Philistines at Gob: then Sibbechai the Hushathite slew Saph, which was of the sons of the giant. And there was again a battle in Gob with the Philistines, where Elhanan the son of Jaareoregim, a Bethlehemite, slew the brother of Goliath the Gittite, the staff of whose spear was like a weaver's beam. And there was yet a battle in Gath, where was a man of great stature, that had on every hand six fingers, and on every foot six toes, four and twenty in number; and he also was born to the giant. And when he defied Israel, Jonathan the son of Shimeah the brother of David slew him. These four were born to the giant in Gath, and fell by the hand of David, and by the hand of his servants" (2 Samuel 21:15-22 KJV).

Combining the information provided in 2 Samuel 21 with that contained in 1 Chronicles 20, we learn that the five sons of the giant of Gath, an unnamed man with twelve fingers and twelve toes, Goliath, Ishbibenob, Saph, and Lahmi were also giants and slain by the hand of David and/or the hand of his servants. "David and all the people returned to Jerusalem. And it came to pass after this, that there arose war at Gezer with the Philistines; at which time Sibbechai the Hushathite slew Sippai, that was of the children of the giant: and they were subdued. And there was war again with the Philistines; and Elhanan the son of Jair slew Lahmi the brother of Goliath the Gittite, whose spear staff was like a weaver's beam. And yet again there was war at Gath, where was a man of great stature, whose fingers and toes were four and twenty, six on each hand, and six on each foot and he also was the son of the giant. But when he defied Israel, Jonathan the son of Shimea David's brother slew him. These were born unto the giant in Gath; and they fell by the hand of David, and by the hand of his servants" (1 Chronicles 20:3-8 KJV).

Not easily explained or accounted for by evolution, the scientific community refuses to acknowledge, comment on, or speculate about the remains of unearthed giants. Rather than admit to any possible short-comings in existing theories or reevaluate newly discovered facts, the scientific community works to maintain the status quo and refuses to change course. The blind eye of science contradicts the archaeological record, documented history, the Bible, and even rational thought. This same blind eye and denial of logical conclusions to presented facts is dem-onstrated by the consensus that bio-organic materials might well survive for millions of years. This is contrary to an earlier understanding that no soft tissue could survive for even 10,000 years, let alone 80 million years in the presence of insects, microbes, rodents, plants, and fungal bod-ies (chapter four), but avoids concluding that dinosaur bones may not be millions of years old. When science claims to have the answers to all things, they place themselves above those of us who don't and assume an arrogance that leaves them little room for reconsideration. Facts are facts and any theory that requires unproven and sometimes far-fetched adjustment to compensate for new and contradicting discoveries is likely invalid. Sometimes it just makes more sense to call the fire department and admit that your house is on fire than it does to ignore the flames and hope that the fire burns itself out.

The evidence is overwhelming. Possibly surviving into the recent past, giants once roamed this planet and the only provided explanation for their existence is that they descended from fallen angels (Genesis 6:4; Enoch 7:2). Assuming that the archaeological record, documented history, and the Bible are correct, the next logical question becomes, what corruption did the fallen angels introduce that was so heinous and widespread that it repented the Lord that he had made man? If the pre-flood corruption of mankind were limited to the interbreeding of fallen angels with the daughters of men, rather than destroying the world that he created, it would seem more likely that in his power and mercy, God would simply bring an end to two-hundred-plus fallen angels (Enoch 6:6), their wives, and offspring. Undoubtedly, the sins of mankind must have been great to warrant God's self-destruction of so much that he created. "And God saw that the wickedness of man was great in the earth, and that every imagination of the thoughts of his heart was only evil continually. And it repented the Lord that he had made man on the earth, and it grieved him at his heart. And the Lord said, I will destroy man whom I have created from the face of the earth; both man, and beast, and the creeping thing, and the fowls of the air; for it repenteth me that I have made them" (Genesis 6:5-7 KJV). Before the pre-flood corruption of man can be sought to be verified by scientific explanation, the archaeological record, or documented history, it must first be clearly defined and bounded. The only source we have that provides this level of detail is the Book of Enoch.

8

MEN LIKE GODS:
THE FORBIDDEN FRUIT

Reiterated numerous times in the New Testament, love is both the root of all commandments and the greatest of all commandments. Speaking to the chief priests and elders of the people at the temple of God in Jerusalem, Jesus asked, ". . . have ye not read that which was spoken unto you by God, saying, I am the God of Abraham, and the God of Isaac, and the God of Jacob? God is not the God of the dead, but of the living. And when the multitude heard this, they were astonished at his doctrine. But when the Pharisees had heard that he had put the Sadducees to silence, they were gathered together. Then one of them, which was a lawyer, asked him a question, tempting him, and saying, Master, which is the great commandment in the law? Jesus said unto him, thou shalt love the Lord thy God with all thy heart, and with all thy soul, and with all thy mind. This is the first and great commandment. And the second is like unto it, thou shalt love thy neighbor as thyself. On these two commandments hang all the law and the prophets" (Matthew 22:32-40 KJV). Later, the apostle Paul would say, ". . . all the law is fulfilled in one word, even in this; Thou shalt love thy neighbor as thyself" (Galatians 5:14 KJV). John the Beloved put it this way, "God is love; and he that dwelleth in love dwelleth in God" (1 John 4:16 KJV).

Just as all the commandments are founded in the love of God, years of study have brought me to the conclusion that sin is founded in the pride of an exaggerated self-worth. Rearing its ugly head just before the expulsion of Adam and Eve from the garden of Eden, the ego first appeared when Eve was told that she too could be as gods. It was this temptation of being as gods, having knowledge greater than the creatures of the kingdom that caused Eve to disobey her Creator. What Adam and Eve found, in fact, was that they were not as gods. They traded their innocence for a secret that they were better off not knowing—the knowledge of good and evil. The cost was the numbering of their days and their expulsion from the garden. "Now the serpent was more subtle than any beast of the field which the Lord God had made. And he said unto the woman, Yea, hath God said, Ye shall not eat of every tree of the garden? And the woman said unto the serpent, we may eat of the fruit of the trees of the garden: But of the fruit of the tree which is in the midst of the garden, God hath said, Ye shall not eat of it, neither shall ye touch it, lest ye die. And the serpent said unto the woman, Ye shall not surely die: For God doth know that in the day ye eat thereof, then your eyes shall be opened, and ye shall be as gods, knowing good and evil. And when the woman saw that the tree was good for food, and that it was pleasant to the eyes, and a tree to be desired to make one wise, she took of the fruit thereof, and did eat, and gave also unto her husband with her; and he did eat" (Genesis 3:1-6 KJV).

We live in a world where everything can be justified, and right and wrong have little to do with it. Why shouldn't we park in the handicapped spot, put the expensive sneakers in the less expensive box before checkout, spend the money from the wallet we found in the bathroom stall, pawn the purple heart that was left on a gravestone, and stop by the Goodwill collection site to confiscate the nice coffee table we saw on the way to the store? After all, who will know? Everyone does it and our neighbors who have not one job between them, still collect their dead mother's social security, have HBO, and can afford to eat out every night. We know good from bad, but bad tastes and looks so good. The fruit of the tree is good and pleasant to the eyes. Unfortunately, the corruption of man doesn't stop here. Often greater than our will to resist, our temptations are fed by the weaknesses of our hearts. We willingly allow attractive shortcuts to supersede hard work. The desire for power and wealth exponentially elevates our depravity. The concept of monopolizing secrets for the acquisition of power and wealth has been around since before the great flood.

Contrary to the desires of heaven, it was Azazel, a fallen angel, that gave early man the secret knowledge to transition from sticks and clubs to daggers and swords. "And Azazel taught men to make swords, and daggers, and shields, and breastplates. And he showed them the things after these, and the art of making them. . . . And the world was changed" (Enoch 8:1). "And God saw that the wickedness of man was great . . ." (Genesis 6:5 KJV). If the revelation of the "eternal secrets that are made in heaven" (Enoch 9:6) was truly the origin of man's wickedness, one would hope that beyond faith, some remnant of the proof of their existence remains. As it turns out, an ancient dagger, an axe, and ingots of an ancient metal alloy have been discovered that even today, remain technically difficult to reproduce.

On November 4, 1922, "British Egyptologist Howard Carter discovered the tomb of Tutankhamun in the Valley of the Kings, Egypt. Tutankhamun, nicknamed King Tut, was an Egyptian pharaoh who ruled from 1333 BCE (when he was just nine years old) until his death in 1323 BCE. After he died, Tutankhamun was mummified, according to tradition, and buried in a tomb filled with artwork, jewelry, and treasures. Shifting desert sands quickly hid the tomb, and it lay undiscovered for more than 3,000 years."[98] Among the beautiful artifacts discovered in King Tut's tomb was a ludicrously beautiful and magnificently fashioned rust-free iron dagger that would later be dubbed the pharaoh's space dagger. In 2016, Albert Jambon, a French archaeo-metallurgist and a professor at the Pierre and Marie Curie University, in Paris performed X-Ray Fluorescence (XRF) spectrometry of the pharaoh's dagger. What Jambon found was that, "Tutankhamun's dagger was made with iron containing nearly 11 percent nickel and traces of cobalt: a characteristic of extraterrestrial iron": iron meteorites.[99] This is particularly interesting because,

"Meteorites are very difficult to fashion into objects. . . . because of the high nickel content, they're very, very brittle." Considering the difficulties in working with meteoric metal, even with today's technology, how did metallurgists 3300 years ago fashion a meteorite into a dagger? "This dagger is completely out of place in the fact that it was not hammered out and rolled, it has been perfected to the point that it has no hammer marks on it, it is completely smooth, it has a nice edge all the way around on it, it almost looks as though it has been cast, but in order to achieve that, you have to reach temperatures of 3000 degrees in order to melt the meteorite and of course add the necessary fluxes to get the impurities out and cast the blade which brings up even more questions for the researchers."[100]

If the Egyptians were smelting iron more than 3300 years ago, it would change history as we know it. "Some archaeologists have proposed that these early iron objects could have been created by 'precocious' smelting of iron ore nearly 2000 years before the technology became widespread in the early Iron Age—perhaps by accident, or through experimentation. But Jambon said his research found no evidence that smelted iron was known until the Iron Age dawned in the Near East, around 1200 BC. The oldest known furnace for smelting iron ore is at Tell Hammeh in Jordan and dates to 930 BC."[101] Similar ancient weapons are few and far between, but they do exist. Professor Jambon also performed XRF spectrometry on a meteoric iron axe from Ugarit on the coast of northern Syria that dated to 1500 BC, about 300 years before the smelting of iron was known to exist. History tells us that these objects should not exist, and yet, here they are. It is as though someone or something brought this technology to earth 2000 years before it was perfected by man. Perhaps Azazel did in fact teach men to make swords, and daggers, and shields, and breastplates (Enoch 8:1). A few thousand years is a short period of time to those who believe that the planet is millions of years old; however, if you accept that the great flood occurred less than 10,000 years ago, 2000 years becomes a much larger block of time.

When considering the origin of metallurgy, it cannot be ignored that, "There seems to be a ubiquitous understanding from ancient cultures that metallurgy is from the heavens."[102] It was, "Hephaestus in the Greek imagination that made the weapons and the armor for the gods. In the Celtic imagination, it was the great goddess Brigid. . . . In Japanese folklore, Kanayago came to earth to teach the people metal working."[103] Always depicted holding a blacksmith's hammer, Ancient Rome believed that it was Vulcan who was the god of fire, metal working, volcanoes, and forging.

In 2015, archaeologist Sebastiano Tusa excavated a shipwreck less than a mile off the coast of Sicily which had remained undisturbed for more than 2600 years. The team salvaged thirty-nine metal ingots from the shipwreck that were unlike anything ever found in the ancient or modern world. Spectrographic analysis of the ingots revealed that they were essentially 80% copper and 20% zinc. Based on their composition, scientists believe that what they have found is orichalcum, a metal associated with the legendary continent of Atlantis.

Mentioned in several ancient writings, including the story of Atlantis (460-403 BC) from the Critias of Plato, orichalcum was first spoken of in seventh century BC by Hesiod. Orichalcum was valued second only to gold. "It was said that the Temple of Poseidon on Atlantis flashed with the red light of orichalcum. This is not just an attractive color. . . . There was something about this metal that was said to resonate with the divine. Perhaps it was its origin, that it had come from heaven."[104] According to Plato's dialogues, "the Greek god Cadmus, the son of Poseidon came down from Mount Olympus and gave orichalcum to the people of Atlantis. Atlantis possessed a power and technology greater than any other civilization on earth."[105] This would be nothing more than a curious story if it were not for the fact that ". . . zinc only occurs in nature as sphalerite, a zinc-sulfur complex" and the ability to extract zinc from sphalerite didn't exist 2600 years ago.[106] There are two methods of smelting zinc: the pyrometallurgical process and the hydrometallurgical process. Over 90% of zinc is produced hydrometallurgically and 90% of the zinc produced hydrometallurgically is produced in electrolytic plants using electrolysis. Both processes begin with roasting, a process of oxidizing zinc sulfide concentrates at high temperatures into an impure zinc oxide, called Zinc Calcine. "In either of the electrolytic processes, each metric ton of zinc production expends about 3,900 kW-h (14 GJ) of electric power."[107]

The Book of Enoch tells us that it was another fallen angel, Amezarak, that taught mankind the secrets of charms and spells, the cutting of roots and trees (Enoch 7:1, 8:3). When we think of modern medicine today, pills, salves, and injections are most likely what come to mind. Thousands of years ago, we would have thought of herbs and roots. When tracking modern medicine back to its beginnings, back to a time of roots and herbs, it becomes apparent that many ancient root remedies have lately experienced a renaissance. They include turmeric, kava-kava, ginger, maca, valerian, echinacea, goldenseal, ashwagandha, licorice, and ginseng. I concede that the medicinal properties of these singular roots may have been stumbled upon by chance or intent; however, the complex chemical interactions of the various ingredients, medicinal benefits, and neurological effects obtained from ingesting a shaman tea prepared from a recipe of roots, vines, barks, and leaves in the Amazon basin, place ayahuasca well beyond the possibility of a chance discovery. In the sixteenth century, "Christian missionaries from Spain first encountered indigenous western Amazonian basin South Americans (modern Peru/Ecuador) using ayahuasca; their earliest reports described it as 'the work of the devil.'"[108] "People in Ecuador, Columbia, Peru, and Brazil have used ayahuasca as a healing medicine or as part of religious ceremonies or tribal rituals for thousands of years."[109] Today, we know that ayahuasca helps patients overcome both physical and mental disease by deconstructing neuron receptors known to affect those suffering from trauma and physical ailments. Although research continues, ayahuasca has been found to be an effective treatment for depression, PTSD, drug abuse, Parkinson's disease, and various blood, liver, and gall bladder disorders.

The two main ingredients of the tea are the leaves of the Psychotria viridis plant and the stalks of the Banisteriopsis caapi vine. The leaves of the Psychotria viridis plant provide an active hallucinogenic compound known as N, N-Dimethyltryptamine (DMT) that is quickly broken down by a Monoamine Oxidase (MAO) enzyme present in the human body. The stalks of the Banisteriopsis caapi vine produce a MAO inhibitor that allows natural diffusion of DMT in the stomach and small intestine. They facilitate crossover of the blood-brain barrier and activate receptors in our brain. "MOA inhibiting carbolines are known to raise serotonin levels." The regulation and/or increase of serotonin levels is commonly associated with the treatment of depression. "It's no wonder that ayahuasca is famously attributed as a natural treatment for depression patients who simply have not seen results with traditional medication." Each natural ingredient of the tea serves to cleanse the body of ailments. Other active ingredients include: "ayahuma bark, capirona bark, chullachaki caspi bark, lopuna blanca bark, punga amarilla bark, remo caspi bark, wyra (huaira) caspi bark, shiwawaku bark, uchu, and huacapurana. It also contains leaves from chacruna, chaliponga, chagropanga, banisteriopsis rusbyana and amyruca" (Spiritual Hand Ayahuasca Center: *Ayahuasca Ingredients* by Ryan Frechette, 2020). Brewed with multiple unrelated and inert ingredients found in nature, containing no unnecessary substances for color or flavor, and all working together to accomplish the singular goal of desired clarity and enlightenment, it is beyond reason to consider that thousands of years ago, native tribes living in the jungles in Peru conjured up the recipe for ayahuasca tea without outside assistance. Just a few hundred years ago, the neurological aspects of the human brain were well beyond the knowledge of literally everyone.

As we will discover in this chapter and the next, knowledge can be used for good or evil. If, as I believe, the cutting of roots and trees (Enoch 7:1; 8:3) refers to the origins of modern medicine (among other things), examples of medical knowledge are found in the artifacts of multiple ancient civilizations at a time well before history tells us that they should exist. The ". . . skull of a twenty-year-old patient was found in northern Greece dating back to around 800 BC, which showed that the patient survived at least twenty years after skull surgery. The patient was hit on the head and part of the projectile went through the skull. The surgical operation that took place didn't use a drill but a special tool sculpting inside the skull in a way that cleaned all debris and fixed cracks on the skull—a method described in texts of Hippocrates."[110] Evidence of early brain surgery has been uncovered in Egypt, India, Assyria, and Sumeria. It is interesting to note that, "Medical knowledge of the past was given to people by the 'gods.' . . . The god Oannes in Babylonian mythology taught the Sumerian people medical techniques and everything they needed to know about civilization according to the Sumerian tablets," and that was 4000 BC.[111] The ancient Egyptians are known to have recorded surgical procedures well before 2500 BC. The Edwin Smith Papyrus tells us of methods used to treat dislocated bones[112] and the Ebers Papyrus tells us of practices related to the removal of cysts and tumors.[113] Therapeutic herbs and foods were extensively used by the ancient physicians of Egypt. They used opiates to alleviate pain and practiced local anesthesia for surgery, where water was mixed with vinegar over a Memphite stone, resulting in the formation of carbon dioxide and its known analgesic effect. The existence of modern medical techniques in ancient Egypt are further evidenced by a collection of recovered ancient surgical instruments in the Cairo museum. They include: scalpels, scissors, copper needles, forceps, spoons, lancets, hooks, probes, and pincers.

The Book of Enoch tells us that it was a fallen angel named Tamiel who taught mankind the secrets of astrology (Enoch 8:3). When looking for documented ancient astrological knowledge capable of challenging twenty-first-century minds and telescopes, nothing stands out more than the Mayan Long Count calendar. "The ancient Maya had a fascination with the cycles of time and were great observers of the sky, using their knowledge of astronomy and mathematics, they managed to develop one of the most accurate calendar systems in human history" (Mayan Peninsula website, *The Mayan Calendar* by Sergio, 2020). "The calendar was based on a ritual cycle of 260 named days and a year of 365 days. Taken together, they form a longer cycle of 18,980 days, or 52 years of 365 days, called a 'Calendar Round.' The original name of the 260-day cycle is unknown; it is variously referred to as the Tzolkin ('Count of Days'). . . . Within the Tzolkin are two smaller cycles of days numbered from 1 to 13 and an ordered series of 20 named days.... The 365-day year was divided into 18 named months (*uinals*) of 20 days plus one month of 5 'nameless' days, called Uayeb. The nameless days were considered extremely unlucky, causing the Maya to observe them with fasting and sacrifices to deities."[114] The Mayan Calendar is a system composed of different intertwining cycles, each having its own ritual, astronomical, or agricultural purpose. The Mayan Long Count calendar was a non-repeating, base-20 calendar used by several pre-Columbian Mesoamerican cultures. It identified a particular day by counting the number of days since what they believed to be the creation date. The creation day corresponded to August 11, 3114 BC in Gregorian calendars. The Mayan Long Count calendar was 5126 years in length and reached its last predicted date, restart, or end of cycle on December 21, 2012.

Although the Mayan Long Count calendar ended on December 21, 2012, it was by no means the world-ending cataclysm that many doomsday theorists had predicted. A more in-depth, after-the-fact examination of Mayan beliefs reveals that the Maya conceived of epochs of time much longer than the Great Cycle being tracked by the Long Count calendar. The present P'iktun does not end until October 13, AD 4772, a date that is carved in the Temple of Inscriptions at Palenque. The Long Count calendar makes a bold and powerful effort to mathematically quantify and define the cycles of world emergence. The Great Cycle is comprised of five distinct units referred to as the kin (1 day), the uinal (20 days), the tun (360 days), the katun (7,200 days), and the baktun (144,000 days). The Long Count is comprised of thirteen baktuns from the start to finish. For the ancient Maya, the thirteenth baktun ended at the beginning of the world's fourth creation. Although the dates of the world's first three creations were lost when the Mayan codices were burned by Diego de Landa during the Spanish inquisition, the Popol Vuh survives to describe the three previous creations (eras) and the fates of their inhabitants. What actually happened on December 21, 2012 was a very rare astrological alignment in which the earth and the sun were in perfect alignment with the center of the Milky Way, an event that is now known to only take place every 25,800 years. One has to wonder how the ancient Mayans predicted such an astrological alignment over 5000 years ago with no computers, telescopes, or assistance. The occurrence of such an extremely rare and only recently identified astrological alignment on the last day of the Mayan Long Count calendar was more than just a coincidence; it was a foretelling of the end of the Great Cycle, a 25,800-year cycle.

Perhaps not yet as conclusive, but just as astronomically interesting and fantastically out of place for an ancient civilization to have known is the 2016 announced discovery of planet 9 by Professor of Planetary Science at Caltech, Konstantin Batygin and his lab partner Mike Brown. Until conclusively proven through a decade or more of further observations, the discovery is for now being called planet 9, or planet 10, depending on who you talk to. This is of course because in August of 2006, the International Astronomical Union (IAU) downgraded Pluto from a planet to a Kuiper Belt Object (KBO), now categorized as a "dwarf planet." The work of Konstantin Batygin and Mike Brown has since been confirmed by Kat Volk and Renu Malhotra of the Planetary and Lunar Laboratory at the University of Arizona. Initial calculations show that the newly discovered planet is up to ten times the mass of Earth, over twenty times farther out than Neptune, and has an elliptical orbit spanning thousands of years. Brown and Batygin said, "they discovered the potential planet by detecting a cluster of six known objects within the Kuiper belt with orbits that funneled toward the sun in a specific formation."[115] "Celestial objects are drawn into the orbits of larger bodies: All the planets in the solar system orbit the Sun and the moon orbits Earth. So, when astronomers find bodies that are not orbiting in the way they should be, it suggests something else is influencing them." When Kat Volk and Renu Malhotra later analyzed the tilt angles and orbits of over six hundred Kuiper Belt Objects, "They discovered the most distant KBOs are tilted away from the orbital plane they should be sitting on, meaning something in this region is warping their orbits" According to their calculations, "something as massive as Mars would be needed to cause the warp that we measured."[116]

Modeling known orbits of known planets and KBOs in our solar system, Batygin and Brown were able to utilize complex computer simulations to predict where to look. When asked how long it might take to have definitive proof of planet 9, Professor Batygin replied, "The search for planet 9 is extremely, extremely difficult. It is just kind of dim enough at the outer parts of its orbit where it can be discovered with current telescopes, but everything has to go right. By everything has to go right, I mean no moon. The atmosphere has to be calm so that the light is not messed up by turbulence. Such nights do come around every year, but they don't come around very often. Since 2017, we've had exactly two successful runs, successful observational runs where we had a sort of a string of nights where we could take pictures of the same part of the sky over and over again. So, we are . . . maybe 25% done with the survey that we are carrying out to search for planet 9. If things go at this rate, it might take about a decade. I think the commencement of the LSST telescope which is coming on line in 2022-23, that's going to help a lot because that is going to first of all, discover many more of these objects and we'll be able to refine the theoretical model better. And also, just by direct observation it'll either find planet 9 or rule out a big chunk of its orbit so that we could kind of zero in. . . . It's an iterative process. I would guesstimate a decade or less."[117] According to Michele Bannister, from the Astrophysics Research Center at Queen's University Belfast, UK, "Planet 10 could be located in one of the only areas of the sky that you could hide any large object—a region covered by the Milky Way. At that point it becomes a lot harder to find distant moving objects because there's just so many stars."[118] The vast majority of astronomers now believe in the existence of the newly discovered planet; however, at least for now, finding it remains a challenge to existing technology.

Zecharia Sitchen, a brilliant scholar with revolutionary ideas about the ancient Sumerian and Babylonian gods, grew up in Palestine where he developed a passion for history and languages. During his time in Palestine, Sitchen studied Hebrew as well as other European and Semitic languages. Later studying at the University of London, Sitchen earned a degree in economic history. Following graduation, he worked as a journalist and editor in Israel. In 1952, he moved to New York where he became an executive for a shipping company. His position with the shipping company gave him the opportunity to travel and visit many archaeological sites. It was during this period of time that Zecharia Sitchen taught himself Sumerian cuneiform. Pooling together his research of ancient Sumerian writings, Sitchen developed a theory of alien visitors who eons ago, created human life. I, of course, am a creationist and in no way ascribe to Sitchen's belief that mankind was created by extraterrestrials; however, I do find his translation of ancient Sumerian to be fascinating. In 1976, Zecharia Sitchen published his first book on ancient astronauts, called *The 12ᵗʰ Planet*. It was the first of the Earth Chronicles volumes, a set that would eventually span seven books. Many ancient astronaut theorists have touted Zecharia Sitchen as arguably the most important proponent of the ancient astronaut hypothesis in the last several decades. Sitchen was a frequent guest on the Coast-to-Coast AM radio show where in 2010 he was presented with a lifetime achievement award.[119] Others have not been so kind. Not surprisingly, Sitchen's ideas have been rejected by scientists and academics alike who dismiss his work as pseudoscience and pseudohistory. His work has been criticized for flawed methodology and mistranslations of ancient texts as well as incorrect astronomical and scientific claims.[120]

What I find fascinating about Zecharia Sitchen is his translation of ancient Sumerian texts and his interpretation of the twelfth planet that now appears validated by the 2016 discoveries of Konstantin Batygin and others. Reaching nearest to the inner solar system roughly every 3600 years, Sitchen determined that the ancient writings told of a planet Nibiru that was beyond Neptune and followed a very long elliptical orbit. According to his translations, Nibiru collided catastrophically with Tiamat, a goddess in the Babylonian creation myth which he considered to be another planet once located between Mars and Jupiter. This collision supposedly formed the planet Earth, the asteroid belt, and the comets. Sitchin states that when struck by one of planet Nibiru's moons, Tiamat split in two, and then on a second pass Nibiru itself struck the broken fragments and one half of Tiamat became the asteroid belt. The second half, struck again by one of Nibiru's moons, was pushed into a new orbit and became today's planet Earth. Nibiru was called "the twelfth planet" because Sitchen claimed that the Sumerian concept of the Solar System counted all eight planets, plus Pluto, the Sun and the Earth's moon. Sitchen alleged that Nibiru was the home of a technologically advanced human-like extraterrestrial race called the Anunnaki in Sumerian myth. He believed that the Anunnaki of Nibiru were actually the Nephilim or fallen angels of Genesis.[121] Zecharia Sitchen had many concepts and interpretations that many would consider "out there" and "beyond belief." However, bearing in mind the recent astronomical discovery of planet 9, I am leaning toward believing his concept of the ancient Sumerian Solar System. If, as many believe, Sitchen correctly translated Sumerian writings, how could an ancient Sumerian people have known about the twelfth planet without the complex computer simulations and telescopes of today?

Lastly, the Book of Enoch tells us that it was a fallen angel named Asradel that taught mankind the path of the moon (Enoch 8:3). When looking for proof that early man had knowledge of lunar cycles and eclipses well beyond what should have been known at the time, my thoughts immediately go to the Antikythera Mechanism described in chapter five. Dated to between 70 and AD 50, the Antikythera Mechanism was discovered in 1901 by a sponge diver in a shipwreck off the coast of the Greek island of Antikythera. This mechanism was recently proven through X-rays, research, and reconstruction to be the world's first known computer. Accounting for the elliptical orbit of the moon and the cyclic variations of that orbit, multiple interlocking brass gears with prime numbers of teeth and variable speed rotations have been shown to accurately predict the location of the planets and the exact hour of future solar and lunar eclipses. The Antikythera Mechanism is a precise astrological computer that existed 1400 years before man was able to measure time independent of the shadow of the sun.

Throughout the world, there is evidence of numerous temples dedicated to the moon and the many deities of the moon. None stands out from the others more than the Well of Santa Cristina in Sardinia, Italy. "The well is part of a shrine complex built in the twelfth or eleventh century BCE by the Nuragic civilization, and is in fact one of the most important remaining Nuragic sites. The Nuragic civilization lived in Sardinia from the eighteenth century BCE to the second century CE, and though they were remarkably skilled masons whose impressive stone structures still stand, they did not leave behind any written record. So, while it is contextually clear that the area around the Well of Santa Cristina was a sacred site complete with a meeting hut and lodgings, the beliefs associated with the site and the rituals that would have taken place there remain unclear. What is clear is that the site was centered around the well, which would have been the focal point of the shrine. The well is composed of an elliptical enclosure surrounding a trapezium-shaped opening in the ground, with stairs leading down to a circular, domed subterranean chamber that housed the spring. The Nuragic religion seems to have involved a lot of symbolic representations of fertility, and included a cult of water that invoked the various aspects of the divine. The well is oriented so that sunlight shines upon the water on the equinoxes, and the moonlight shines upon the water at the maximum declination of the moon, which occurs every eighteen years and six months. The stonework in the steps and the wall of the well entrance still showcase the smooth, perfectly squared stonework typical of Nuragic structures." [122]

Certainly, the archeological remnants of our past have shown us that early man was capable of tracking the shadows of the sun with standing sticks and stones. After a year of watching the projected shadows, the cycle showed our ancestors that it repeated itself and the equinoxes were identified for planting and harvesting. This, however, does not explain how an ancient culture with no known written language could have identified the maximum declination of the moon. Although during the moon's maximum declination the diameter of the moon would be at its smallest when observed from earth, this slight variation is also indiscernible with the naked eye. Without complex mathematics to consider the tilt and spin of the earth and the cyclic variations of the moon's orbit or photographic plates to superimpose over one another for comparison of the moon's diameter, it is hard to imagine how early man could have identified such subtle changes without help. The maximum declination of the moon occurs every eighteen and a half years and it looks just the same as it did the night before and after.

With all things there is a yin and a yang perspective, a positive and a negative, a door to light and darkness, a choice between good and evil. Knowledge by itself is neither good nor bad, but it was for some reason that the angels of heaven declared the gifts of the fallen to be the undesired revelation of the "eternal secrets that are made in heaven" (Enoch 9:6). Perhaps knowing that mankind had knowledge of good and evil, God also knew that much of mankind would choose an evil path to exploit the knowledge of heaven. Secret knowledge has always been synonymous with power and wealth. It was daggers and swords that replaced sticks and clubs, guns and bullets that took the Native American lands from those who protected them with bows and arrows, and the atomic bomb that brought about the surrender of Japan in World War II. Perhaps knowing that mankind had knowledge of good and evil, God also knew that much of mankind would worship the source of their knowledge and place science above their Creator.

Starting nearly 2700 years before Christ and lasting for well over 3000 years, tiny creatures in China were secretly spinning a mysterious and highly sought-after fabric that was made available to the world through a vast trade route known as the Silk Road. The Silk Road stretched from Asia through the Middle East and onto Europe. Traders returning from the East brought with them a strong but soft and shimmering material that kept wearers cool in hot weather and warm in cold weather. Ancient Rome had never seen anything like it and the highly desired material commanded high prices. Once exported, China recognized the value of silk and issued an imperial decree condemning to death anyone who tried to smuggle silkworms or their eggs out of the Empire. While the Bombyx mori silk moth remained a guarded secret for thousands of years, great wealth was amassed by the silk farmers of China and the traders of the Silk Road. Monopolizing the production of silk for thousands of years, the silk farmers of China enjoyed a lack of competition and ample time to finely tune their craft. Even after losing their exclusivity and having to compete in the world marketplace, China remains, to this day, the greatest silk producer in the world. It is believed that the secrets of silk finally made it to Europe around AD 552, when two monks who, as the story goes, smuggled silk moth eggs out of China inside hollow walking sticks made of bamboo.

Secret knowledge is no less guarded today than it was when China decreed that anyone revealing the secrets of silk would be put to death. Nevertheless, fueled by greed and power, modern white-collar crime is founded on dishonest and often illegal shortcuts. The less fortunate and disadvantaged are dehumanized and exploited for personal gain. Ignoring all warning lights and designated stops, the unscrupulous barrel down the tracks, running full-steam ahead to their profits and the power that their profits bring. Nothing is sacred and everybody is expendable. The prideful and self-aggrandizing hearts of man have tasted the forbidden fruit and the fallen have shown us that knowledge can be woven into positions of power and wealth. We worship the source of our knowledge and demand the respect of those who do not have it. "See then what Azazel has done; how he has taught all iniquity . . ." (Enoch 9:6). Masked as white-collar crime, the illicit manipulation of today's multi-million-dollar secrets includes insider trading, the credit collapse of Fannie Mae and Freddie Mac, the downfall of Enron, China's theft of US personal identity information, and the church coverup of known predator priests.

There is no more blatant example of secret information being exploited for personal gain than insider trading, which will forever be synonymous with the name of Michael Milken. Milken received considerable attention "because he was the biggest target for the Securities and Exchange Commission (SEC), but it was actually Boesky who was the spider in the center of the web." Boesky had ". . . an uncanny ability to pick out potential takeover targets and invest before an offer was made. When the fated offer came, the target firm's stock would shoot up and Boesky would sell his shares for a profit. Sometimes, Boesky would buy mere days before an unsolicited bid was made public—a feat of precognition rivaling the mental powers of spoon bender Uri Geller. Like Geller, Boesky's precognition turned out to be a fraud." Rather than using any standard or recognized investment model, "Boesky went straight to the source—the mergers and acquisitions arms of the major investment banks. Boesky paid Levine and Siegel for pre-takeover information that guided his prescient buys. When Boesky hit home runs on nearly every major deal in the 1980s—Getty Oil, Nabisco, Gulf Oil, Chevron (NYSE: CVX), Texaco—the people at the SEC became suspicious." Suspicions were confirmed when Merrill Lynch was tipped off that, "someone in the firm was leaking info, and, as a result, Levine's Swiss bank account was uncovered." Pressured by the SEC, Levine promptly gave up Boesky and, "watching Boesky, particularly during the Getty Oil fiasco, the SEC caught Siegel. Having three in the bag, they went after Michael Milken." While not all charges would stick, the SEC initially filed charges against the junk bond king punishable by 520 years in prison.[123]

Lies beget lies and in today's world, secret knowledge may be nothing more than a secret cooking of the books and an ongoing coverup of known fraud. After accounting issues arose at Freddie Mac, "the Office of Federal Housing Enterprise Oversight (OFHEO) began to examine Fannie Mae's accounting practices. The result of the probe, detailed in a 211-page report . . . paints Fannie Mae as an Enron-in-the-making. At the company that prides itself on being a cuddly enabler of the American dream, OFHEO unearthed a 'pervasive' misapplication of accounting standards, poor internal controls, and . . . a pay structure that rewarded executives for meeting earnings goals, which encouraged executives to manipulate earnings to hit the number."[124] A civil fraud lawsuit was later filed by the Securities and Exchange Commission in an attempt to hold the executives of Fannie Mae and Freddie Mac accountable for their sins. "According to the lawsuit, Fannie told investors in 2007 that it had roughly $4.8 billion worth of subprime loans on its books, or just 0.2 percent of its portfolio. The SEC says that Fannie actually had about $43 billion worth of products targeted to borrowers with weak credit, or 11 percent of its holdings. The suit cites similar numbers for Freddie." In September of 2008, a federal takeover of Fannie Mae and Freddie Mac by the US Treasury placed the Government-Sponsored Enterprises (GSEs) into conservatorship. The US Treasury Secretary, Henry Paulson conceded, "conservatorship was the only form in which I would commit tax-payer money to the GSEs."[125] So far, Fannie Mae and Freddie Mac have cost taxpayers $150 billion and according to the Federal Housing Finance Agency, the final burden to taxpayers may go as high as $259 billion.[126]

In the case of Enron, projected profits for newly built assets were reported as actual profits before a penny of actual profits was ever generated. When actual profits were less than projected, losing assets were transferred to an off-the-books corporation where losses remained unreported. This was the secret that Enron kept, an orchestrated scheme that was designed to hide losses and make the company appear to be more profitable than it actually was. Also known as Special Purpose Vehicles (SPVs), off-balance-sheets allowed Enron to hide, "mountains of debt and toxic assets from investors and creditors." The tale of Enron is the story of ". . . a company that reached dramatic heights only to face a dizzying fall. The fated company's collapse affected thousands of employees and shook Wall Street to its core. At Enron's peak, its shares were worth $90.75; when the firm declared bankruptcy on December 2, 2001, they were trading at $0.26. . . . At the time, Enron's collapse was the biggest corporate bankruptcy to ever hit the financial world (since then, the failures of WorldCom, Lehman Brothers, and Washington Mutual have surpassed it). The Enron scandal drew attention to accounting and corporate fraud as its shareholders lost $74 billion in the four years leading up to its bankruptcy, and its employees lost billions in pension benefits." Already in freefall, in October of 2001, Enron "reported its first quarterly loss and closed its 'Raptor' SPV so that it would not have to distribute 58 million shares of stock, . . . This action caught the attention of the SEC." Despite shredding financial documents to conceal them from the Securities and Exchange Commission, the SEC found that Enron had, "losses of $591 million and . . . $628 million in debt by the end of 2000."[127]

The unscrupulous now weaponize the secret information of others to establish new identities, peddle to telemarketers and scammers, extort money, and bankrupt the targeted. Credit card theft occurs in a variety of ways, everything from low-tech dumpster diving or high-tech computer hacking. Fully exploited, the secret information of others can be as valuable as the secret Radar Cross Section (RCS) design of the B-2 Spirit Stealth Bomber. In 2017, a data breach of consumer credit reporting agency Equifax compromised the personal data of nearly half of all Americans, ". . . with the hackers successfully stealing names, addresses, Social Security and driver's license numbers and other personal information stored in the company's databases."[128] In February of 2020, "The U.S. Department of Justice filed an indictment against four Chinese nationals with alleged ties to the Chinese military, charging them with compromising the personal information of 145 million Americans in the . . . Equifax data breach. The nine-count indictment claims Wu Zhiyong, Wang Qian, Xu Ke, and Liu Lei were members of the People's Liberation Army's 54th Research Institute, and they routed files through approximately 34 servers in almost 20 countries to avoid detection." According to security expert Brian Vecci, "China's intended target is more likely high-level political operatives than U.S. citizens. The fact that we haven't seen China sell this information on the Dark Web says to me that whatever they're using it for is more valuable to them."[129]

Sometimes it becomes necessary to keep secrets so that existing power and wealth can be maintained. In December of 2002, the former archbishop of Boston resigned after The Boston Globe broke the story of what will forever will be known as the Catholic sex abuse scandal, revealing that Cardinal Law "had done little to punish abusers and protect children despite extensive knowledge of sex abuse . . ."[130] Still an issue in 2018, a grand jury report concluded that "Church leaders protected more than 300 'predator priests' in six Roman Catholic dioceses across Pennsylvania for decades because they were more interested in safeguarding the church and the abusers than tending to their victims . . ."[131] In a more recent 2019 report, attorney Gerald Williams acknowledged, "we've heard a lot about the church's desire to be accountable and turn over a new leaf." But when we turn to the forum where we can most help, the courts of justice, "the church has been there blocking our efforts."[132] Pedophilia is an offense to God and, as the church had feared, when the extent of the coverup was exposed, the church pews began to empty and millions of parishioners began to question their beliefs and allegiance to the church. The extent of the sickness nearly reached the pinnacle of the church and Catholics began to question the doctrines of the pope. In February of 2019, the pope's top financial adviser and the church's third-most-powerful official, Cardinal George Pell, ". . . was convicted . . . of molesting two 13-year-old choir boys . . ."[133] And "For such a high priest became us, who is holy, harmless, undefiled, separate from sinners, and made higher than the heavens" (Hebrews 7:26 KJV). Clearly, the high honors intended to accompany elevation to the priesthood and God's proctor on earth have fallen a great distance from the values appreciated by God and demonstrated by Christ. To the contrary, man seems to have placed himself and the pleasures of the flesh above the Spirit. Pride and arrogance are abundant, just as they were before the fall of Babel. Only God's grace and man's prayers keep us from our destruction.

Barely a crime, the law now allows, even encourages the financial exploitation of those least able to afford it. Modern patent laws have replaced the secrecy once necessary for the accumulation of wealth with intellectual property rights. Prior to 1980, the United States issued three categories of patents; utility patents, design patents, and plant patents. Valid for years, these patents prevented competitors from making, using, or selling the patented items or processes. Utility patents applied to machines, processes, and manufactured objects. Design patents applied to the ornamental design of functional items such as jewelry, furniture, beverage containers, and computer icons. Plant patents applied to the intellectual property rights of new and unique plant key characteristics.

In 1980, a Supreme Court ruling made it possible to patent living, man-made organisms, a key concept to the success of biotechnology companies. Biotech firms use patents to protect the intellectual property rights of newly developed drugs. Intended to allow the developers of new medicines to earn profits as compensation for the high research and development costs associated with bringing them to market, patented drugs are protected against generic competition. The unfortunate biproduct of this protection is to make new drugs unaffordable to many low-income patients. Secrecy is no longer required, and the practice is fully justified by an exaggerated and protected self-worth. One needs to look no further than the recent 2017 EpiPen debacle of pharmaceutical giant Mylan for an example of corruption born in the entitlement of patent protection.

The EpiPen is designed to ". . . ward off anaphylaxis—a potentially fatal allergic reaction that can result from exposure to anything from peanuts to insect bites. The drug itself (epinephrine) is over 100 years old, but the device makes it easy to inject," an attractive alternative when flirting with death.[134] Literally manufactured for less than $50, the EpiPen initially sold for $57, was priced at $103.50 in 2009, and skyrocketed to $608.61 by 2016. By 2017, the EpiPen manufacturer (Mylan) was being investigated by the Federal Trade Commission to determine ". . . whether the company violated antitrust laws by tweaking EpiPen's design slightly to extend its patent, and . . . delayed the entry of potential EpiPen competitors to the marketplace. Mylan has strongly denied that it did anything wrong."[135] When asked by Norah O'Donnell of CBS This Morning why the price of the EpiPen had increased 500 percent over the past decade, Mylan CEO Heather Bresch responded, "Because we realized there was an unmet need. . . . And so, we made a conscious decision, the board, we put a business plan together to invest, to build public awareness and access,"[136] Following congressional hearings and the resulting public outrage, "Institutional Shareholder Services, a shareholder advisory firm, took the rare step of urging investors to oust all of Mylan's existing directors." As a result, former CEO Robert Coury was transitioned to the position of Executive Chairman with a 2016 pay package of $98 million.[137]

If the corruption of mankind from the revelation of heaven's eternal secrets (Enoch 9:6) were so complete that ". . . the world was changed" (Enoch 8:1), one might expect to see similar widespread exploitation of secret knowledge today. Why are the airwaves not inundated with stories of corruption? Unfortunately, to make the news today, stories of corruption must be so severe and unique that they overshadow the headlines of the day. They have to compete with the discovery of water on Mars, the attempted congressional impeachment of the president of the United States, the lack of PPE to fight COVID-19, a shooting in the Detroit police station, and the mob-established autonomous zone in Seattle. A close look beyond the headlines reveals that the pervasive corruption of yesteryear is alive and well and flourishing. The egocentric power that is possible with the possession of secret knowledge is often camouflaged as the opportunity of the privileged. Now self-empowered and independent of any common good, the elite set lofty goals of world domination and stack the deck in their favor. They recruit the future knights and bishops of the world's chess board. The advantaged groom the select and the privileged beget the privileged. Secret societies are formed for just this purpose. Some of the most powerful and well known of today's secret societies include the Illuminati, the Freemasons, Skull and Bones, the Bohemian Club, and the Bilderberg Group.

The Illuminati was founded in Bavaria by Professor Adam Weishaupt in 1776. Aggravated by the power of the Catholic Church, Professor Weishaupt sought to cast aside organized religion in favor of a new form of "illumination" through reason. Inspired by the spread of the Enlightenment, Weishaupt drew upon the ideas of the Jesuits, the Mysteries of the Seven Sages of Memphis, the Kabbalah, and the Freemasons. His right-hand man, Baron Adolph von Knigge expanded the Order from a five-man secret society to an organization with thousands of underground members. The baron helped to implement a hierarchy with degrees, classes, and secret symbolic member names. The organization flourished before being abolished in 1787 by Karl Theodor of Bavaria, who issued an edict making membership in the Illuminati punishable by death. Conspiracy theories formed almost immediately. Many believed the members of the Order carried on with their plans in secret. Some even claim that they wanted to get disbanded, and used the public abolishment to their advantage to deflect curious eyes. Shortly after the Illuminati was abolished, Albert Pike had a vision that portrayed a New World Order. Pike then outlined the blueprints for the Third and Final World War— the blueprints that, according to Illuminati truthers, the society's leaders are still following today. There is no definitive proof of membership, because there is no real proof of the Illuminati beyond the original Order. Reported members include the royal families of several nations as well as a large handful of prominent leaders in finance, technology, and government. Well-publicized theories of Illuminati membership claim that it is only open to people born into one of thirteen powerful families, some of which have famous names like Kennedy, Rothchild, and Rockefeller.

The Order of Skull and Bones was co-founded in 1832 by William Huntington Russell and Alphonso Taft after a dispute among Yale debating societies over that season's Phi Beta Kappa awards. Members are rumored to worship Euloga, the goddess of eloquence who died with Demosthenes, a Greek orator in AD 322. This is based on the skull and crossbones emblem having the number "322" beneath it. The initiation ritual is said to require new Bonesmen to swear allegiance to the devil while in a coffin and holding a skull. Members meet in a windowless brownstone Egypto-Doric style building known as the tomb where it is believed that they keep the skulls of Geronimo and Martin Van Buren. Most known for its powerful alumni, Yale University's most famous and most secret society has inspired sinister conspiracy theories since its foundation. Many believe that Skull and Bones controls the CIA, while others think it's a branch of the Illuminati, seeking a global totalitarian government. These theories have help from at least one of the society's famous members, James Jesus Angleton who headed CIA counterintelligence for nearly two decades. Prominent alumni include: Chief Justice William Howard Taft (son of Alphonso Taft); former presidents George Herbert Walker Bush and George Walker Bush; Chauncey York; Supreme Court

Justices Morrison R. Waite and Potter Stewart; Henry Stimson, US Secretary of War (1940–1945); Robert A. Lovett, US Secretary of Defense (1951–1953); William B. Washburn, Governor of Massachusetts; and Henry Luce, founder and publisher of *Time, Life, Fortune,* and *Sports Illustrated* magazines.[138]

The earliest Masonic texts contain what might loosely be called a history of the craft. The oldest known work of this type, the Halliwell Manuscript dates to sometime between 1390 and 1425. This document states that the "craft of Masonry" began with Euclid in Egypt, and came to England in the reign of King Athelstan (927–939). Shortly afterward, the Cooke Manuscript traces Masonry to Jabal son of Lamech (Genesis 4: 20–22), and tells how this knowledge came to Euclid, from him to the children of Israel. According to Dan Brown, "The secrecy of the Masons is what allowed prominent disgruntled colonists to gather, to conspire against British tyranny, and eventually to establish the new and independent country of the United States.... At the time of independence in 1776, Masons were highly respected. Yet as they became more powerful after the revolution, they also became more corrupt."[139] Freemasons have been accused of everything from murder to devil worship to secretly controlling the US government. Masons who became Presidents of the United States are: George Washington, James Monroe, Andrew Jackson, James K. Polk, James Buchanan, Andrew Johnson, James A. Garfield, William McKinley, Theodore Roosevelt, William Howard Taft, Warren G. Harding, Franklin D. Roosevelt, Harry S. Truman, Lyndon B. Johnson, and Gerald Ford. Other prominent Freemasons include: Benjamin Franklin, John Hancock, Samuel Adams, Albert Einstein, Thomas Edison, Henry Ford, Douglas MacArthur, Winston Churchill, J. Edgar Hoover, Roy Rogers, Gene Autry, Buzz Aldrin, Wolfgang Amadeus Mozart, Ludwig Von Beethoven, and Johannes Brahms.

Receiving very little press since their inception, a confederation of the world's most powerful men came together in 1872 to form a San Francisco-based art club known as the Bohemian Club. The Bohemian Club meets each year in mid-July at a 2700-acre campground known as the Bohemian Grove in Monte Rio, California. Members participate in ancient pagan rituals that, for the most part, remain shrouded in secrecy. According to G. William Domhoff, a Bohemian Club researcher and Professor of Psychology and Sociology at the University of California, Santa Cruz, the apex of the Bohemian rituals is a ceremony known as the Cremation of Care. According to Domhoff, dressed in robes and chanting incantations, members watch as a ferryman transports a small boat across a lake to deliver an effigy of Care ("Dull Care") to hooded individuals that then receive and burn the effigy at the foot of a forty-foot statue of an owl. Domhoff notes: ". . . this is the body of Care, symbolizing the concerns and woes that afflict all men during their daily lives." The occult meaning of this ceremony is clear. These men carry the cares of the world on their shoulders and cast them off with symbolic gesture. Previous members of the Bohemian Club have included: George H. Bush, George W. Bush, Ronald Reagan, Henry Kissinger, Casper Weinberger, Dick Cheney, Malcom Forbes, Stephen Bechtel, James Baker, David Rockefeller, Tom Johnson, William Randolph Hearst Jr., Jack Howard, Charles Scripps, and Walter Cronkite.

According to Daniel Estulin, ". . . in 1954, 'the most powerful men in the world met for the first time' in Oosterbeek, Netherlands, 'debated the future of the world,' and decided to meet annually in secret."[140] They called themselves the Bilderberg Group and their membership represented a who's who of world power elites. Familiar names included: David Rockefeller, Henry Kissinger, Bill Clinton, Gordon Brown, Angela Merkel, Alan Greenspan, Ben Bernanke, Larry Summers, Tim Geithner, Lloyd Blankfein, George Soros, Donald Rumsfeld, and Rupert Murdoch. Private discussions are held at group meetings under Chatham House Rule, which means participants can use any information they receive during the meetings but cannot reveal their source. Whatever their earlier mission, "the Group is now 'a shadow world government . . . threatening to take away our right to direct our own destinies (by creating) a disturbing reality' very much harming the public's welfare." Supporters of a One World Order, the Bilderbergers hope to, "supplant individual nation-state sovereignty with an all-powerful global government, corporate controlled, and check-mated by militarized enforcement."[141] Meeting at the Hotel Montreux Palace, Montreux from May 30 to June 2, 2019, the latest meeting of the Bilderberg Group included: Henry Kissinger, Jared Kushner, Jens Stoltenberg, Mike Pompeo, and Mark Carney (Governor of the Bank of England).

Corruption now invades nearly every aspect of our lives. Our own government is infested and as the 2018 appointment of Brett Kavanaugh to the Supreme Court has demonstrated, the accused are now guilty until proven innocent. Pandora's box has been opened; the genie has escaped and the corruption of mankind is near complete. First experienced as the knowledge of good and evil, magnified by the revelations of the fallen angels, and fully embraced since before the great flood, every imagination of the thoughts of our hearts are only evil continually. As it is now and as it was before the great flood, the wickedness of man is great in the earth (Genesis 6:5). So great were the sins of man when given the eternal secrets of heaven, that the bringer of swords and metallurgy (Enoch 8:1), Azazel, was bound and buried in the desert, forever recorded as, "ALL SIN." And ". . . the Lord said to Raphael: 'Bind Azazel by his hands and his feet and throw him into the darkness. And split open the desert, which is in Dudael, and throw him there. And throw on him jagged and sharp stones and cover him with darkness. And let him stay there forever. And cover his face so that he may not see the light. And so that, on the Great Day of Judgment, he may be hurled into the fire. And restore the Earth which the Angels have ruined. And announce the restoration of the Earth. For I shall restore the Earth so that not all the sons of men shall be destroyed because of the knowledge which the Watchers made known and taught to their sons. And the whole Earth has been ruined by the teaching of the works of Azazel; and against him write: ALL SIN'" (Enoch 10:4-8).

As if our offenses were not yet enough, the prophet Isaiah reminds us that mankind managed to further distance himself from God when our ancestors declared the bearer of their gifts as their gods and counselors.

God himself said, I alone am God and I am a jealous God (Isaiah 45:5; Exodus 20:5). "Remember the former things of old: for I am God, and there is none else; I am God, and there is none like me. Declaring the end from the beginning, and from ancient times the things that are not yet done, saying, my counsel shall stand, and I will do all my pleasure. . . . I have spoken it; I will also bring it to pass" (Isaiah 46:9-11 KJV). The prophet Isaiah then went on to warn the house of Jacob and the remnant of the house of Israel, ". . . thou hast trusted in thy wickedness: thou hast said, None seeth me. Thy wisdom and thy knowledge, it hath perverted thee; and thou hast said in thine heart, I am, and none else beside me. Therefore, shall evil come upon thee; thou shalt not know from whence it riseth: and mischief shall fall upon thee; thou shalt not be able to put it off: and desolation shall come upon thee suddenly, which thou shalt not know. Stand now with thine enchantments, and with the multitude of thy sorceries, wherein thou hast labored from thy youth; if so be thou shalt be able to profit, if so be thou mayest prevail. Thou art wearied in the multitude of thy counsels. Let now the astrologers, the stargazers, the monthly prognosticators, stand up, and save thee from these things that shall come upon thee. Behold, they shall be as stubble; the fire shall burn them; they shall not deliver themselves from the power of the flame" (Isaiah 47:10-14 KJV).

— 9 —

BLOOD SACRIFICE:
FALLEN ANGELS ON HIGH ALTARS

The intent of this chapter is to define, as best I can, what I believe that God must have seen as the total corruption of mankind when, ". . . it repented the Lord that he had made man on the earth" (Genesis 6:5-6 KJV). I also hope to demonstrate that it was the fallen angels and their descendants who were most often responsible for jump-starting and fueling the continued corruption of man. The recurring events of our written and archeological record show us that as we exercised our innate desire for power, our pride and elevated self-worth corrupted our doings and we foolishly justified evil actions over good works. We elevated the importance of those who brought us the knowledge to achieve the power that we so desperately desired and we called them our gods.

The secrets of charms and spells and the cutting of roots and trees are forever intertwined and purposely bunched together when speaking of the gifts of the fallen. Unlike the other gifts of the fallen, these gifts are attributed to more than one fallen angel. "Amezarak taught all those who cast spells and cut roots, Armaros the release of spells. . . . And Semyaza has made known spells, he to whom you gave authority to rule over those who are with him" (Enoch 8:3; 9:7). Previously, we talked about the tie between the cutting of roots and trees and the application of herbs and roots to the beginnings of modern medicine (Chapter 8). We also briefly discussed yin and yang, the fact that knowledge by itself is neither good nor bad. With all things, there is a positive and a negative, a door to light and darkness, a choice between good and evil. To this end, we see that the secrets of charms and spells and the cutting of roots and trees are also the essential tools employed in the pagan ritual practices of Wicca, Satanism, and Voodoo.

As witchcraft practitioner Margot Adler claims, "A spiritual path that is not stagnant ultimately leads one to the understanding of one's own divine nature. Thou art Goddess. Thou art God. Divinity is imminent in all Nature. It is as much within you as without. The practice of the occult arts is thus an endeavor to actualize one's own divinity."[142] Witchcraft deals with various rituals and activities that can be perfected to manipulate or utilize a cosmic or psychic force to do one's bidding. With only minimal research at the local library, one can find instruction on ". . . the tools to use (candles, herbs, tarot cards, talismans, fetishes); and rituals to perform (spells, incantations, chanting, music, dancing)—all of which enables the practitioner to become open to these forces (if they exist outside) or to conjure up these forces (if they originate from within). One will learn how to interpret dreams, meditate, have out-of-body experiences, speak with the dead, heal, and read auras. One can seek to develop one's own powers within the context of other witches (in a coven) or alone (in solitary practice). There are no obligations to follow any previously prescribed method. If what others have done before works, that is fine. If one sees the need to change the ritual or tools to get better results, then that is fine as well. All of these activities are designed to do two things: to enhance the well-being of one's self or those around him or her and to actualize one's own divinity"[143] Indicative of the close relationship between good and evil, medicine and the occult, the Wiccan Rede is in part similar to the Hippocratic oath in that it reads, "An' it harm none, do what ye will."

At its foundation, "Wicca holds a duo-theistic belief system that includes a female Mother Goddess and a male Horned God." In the words of Jone Salomonsen, "Witches perceive of themselves as having left the Father's House (Jewish and Christian religion) and returned home to the Self (Goddess religion) with a call to heal western women's (and men's) alienation from community and spirituality and to become benders of human and societal developments." According to Michael F. Strmiska, this flexibility in excluding/including deities has, "allowed people with interest in different deities and religious traditions to customize Wicca to suit their specific interests, thus enhancing the religion's appeal to a broad and growing membership"[144] Officially recognized by the US government as a religion in 1985, Wiccans have a commonly shared core belief in magic and magic has been around since the dawn of time. "The Wiccan view is similar to that of Aleister Crowley, who defined magic as 'the science and art of causing change to occur in conformity with will.' As Wesley Baines says, 'Many believe magic to be simply another law of nature, albeit one that is poorly understood and written off as fakery. As such, magic is not supernatural, but just as natural as gravity and wind, and often involves a combination of invocations, movements, music, meditation, and tools.' And as one Wiccan site explains, 'Magick [sic] is another word for transformation, creation, and manifestation. Wicca magick is a tool we use to act on the subtle—or energy, or quantum—level of reality. The quantum level is the causal realm. It is the subtle influences at the quantum level that decide which way reality will go.'"[145]

Clearly, man's desire to be as God remained and sorcery (magic) survived the great flood to flourish at a time before Christ. We know this because the Bible tells us that the magicians of Egypt were called upon to discredit Moses by reproducing the miracles of Exodus until they couldn't and had to acknowledge the finger of God. ". . . Moses and Aaron went in unto Pharaoh, and they did so as the Lord had commanded: and Aaron cast down his rod before Pharaoh, and before his servants, and it became a serpent. Then Pharaoh also called the wise men and the sorcerers: now the magicians of Egypt, they also did in like manner with their enchantments. For they cast down every man his rod, and they became serpents: but Aaron's rod swallowed up their rods" (Exodus 7:10-12 KJV). Finally,

". . . Aaron stretched out his hand with his rod, and smote the dust of the earth, and it became lice in man, and in beast; all the dust of the land became lice throughout all the land of Egypt. And the magicians did so with their enchantments to bring forth lice, but they could not: so, there were lice upon man, and upon beast. Then the magicians said unto Pharaoh, this is the finger of God: and Pharaoh's heart was hardened, and he hearkened not unto them; as the Lord had said" (Exodus 8:17-19 KJV). The Bible tells us that the pursuit of such things is an offense to God. "There shall not be found among you any one that . . . useth divination, or an observer of times, or an enchanter, or a witch, or a charmer, or a consulter with familiar spirits, or a wizard, or a necromancer. For all that do these things are an abomination unto the Lord: and because of these abominations the Lord thy God doth drive them out from before thee" (Deuteronomy 18:10-12 KJV).

Testifying to the Wicca intent of opening up one's self to outside forces, the apostle Paul viewed those having the spirit of divination as possessed. "And it came to pass, as we went to prayer, a certain damsel possessed with a spirit of divination met us, which brought her masters much gain by soothsaying: The same followed Paul and us, and cried, saying, these men are the servants of the Most High God, which shew unto us the way of salvation. And this did she many days. But Paul, being grieved, turned and said to the spirit, I command thee in the name of Jesus Christ to come out of her. And he came out the same hour" (Acts 16:16-18 KJV). Demonic spirits are also referred to as evil spirits and are depicted in the Bible as fallen angels (Revelation 12:4-9). "Subject to debate, and depending upon different religious doctrines, the premise of demonic energy is the same: It stems from a lower order of angels that fell to Earth from God, or the Creator's grace."[146] The gifts of the fallen seem to be the gifts that keep on giving. In Hinduism, a religion of over 900 million practitioners worldwide, divine possession is both expected and acceptable. Worshiping the gods and goddesses implies acknowledging their ultimate control over our lives. In her 1996 book *Devi, Goddesses of India*, Kathleen M. Erndl discusses at length the fact that "Hinduism does not draw a clear dividing line between divine and human; gods can become humans and humans can become god."[147]

The first satanic church was formed by Anton LaVey in 1966. Much like Wicca, Satanism is based on the manipulation of energy and consciousness through mind control, possession, deception, and ritual abuse. Whether actively seeking to facilitate demonic possession or not, there is literally a laundry list of intentional actions that are employed to open the channels and create a conducive environment for a dark or demonic energy to inhabit a space or possess the weakened individual. "Instances of intent include a willingness to conduct unholy chants, recite Satanic spells or incantations, use of Ouija Boards, actively seeking Satanic or dark energies for entertainment, and misuse of Tarot or other divination tools. Each of these actions opens the door for a demonic force to cross, and makes way for horrific, and often tragic, opportunity."[148] Demonic forces seek the weak (male or female) and attempt to take over the physical body to carry out their work. Indications of demonic possession sometimes include, but are not limited to: denouncement of God, lack of self-respect or respect of others, uncontrolled sexual expression and behaviors, vocal annunciations and vulgarities, split-personality, altered appearance (black, soulless eyes), affirmation of Satan, despondency, and thoughts of murder and/or suicide. Demonic possession is a state in which one or several demonic spirits have gained access to the body of an individual and then proceed to take full control over the person's will. In such a condition, the demonic spirits use the body of the individual to express its personality and to carry out its evil intent.

Both Satanism and witchcraft "... stand in stark contrast to Christianity in their repudiation not only of God but also of the role of Jesus in effecting the salvation of mankind; indeed, there is a sense in which both Satanism and witchcraft deny that mankind is in any need of salvation."[149] Two of the most important rituals in Satanism are the Initiation Ritual and the Dedication Ritual. "In some cases, the Initiation Ritual represents the introduction of the adept in the satanic religion and the Dedication Ritual represents the dedication of one's life to Lucifer's cause. In other cases, the Initiation Ritual represents the individual's intention to choose another path. Leaving back the past, the previous religion, the former god and former self. This ritual is pure blasphemy towards the practitioner's former self and his anterior god. . . . The Dedication Ritual however, consists, in the satanist's case, in his intention to dedicate his soul and life to Satan."[150] Echoing of charms and spells, the basic tools necessary for satanic rituals include a bowl of steel or silver to burn objects belonging to others, either enemies or friends, for rituals of revenge, love, or health. This same bowl holds water blessed by leviathan and used in satanic baptisms, where water is mixed with the blood of the baptized person. Satanism is a blood cult where demons are not bought with gold or silver; they are bought with blood. There is no shortage of demons to carry out the work of Satan. These demons are sometimes referred to as spirit guides, angels, wizards, ghosts, aliens, or a number of other disguises. Satan is trying to develop man's hidden abilities as well as to provide him with some extraordinary supernatural powers, to encourage his independence from God as opposed to his faith in, fellowship with, and dependence upon his Creator. As man develops these hidden powers, he increasingly feels more like God.

Evil comes in many colors and the devil uses many tools to build his house of deception. From the beginning, "Satan's strategy has been to ask 'Did God Say?' (Genesis 3:1). He is saying the same today and many people are listening. More and more prefer to believe the world's view of origins rather than the plain teaching of the Bible. . . . People do not reject Christ because of the preaching of any biblical truth, including the truth about creation, but because they love darkness (John 3:19). Moreover, it appears that many justify their atheism by embracing evolution. Religious studies scholar Professor Huston Smith wrote, 'Martin Lings is probably right in saying that more cases of the loss of religious faith are to be traced to the theory of evolution . . . than anything else.' According to evangelist Mark Cahill, 'The number one answer I get for there not being a God . . . is evolution.' This suggests that people have great difficulty reconciling the doctrine of evolution with Christianity, rather than a belief in biblical creation. Young people, raised as creationists, leave the church because they have not been taught the facts. They suffer years of secular, evolutionary indoctrination at school and are never told the other side of the story. The bankruptcy of the claim that evolution is well supported by science is easily exposed. At the same time, the evidence supporting the biblical account of creation and Earth history grows by the month. Despite this, many youngsters in churches reach adulthood never having been told these things."[151] Scientific arguments against evolution are typically recognized by Christians who fully embrace science (chapter 4). According to Nobel prize-winning Professor Ernst Chain, "Evolution is a hypothesis based on no evidence and irreconcilable with the facts."[152]

Recognized as one of the key texts of modern Satanism, Anton LaVey published *The Satanic Bible* in 1969. This gave the church a national reputation and served as a strong vehicle for its significant growth. Since publication, many branches and sects of Satanism have sprung up throughout the world. They include, but are not limited to: The Order of Nine Angels, Temple of Set, Luciferian Children of Satan, Order of the Left-Hand Path, and The Satanic Reds. As proof of Satanism's growth, the US Army included Satanism in its manual for chaplains *Religious Requirements and Practices* beginning in 1978. Again, echoing of charms and spells, although satanists do not advocate murder, *The Satanic Bible* does promote symbolic human sacrifice "through hexing, a magical working that 'leads to the physical, mental or emotional destruction of the sacrifice in ways and means not attributable to the magician.' The primary goal, however, is not the destruction of the individual but rather the anger and wrath summoned up within the magician during the course of the ritual. Anything that happens to the sacrifice is of secondary importance. The only people satanists will consider targeting with such a sacrificial hex is a 'totally noxious and deserving individual' who 'by his reprehensible behavior, practically cries out to be destroyed.' In fact, satanists see the elimination of such obnoxious influences as something of a duty. These people are emotional leeches, dragging everyone else down to feed their starved egos."[153] Most satanists in America today, including most theistic satanists, do *not* practice animal sacrifice. However, some do. The original La Vey Satanists claim to strongly oppose animal sacrifice; however, comments in *The Satanic Bible* imply that if you do practice animal sacrifice, you should do so in a deliberately cruel manner, to maximize the animal's "death throes."[154]

Despite fully embracing possession and animal sacrifice, practitioners of Voodoo claim to be a Christian offshoot of Catholicism, a religion whose doctrine opposes both. Voodoo is also known as Vodou, Vaudin, Vodun, Vodoun, Vaudoux, and several other variants. Believed transplanted to Louisiana in 1804 by displaced Cuban plantation owners who brought their slaves with them, Voodoo is alleged to have started in Haiti in 1724 as a snake cult. "Vodou is a monotheistic religion. Followers of Vodou—known as Vodouisants—believe in a single, supreme godhead that can be equated with the Catholic God. This deity is known as *Bondye*, 'the good god.' Vodouisants also accept the existence of lesser beings, which they call *loa* or *lwa*. These are more intimately involved in day-to-day life than Bondye, who is a remote figure. The lwa are divided into three families: Rada, Petro, and Ghede. The relationship between humans and the lwa is a reciprocal one. Believers provide food and other items that appeal to the lwa in exchange for their assistance. The lwa are frequently invited to possess a believer during rituals so the community can directly interact with them. . . . It is a syncretic religion that combines Roman Catholicism and native African religion, particularly from the religion of the Dahomey region of West Africa" (the modern-day nation of Benin).[155] Voodoo is primarily practiced in Haiti, New Orleans, and other locations within the Caribbean. Modern Voodoo "began when African slaves brought their native traditions with them as they were forcefully transported to the new world. However, they were generally forbidden from practicing their religion. To get around these restrictions, the slaves started to equate their gods with Catholic saints. They also performed their rituals using the items and imagery of the Catholic Church."[156] Many Vodouisants consider themselves Catholics. They see the saints and spirits as one and the same.

Nothing smacks more of charms and spells than Voodoo. Voodoo embraces elaborate rituals that invoke spirit-possessed dancing and are immersed in secret languages. The ancestral dead are believed to walk among the living during ritual hooded dances. Even touching one of these dancers while in their spirit-possessed trance is thought to bring about death. Talismans are bought and sold as charms possessing medicinal and/or spiritual powers. These totems are often statues of Voodoo gods, dried animal heads, or other body parts. Participants summon evil spirits and cast hexing spells upon their adversaries. Adhering to a special diet, the priesthood is held by both Voodoo priests and priestesses. Their primary responsibilities include initiating new priests or priestesses, conducting rituals, shepherding religious ceremonies to call upon or pacify the spirits, initiating healings, telling fortunes, reading dreams, casting spells, invoking protections, and creating various potions. Voodoo potions are intended to petition spells for everything from love to death. "Rituals commonly involve the drawing of certain symbols known as veves with cornmeal or another powder. Each lwa has its own symbol and some have multiple symbols associated with them."[157] The Voodoo temple is called a Hounfour and the leader of the ceremony is a male priest called a Houngan, or a female priest called a Mambo. The term is believed to derive from the Fon houn for, "abode of spirits." Items placed on the altar and used in ritual practices include objects of symbolic meaning, such as candles, food, money, amulets, ritual necklaces, ceremonial rattles, pictures of Catholic saints, bottles of rum, bells, flags, drums, sacred stones, and knives.

Regardless of any shared terminology, use of crosses, or recognized saints, Voodoo practices are about as far from Christianity as the East is from the West. The distinction between a monotheistic loving Creator God who made angels to help oversee and guide his creation and a distant Voodoo godhead named Bondye who remains absent while his lesser lwa gods answer prayer and interact with mankind is enormous. In Christianity there is only one God and it is he who answers prayers. As pointed out in the previous chapter, God himself said that he alone is God (Isaiah

45:5-6; 45:21; 46:9-11)."Thou shalt worship no other god: for the Lord, whose name is Jealous, is a jealous God" (Exodus 34:14 KJV). As a further insult to God, Voodoo priests and priestesses routinely practice animal sacrifice. A variety of animals are "... killed during a Vodou ritual, depending upon the lwa being addressed. It provides spiritual sustenance for the lwa, while the flesh of the animal is then cooked and eaten by participants."[158] Animal flesh is of no value when compared to the sacrificial flesh of the Son of the living God. Clearly, practitioners of Voodoo do not understand the significance of God sacrificing his only begotten Son so that man might have everlasting life (John 3:16). They do not understand the difference between the Old Testament and the New Testament.

In the words of the apostle Paul, "Neither by the blood of goats and calves, but by his own blood he (Christ) entered in once into the holy place, having obtained eternal redemption for us. For if the blood of bulls and of goats, and the ashes of a heifer sprinkling the unclean, sanctifieth to the purifying of the flesh: How much more shall the blood of Christ, who through the eternal Spirit offered himself without spot to God, purge your conscience from dead works to serve the living God?" (Hebrews 9:12-14 KJV). Paul goes on to explain, "For it is not possible that the blood of bulls and of goats should take away sins. Wherefore when he cometh into the world, he saith, Sacrifice and offering thou wouldest not, but a body hast thou prepared me. . . . Then said I, Lo, I come (in the volume of the book it is written of me,) to do thy will, O God. Above when he said, Sacrifice and offering and burnt offerings and offering for sin thou wouldest not, neither hadst pleasure therein; which are offered by the law; Then said he, Lo, I come to do thy will, O God. He taketh away the first, that he may establish the second. By the which will we are sanctified through the offering of the body of Jesus Christ once for all. And every priest standeth daily ministering and offering oftentimes the same sacrifices, which can never take away sins: But this man, after he had offered one sacrifice for sins forever, sat down on the right hand of God; From henceforth expecting till his enemies be made his footstool. For by one offering he hath perfected forever them that are sanctified. Whereof the Holy Ghost also is a witness to us: for after that he had said before, this is the covenant that I will make with them after those days, saith the Lord, I will put my laws into their hearts, and in their minds will I write them; And their sins and iniquities will I remember no more. Now where remission of these is, there is no more offering for sin" (Hebrews 10:4-5, 7-18 KJV).

Although the Book of Enoch tells us that there were two hundred fallen angels (Enoch 6:6), of the "eternal secrets that are made in heaven" (Enoch 9:6), only those eternal secrets that have thus far been discussed are documented in the Book of Enoch as having been shared with mankind. Examining the archaeological evidence of technologies not currently understood by science and taking into account that there were two hundred fallen angels, it seems a safe presumption to assume that additional (as yet) unknown eternal secrets were also shared. The megalithic stones of Baalbek provide just such an example of an ancient and still secret technology that has been lost to time. So massive are the stones of Baalbek that they have been given names. The recently unearthed "Hajjar al-Hibla" measures 19.6 meters (64.3 feet) long by 6.0 meters (19.7 feet) wide by 5.5 meters (18.0 feet) tall, and is estimated to weigh 1650 tons or 3,300,000 pounds. The "Stone of the South" measures 20.5 meters (67.3 feet) long by 4.6 meters (15.0 feet) wide by 4.5 meters (14.8 feet) tall, and is estimated to weigh 1242 tons or 2,484,000 pounds. The "Stone of the Pregnant Woman" measures 20.8 meters (68.1 feet) long by 5.3 meters (17.4 feet) wide by 4.3 meters (14.2 feet) tall, and is estimated to weigh just over 1000 tons or 2,000,240 pounds. These are the most massive stones ever known to have been quarried. Science and archaeology have only recently acknowledged that modern man has no idea how these colossal stones were cut from solid bedrock, transported sometimes hundreds of miles, and in the case of the Temple of Jupiter, ever so gently and precisely romanced into place. Just under three thousand feet to the northeast of the Stone of the Pregnant Woman, eight-hundred-ton stones were raised twenty feet in the air and placed with machine-like precision into the foundations of the mighty Temple of Jupiter. Initially thought to have been transported on rollers, experimentation has since shown that regardless of the materials used, rollers would have been crushed by the sheer weight of these monoliths.

To give some perspective of just how massive these stones are, the Liebherr LTM 11200-9.1 was the world's strongest mobile crane in 2011. The LTM 11200-9.1 was said to be ". . . both the strongest and tallest telescopic crane in the world, lifting up to 1,200 tons (that's 2,645,000 pounds or 12 adult Blue Whales, depending on who's counting). Its eight-part telescoping boom extends up to 328 feet (50 feet taller than the last record holder) and, with the addition of a lattice jib, has a maximum lift height of 630 feet, more than 50 stories high! Despite its 445,000 pounds of counter-weight, when the LTM 11200 is picking up over two million pounds, it can only extend about eight feet laterally without tipping."[159] Although a handful of larger cranes have since been built, if the LTM 11200-9.1 were able to be positioned over the Baalbek stones and the proper rigging applied in 2011, it still would not have been capable of lifting either the "Hajjar al-Hibla" or the "Stone of the South," both weighing over 1200 tons. Modern science now believes that sound waves, resonant frequencies, or super conducting magnets might have been employed to lift these massive stones. Regardless of how these massive stones were transported, it seems like magic today and I am sure that it must have seemed like magic thousands of years ago. It is not beyond reason to assume that this lost technology may have also been given to mankind by the fallen angels.

The secrets of the cutting, transporting, and placing of these mega-stones was not confined to Baalbek. West of the River Nile, in the Theban necropolis stands the Colossi of Memnon. They are two giant statues that were each built from a single block of quartzite sandstone and according to researchers, quarried and transported 430 miles from a quarry in El-Gabal. Each statue is 18 meters (60 feet) tall and has an estimated weight of 720 tons. Another incredible stone quarried thousands of years ago in ancient Egypt is the Unfinished Obelisk of Aswan. The Obelisk of Aswan is more than twice the size of any known obelisk ever raised. When erected, it would have measured a staggering 42 meters (137.8 feet) tall and have weighed nearly 1200 tons. Again, in 2011, with only minimal rigging applied, the Obelisk of Aswan would have been beyond the lifting capability of the world's largest mobile crane. In Peru, the andesite stones used in the construction of the terraces at Sacsayhuamán weigh over 220 tons and display a precision of fitting that is unmatched in the Americas. The stones are so closely spaced together that in most cases, a single piece of paper will not fit between them. "This precision, combined with the rounded corners of the blocks, the variety of their interlocking shapes, and the way the walls lean inward have puzzled scientists for decades."[160] Also, in Peru, the massive pink granite blocks of the Wall of the Six Monoliths at Ollantaytambo are likewise joined together so precisely that a piece of paper could not pass between them. The Western Stone is a monolithic stone ashlar block that forms a portion of the lower level of the Western Wall in Jerusalem. Considered one of the largest building blocks in history, the Western Stone is the largest visible stone in the Western Wall Tunnel. The stone's face is measured at 13.6 meters (44.5 feet) long by 3.3 meters (11 feet) high, but its width, or depth, is hidden within the wall. Estimated to weigh between 275 and 625 tons, Ground-Penetrating Radar (GPR) measurements have shown the Western Stone to be between 1.8 and 2.5 meters (5.9 and 8.2 feet) deep.

Bearing in mind that the world still has knowledge of astronomy, lunar eclipses, metallurgy, swords and daggers, and medicinal roots and herbs, one might wonder why we have lost the secrets of transporting and placing the mega-stones of antiquity. In all honesty, it might well be for any of a number of reasons, anything from the Dark Ages to the ice age. Because we have no written record, every answer is, at this time, speculation. What we do know is that Baalbek, the home of the largest and arguably oldest hand-hewed stones on the planet was also home to one of the world's oldest and most vile religions. The inhabitants of Baalbek are known to have worshipped Baal and practiced human sacrifice since the founding of Carthage near 813 BC. The tablets of Ugarit tell us that

Baal was the god of rain, thunder, and extraordinary bolts of lightning. The people of Baalbek feared their god and practiced human sacrifice to pacify him; thereby preventing calamities such as earthquakes, droughts, and plagues. They believed that by their actions, they could control and manipulate their gods. Under the influence of his wife, Jezebel, King Ahab built altars to Baal. "And he reared up an altar for Baal in the house of Baal, which he had built in Samaria. And Ahab made a grove; and Ahab did more to provoke the Lord God of Israel to anger than all the kings of Israel that were before him" (1 Kings 16:32-33 KJV). Equally as morally bankrupt, King Hiel rebuilt Jericho wherein he sacrificed his firstborn son, Abriam. "In his days did Hiel the Bethelite build Jericho: he laid the foundation thereof in Abiram his firstborn, and set up the gates thereof in his youngest son Segub, according to the word of the LORD, which he spake by Joshua the son of Nun" (1 Kings 16:34 KJV). This is an explicit reference to what are called foundational sacrifices. Common enough in biblical times, humans were ritually sacrificed, typically children to a patron deity. Seeking favor, bodies of the victims were placed under the foundations or in the walls at the place where they were sacrificed.

The Bible refers to the sacrifice of children to Baal as causing them to "pass through fire." Officiating priests are said to have danced around altars, chanting frantically and cutting themselves with knives to inspire the attention and compassion of Baal. Worshipers worked themselves into frenzies at the thought of possibly offending him. It is believed that on a moonlit night, the priests would light a fire at the base of a brass effigy of Baal. Then, one at a time, they placed still-alive children across the burning hot outstretched arms of Baal. As children were burned alive, they vehemently cried out and the priests beat their drums, sounded flutes, lyres, and tambourines to drown out the cries of the anguished parents. Worshipers of Baal disgustingly referred to this ritual burning of children as "the act of laughing." "Manasseh was twelve years old when he began to reign, and he reigned fifty and five years in Jerusalem: But did that which was evil in the sight of the Lord, like unto the abominations of the heathen, whom the Lord had cast out before the children of

Israel. For he built again the high places which Hezekiah his father had broken down, and he reared up altars for Baalim, and made groves, and worshipped all the host of heaven, and served them. Also, he built altars in the house of the Lord, whereof the Lord had said, In Jerusalem shall my name be forever. And he built altars for all the host of heaven in the two courts of the house of the Lord. And he caused his children to pass through the fire in the valley of the son of Hinnom: also, he observed times, and used enchantments, and used witchcraft, and dealt with a familiar spirit, and with wizards: he wrought much evil in the sight of the Lord, to provoke him to anger" (2 Chronicles 33:1-6 KJV). "And they left all the commandments of the Lord their God, and made them molten images, even two calves, and made a grove, and worshipped all the host of heaven, and served Baal" (2 Kings 17:16 KJV).

The worship of Baal was widespread. According to Herodotus, the deity of the Canaanites and the Phoenicians was also known as Jupiter to the Romans, Zeus to the Greeks, Mazda to the Persians, and Amon to the Egyptians. "For according to the number of thy cities were thy gods, O Judah; and according to the number of the streets of Jerusalem have ye set up altars to that shameful thing, even altars to burn incense unto Baal" (Jeremiah 11:13 KJV). The Bible tells us that the altars of Baal were destroyed and rebuilt many times. "And all the people of the land went into the house of Baal, and break it down; his altars and his images break they in pieces thoroughly, and slew Mattan the priest of Baal before the altars. And the priest appointed officers over the house of the LORD" (2 Kings 11:18 KJV).[161] Manasseh ". . . built up again the high places which Hezekiah his father had destroyed; and he reared up altars for Baal, and made a grove, as did Ahab king of Israel; and worshipped all the host of heaven, and served them" (2 Kings 21:3 KJV).[162] As God commanded Moses to utterly destroy the inhabitants of the Promised Land, destroy their altars, break their images, and cut down their groves so also did Joshua.[163] "And they smote all the souls that were therein with the edge of the sword, utterly destroying them: there was not any left to breathe: and he burnt Hazor with fire. And all the cities of those kings, and all the kings of them, did Joshua take, and smote them with the edge of the sword, and he utterly destroyed them, as Moses the servant of the LORD commanded" (Joshua 11:11-12 KJV).[164] I like to think that together, Moses and Joshua successfully destroyed all the worshippers and altars of Baal as God had commanded and with their annihilation, the secrets of transporting and placing the mega-stones of antiquity was also lost. There is of course no proof of this, but if true, the loss would certainly have been worth the cost.

Perhaps not so coincidently, the above described precisely made and exactly placed mega-stones of the terraces at Sacsayhuamán and the Wall of the Six Monoliths are the lost remnants of a technology possessed by an empire that routinely practiced human sacrifice. "Qhapaq hucha was the Inca practice of human sacrifice, mainly using children. The Incas performed child sacrifices during or after important events, such as the death of the Sapa Inca (emperor) or during a famine. Children were selected as sacrificial victims, as they were considered to be the purest of beings. These children were also physically perfect and healthy, because they were the best the people could present to their gods. The victims may be as young as six and as old as fifteen. Months or even years before the sacrifice pilgrimage, the children were fattened up. Their diets were those of the elite, consisting of maize and animal proteins. They were dressed in fine clothing and jewelry and escorted to Cusco to meet the emperor where a feast was held in their honor. More than one hundred precious ornaments were found to be buried with these children in the burial site. The Incan high priests took the children to high mountaintops for sacrifice. As the journey was extremely long and arduous, especially so for the younger, coca leaves were fed to them to aid them in their breathing so as to allow them to reach the burial site alive. Upon reaching the burial site, the children were given an intoxicating drink to minimize pain, fear, and resistance. They were then killed either by strangulation, a blow to the head, or by leaving them to lose consciousness in the extreme cold and die of exposure."[165] "Early colonial Spanish missionaries wrote about this practice but only recently have archaeologists such as Johan Reinhard begun to find the bodies of these victims on Andean mountaintops, naturally mummified due to the freezing temperatures and dry windy mountain air."[166]

Similar to Baal, the Canaanite god of rain and thunder and lightning, the Inca also worshipped a god of thunder known as Illapa. According to Gordon McEwan, "The Inca pantheon had an array of gods that included the creator god Viracocha, sun god Inti, thunder god Illapa and earth-mother goddess Pachamama, among others. There were also regional deities worshipped by people whom the Inca conquered."[167] Already offending God in their worship of many deities and the practicing of child sacrifice, the Inca added insult to injury by practiced acts of cannibalism. Cannibalism was practiced in rituals of sacrifice, war, death, and renewal. The Inca believed that in consumption of flesh, the dead person's power, accomplishments, and skills would be inherited. The Inca practiced both exocannibalism and endocannibalism. Exocannibalism involved eating the flesh of an enemy. This served to prove one's power, to humiliate the defeated, and to exact revenge upon the companions of the defeated. Endocannibalism was more respectful of the dead. In endocannibalism, the dead person's bones were ground to dust and mixed with roots to be drunk by the family and relatives to preserve the essence of the dead person. Regardless of the circumstance, cannibalism was an offense to God. "And I said, Hear, I pray you, O heads of Jacob, and ye princes of the house of Israel; Is it not for you to know judgment? Who hate the good, and love the evil; who pluck off their skin from off them, and their flesh from off their bones; Who also eat the flesh of my people, and flay their skin from off them; and they break their bones, and chop them in pieces, as for the pot, and as flesh within the caldron. Then shall they cry unto the Lord, but he will not hear them: he will even hide his face from them at that time, as they have behaved themselves ill in their doings" (Micah 3:1-4 KJV).

Not wishing to mislead or hide any pertinent facts, it should be noted that although nearly identical in every aspect, only the stones of the Wall of the Six Monoliths at Ollantaytambo are attributed to having been quarried and placed by the Inca. Some claim that the mega-stones at the base of the terraces at Sacsayhuamán were quarried and placed by an earlier culture known as the Killke. The Killke people were determined by archeologists to have occupied the South American region of Cusco from 900 to AD 1200, prior to the arrival of the Inca in the thirteenth century. Having no known written records, little else is known of the Killke. However, according to David Childress, "Sacsayhuamán may still be hundreds or even thousands of years older than the Killke culture. There seems to be no reason why building in the Cuzco and Sacsayhuamán area would have only begun in AD 1100 when megalithic building had begun much earlier in other areas."[168] The Inca are believed to have built the terraces at Sacsayhuamán atop Killke ruins. The ninety-ton stones of the Wall of the Six Monoliths at Ollantaytambo are, however, unilaterally accepted as having been quarried and put in place by the Inca. They are known to have been quarried some four miles away, on the side of an adjoining mountain. The responsibility for placing the foundation stones of the terraces at Sacsayhuamán is inconsequential. What is important is that the Inca once had an ability to exactly fashion large stones and so precisely place them together that theorists have speculated as to whether or not the Inca might have had an ability to melt rocks. Perhaps given to the Inca by fallen angels and long since lost to time, the secret knowledge of an ancient culture that believed in many deities, sacrificed children, and practiced cannibalism was well beyond what should have been known at that time. In this regard, the stones of the Wall of the Six Monoliths and the terraces at Sacsayhuamán are very similar to the stones of Baalbek.

The Wall of the Six Monoliths that form the high altar for the Temple of the Sun at Ollantaytambo are believed to have once been covered in gold. After the Battle of Cajamarca during the Spanish Conquest of the Inca, Francisco Pizarro sent Martin Bueno and two other Spaniards to transport the gold and silver from the temple of Coricancha to Cajamarca.[169] "They found the Temple of the Sun 'covered with plates of gold,' which the Spanish ordered removed in payment for Atahualpa's ransom. Seven hundred plates were removed, and added to two hundred *cargas* (loads) of gold transported back to Cajamarca. The royal mummies, draped in robes, and seated in gold embossed chairs, were left alone. But, while desecrating the temple, Pizarro's three men also defiled the Virgins of the Sun, sequestered women considered sacred, who served at the temple."[170] When the Spanish conquered Cusco, they began to tear down the structure and took off with rocks to build the new city, as well as the houses of the wealthiest Spaniards. Today, only the stones that were too large to be moved remain at the site. The Bible tells us how God made himself known to Assyria and the surrounding lands of the Ancient Near East and how through Jesus and the apostles, he continues to spread his word to the rest of the world. It tells us how God worked through the prophets, Moses and Joshua, to rid the Ancient Near East of idolatry and to establish his people in the promised land. What it does not tell us is who God worked through to accomplish his will in the remainder of the world. One thing we know for sure is that if the God who speaks life into existence says it, it will happen. The Bible is clear that the laws of man apply to all mankind and if God proclaims it there, he proclaims it here. His will be done, and it is. The child sacrificing and sometimes cannibalistic Incan empire of many deities is now gone and with it, the unmatched exacting large stone masonry skills of the Inca have been lost to antiquity.

Believing that the secrets of the mega-stones are a gift from the fallen angels, it is worth mentioning that according to Pohnpeian legend, it was two giant twin brothers named Olisihpa and Olosohpa that constructed the megalithic basalt stone walls of Nan Madol. Adjacent to the eastern shore of the island of Pohnpei, now part of the Madolenihmw district of Pohnpei state in the Federated States of Micronesia, Nan Madol was the ceremonial and political seat of the Saudeleur Dynasty until approximately 1628. The stone walls of Nam Madol are constructed of multi-ton rectangular prisms of volcanic basalt that are sometimes stacked as high as forty-feet tall. Although 20% of the stones are believed to have come from an ancient volcano some twenty miles away, archaeologists do not know where the other 80% of the stones came from. "The city, constructed in a lagoon, consists of a series of small artificial islands linked by a network of canals. The stone walls of Nan Madol enclose an area approximately 1.5 km long by 0.5 km wide. Nan Madol contains nearly 100 artificial islets—stone and coral filled platforms—bordered by tidal canals. The name Nan Madol means 'within the intervals' and is a reference to the canals that crisscross the ruins."[171] Legend has it that the brothers levitated the huge stones with the help of a dragon to transport them to the site and stack them in place. Olisihpa and Olosohpa apparently arrived by boat and were looking for a place to build an altar to worship Nahnisohn Sahpw, the god of agriculture. When Olisihpa died of old age, Olosohpa became the first Saudeleur. Olosohpa married a local woman and sired twelve generations, producing many other Saudeleur rulers.

Just as interesting, the Rapa Nui people of Easter Island have a similar folklore to explain how the ninety-plus ton Moai statues of their ancestors were transported and levitated into place. "Oral histories recount how various people used divine power to command the statues to walk. The earliest accounts say a king named Tuu Ku Ihu moved them with the help of the god Make-Make, while later stories tell of a woman who lived alone on the mountain ordering them about at her will."[172] As legend goes, god Make-Make was amazed at seeing himself and a bird who came to rest on his shoulder in the water's reflection. Seeing the union of the two reflections, Make-Make decided to create man by making his firstborn son. Whether combined with more recently encountered Christian beliefs or just another testimony to creation, the similarities between Rapa Nui tradition and Christian beliefs is stunning. Make-Make fertilized the red clay earth and from it made man. But the man was lonely and Make-Make caused him to go to sleep and from his rib, created woman.

Archaeological evidence suggests that despite elaborate writings, the Long Count calendar, and impressive artwork and architecture that survive to this day, the early Mayan also possessed technologies that remain secret. Teotihuacán ". . . was the largest, most influential, and certainly most revered city in the history of the New World, and it flourished in Mesoamerica's Golden Age, the Classic Period of the first millennium CE. Dominated by two gigantic pyramids and a huge sacred avenue, the city, its architecture, art, and religion would influence all subsequent Mesoamerican cultures, and it remains today the most visited ancient site in Mexico." It is believed that the inhabitants of the pre-Aztec city of Teotihuacán were a mixture of native people of Mesoamerica. Compared to other Mesoamerican cultures, Teotihuacán corresponds to early Classic Maya (250-900 CE). Located in the valley of the same name, the city is believed to have been founded between 150 BCE and 200 CE. "The largest structures at the site were completed before the 3rd century CE, and the city reached its peak in the 4th century CE with a population as high as 200,000."[173]

When first discovered, the Pyramid of the Sun was buried under four meters (13.1 feet) of dirt which researchers believe was placed there intentionally. I can't help but consider that perhaps our archaeological timeline is off and it may have instead been buried by the turbulence of a great flood (chapter 3, Gobekli Tepe). It took researchers five years to remove the thousands of tons of dirt covering the pyramid to reveal the surface. To their amazement, in 1906, researchers found that the top of the temple was covered in a thick layer of mica. Unfortunately, because of its value, most of the mica was removed from the Pyramid of the Sun and sold in the 1900s. Approximately 300 meters south of the west face of the Pyramid of the Sun, under a patio floor paved with heavy rock slabs, archaeologists discovered two massive ninety-foot square sheets of mica, one on top of the other in 1983. What they stumbled upon were chambers insulated by a layer of mica inserted between two layers of stone. Each stone-mica-stone interface is approximately 6 inches thick. The type of mica found at Teotihuacán is indicative of a type only found in Brazil, more than 2000 miles away. Mica is resistant to sudden temperature changes and organic acids, highly elastic, and impervious to temperatures as great 1470 degrees F. The purpose of the insulated chambers remains unknown.

Covering a large area of Teotihuacán are burn marks that appear to have come from a giant explosion or fire that is believed to have coincided with the collapse and abandonment of Teotihuacán around AD 650.

Theories range from the explosion of a hypothetical power plant to the intentional fires of an uprising where the poor rose up against the elite. Whatever the cause, Teotihuacán remained uninhabited until found abandoned many years later by the Aztecs. In 2003, a heavy rainstorm opened up a three-foot-wide sinkhole at the base of a large pyramid known as the Temple of the Plumed Serpent. By 2005, high-resolution, ground-penetrating radar had identified a 338-foot corridor sealed off with boulders some two thousand years ago and located sixty feet below the temple. In 2009, the government granted lead archaeologist Sergio Gómez permission to excavate and he broke ground at the entrance of the tunnel. Among the ancient artifacts so far recovered, the team has found deposits of mercury, walls embedded with pyrite, and mysterious yellow orbs ranging from four to twelve centimeters across. Scientists are baffled and theories abound. Clearly there is something here that is not fully understood. In the words of Matthew Shaer, "Fifty feet in, we stopped at a small inlet carved into the wall. Not long before, Gómez and his colleagues had discovered traces of mercury in the tunnel, which Gómez believed served as symbolic representations of water, as well as the mineral pyrite, which was embedded in the rock by hand. In semi-darkness, Gómez explained, the shards of pyrite emit a throbbing, metallic glow. To demonstrate, he unscrewed the nearest light bulb. The pyrite came to life, like a distant galaxy. It was possible, in that moment, to imagine what the tunnel's designers might have felt more than a thousand years ago: 40 feet underground, they'd replicated the experience of standing amid the stars."[174] Other recovered artifacts to date include seashells, pottery shards, elaborate necklaces, rings, balls of amber, finely carved jade and black stone statues, jaguar bones, boxes of beetle wings, and fragments of human skin.

Like the Pyramids of Giza and the Xi'an Pyramids of China, the footprints of the Pyramids of Teotihuacán appear to be in perfect alignment with the stars of Orion's Belt. The Teotihuacán complex is comprised of three pyramids, two larger than the third and identical to the layout of the pyramids at Giza and correlating to the belt Orion. Another constellation of great myth and lore often linked to the constellation of Orion, many believe that the Pyramid of the Sun at Teotihuacán aligns with the Pleiades.[175] The west face of Pyramid of the Sun and many of the surrounding streets were aligned directly with the setting point of the Pleiades on midnight of the night when it is at its highest point. There are many theories that link the Pleiades, also known in Greek mythology as the seven daughters of Atlas and Pleione to the seven wells of Abraham and/or the seven daughters of Jethro as a symbol of our origins here on Earth. I don't put much merit in these theories, but mention them to show that others have wondered why so many ancient sites were built to such precise astronomical alignments. The Bible is clear. Man was formed from the dust of the Earth and placed in the garden that God created east of Eden (Genesis 2:7-8). While the stars of the Pleiades and/or Orion's Belt may in some way represent where the fallen angels originated from (Revelation 12:4-9), they in no way have anything to do with the birthplace of man. For agricultural tribes in the northern hemisphere, the course of the Pleiades indicated the beginning and ending of the growing seasons. For the contention being made here, my concern is how, not why. Where did the builders of Teotihuacán acquire the knowledge to construct a group of structures that so precisely align with the stars? Other archaeologists and surveyors have claimed that selected monuments at Teotihuacán also form a precise scale model of the universe, including Uranus, Neptune, and Pluto.

Noted for their far-advanced mathematical and astronomical understanding of the cosmos, the Maya were also recognized for their extremely barbaric acts of torture, bloodletting, human sacrifice, and cannibalism. "The Maya had a complex religion with a huge pantheon of gods. In the Mayan worldview, the plane on which we live is just one level of a multilayered universe made up of thirteen heavens and nine underworlds. Each of these planes is ruled by a specific god and inhabited by others. Hunab Ku was the creator god and various other gods were responsible for forces of nature, such as Chac, the rain god. Mayan rulers were considered to be divine and traced their genealogies back to prove their descendance from the gods. Maya religious ceremonies included the ball game, human sacrifice and bloodletting ceremonies in which nobles pierced their tongues or genitals to shed blood as an offering to the gods."[176] Human sacrifice and beheading were often an integral part the ball game. "The game, in which a hard rubber ball was knocked around by players mostly using their hips, often had religious, symbolic, or spiritual meaning. Maya images show a clear connection between the ball and decapitated heads: the balls were even sometimes made from skulls. Sometimes, a ballgame would be a sort of continuation of a victorious battle. Captive warriors from the vanquished tribe or city-state would be forced to play and then sacrificed afterwards. A famous image carved in stone at Chichén Itzá shows a victorious ballplayer holding aloft the decapitated head of the opposing team leader."[177]

Sacrifice by heart extraction eventually became the most common form of Mayan sacrifice. This is in part believed to be influenced by a similar practice of the contemporary Aztecs in the Valley of Mexico. This sacrifice typically took place in the court of a temple or on the top of a pyramid where all could see. The victims were placed over a stone, pushing their chests upward while a sacrificial knife made of flint was used to cut into their ribs just below the left breast and remove their still-beating heart. The body was then ritually eaten. While heart extraction and the beheading of the ball game were the most common forms of human sacrifice, there were also less widely used methods. One such method involved the tying of a victim's hands behind his head and disemboweling him. Another was death by multiple arrows where the victim was tied to a stake and a symbol was painted on his chest to serve as a target. Multiple archers then released their arrows at the symbol until the victim's chest was filled with arrows.

Thought to have been around since the earliest known Maya settlement, which is believed to have been established around 1800 BC, most of the great stone cities of the Maya were inexplicably abandoned around AD 900. With the abandonment of cities came the start of the decline of Mayan civilization and culture. The fall of the Maya has long been one of the great mysteries of the ancient world. Most agree that the collapse was due to a combination of problems, but none seem to agree on what was the dominant cause. Perhaps there was a series of natural disasters— drought, earthquakes, volcanoes, hurricanes, or maybe even crop failures. Again, God's will be done. Not unlike the Incan Empire, the human sacrificing and cannibalistic Mayan worship of many deities is now gone and with it, the secrets of the mica chambers, mercury deposits, and mysterious yellow balls at Teotihuacán.

Centuries after the great stone city was abandoned by the Mayans, it was found deserted and taken over by the Aztecs of Mexico in the 1300s. The Aztecs are believed to have concluded that the city must have been constructed by the powerful Ur culture, an ancestor of theirs. Not knowing the name of the great city, the Aztecs named it Teotihuacán. In Nahuatl, the language of the Aztecs, Teotihuacán translates as "the place where men become gods." The Aztecs ". . . believed Teotihuacán was where the gods had created the present era, including the fifth and present sun. The Aztec king Montezuma, made several pilgrimages to the site during his reign in homage to the gods and the early rulers of Teotihuacán, who were 'wise men, knowers of occult things, possessors of the traditions' and whose tombs were the site's great pyramids, built for them, according to legend, by giants in the distant but not forgotten past."[178] When Hernan Cortez and his men conquered the Aztec empire in the sixteenth century, they asked the natives who it was that built Teotihuacán. The Aztecs replied that Teotihuacán was built by Quinanatzin, a race of giants who came from the heavens in the times of the Second Sun.

Further bolstering the premise that gift-giving fallen angels once existed are the myths and folklores of numerous surviving ancient cultures that tell us of gods that long ago came from the stars to impart secret knowledge to mankind. Even today, the star gods are often honored and worshipped in ceremonies as believers sometimes await their promised return. In ancient Mesopotamia, Anu was the divine personification of the sky, supreme god, and ancestor of all deities. Anu was believed to be the supreme source of all authority for all the other gods and mortal rulers. Described as the one who contains the entire universe, he is identified with the north ecliptic pole centered in the constellation Draco. Along with his sons Enlil and Enki, Anu constitutes the highest divine triad personifying the three bands of constellations of the vault of the sky. The divine triad were exclusively anthropomorphic. They were thought to possess extraordinary powers and were often portrayed as being of tremendous physical size.[179] In astral theology, the three—Anu, Enlil, and Enki—also personified the three bands of the sky, and the contained constellations, spinning around the ecliptic, respectively the middle, northern, and southern sky.[180] Anu's primary role in the Sumerian pantheon was as an ancestor figure; the most powerful and important deities were believed to be the offspring of Anu and his consort Ki, the earth goddess. These deities were known as the Anunnaki which means offspring of Anu.[181] The ancient Sumerians believed that the Anunnaki were fallen angels that descended from the heavens to indirectly determine the fate of mankind. The Cylinder of Adda and other ancient Sumerian texts define the Anunnaki as, "those who from heaven to earth came."[182]

According to the Kojiki and Nihon Shoki chronicles in Japanese mythology, the Emperors of Japan are considered to be the direct descendants of Amaterasu, the Shinto sun goddess and goddess of the universe. Appearing in the two earliest written works, the Kojiki and Nihon Shoki, Amaterasu also appears in Japanese mythology. "Amaterasu was said to have been created by the divine couple, Izanagi and Izanami, who were themselves created by, or grew from, the originator of the universe, Amenominakanushi."[183] A ceremony known as Shikinen Sengū is held every twenty years at the Ise Grand Shrine to honor the many deities enshrined. The Ise Grand Shrine, located in Ise, Mie Prefecture, Japan, houses the inner shrine, Naiku, dedicated to Amaterasu. "Her sacred mirror, Yata no Kagami, is said to be kept at this shrine as one of the Imperial regalia objects."[184] The Yata no Kagami represents wisdom or honesty, depending on the source. Mirrors in ancient Japan represented truth because they merely reflected what was shown, and were a source of much mystique and reverence.

The Zulu, a Bantu ethnic group of ten to twelve million people living mostly in the KwaZulu-Natal province of South Africa, believe Ukhulukhulwana or UkhuluKhukwan is an ancestor who came from the stars and found the ancient Zulus living like animals and without laws. He taught them to build huts and the high laws of mankind. The Zulu have many deities—among them are uNgungi, the deity of the blacksmiths and Unsondo, the god of thunder and earthquakes.[185]

In Australian Aboriginal mythology, Baiame was the creator god and Sky Father.[186] The Aboriginal creation story is recalled in a traditional ceremony known as the dreaming in several language groups of the Indigenous Australians of southeast Australia. The story recalls how Baiame came down from the sky to the land where he is said to have created the rivers, mountains, and forests. He then gave the people their laws of life, traditions, songs, and culture. He also created the first initiation site, also known as a bora, where boys were initiated into manhood. When Baiame had finished, he returned to the sky and the people called him the Sky Hero of Sky Father.[187] Baiame is said to have been married to Birrahgnooloo (Birran-gnulu), who was often depicted as an emu, and with whom he had a son named Daramulum (Dharramalan).

In Native American Blackfoot culture, the Above People, or Sky Beings, were the first creations of the Blackfoot god Apistotoke. The first Sky Being created was the Sun, Natosi, who is highly venerated by Blackfoot people. Other Sky Beings included the moon goddess, Komorkis, the immortal hero Morning Star, and all the stars in the sky. The Above People are said to have their own land and their own society above the clouds. Star-Boy is a magical hero of Blackfoot mythology who is the son of a mortal woman named Feather Woman and the immortal Morning Star. Important to the Blackfoot Sun Dance, Star-Boy is credited with bringing the Blackfoot forgiveness for his mother's fall from grace.

Overwhelmingly, the facts indicate that the fallen angels shared the desires of Adam and Eve to become as gods (Genesis 3:1-6). They became as gods to mankind, and together, we provoked the jealous wrath (Exodus 34:14) of the one true God who created man (Genesis 2:7) and declared the end from the beginning (Isaiah 46:10). The fallen angels showed us the eternal secrets that are made in heaven (Enoch 9:6) and we were enamored and awestruck. Their gifts appeared to us as magic and we worshipped the all-knowing gift givers as our gods. Unlike Christ, whose yoke is easy and burden is light (Matthew 11:30), the yoke of the fallen angels was hard and their burden heavy. Where Christ brings us rest (Matthew 11:28-29), the fallen brought torment and the weeping of souls. The worship of the fallen required the passing of children through fire, live heart extraction, human sacrifice, bloodletting, and cannibalism. "... God saw that the wickedness of man was great in the earth, and that every imagination of the thoughts of his heart was only evil continually. And it repented the Lord that he had made man on the earth, and it grieved him at his heart. And the Lord said, I will destroy man whom I have created from the face of the earth; both man, and beast, and the creeping thing, and the fowls of the air; for it repents me that I have made them" (Genesis 6:5-7 KJV).

Not so long ago, an occult driven, self-proclaimed Messiah arose in Germany with aspirations of world domination. He was able to successfully conquer nearly all of Europe before being stopped by the combined allied forces of Britain, France, Russia, and the United States. When I saw the black-and-white film footage of hundreds of thousands of people with their hands in the air, chanting hail to Hitler, I knew that the false prophet had been worshipped. Claiming divinity, promising to restore the pure Aryan race, employing secret advanced technology, and attempting to sacrifice an entire race of people, it was clear that mankind had not changed all that much in the last few thousand years. The pattern remained the same. We were born in wonderment and we were happy to follow our charismatic savior who possessed secret knowledge of the answers we sought. There will always be another Jim Jones, David Koresh, or Heaven's Gate, ready and willing to step in and fill an empty vessel. It is arrogant to think that we are far too wise to be so easily mislead today; we are an educated and scientifically astute people who know right from wrong. We can, we have, and we will again repeat the mistakes of our past. To think otherwise echoes the prideful self-image that first brought about our fall from grace. I have more faith in God than in science and mankind. History tells us that if the fallen angels returned tomorrow and brought with them the secrets of space travel, anti-gravity propulsion, and teleportation, we would again see them and worship them as our gods.

Home to some of the greatest scientific and mathematical minds of the time, the German war machine under Hitler was responsible for the creation and/or planned production of weaponry that was far in advance of anything previously known to man. Despite the Fletcher factory being destroyed by allied bombing after producing only twenty-four aircraft, the ". . . Fletcher Fl 282 became the world's first large-scale produced helicopter, with prototypes taking off in 1941, and a full order for 1000 machines placed in 1944."[188] Still in the design phase at the war's end was the Silbervogel, a sub-orbital bomber that ". . . would have been able to attain 90 miles in height and bomb New York when launched from Germany. . . . [W]ork done on the design continues to influence rocket and ramjet technology today."[189] The Arado E.555 and Horton HO 229 jet bombers were, however, Germany's prime candidates to fly from Europe to New York and drop an atomic bomb. "They used the same flying wing designs and low radar profile that the B-2 bomber would later adapt. If the war had dragged on and Germany had the resources to complete the bomber and nuclear projects, they could have destroyed Manhattan without anyone seeing it coming."[190] While the Messerschmitt ME-262 became famous as the first operational jet fighter, Germany had a wide range of other jet fighters and bombers in various stages of development. "The most effective was the Arado AR-234 jet bomber, used in very limited numbers at the end of the war and virtually impossible to intercept in flight."[191] Pioneering the technology that would form the core of modern armies for decades to come, the Germans ". . . had prototypes for man-portable guided missiles, television-guided surface to air missiles, and wire-guided air to air missiles."[192] Best known for their use of the V1 and V2 rockets, the Germans also "made use of guided anti-ship glide bombs (the "Fritz X") and guided air-dropped anti-ship missiles."[193]

Rumored to have been reverse-engineering at least one crashed UFO, Nazi scientists were said to have been developing anti-gravity technology at the end of the war in an ultra-secret project known as Die Glocke (the Bell) at a secret Nazi base known as Der Riese. According to Polish writer Igor Witkowski, who claimed to have access to stolen transcripts of an SS interrogation, "The Nazis built a massive rig to hold up a bell-shaped craft. This craft was able to launch itself off the ground using the power of 'red mercury' and achieve propulsion without an engine. As the war was coming to an end, all of the scientists involved were supposedly killed and the Bell itself was taken away by the US."[194] The Bell was reported to have been made from an especially heavy metal, had some kind of Nazi symbol on the front of it, and was chained to the ground. It measured five meters high by three meters in diameter, held two rotating cylinders containing a substance similar to mercury called Xerum 525, and had an exterior lined with a ceramic material. Many of the scientists who worked on the Bell while it was energized were said to have died of cancer. Although the Bell itself was rumored to have been taken away by the US, the original plans were lost when Der Riese was destroyed in 1945. As theorized by author Henry Stevens, another feature of the Bell was "an ability to see through time." Others have speculated that the Bell itself was a time machine, giving the person inside the capability to move into the past. On December 9, 1965, an unknown flying object, acorn-shaped or bell-shaped, crashed in the vicinity of the US town of Kecksburg, Pennsylvania. This event was known in the study of Ufology as the case of Kecksburg. The artifact had strange inscriptions, like the Nazi bell, and was said to have been quickly recovered by military forces. Although one of the most compelling Nazi wonder weapon (wunderwaffen) stories ever told, most believe that the Die Glocke is sheer fantasy and Witkowski's evidence is complete conjecture.

Hitler was engineering a new religion and a master race. He once told General Rommel, "Your God is for the weak ones and my God is for the strong ones."[195] Hitler convinced the German people that they were once a proud race of Aryan giants until the gene pool was diluted by interbreeding with the Jews. The Jews were animals and the sworn enemy of the Third Reich. "Under the sway of symbols, engulfed in ardent ritual, Nazism enshrined itself as more than political doctrine. The reign of the swastika was rooted in occultism, a belief in magical forces that could unlock the secrets of the universe."[196] Deputy Führer and second in charge, Rudolf Hess employed the services of astrologers and was known to coordinate many of his actions with favorable astrological alignments. Carefully chosen by Hitler, Heinrich Himmler was appointed as the leader of the Saal-Schutz (SS). "Consumed by Arian myth, Himmler sought SS officers whose pure Aryan descent dated back at least 175 years."[197] Swearing personal allegiance to Hitler, "the SS was as notorious for its occult orientation and practices as it was feared for the torture and murder it committed."[198] Beneath the main hall of the castle, where the SS indoctrinations took place, "was a crypt that Himmler envisioned would one day contain twelve pedestals to support urns filled with the ashes of SS heroes destined for worship."[199] Heinrich Himmler "unhesitatingly employed his deviant imagination in service to the occult."[200] It is alleged that a deposition of the Nuremberg trial described secret rituals in which select members of the SS were beheaded and their severed heads used in an attempt to communicate with the spirits of dead. Publishing lists of suitable cemeteries for breeding, it is no secret that Himmler believed, "children conceived in Nordic cemeteries inherited the spirits of the heroes buried there."[201] When it was all said and done, nearly six million Jews were sacrificed as the final solution in preparation for the new world order and master race of blond-haired, blue-eyed Aryan superhumans that would be conceived by the pure Aryan SS and Hitler Youth.

Again and again, our written and archeological records demonstrate that our pride and elevated self-worth have corrupted our doings and caused us to foolishly justify evil actions over good works. Whether profiting from the disadvantaged, sacrificing children to Baal, performing live heart extractions, or committing genocide, the cost of elevating those who gave us the knowledge to achieve power to the status of gods has always been expensive, and we have always paid it. The legends and folklores of many tell us that in our pursuit for power, we have worshiped giants and gods who have fallen from the heavens. We have replaced the one true God with multiple gods and worshipped everyone, except God. Championed by the fallen angels, this is the total and complete corruption of man. "There were giants in the earth in those days; and also, after that, when the sons of God came in unto the daughters of men, and they bare children to them, the same became mighty men which were of old, men of renown. And God saw that the wickedness of man was great in the earth, and that every imagination of the thoughts of his heart was only evil continually. And it repented the Lord that he had made man on the earth, and it grieved him at his heart" (Genesis 6:4-6 KJV). I am comforted to know that I have no more sacrifices to make and the knowledge my Savior brings is bought and paid for. "We are sanctified through the offering of the body of Jesus Christ once for all" (Hebrews 10:10 KJV).

At the time of this writing, many businesses remain closed and my wife and I continue under a government-imposed quarantine to combat the spread of the coronavirus (COVID-19). Motivated by greed, rumors abound that deep state globalists have manufactured the largest political hoax and coordinated mass-media disinformation campaign in history. Yesterday, I watched a YouTube video in which Bill Gates vowed that countries not significantly impacted by COVID-19 would eventually come around after the second wave. Today, the video has been taken down for apparently violating YouTube content policy. Seeking increased government oversight and control, globalists employ fear in the hopes that we will embrace compliance. Normal influenza deaths are recorded as COVID-19 and the sick and elderly are housed together to inflate the number of recorded pandemic deaths. Under the guise of safety, even going to church is banned. It should be no surprise to anyone that as we slept, COVID-19 trackers were added to our smartphones without our consent. I pray that humility will conquer the pride and self-worth of the few. Follow Christ and he will turn to meet you on your path.

— 10 —

SPACE FORCE:
CHARIOTS OF THE FALLEN

Several very significant and related events have quietly taken place since December of 2017 with very little fanfare or media coverage. Remaining relatively unnoticed, these events are verified with a quick search of the internet and little effort. First, in December of 2017, news broke of a secret US government funded program known as the Advanced Aerospace Threat Identification Program (AATIP) when the former Director, Lou Elizondo left the Pentagon due a disagreement in policy. Next, in April of 2018, the US military updated and formalized a process for pilots to report UFO sightings without threat of a psychological evaluation or loss of their clearance and pilot status. On June 18, 2018, President Donald Trump announced that he had directed the Pentagon to create a Space Force as a new, sixth military branch to oversee missions and operations in the domain of space. Ten months later, on April 29, 2019, Senator Mark Warner, the vice chairman of the Senate Intelligence Committee, and two other US senators received a US Navy-delivered Pentagon briefing on reported UFO sightings by US Navy pilots who witnessed objects flying at hypersonic speed. Finally, on April 27, 2020, the Pentagon authenticated, declassified, and released three UFO videos taken by US Navy fighter pilots on CVN-71, the USS Theodore Roosevelt in 2015 and CVAN-68, the USS Nimitz in 2004.

The USS Theodore Roosevelt, fighter pilot instrument-captured UFOs were designated the GIMBAL and GOFAST videos. Initially dubbed the FLIR video, the video taken from the cockpit of the USS Nimitz F/A-18F Super Hornet was later nicknamed the TIC-TAC video. Although first published by *The New York Times* and Tom DeLong's UFO research organization, To the Stars Academy, in 2017 and 2018, the Pentagon authentication, declassification, and release of these videos would not have been possible if it were not for the work of Lou Elizondo. Before leaving the Pentagon and while still the Director of AATIP, Lou initiated the paperwork to declassify these videos and several others. The GIMBAL, GOFAST, and TIC-TAC videos were no doubt declassified first because they were already in the public domain.

Prior to its authentication, analysis of the GIMBAL video was performed by Physicist and Aerospace Engineer, Travis Taylor and Hollywood Visual Effects Supervisor, Sam Edwards on March 9, 2019. The GIMBAL video was filmed in what is called "Black-Hot" Mode, which means that the hotter an object is, the darker it will appear in the video. The craft was not surprisingly black; however, unlike what would be expected, the craft was sustained in a white bubble. This was unusual in that the generated heat from the craft would typically be expected to heat up the atmosphere around it and would cause it to appear with blurry edges, much like looking at bright light. The cold region around the craft was indicative of a non-conventional and theoretical propulsion system known as an Alcubierre Warp Drive. Scientists believe that an Alcubierre Warp Drive would form a bubble around the craft as space is theoretically contracted in front of the craft and expanded behind the craft through initiation of an artificial gravitational field. The Alcubierre Warp Bubble would be so much cooler than the atmosphere around it that it would be visible in infrared, as it was. The concept of the Alcubierre Warp Drive was first introduced to the public by former Los Alamos National Laboratory scientist and renowned Area 51 whistleblower Bob Lazar in 1989.

Scrambling for a story when a scheduled interview was canceled in May of 1989, KLAS-TV Channel 8 Eyewitness News Chief Investigative Reporter George Knapp arranged through a contact for a last-minute interview with a man claiming to have been reverse engineering UFOs at a top-secret military base in the desert. In his first interview, Bob Lazar's face was obscured and his name unreported. He sat in the shadows and claimed that the US government had in its possession nine UFOs, all differing models. Some were fully operational and some appeared to have been shot down. Bob alleged that he had been working at a facility designated as S-4, fifteen miles south of Groom Lake on a top-secret military base known as Area 51. S-4 was comprised of nine ground-level aircraft hangers that had been carved out of the foot of the Papoose Mountains. Bob said that his life was in danger, he had been threatened with charges of espionage, and his was a story that needed to be told. I cannot say one way or another whether the claims of Bob Lazar are true, but I can present what I believe to be verifiable facts and let the reader make his or her own determination.

A few months after his initial interview with George Knapp, while attempting to acquire a new ID and a copy of his birth certificate, Lazar found that much of the record of his existence was being expunged and he reached out to George Knapp directly. This time, Bob was forthcoming and brought with him his previous tax forms to show who he was and that he had been working for and paid by US Naval Intelligence. He brought with him a photo ID and a phonebook from Los Alamos National Laboratory to show that he had been listed as an employee. Most significantly, Bob produced witnesses to two separate Groom Lake saucer test flights. He said that he knew the current schedule for flights of the craft that he had been working on at S-4. Witnesses included decorated pilot and former candidate for Nevada State Senator Captain John Lear, Las Vegas Real Estate Appraiser and friend Gene Huff, and his ex-wife, Tracy. On three separate occasions, Lazar took the group in the middle of the night to a spot on a secluded dirt road, adjacent to Area 51, where he pointed to a spot over the mountains at a preordained time and a UFO appeared on cue to demonstrate what seemed like impossible maneuvers. One of the test flights was captured and provided on VHS tape. The tape was filmed at a distance, in the dark with no reference points, and verified only an elliptical-shaped light that varied in intensity. Lazar's group of friends were getting careless and were caught while waiting to observe a third UFO test flight. Everyone was disbanded and Bob was whisked off to be debriefed and threatened, before being released. Arranged by George Knapp and others, Bob Lazar passed four separate polygraph tests with "no indication of deception," and underwent hypnosis in August of 1989 where he revealed additional missing details of his claims. The provided evidence doesn't amount to much; but when combined with the knowledge that some of Bob Lazar's claims have since been proven plausible, it increases the believability.

Through the course of several interviews with George Knapp and (later) others, Bob Lazar made some pretty spectacular claims. My favorite was his claim that captured extraterrestrial crafts were propelled by Element 115, something that didn't then exist in a periodic table. According to Lazar, ". . . bombarding Element 115 with protons leads to it creating Element 116 (Livermorium) which immediately decays and produces antimatter. The antimatter collides with normal particles creating a massive energy burst, which can be used for propulsion." Lazar goes on to say, "Given recent studies showing that suns regularly undergo micro-nova or 'solar flash' events, we have another process by which a star can produce and eject heavy elements, which are subsequently mined by advanced extraterrestrial civilizations in a cyclic manner." Michael Salla, PhD, is in agreement with Lazar when he speculates, "If element 115 is naturally formed in the core of some massive stars and element 115 is used in the propulsion system of extraterrestrial races, then it would be fair to assume that some extraterrestrials may have discovered how to mine stars of their heavy elements to use as a propulsion fuel." Dr. Stella goes on to say, "It's quite likely Element 115 could also be the famed exotic matter that is needed to create traversable wormholes that physicists such as Drs Kip Thorne and Carl Sagan have speculated."[202]

Bob also claimed that the US government had five hundred pounds of Element 115 in their possession that had been given to them in the form of discs by extraterrestrials at S-4. Scientists at S-4 had apparently sent the discs to Los Alamos National Laboratory to be milled into wedges for use in an Antimatter Reactor. The Los Alamos personnel were told that the wedges were being milled for a new form of armor. They simply followed orders, milled the discs as specified, and sent the finished products back to Groom Lake. The machining process produced a tremendous amount of waste and it was during this process that some of the Element 115 was said to have turned up missing. Although asked many times if he had a sample of heavy Element 115, Bob never answered the question. He does, however, seem to get into trouble whenever he discusses it. On July 19, 2017, documentary filmmaker, Jeremy Corbell asked Lazar if he had taken any Element 115 home with him. The next day, the FBI turned the offices of Bob Lazar and the company that he founded, United Nuclear, upside down. To be fair, the FBI did produce a search warrant that was drawn up two days earlier and claimed to be searching for the sales records of a polonium isotope used to kill someone. The FBI first raided United Nuclear in 2003 on similar grounds when searching for the sales records of the same polonium isotope, then used to kill a Russian spy.

Initially introduced by Bob Lazar in May of 1989, Element 115 was synthesized for the first time in May of 2003, fourteen years after the whistleblower tapes, by a team of Russian and American scientists at the Joint Institute for Nuclear Research (JINR) in Dubna, Russia. The new element, Moscovium is described as a synthetic chemical element with the symbol MC and an atomic number 115. "Moscovium is an extremely radioactive element: its most stable known isotope, moscovium-290, has a half-life of only 0.65 seconds."[203] In December 2015, it was recognized as one of four new elements by the Joint Working Group of International Scientific Organizations IUPAC/IUPAP. On November 28, 2016, it was officially named in honor of the Moscow region in which JINR is located. Over a dozen years after Bob Lazar's fantastical claims of Element 115 that mainstream media almost universally discarded as the rantings of a lunatic, science has now shown that the development of a stable Element 115 may be entirely possible. Element 116, antimatter, and unlimited energy may be just around the corner.

Adding credibility to Lazar's claim of a stable Element 115 are the views and opinions of physicists like Michio Kaku, PhD, who was recently quoted as saying, "We physicists think that we can make use of it to create nuclear energy on a much more efficient scale than Plutonium and variations of it could be stable and might eventually provide fuel for a starship."[204] Adding to the believability of Lazar's claim that the US government housed nine UFOs at S-4 in 1989, in 2007, the FBI declassified a 03/22/1950 memo in which J. Edgar Hoover was debriefed on three recovered flying saucers. The J. Edgar Hoover memo was quietly declassified a full sixty years after the famed 1947 weather balloon/flying saucer debacle that took place in Roswell, New Mexico. Lastly, the possibility of extraterrestrial civilizations mastering the technology to produce a viable Alcubierre Warp Drive was demonstrated in the 2019 analysis of the GIMBAL video. Whether or not you believe Bob Lazar is up to you. In the end, it makes no difference if Bob Lazar is telling the truth or not; he is just one book in a library of documentation that directs the curious to the knowledge and acceptance of star-traveling extraterrestrials.

In April of 2013, Citizen Hearings on UFO Disclosure were held with former members of Congress: California Congresswoman, Lynn Woolsey (Chair); Maryland Congressman, Roscoe G. Bartlett (Co-Chair); Oregon Congresswoman, Darlene Hooley; Michigan Congresswoman, Carolyn Kilpatrick; Utah Congressman, Merrill Cook; Joseph Buchman PhD (Moderator); and former United States Senator from Alaska, Mike Gravel. The purpose of the meeting was stated in part as, "We would like to make the public more aware and we would like to have a hearing that could lead possibly to legislation or policy making."[205]

The opening statement was by the Honorable Paul Hellyer, former Minister of Defense of Canada, "Over many decades of service to the Canadian people, I have come to understand and appreciate the importance of open, transparent government, and the power of truth—as antidote to the many afflictions that the body politic is heir to. The true currency of the twenty-first century . . . will be trust. Without that commodity, progress and right action are undermined and delayed. There is only one way to regain trust; find and tell the truth. . . . And like my friend, Edgar Mitchell, I say without equivocation, we are not alone in the cosmos. We have neighbors. We should try to get to understand them and to cooperate with them." A few days later, Hellyer went on to clarify that he had been privy to a study undertaken for a UFO incident and read the resulting summary report which concluded that, "at least four species have been visiting earth for thousands of years." Hellyer stated, ". . . this is my own view at this stage, as well. . . . We were referring to them as 'they' until this morning when Linda Moulton Howe, I think she was the first one, actually named three different species. . . . I name five different species here. I am aware of more now. As a matter of fact, I saw a document just a few days ago that mentioned twenty." Hellyer closed with a quote from the late Dr. John Mack, an American secular Jewish psychiatrist who became a world leader in interviewing abductees or "experiencers" as he called them. "Although the aliens are not themselves gods and their behavior is sometimes anything but godlike, abductees consistently report that the beings seem closer to the godhead than we are; acting as messengers, guardian spirits, or angels, intermediaries between us and the divine source."[206] This makes my hair stand up. I have one intermediary to God and it is my Lord, Jesus Christ.

Substantiated by taped phone conversations and interviews with Colonel Walter Figel (see also, Robert Hastings interview of Col. Walter Figel, October 20, 2008), retired USAF Captain Robert Salas, previous Deputy Missile Combat Crew Commander at Malmstrom Airforce Base in Montana, recalled an event that occurred when he was a First Lieutenant, assigned duties as a missile launch officer for the Minuteman-1 intercontinental ballistic missile in March of 1967. Together, Captain Robert Salas and Colonel Walter Figel detail two separate instances in which all the missiles on a United States Military facility were somehow remotely disabled concurrently with reports of UFOs being spotted at or above the base (March 16 and 24, 1967). The flying saucers were only present for a short period of time and left immediately after all missile silos had been disabled. Captain Salas explained that systems were shut down despite the fact that the Sensitive Information Network (SIN) cables that carried the signals to the missile systems were triply shielded from electro-magnetic interference, and despite the use of redundant logic override protection. "The preliminary investigation isolated the failure to the logic coupler at each missile. The logic coupler is associated with the missile guidance system. . . . In the opinion of the team, . . . externally generated signals caused the generation of these two channels and shut down the launch facilities. The possibility of this is very remote due to the fact that all ten couplers would have to fail . . . within a few seconds of each other. . . . This statement confirms that signals were sent to each individual missile separately, in order to disable them. From my knowledge of the operating system at the time, neither I, nor the investigating team could define the method or means by which these signals were sent to disable the missiles, each in the same manner." Retired ASAF Captain Bruce Fenstermacher recalled a later UFO encounter that occurred in 1976 at Francis E. Warren Air Force Base in Wyoming. Captain Fenstermacher was told that as the SAT team approached, ". . . they saw a bright pulsating light with a beam of light extending down to the launch facility." The missiles were at no time disabled or shut down by the visitors during the 1976 encounter in Wyoming.

Scientific UFO studies and documentation of incidents were added to the record by Stanton Friedman, a nuclear physicist who previously worked on fission/fusion rockets and compact nuclear power plants for space applications. He stated that, "There are at least five large scale scientific studies. . . . These include Project Blue Book—Special Report Number 14, the largest study ever done for the United States Air Force, covering more than 3200 cases, with over 200 charts, tables, graphs and maps. It is a quality evaluation, cross-comparisons between unknowns and knowns. . . . The unknowns comprise 21-½ % of the cases, completely separate from the 9.3% listed as insufficient information. . . . It is a very valuable source of information. . . . Another primary source of valuable data . . . are the Congressional hearings of July 29th, 1968, which included testimony from twelve scientists. The most important paper was by Dr. James E. McDonald, Professor of Physics at the University of Arizona. He had talked to five hundred witnesses, but he presented forty-one outstanding cases, including multiple witness radar visual sightings, sightings by pilots, by astronomers, by meteorologists. He noted physical trace cases; of which by now, more than five thousand have been collected . . . from ninety-five countries. . . . The same thing is happening all over the world. A saucer is seen on the ground; it leaves; they find physical changes. . . . One sixth of those cases involved reports of small beings associated with the craft while it was on the ground. Friedman introduced us to a report called, *The UFO Evidence* which documents hundreds of UFOs that remain unidentified and *The COMETA Report* from France which goes into numerous, excellent, officially involved cases."[207]

For five days, the speakers answered questions, introduced evidence, and provided eyewitness accounts of star-traveling extraterrestrial crafts that demonstrated maneuvering capabilities well beyond our current understanding. We learned that no military encounters were evaluated in Special Report Number 14. Project Blue Book, Special Report Number 14 was one of many Project Blue Books, having varying levels of classification, and Special Report Number 14 is the only declassified Blue Book. Combined with the July 1947 report of a crashed UFO in Roswell, New Mexico, the encounter of pilot Kenneth Arnold is generally accepted as the initiating event that triggered the creation of Project Blue Book. "In June 1947, while flying his small plane, businessman and civilian pilot, Kenneth Arnold, reported seeing nine objects moving at high speeds through the skies over Washington's Mount Rainier. Widely publicized reports of Arnold's experience, followed by an increasing number of reported UFO sightings, led the US Air Force to begin an investigation into the sightings, called Operation Sign in 1948. The initial investigation resulted in the formation of Project Blue Book in 1952. That project became the longest running of the US government's official inquiries

into UFO sightings. . . . In 1966, the Air Force had requested the formation of another committee to look into the details of 59 UFO sightings
investigated by Project Blue Book. The committee, headed by Dr. Edward
Condon and based at the University of Colorado, released its Scientific
Study of Unidentified Flying Objects—better known as the Condon
Report—in 1968. According to the Condon Report, the sightings they
examined showed no evidence of any unusual activity, and recommended
that the Air Force stop investigations into UFO-related incidents. In
1969, in response to the Condon Report as well as a declining number
of UFO sightings, Project Blue Book was officially brought to an end."[208]

Perhaps motivated by the end of Project Blue Book in 1969, or the
inaccessibility to classified Project Blue Book investigations of military
encounters with extraterrestrial crafts, while still the majority whip,
Nevada State Senator, Harry Reid allocated $22 million of a massive
defense budget to the study of military sightings of UFOs in 2007. Ten
years later, when Lou Elizondo left the Pentagon, it was confirmed that
the allocated money was used to fund the Advanced Aerospace Threat
Identification Program (AATIP). After the AATIP story broke, Senator Reid told KNPR, ". . . money was spent developing page after page
of information. There's been a lot of activity since that."[209] Three years
later, after the Pentagon declassified and authenticated the three AATIP
captured videos from the USS Theodore Roosevelt and the USS Nimitz,
Senator Reid tweeted, "I'm glad the Pentagon is finally releasing this footage, but it only scratches the surface of research and materials available.
The US needs to take a serious, scientific look at this and any potential national security implications. The American people deserve to be
informed."[210]

Despite the GIMBAL video showing a craft that was shaped much
like a conventional flying saucer and the TIC-TAC video showing a craft
shaped like a tic-tac, both videos are (at least partially) recorded in "Black
Hot" Mode and both demonstrate unworldly crafts of unknown origin
that are driven by an unknown propulsion system which generates no
heat. Chad Underwood, the Nimitz Super Hornet pilot who recorded

the 2004 TIC-TAC video spoke publicly in 2019. The story began when radar operator Kevin Day reported seeing odd and slow-moving objects flying in groups of five to ten, off of San Clemente Island, west of the San Diego coast. The clusters were at an elevation of 28,000 feet and moving at 120 knots, or about 138 miles per hour. In a military report made public by KLAS-TV in Las Vegas, Day would later observe that the objects "exhibited ballistic-missile characteristics." Causing no sonic boom, the crafts zoomed from 60,000 feet to 50 feet above the Pacific Ocean. "Eventually, David Fravor, Commanding Officer of the Black Aces, made visual confirmation of one of the objects midair during a flight-training exercise. An hour later, Underwood made his infrared recording on a second flight. . . . The footage appears to depict what Fravor had identified as a 40-foot-long, white, oblong shape (hence 'Tic-Tac'), hovering somewhere between 15,000 and 24,000 feet in midair and exhibiting no notable exhaust from conventional propulsion sources, even as it makes a surprising dart leftward in the video's final moments."[211] The GOFAST video was appropriately named and speaks for itself.

At this point, three facts ought to lift your eyebrows; the Pentagon has just admitted that there are extraterrestrial crafts having technology beyond that currently understood by mankind, US Navy fighter pilots are now encouraged to report UFO sightings, and the president of the United States has just established a Space Force to oversee missions and operations in the domain of space. It appears that perhaps continued pressure on the US government by civilian UFO organizations, along with the occasional assist from Nevada State Senator, Harry Reid, have caused the US government to finally crack open the door to a topic beyond full understanding. Chances are good that the door will open further over time and that the deeper we look into the dark, the scarier the possibilities will become. Still in the fight, the Advanced Aerospace Threat Identification Program (AATIP) is still active, many additional videos of extraterrestrial crafts have been declassified (but not yet released), civilian UFO investigative organizations continue to investigate new sightings, and driving forces like Lou Elizondo, Tom DeLong, and Senator Harry

Reid are still out there. Trump declared, "When it comes to defending America, it is not enough to merely have an American presence in space. We must have American dominance in space." Regardless of what is shared with the public, of one thing we can be sure: whatever we are told will not be the full story, and the information we are provided will always be at least twenty years old. I base this conclusion on previously holding a Final Top-Secret clearance, UFO debriefing with J. Edgar Hoover that remained hidden for fifty-seven years, and the Manhattan Project. When Trump says, ". . . establish a presence in space," I hear, "We now have a manned military facility on the dark side of the moon."

When President Trump announced that he had directed the Pentagon to create a Space Force, I was reminded of Ronald Reagan's September 16, 1983, address to the United Nations where he said, "I occasionally think how quickly our differences, worldwide, would vanish if we were facing an alien threat from outside this world." What at first may have appeared to be nothing more than the President of the United States telling the nations of the world to work out their differences, now seems more significant. Assuming that just a small fraction of the warehouses of UFO information, accounts, and evidence hold any merit, the only logical conclusion is that other intelligent life must exist elsewhere in the cosmos. If there are cognitive, acting beings living in the vast regions of space, surly they've heard of us by now. After all, this is a planet that makes a lot of racket. Planet Earth has been broadcasting radio signals unintentionally into space since 1910 and nations have been test-firing atomic bombs since 1945.

We have called the extraterrestrials and provided them with our GPS coordinates. Two of our unmistakable calling cards are Dr. Carl Sagan's golden phonograph records, attached to the Voyager spacecraft of 1977, and the Arecibo radio telescope message of 1974. A golden phonograph record was attached to both the Voyager 1 and the Voyager 2 spacecraft. The purpose was to send a message to the extraterrestrials who might find the spacecraft as they journeyed through interstellar space. Among other things, each record provided greetings to the universe in fifty-five languages. The Arecibo radio telescope message transmitted numbers one through ten, the atomic numbers of the elements that make up DNA, formulas in the nucleotides of DNA, the number of nucleotides in DNA, a graphic of the double helix structure, a graphic representation of man, a graphic of our solar system, and a graphic of the Arecibo radio telescope. The Chilbolton Crop Circle, otherwise known as the Arecibo Response, was a mysterious crop circle that appeared in the farmland adjacent to the Chilbolton radio telescope in 2001. Many believe that the design was perhaps in response to the famous Arecibo radio telescope message, sent from Puerto Rico to the cosmos in 1974. The format and content of the Arecibo Response appear strikingly similar to the message of peace that was sent into space on the Voyager spacecraft in 1977. Interpretations of the 2001 Chilbolton Crop Circle are many and varied. In 2002, another interesting crop circle appeared in the same field depicting an extraterrestrial being holding a disc embedded with binary code. The decoded disc was interpreted to read "Beware of the bearers of false gifts and their broken promises. Much pain, but still time. There is good out there. We oppose deception. Conduit closing (Bell Sound)."

Perhaps things are as they seem and other intelligent life does exist elsewhere in the cosmos. Other than the testimonies of those who claim to be aware of communications between star-travelling extraterrestrials and mankind, is there any hard evidence to substantiate the many claims that extraterrestrials have been visiting mankind for thousands of years? Here is where things get a bit sketchy. As it turns out, much of the evidence supporting thousands of years of occupation is disputed by experts with sometimes credible arguments. Prime examples are the tomb of King Pakal in Palenque, Mexico, the Egyptian Helicopter Hieroglyph, and the Golden Flyer. What was once interpreted by proponents of ancient aliens to be an engraving of King Pakal piloting a spaceship to the stars on his funeral slab now seems far less likely. Experts in Maya epigraphy and iconography, Linda Schele and Ian Graham believe that what is often mistaken for a rocket engine below King Pakal is actually the Mayan god of death, Ah Puch who also appears in sacrificial altars at

Copán and Chichén Itzá. What Erich von Däniken believed was the tip of the spaceship that King Pakal was piloting was in fact, a representation of the Wacah Chan or World Tree that lives in all three of the Mayan Great Worlds. The so-called rocket flames are apparently the beard of a dragon who holds open his mouth to encapsulate King Pakal between his jaws that form the outer shell of the spacecraft. While suspended in the Central-World, King Pakal gazes at the Upper-World where the gods live and the dragon pulls King Pakal to the Under-World, where everyone goes after death. Both arguments are pretty convincing.

The Helicopter Hieroglyph refers to a 3000-year-old Egyptian hiero-glyph in the Temple of Seti I at Abydos. At some point, the initial glyph was plastered over and re-carved. After centuries of time, the plaster came off, revealing what we see today. Egyptologists tell us that what we see are two sets of hieroglyphs superimposed. That is why some of the shapes on this panel are unlike any others in Egypt. When I look at the panel, I see what everyone else sees; a George Jetson looking spacecraft, a standard flying saucer, a blimp or a cigar-shaped craft, a helicopter, a fish, and an insect. The problem is that when I superimpose the previous hieroglyph over the current hieroglyph, I also see what the experts are talking about.

The Golden Flyer is one of many trinkets that were unearthed with golden fish and insect figurines in the jungles of Columbia. Alien theo-rists have promoted this and other trinkets as being eerily similar to mod-ern fighter jets. To test the aerodynamic properties of the Golden Flyer design, they made a near-scale model, attached a propeller, and remotely flew the craft. However, a comparison of the finished model to the origi-nal shows that the strange frills on the cutting edge of the wings were removed and the wings were re-shaped to make them more aerodynami-cally tapered, instead of flat, as they actually were. Whether or not the original design would fly is still in question. Close examination shows that the nose of the Golden Flyer is actually a face with eyes and a mouth.

Like fool's gold, there is a ton of disinformation to distort our per-ception of the real treasures as we stumble across them. Not so easily ignored are the ancient Sanskrit texts of India. In addition to the many folklores and legends of a world that tells us of gods coming from the stars, the ancient Sanskrit texts of India contain descriptions of wonderous aeronautical crafts, said to have flown the skies many thousands of years before modern flight. While some find the ancient Sanskrit texts to be more myth than fact, there is still a large portion of India that believes them to be an accurate historical record. The Sanskrit texts tell us of ancient flying machines known as Vimana. The Ramayana is one of the two epic Indian poems. It is the first to mention the flying Vimana in existing Hindu texts. "The Pushpaka Vimana that resembles the Sun and belongs to my brother was brought by the powerful Ravana; that aerial and excellent Vimana going everywhere at will . . . that chariot resembling a bright cloud in the sky . . . and the king [Rama] got in, and the excellent chariot at the command of the Raghira, rose up into the higher atmosphere."[212]

The other epic poem, the Mahabharata (800 to 900 BC) documents seeing thousands of flying Vimana and describes the cloaking ability and advanced weaponry of one in particular. "The Vimana had all necessary equipment. It could not be conquered by gods or demons. And it radiated light and reverberated with a deep rumbling sound. Its beauty captivated the minds of all who beheld it. Visvakarma, the lord of its design and construction, had created it by the power of his austerities, and its outline, like that of the sun, could not be easily delineated. . . . And he also gave [unto Arjuna] a car furnished with celestial weapons whose banner bore a large ape . . . And its splendor, like that of the sun, was so great that no one could gaze at it. It was the very car riding upon which the lord Soma had vanquished the Danavas. Resplendent with beauty, it looked like an evening cloud reflecting the effulgence of the setting sun. . . . Bhima flew along in his car, resplendent as the sun and loud as thunder. . . . The flying chariot shone like a flame in the night sky of summer . . . it swept by like a comet. . . . It was as if two suns were shining. Then the chariot rose up and all the heavens brightened. . . . And on this sun-like, divine, wonderful chariot the wise disciple of Kuru flew joyously upward. When becoming invisible to the mortals who walk the earth, he saw wonderous airborne chariots by the thousands."[213] In Vedic literature, ". . . one finds the predecessors of the flying Vimanas of the Sanskrit epics. Vimana were the flying chariots employed by various gods. The Vedas are considered the earliest literary record of Indo-Aryan civilization and the most sacred books of India."[214] Occurring between 1500 and 500 BC, the Vedic Age was responsible for developing many of the founding principles of Indian civilization, instituting the caste system, and establishing early Hinduism.

In the Controller of the Battlefield, the Samarangana Sutradhara, it is written, "Strong and durable must the body of the Vimana be made, like a great flying bird of light material. Inside one must put the mercury engine with its iron heating apparatus underneath. By means of the power latent in the mercury which sets the driving whirlwind in motion, a man sitting inside may travel a great distance in the sky. The movements of the Vimana are such that it can vertically ascend, vertically descend, move slanting forwards and backwards. With the help of the machines human beings can fly in the air and heavenly beings can come down to earth. . . . In such a manner the High-Souled ones flew, while the lower classes walked. All those friends succeeded in their much-deserved acquisition of a Yantra, by means of which human beings can fly in the air, and non-earthling, Celestial Beings can move down to mortals when visiting the Earth." Often omitted from English translations of the Samarangana Sutradhara, "At the critical time the beam of fire must be released, which will make the action possible. The time-beam expands, accompanied by the thunder of the expanding medium. This resultant expansion performs work like an elephant in an endless cycle."[215] Many forms of propulsion are discussed for use in different Vimana. So detailed are the descriptions of the Vimana that in 1923, under the instruction of Pandit Subbaraya Sastry of Anckal, Bandalore, T.K. Ellappa was commissioned to fabricate construction drawings of the Rukma Vimana, the Tripura Vimana, the Shakura Vimana, and the Sundra Vimana. These drawings are easily retrievable on the internet today. Designed by the author of *Reverse Engineering Vedic Vimanas*, Aircraft Design Engineer, Kavya Vaddadi created multiple 3D-printed Vimana in 2017. Kavya recreated the

2500-year-old Marut Sakha as a digital 3D model and shared it with Aerospace Engineer Travis Taylor PhD, so that he could 3D print it and test its aerodynamic properties in the University of California at Irvine's wind tunnel. In April of 2017, Travis categorized the shape of the model as "... a viable aerodynamic structure."[216]

Obviously open to interpretation, there are dozens of petroglyphs and cave paintings claiming to depict ancient aliens, astronauts, and spacecraft. Despite these illustrations being scattered across the entire planet, many depictions appear similar. This has caused many to speculate that mankind must have previously seen these beings. Of particular interest is the fact that many of the ancient drawings are nearly identical to more recent eyewitness accounts. Believed by many to predate both Stonehenge and the Pyramids of Giza, the Petroglyphs at Karahunj, Armenia's Stonehenge, include strange beings with elongated heads and almond-shaped eyes, identical to modern-day Grey Aliens. Intertwined with butterfly-shaped flying things, the Picasso-looking Wandjina cave paintings depict the heads of numerous big-eyed, otherworldly-looking creatures; known locally as the Wandjinas. Believed by some to be 100,000 years old, this cave art was discovered in Kimberly, Australia, in 1838. Like the legends of many ancient cultures around the globe, the Wandjinas are said to come from the sky, bringing civilization and prosperity. Demonstrating that the Sahara was teeming with life 10,000 to 15,000 years ago, cave art located at Tassili n'Ajjer National Park in southeastern Algeria depicts giraffes, ostriches, elephants, oxen, alligators, and even hippos. Also found are mysterious creatures with helmets, gloves, and strange suits, which according to many, resemble modern-day astronauts. My favorite prehistoric cave art comes from a remote region of Algeria, in the Tassili Mountains, on the edge of the Sahara Desert. It dates back to around 6000 BC and has been dubbed the Martian. The drawings are very well done and depict what can only be characterized as creatures in pressure suits, having helmets similar to those used for deep-water diving, and standing with several renderings of what can easily be interpreted as flying saucers.

There is a rock carving known as the spaceman in northern Italy, on the side of a mountain overlooking the city of Val Camonica. Dating to a thousand years before Christ, the carving depicts two human-like figures, each having a circle carved out around their head and appearing to wear a modern space helmet that emits rays of light. A hike away on the same mountain, there is a single spaceman carving on a large flat rock, among many other carvings. Each holding a similar, but unknown device in their hand, the spacemen seem to be dancing. Located in the same alpine valley is the city of Turin. Best known for the Turin Shroud, ". . . locals are aware of another legacy that may be unfamiliar to those visiting the city as tourists. In fact, Turin is a city known for being mysterious and has been associated with magic since its beginnings—both white magic, and black. According to legend, the city was founded by the son of the goddess Isis, Phaeton. He established the city in order to honor the cult of Apis, which had the features of a bull and this is the animal that was to become the very symbol of Turin."[217] Phaeton is said to have come to earth in a fiery chariot, bringing with him the skills of metallurgy and many other gifts. Perhaps somehow related, but perhaps not, Val Camonica is 165 miles from Monte Musinè, a modern UFO hot spot in the Susa Valley.

Going back just five hundred years, the first documented and indisputable mass UFO sighting occurred at dawn, in Nuremberg, Germany. Citizens awoke on April 14, 1561, to an upheaval in the sky that was unlike anything ever witnessed. Leaving their homes to determine the source of the commotion, witnesses described what they saw as a celestial battle. There were hundreds of strange shaped objects occupying the skies over Nuremberg. Thousands of witnesses claimed to have seen the flying shapes hurling projectiles at one another. As shown in an illustration made from a Hans Glasser woodcut of the event, the projectiles occasionally came crashing down to earth. The illustration is held in the Zurich Central Library, but available on the internet and documented through numerous television broadcasts. Just five years later, a similar event occurred in the skies over Basel, Switzerland. The 1566 event is captured in a broadsheet picture by Samuel Coccius that is also held in the Wickiana Collection at the Zurich Central Library, but available on the internet. The broadsheet picture lacks the diversity of flying crafts depicted in the Nuremberg illustration. It depicts a half-dozen people standing in the streets of Basel and pointing upward, toward black and sometimes fiery globes cluttering the skies.

Indicating that UFOs were perhaps being sighted in medieval times, a few hundred years before the Nuremberg and Basel sightings, fiery chariots and hovering discs began showing up in Renaissance Era art. As demonstrated in the works of Michelangelo and Leonardo Da Vinci, secrets were sometimes hidden in works of art. Concepts contradicting church doctrine were not advertised in medieval times (see Giordano Bruno—chapter 2). Created by an unknown Tuscan School painter in 1350, *The Crucifixion* hangs above the altar at the Visoki Decani Monastery in Kosovo, Yugoslavia. Flying left to right, a futuristic spacecraft flies on both sides of the crucified Christ, one chasing the other. The spacecraft have transparent cockpits and clearly show that each is driven by a human-looking pilot. Each craft has a different, but similar design and each pilot is dressed in distinctly different clothing. A seventeenth-century fresco depicting the crucifixion of Christ, located in the Svetishoveli Cathedral in Mtskheta, Georgia, also depicts two very out-of-place looking UFOs, one on each side of the crucified Christ.

Painted by Masolino da Panicale for the church of Santa Maria Maggiore, the *Miracle of the Snow* can be seen at the National Gallery of Capodimonte in Naples, Italy. To my eye, the painting depicts Jesus and Mary, mother of God looking through a hole that has opened up in the sky. The right hand of Jesus is clearly reaching out past and in front of the portal as he extends his hand, bringing attention to the armada of dark saucer-like looking craft that fill the sky below the window. More likely, the painting is based on a legend from AD 352, in which the Virgin Mary appeared to Pope Liberius and a Roman nobleman named John on the Esquiline Hill in Rome. The Virgin Mother told the pope and the nobleman that there would be snow in the morning that would outline the foundation for a basilica that was to be built there. The next morning the snow appeared and plans for the first major church to honor the Virgin Mary in Rome began. Local Roman Catholics commemorate the miracle each year with white rose petals during a special dedicated mass. Believers interpret the saucers as the dark lenticular clouds that brought the predicted snow.

Created by an unknown Lippi School painter in the fifteenth century, *The Madonna with Saint Giovannino* is oftentimes attributed to Domenico Ghirlandaio. The painting currently hangs in the Palazzo Vecchio in Venice as part of a collection known as the Loeser Bequest. In the distance, behind Mary's left shoulder, as if to block the sun, a man holds his hand up to his forehead and looks to the sky, at a single flying craft that seems to be emitting rays of light. Perhaps howling in response to the noise of the craft, a dog sits by the feet of the man with an open mouth, also looking up at the strange object in the sky. Close examination of the flying object shows that great care was taken in painting the craft. It is not just a blob in the sky. There are details to the distinct shape of the craft that are not by accident, the upper portion contains viewing portals and numerous tiny, yellow-gold rays of light are painted streaming out from the craft. I have to concede that if this is not a rendering of a UFO, I have no idea what it is.

Aert De Gelder's 1710 *The Baptism of Christ* (housed in the Fitzwilliam Museum in Cambridge) and Carlo Crivelli's 1486 *The Annunciation, with Saint Emidius* (housed in the National Gallery in London) both depict an aerial disc, shining a directed beam of light down from the heavens. The painted discs are seen by alien enthusiasts as flying saucers. What is often interpreted as flying saucers can just as easily be interpreted as what the artists must have imagined that the intercession of God would have looked like. I am sure that it is not an easy task to capture in paint the Spirit of God descending like a dove when Christ is baptized. "And Jesus, when he was baptized, went up straightway out of the water: and, lo, the heavens were opened unto him, and he saw the Spirit of God descending like a dove, and lighting upon him: And lo a voice from heaven, saying, this is my beloved Son, in whom I am well pleased" (Matthew 3:16-17 KJV).

As it turns out, when it comes to UFOs, a lot of things are open to interpretation. There are claims that are easily disputed, hard evidence that is found sketchy, and other things that are not so easily discredited. It is the other things that are hard to ignore. Shortly after the release of the Nimitz and Theodore Roosevelt fighter-pilot videos, Chili, the world hotspot for encounters with extraterrestrial crafts, released a video from a Chilean Navy helicopter, now known as the Helicopter video. The quality of the Helicopter video is comparable to that of the GIMBAL, GOFAST, and TIC-TAC videos. Like the Nimitz and Theodore Roosevelt videos, the Chilean Helicopter video was analyzed by Physicist and Aerospace Engineer, Travis Taylor. What he found was that the craft was only visible in Black-Hot Mode/Infrared, it could not be seen by the naked eye or radar. It appeared to be a peanut-shaped craft that was extremely hot and again, surrounded by a blanket of cold air. Contrary to known physics, the Black-Hot craft left no heat signature in the surrounding atmosphere. Unlike a vapor cloud that would dissipate in the air, several minutes into the flight, the unidentified craft began emitting a heat trace that trailed behind it. It looks like someone swiping a paint brush across the sky, painting a wide black line behind the craft as it moved. The discharge only lasted for a few seconds, but the streak remained stationary, again defying the laws of known physics. At no point could anything be seen with the naked eye or radar.

For me, if star traveling extraterrestrials are visiting our planet, it really doesn't make much difference if they have been stopping by for thousands of years or not. Numerous mass sightings by reliable witnesses occurring in my lifetime have added to the growing pile of data that tells me we are not alone in the cosmos. The largest single UFO mass sighting to ever occur in Australia happened in 1966 when a saucer-like craft briefly hovered over a schoolyard of children and then momentarily landed in a nearby reserve clearing. The encounter was witnessed by the majority of the student body from the Westall High School in 1966, several teachers, various residents, and employees working in the suburb of Westall, Melbourne, Victoria, Australia. Although the story has been told on various UFO programs and was once featured on a recent episode of *Ancient Aliens*, the most detailed recollection of the event that I could find was captured in a 2008 documentary by Shane Ryan. A local resident, Shane remembering the rumors of a UFO sighting at the Westall High School that he had heard as a child. He made the documentary at a time when many of the witnesses were still alive and eager to talk. The documentary was entitled *Westall '66: A Suburban UFO Mystery* and was uploaded to YouTube as "UFO Encounter at Australian High School" by Charan Oblate in 2014. Later accounts of the event are a derivative of Shane's documentary. Nearly every detail of the event was witnessed and the entire story can be retold through eyewitness accounts.

For Marilyn Smith (nee Eastwood) from homeroom 2D (1966), the ordeal began when, "A student came in, was hysterical, leaned up against the sliding door, screaming, 'There is a flying saucer in the oval' and of course, everyone started heading toward the door and the teacher said, 'Sit down, it's not recess yet,' and a few minutes later, the bell went off. Everyone just took off to the oval in time to see it lifting off from the oval, it was probably, I don't know, maybe fifty feet or more, in the air, at that stage. . . . All the students were just running all over the place, hysterical. My girlfriend and I sat on the fence, climbed the fence to the school boundary, and we were crying, thinking that it was the end of the world." Terry Peck (nee Clarke) from homeroom 1A (1966), was playing outside when it arrived, "We all looked up and it really was a flying saucer; I mean from what you imagine a flying saucer, it was a round, silver disc. It seemed to be very low over the school. I remember kids screaming and running inside. A lot of kids took off toward where it seemed to go and it disappeared down behind the trees. So we all got through this fence and ran toward where it had appeared to land. A couple of girls got there faster than me, I was a bit slow, and they actually passed out." As Jacqueline Argent from homeroom 2A (1966), recalled, once the craft departed from the oval, "Tanya and I, and this other girl, we were over the fence. Tanya was in the lead and we ran towards where it was coming down. I lost sight of Tanya. She was in front of me. Before I got there, the disc came back up again so I stopped chasing it." Asked by the interviewer about her friend, Tanya, Jacqueline recalled, "I believe she did see it on the ground. . . . but I went back to school and Tanya went back to school and, basically had gone into pieces. There was definitely an ambulance on the oval and I was told that she had been taken away in the ambulance, and that was the last time I ever saw her. She was just gone and she never came back to school."[218]

Working as a marketing gardener on the property next door, Paul Smith recalled, "We were loading up for market and as we were pulling the carrot top, I looked up and I was facing the object in the sky and, um, and I just thought, oh, somebody's got some way of projecting a film or something into the sky. I didn't believe that it was really happening. . . . My boss turned around and he saw it and we stood there looking at it for several minutes." An apprentice mechanic in 1966, Les Medew said that he went to the landing site sometime later, with his younger sister: "We hid behind this tree, but fortunately with this tree, the branches came down to the ground. Here we are crouched down on our knees, we can only look so often as this tractor came around. He was on guard duty. This was a farmer who has decided to help out. We observed two army trucks, two men in camouflage, and two men in blue uniforms. And, it appeared that a soldier was using a metal mine detector. He was walking around, sweeping back and forth. The next time I saw them, they've turned and they started kicking violently at the ground. The two officers decide then, time to come back. They come back to the truck and they were gone, and then we could enter the paddock." As Terry Peck remembered from just after the landing, ". . . there was a great big round patch of like flattened, yellow, almost burnt, but I am a bit sketchy on that. I can't remember if it was really burnt or just flattened, but it was sort of yellow and the grass was all flattened in a swirly sort of a pattern." Within days of the event, students recalled that the field in the Grange Reserve where the craft had landed was mowed and the actual spot where it touched down was intentionally burned.[219]

Not considering the long-term effects of suppressing childhood memories and fearing that the children might be denounced as unstable for claiming to have witnessed a UFO landing, the coverup began almost immediately. The chemistry teacher, Barbara Robins, had grabbed a camera and been taking pictures. After everyone had returned to their classrooms, the school captain, Graham Simmonds, remembered, "There was a confrontation between Mr. Samblebe, Barbara Robins, and a man I'd never seen before. . . . He demanded that she hand over not the film, but the entire camera." Joy Clarke (nee Tighe) from homeroom 2C (1966) remembered, "That afternoon, our principal called a special assembly and told us all not to talk about it." According to Brendan Dickson, from homeroom 3B (1966), "I just got called into the gymnasium and then these people spoke and, um, they just sort of said, oh, what you saw was sort of an experimental thing and you know, we just don't want anybody talking about it or it going any further." Marilyn Smith confessed, "We were told that we weren't allowed to speak to the media in school grounds. After the school finished, there was a TV crew outside school grounds so we undertook an interview with them. Now, I can't remember if it was the principal or a school representative that came out and ordered us to go home and the film crew to leave." Marilyn went on to explain, "Because I was a mischievous sort of person, I was always getting into trouble. I had detention for actually appearing on the show and then I got detention again, at a later date, after my picture and story was in the Dandenong Journal." She snickered, ". . . it didn't go unpunished, but it was worth it." Around the same time, Joy Clarke (nee Tighe) from homeroom 2C (1966) was also giving an interview to Channel 9 News. As she recalled, "a policeman walked up to them and said, 'Stop filming and you go back into the schoolground.' Ok, so, that is what I did. I was twelve-and-a-half years old."[220]

Shane interviewed dozens of students, surviving teachers, and anyone else that remembered the event and was willing to talk about it. The event remains the largest single UFO mass sighting to ever take place in Australia and plenty of witnesses were surviving when the documentary was produced, forty-two years after the event took place. Channel 9 News was still in business and Shane attempted to retrieve film footage of the Joy Clarke interview. What he found was an index card that read, "NGV 248-275, Flying Saucer at School" and an empty canister labeled, "NGV 248-275." The station had no idea or record of what might have happened to the film that should have been in the canister. Shane had better luck with the Dandenong Journal. Although the paper was no longer in business, original copies of early editions could still be found at the State Library of Victoria. These records have since been scanned and uploaded to the internet for all to see. Although the Head Master, Frank Samblebe, had passed away by the time of filming, Shane came into the possession of a recording of Mr. Samblebe verifying that US Air Force personnel were present on the day of the sighting. Still with a heavy impact in 2008 and likely consequences to their reputations and/or careers, no surviving local policemen, ambulance drivers, or military personnel could be found that were willing to come forward and verify observing or taking part in any portion of the 1966 mass sighting.

The Rendlesham Forest incident took place over the course of three days in December of 1980. It happened in a three-mile stretch of forest that exists between two US leased military bases in the UK: RAF Bentwaters and RAF Woodbridge. Seeing strange lights in the Rendlesham Forrest, three men were dispatched to investigate—two men encountered a small, triangular-shaped craft, and one got close enough to touch the side of the craft. Promoting his 2019 book, *The Rendlesham Enigma*, a book detailing his involvement in Britain's Roswell (also known as the Rendelsham Forest Incident), retired US Air Force Tech Sgt. Jim Penniston gave an interview to Eric Mintel of Bucks County Paranormal Investigations. The interview has been uploaded to YouTube as "Exclusive Interview: Jim Penniston Rendlesham Forest UFO Incident."[221] As the head of security for RAF Woodbridge, Tech Sgt. Penniston was called to the front gate shortly after midnight on December 25, 1980. There, he spoke with the senior security law enforcement official, Staff Sgt. Bud Stephens. Asked what was going on, Bud pointed over to the forest where various colored lights flickered through the trees. After some discussion, Tech Sgt. Penniston initiated an SRO security response option for a downed aircraft. Within seconds of initiating the security response, Staff Sgt. Coffee notified Tech Sgt. Penniston that he spoke with London radar, Eastern radar, and Bentwaters radar. They confirmed that they had lost track of a bogie fifteen minutes earlier, over Woodbridge Base. Under the Standards of Forces Agreement (SOFA), this confirmation granted authorization to deploy US forces on British soil. Tech Sgt. Penniston then made the necessary notifications to deploy, assembled a response team, and took a jeep with two airmen to the edge of the forest. At the edge of the forest, Penniston established an entry control point and posted one of the airmen.

Penniston recalled, "As we entered the forest, and over the berm, there was a bright flash of light. . . . The reaction was to hit the ground, thinking that it was an explosion or something like that. And there was no explosion, no noise, nothing. Once I gained my wits on me over that, I got back up, brushed myself off. The other airman is about twenty-five feet away from me, behind me and to my right. I was feeling sensations that normally you don't have. I started writing things off as adrenaline, or something like that. I knew that wasn't it. Things like, I could feel static electricity on my face and skin, hair. Then, as I came closer to the berm, . . . my movements became labored. Like, the best way to describe it would be, oh, like walking through a pool of water, waist deep. . . . I was pretty concerned about it because it just wasn't, it wasn't normal. Anyway, the other oddity was, um, and I am probably about from the edge of the berm to where the light is, maybe fifteen feet away at the time, maybe twenty; it wasn't very far. I wasn't hearing no, no sounds. I couldn't hear my feet breaking the branches and the debris on the bottom of the forest floor. Which is, I was more than concerned with that, believe me. Just that, nothing made sense. I was trying to rationalize everything. I get up over the berm. I see a bright, white light that starts to dissipate. It's slowly getting smaller and not as bright, and ahh, I am just standing there and as it gets down to a certain point, a structured craft forms, a triangular craft. And finally, the light that was all around it is gone. There is some little white light coming out of the bottom of it. The fabric of the craft was globular type color that was running sporadically through the skin of it. And then, that speed started to slow and . . . finally disappeared. All that is left is a black, opaque craft. The physical effects like the um, labored movements started to dissipate, especially since I went over the top of the berm. I look over to my right, the other airman is outside this sphere, or what I call the sphere of influence. It is the immediate area around the craft. It measured out maybe fifteen feet. . . . I called that the sphere of influence because weird things happen inside there."[222]

Penniston continued, "I get on the radio and I terminate the SRO security response option for downed aircraft. I implement a security response option which is called a Helping Hands situation. It is a security up-channel report . . . saying that there is a possible hostile threat outside an airbase. . . . That was what I implemented. . . . I was in fear, obviously. You know, what is this thing doing outside of the largest tactical fighter wing in the Air Force at the time? I mean, there's something not right about it. It's got to be hostile. That was . . . my first thought. Of course, I am not receiving nothing back on the radio. I am just transmitting, but I hoped that they would hear my transmissions. . . . I started wondering about my own safety. You know, am I going to survive this? I didn't know. So, I said, I better go ahead and do my job. If nothing else, do your job. Get as much information as you can. Write it down. Continue to make transmissions and hopefully, you give enough information to headquarters where they can make a determination or something like that, or at least, be aware of it. . . . I started looking for things that airplanes, aircraft must have to fly. . . . One of them is flaps, didn't have any. It had to have intake; it didn't have that. It didn't have no exhaust. . . . I was looking for . . . things like that. Then I looked underneath the craft because there is still that white light coming out from under it. I see no landing gear. It's sitting about three feet off the ground, and then, there's indentions in the ground. . . . I think one of the things that kept me grounded with it is that I was running checklists. . . . Even though it was nothing that I experienced before, running the security checklists in my head helped. . . . I wrote my notes down and that. I figured I'd go ahead and try to put size and that. So I paced it off. I have a three-foot stride, so its nine feet long and it looks like it's all the same on . . . all three sides anyway. . . . So I am standing about six-foot-two, you know, I am trying to get my position and I said, this thing looks about six and a half feet high and I write that down."

Penniston remembered that as he walked around the craft, experiencing panic and fear, "I see what possibly looks like writing on the sides of the craft and I felt relieved. . . . I said there's some kind of writing, well, because I know this is nothing in the US Air Force inventory or in a prototype. I know that. . . . As I walk around to it, and I am running my hand on it because it looks like black glass, but it feels like metal. I mean, there's no rivets or nothing like that. It's just completely smooth. So, you know, I am still fascinated by it. And then when I get around to what I thought was writing, it turns out they're like what I would call glyphs. And um, I, I didn't know what to think of that. . . . And I said, well, it's not writing, because I was looking for obvious, nice relieving things, like it would say NASA, or experimental, or Russian, anything, I mean anything on there would have been great for me. I would have been ok with it. . . . They measured, . . . four to five inches high, the writing on the symbols and they were about three-feet long, spread out. . . . So, I run from the smoothness of the craft, feeling it to where the first glyph is and it is like going from completely smooth to maybe like sandpaper. That's how it felt, the actual etching. It felt like it was etched in. So I ran across those on the bottom and walked around, still taking notes. And I said, I'll do another 360. So I did another 360 walk-around and of course at this point, I haven't died. It hasn't, you know, it hasn't exploded. So I felt a little bit better, and more comfortable than I did initially. Then I said, well, that's a fascinating symbol on there. The one on the top was a circular thing and it was a larger one, and it had a triangle, and it had three little things so I wrote what that looked like. And I said, I was going to feel it. . . . So, when I touched it, there was like a blinding, blinding white light. I mean, I can't see anything else. All I see is this white, bright light. And then, during the course of it,

I am seeing all kinds of flashes of ones and zeros (Jim later said, it was like looking at a full page of ones and zeros, flashing). I am stunned. And ahh, then I don't know what happened, whether it was for ten seconds or what. I gained my wits with me and all I did was just lift my hand back off and it stopped immediately. . . . I figured, wow, I am not going to touch that again."[223]

Seconds later, the craft powered up, backed up into the forest, and rose to the top of the trees, where it disappeared into the night. Two days later, the craft returned. When a US Air Force memorandum describing the incident was released under a freedom of information request, numerous eyewitnesses came forth to recall the encounter. While attending the Combat Support Group Christmas party, the on-duty Flight Commander notified Lt. Colonel Charles Halt that the UFO was back. This time, Lt. Colonel Halt pocketed a small micro-cassette recorder and recorded most of the in-field conversations by the response team. Lt. Colonel Halt's audio recordings of the encounter have since been released to the public. As Lt. Colonel Halt recalled in an interview with the History Channel, "We moved forward and came to a spot where the Flight Lieutenant told me, this is where it had landed. He was quite alarmed because he was getting higher readings than normal background radiation. That's when I started getting a little bit nervous and, how did I get into this and what am I doing here? And I noticed off to the side some activity and the lieutenant started hollering, 'Look over there! Look over there!' And, we could see something. It moved through the trees as though it were under some kind of intelligent control. The whole time, it appeared to be shedding something like molten metals. We moved forward to try and find out what it was. We were really concerned and wanted to know. We wanted some answers. It suddenly exploded without a noise and broke into several objects, white objects and they disappeared. Is this a signal? Is this a warning, some type of a weapon, what is it? We didn't know. We were really concerned."[224] Lt. Colonel Charles Halt documented the details of the Rendlesham incident in a memo to the Ministry of Defense (MOD) that was later declassified and released to the public through a freedom of information request. This was the memorandum that first made the world aware of the Rendlesham Forest encounter. Despite a MOD investigation, the Rendlesham Forest encounter remains unexplained.

The All-Union UFO Center in Moscow, houses a work by Dr. Felix Zeigel that documents over fifty thousand UFO sightings, all taking place in the Soviet Union. There are more than seventy UFO encounters documented in the logs of the Bhunice Atomic Energy Plant, Slovak Republic. The list goes on, all around the world. Every nation has reported sightings. Nations have established government agencies for investigating UFOs. Many nations capable of supporting their own military have documented military film footage of unidentified crafts capable of performing maneuvers that under normal laws of physics, would kill any human pilot. Several nations have their own Roswell incident and are reported to have captured alien craft. The ever-growing mountain of evidence for UFOs is admittedly overwhelming. I was surprised to discover how many often-told, cited examples of proof were able to be debunked or found tampered with. Just as surprising, the longer I dug into this endless mountain of evidence, the more I found accounts that could not be debunked or found tampered with. The more I looked, the bigger the believable pile became. At some point, the number of verifiable and believable accounts became just too big to ignore. Surely, if we allow ourselves to believe for a moment that star-traveling extraterrestrials are visiting our planet, we must also acknowledge that the visitors possess secret knowledge of technologies beyond our current human understanding and known physics. The public now possesses declassified and released records from high-ranking government officials and military personnel to support whistle-blower claims of reverse engineering of captured extraterrestrial crafts in Germany, Russia, and the United States.

In November of 2018, Canadian UFO researcher, Grant Cameron received a 15-page document in which the former Director of the Defense Intelligence Agency, US Navy Admiral Thomas Wilson, confirmed military involvement in reverse engineering of extraterrestrial technologies. In a 10/16/02 transcript of what is most likely a telephone conversation between US Navy Admiral Thomas Wilson and the CEO of Warp Drive Metrics, Dr. Eric W. Davis, the Admiral told Eric that he ". . . didn't tell Miller EVERYTHING! Miller knows what I did in Pentagon Records Group search but no more. Miller can make a good educated guess on who (contractors) has alien hardware." They were discussing an earlier (04/25/02) letter from Will Miller to Eric Davis (included with Grant Cameron released documents) in which Mr. Miller said that he ". . . would be willing to assist . . . with . . . ongoing research into UFO crash retrievals and the entities within the government (or outside of it) that are involved in that business." He went on to say that he could provide, "The name and last location of a senior officer who I believe had first-hand knowledge of US government Alien Reproduction Vehicles (ARVs) at Area 51 and associated locations."[225] Unable to fathom the fifty-year technological jump required to transition from needing a computer the size of a house to land a man on the moon, to everyone having a computer ten times as powerful in the palm of their hand (in their smartphone), alien theorists attribute nearly every technological advance to the reverse engineering of captured UFOs. Some of the advances attributed to the reverse engineering of alien technologies include: fiber optics, lasers, transistors, microchips, night vision, stealth technology, and cloaking. None of this can of course be proven, but it makes you wonder. Has mankind again begun to accept gifts from beings beyond this world? Will we again accept these beings as our gods?

Who are these star-traveling extraterrestrials and where do they come from? Are they the creation of our God elsewhere in the universe, the descendants of fallen angels, possibly our former taskmasters? Only a select group of high-ranking government officials, military personnel, and God seem to know for sure. Despite knowledge of the unknown and an apparent desire for the advancement of the human race, we can be confident that the star-traveling extraterrestrials are not our gods. The Bible (proven correct to this point) foretells of the second coming of the Son of God. The Bible tells us what must first take place, before the second coming, so that we might recognize the signs of the times, and prepare ourselves. We are the free brothers and sisters of the Son of the living God and we worship only the Father and the Son. Jesus stretched forth his hand". . . toward his disciples, and said, Behold my mother and my brethren! For whosoever shall do the will of my Father which is in heaven, the same is my brother, and sister, and mother'" (Matthew 12:49-50 KJV). The Son of the only God to speak life into existence needs no craft or ship to ascend into the heavens. "And when he had spoken these things, while they beheld, he was taken up; and a cloud received him out of their sight. And while they looked steadfastly toward heaven as he went up, behold, two men stood by them in white apparel; Which also said, Ye men of Galilee, why stand ye gazing up into heaven? this same Jesus, which is taken up from you into heaven, shall so come in like manner as ye have seen him go into heaven" (Acts 1:9-11 KJV). The Bible tells us how we will know that the Son of the living God has returned. We must be vigilant to ensure that we do not repeat the mistakes of our past. Each foretold sign that precedes the second coming of the Son of the living God is another reason why star-traveling extraterrestrials are not our gods. "Be sober, be vigilant; because your adversary the devil, as a roaring lion, walketh about, seeking whom he may devour" (1 Peter 5:8 KJV).

— 11 —

ONE JERUSALEM:
THE SIGNS OF THE TIMES

L et me start by giving you my perspective so that you will know my natural predispositions. I believe that the events predicted in the Bible have, can, and will continue to unfold as foretold in the documented Word of God. My conclusions are based on the truths that I have found and continue to find in the Word of God. Moreover, I have found no falsehoods in my search of the Bible for truth. Years of searching have shown me that regardless of faith or religion, those who seek to find the truth of God in his Word ultimately reach a common truth and understanding on nearly 99% of the Scriptures. This tells me that we got it right. Every answered prayer and witnessed act of God's intercession tells me that the Bible is the true Word of our loving God. Knowing full well that it is only by his grace that he so loves me and that I am so loved, still I seek to please him and be worthy of the Father's love that never fails. These truths are my living testimony and not the intention of this book. The case for believing that Bible prophecy must be fulfilled before the return of the Son of God is bolstered by prophecies that have happened as predicted throughout history, and within our lifetimes. This is verifiable evidence that should be taken into consideration when determining the merit of future prophecies. For this purpose, before we talk about what is going to happen, we need to talk about what has happened. The difference between the two is where we are today and the signs of the times.

The Hebrew Scriptures contain more than three hundred prophecies of the Messiah: when and where the Messiah would be born and how we would recognize him when he came. All Torah and Old Testament prophecies of the coming Messiah have been fulfilled in the life, death, and resurrection of Jesus. If Jesus is not the Messiah, there is no Messiah. Jesus is the very one who, on the exact day that the angel Gabriel foretold to Daniel, rode into Jerusalem, was hailed as the Messiah, and then rejected and crucified as the Jewish prophets had foretold. The angel Gabriel told Daniel that Jerusalem would again be rebuilt and in another 483 years, the Messiah would come and his own people, Israel, would reject and crucify Him. "Know therefore and understand, that from the going forth of the commandment to restore and to build Jerusalem unto the Messiah the Prince shall be seven weeks, and threescore and two weeks: the street shall be built again, and the wall, even in troublous times. And after threescore and two weeks shall Messiah be cut off, but not for himself" (Daniel 9:25-26 KJV). As the Lord told Ahaz, "Behold, a virgin shall conceive, and bear a son, and shall call his name Immanuel" (Isaiah 7:14 KJV). Every word of this prophecy echoes of God. Mary referred to the Son of God as Immanuel, which is Hebrew for "God with us." Mary knew that her son, the Son of God, belonged to the world more than to herself, and she not only accepted this, but welcomed the will of God. "Blessed art thou among women and blessed is the fruit of thy womb" (Luke 1:42 KJV).

Jeremiah prophesied that if the people of Jerusalem did not turn from their evil ways, the city would be made a desolation and the people would be made captive of Babylon for seventy years. "And the Lord hath sent unto you all his servants the prophets, rising early and sending them; but ye have not hearkened, nor inclined your ear to hear. They said, turn ye again now everyone from his evil way, and from the evil of your doings, and dwell in the land that the Lord hath given unto you and to your fathers for ever and ever: And go not after other gods to serve them, and to worship them, and provoke me not to anger with the works of your hands; and I will do you no hurt. Yet ye have not hearkened unto me, saith the Lord; that ye might provoke me to anger with the works of your hands to your own hurt. Therefore, thus saith the Lord of hosts; Because ye have not heard my words, Behold, I will send and take all the families of the north, saith the Lord, and Nebuchadnezzar the king of Babylon, my servant, and will bring them against this land, and against the inhabitants thereof, and against all these nations round about, and will utterly destroy them, and make them an astonishment, and an hissing, and perpetual desolations. Moreover, I will take from them the voice of mirth, and the voice of gladness, the voice of the bridegroom, and the voice of the bride, the sound of the millstones, and the light of the candle. And this whole land shall be a desolation, and an astonishment; and these nations shall serve the king of Babylon seventy years" (Jeremiah 25:4-11 KJV).

Despite the words of Jeremiah, Israel did not turn from her evil ways and Nebuchadnezzar besieged, conquered, and destroyed Jerusalem (606 BC). The once proud inhabitants of the Promised Land were slaughtered and carried off to Babylon. Israel became a wasteland: uninhabited except for a few peasants eking out a bare existence. Nebuchadnezzar destroyed the city wall and the temple, together with the houses of prominent citizens. "And the king of Babylon slew the sons of Zedekiah before his eyes: he slew also all the princes of Judah in Riblah. Then he put out the eyes of Zedekiah; and the king of Babylon bound him in chains, and carried him to Babylon, and put him in prison till the day of his death. Now in the fifth month, in the tenth day of the month, which was the nineteenth year of Nebuchadnezzar king of Babylon, came Nebuzaradan, captain of the guard, which served the king of Babylon, into Jerusalem, and burned the house of the Lord, and the king's house; and all the houses of Jerusalem, and all the houses of the great men, burned he with fire: And all the army of the Chaldeans, that were with the captain of the guard, brake down all the walls of Jerusalem round about. Then Nebuzaradan the captain of the guard carried away captive certain of the poor of the people, and the residue of the people that remained in the city, and those that fell away, that fell to the king of Babylon, and the rest of the multitude" (Jeremiah 52:10-15 KJV).

Fulfilling Jeremiah's prophesy that Israel would be the servant of Babylon for seventy years, captivity ended under Cyrus the Great (the king of Persia) seventy years later. In the first year of his reign (539 BC) he decreed that by the will of God, the temple in Jerusalem should be rebuilt and that such Jews as cared to might return to their land for this purpose. Moreover, he sent back with them the sacred vessels which had been taken from the first temple and a considerable sum of money with which to buy building materials.[226] "Now when the adversaries of Judah and Benjamin heard that the children of the captivity were building the temple unto the Lord God of Israel; Then they came to Zerubbabel, and to the chief of the fathers, and said unto them, let us build with you: for we seek your God, as ye do; and we do sacrifice unto him since the days of Esarhaddon king of Assur, which brought us up hither. But Zerubbabel, and Jeshua, and the rest of the chief of the fathers of Israel, said unto them, Ye have nothing to do with us to build an house unto our God; but we ourselves together will build unto the Lord God of Israel, as king Cyrus the king of Persia hath commanded us" (Ezra 4:1-3 KJV). The Cyrus decree ended the foretold seventy years of Jewish captivity in Babylon.

Many Jews returned to Jerusalem to rebuild the temple, but the city itself was still desolate, its walls broken down and its gates burned. In that hopeless hour, God spoke through Zechariah—one of the most remarkable prophesies ever recorded. It concerned what the Bible calls the last days. "Behold, I will make Jerusalem a cup of trembling unto all the people round about, when they shall be in the siege both against Judah and against Jerusalem. And in that day will I make Jerusalem a burdensome stone for all people: all that burden themselves with it shall be cut in pieces, though all the people of the earth be gathered together against it" (Zechariah 12:2-3 KJV). Following the rebirth of Israel in 1948, fulfillment of this prophecy has been witnessed by the entire world. Tiny Jerusalem is the world's greatest burden. On average, the United Nations Security Council devotes nearly a third of its deliberations to

Israel, which accounts for only one-one-thousandth of the world's total population.[227]

Zechariah also prophesied that, "In that day will I make the governors of Judah like a hearth of fire among the wood, and like a torch of fire in a sheaf; and they shall devour all the people round about, on the right hand and on the left: and Jerusalem shall be inhabited again in her own place, even in Jerusalem. In that day shall the Lord defend the inhabitants of Jerusalem; and he that is feeble among them at that day shall be as David; and the house of David shall be as God, as the angel of the Lord before them" (Zechariah 12:6, 8 KJV). As foretold, the new nation of Israel has devoured her attackers, winning every war against overwhelming odds. May 14, 1948, Israel declared their independence. It was immediately invaded by six Arab nations. These armies outnumbered the Jewish settlers many times over and had overwhelming superiority in weapons, tanks, and planes. Given an indefensible narrow strip of land by the UN and attacked by enemies determined to exterminate her, Israel should have been annihilated, but to the astonishment of a watching world, the Israeli settlers soundly defeated their would-be destroyers, exactly as God had promised. And so it has been, in war after war. In the Yom Kippur War of 1973, thousands of tanks swept simultaneously across Sinai from Egypt and down the Golan from Syria in a carefully coordinated sneak attack. Israel's military forces were all on leave, celebrating the holiest of Jewish religious holidays, and it took three days to fully mobilize. Heavily outnumbered, 300,000 Israelis fought 1.2 million Arabs. Teetering on the brink of defeat, Israel's casualties were heavy, but in undeniable fulfillment of Zechariah's astonishing prophesy, the Jewish forces were like fire to devour the surrounding nations.

Gabriel told Daniel that at the end of seventy weeks of years—490 years—all prophesies would be fulfilled, Israel would be fully restored and would never dishonor God again. At the end of the first sixty-nine weeks of years (483 years), the Messiah would come and be cut off. The time would be counted from the date authorization to rebuild Jerusalem was given. "Seventy weeks are determined upon thy people and upon thy holy city, to finish the transgression, and to make an end of sins, and to make reconciliation for iniquity, and to bring in everlasting righteousness, and to seal up the vision and prophecy, and to anoint the most Holy. Know therefore and understand, that from the going forth of the commandment to restore and to build Jerusalem unto the Messiah the Prince shall be seven weeks, and threescore and two weeks: the street shall be built again, and the wall, even in troublous times" (Daniel 9:24-25 KJV). Nehemiah says that he received the authority to rebuild Jerusalem on Nisan 1st, in the twentieth year of the reign of King Artaxerxes, which was 445 BC. According to the Hebrew calendar, on Sunday, April 6, AD 32, exactly 483 years to the day after Israel was given authority to rebuild Jerusalem, Jesus rode into Jerusalem on a donkey, humbly bringing salvation as foretold. "Rejoice greatly, O daughter of Zion; shout, O daughter of Jerusalem: behold, thy King cometh unto thee: he is just, and having salvation; lowly, and riding upon an ass, and upon a colt the foal of an ass" (Zechariah 9:9 KJV). It was the 10th of Nisan, the day the Passover lambs were being taken from the flock when Jesus rode into Jerusalem, presenting himself to his People. On the 14th of Nisan, when those lambs were being slain all over Israel, he, the Lamb of God, nailed to a cross, died for the sins of the world in fulfillment of Moses's prophesy. "Your lamb shall be without blemish, a male of the first year: ye shall take it out from the sheep, or from the goats: And ye shall keep it up until the fourteenth day of the same month: and the whole assembly of the congregation of Israel shall kill it in the evening" (Exodus 12:5-6 KJV).

In the words of Isaiah who also predicted the coming of Christ (Isaiah 7:14), "He is despised and rejected of men; a man of sorrows, and acquainted with grief: and we hid as it were our faces from him; he was despised, and we esteemed him not. Surely, he hath borne our griefs, and carried our sorrows: yet we did esteem him stricken, smitten of God, and afflicted. But he was wounded for our transgressions, he was bruised for our iniquities: the chastisement of our peace was upon him; and with his stripes we are healed. All we like sheep have gone astray; we have turned everyone to his own way; and the Lord hath laid on him the iniquity of us all. He was oppressed, and he was afflicted, yet he opened not his mouth: he is brought as a lamb to the slaughter, and as a sheep before her shearers is dumb, so he opens not his mouth. He was taken from prison and from judgment: and who shall declare his generation? for he was cut off out of the land of the living: for the transgression of my people was he stricken" (Isaiah 53:3-8 KJV).

When the disciples of Jesus came to him to show him the work that was being done on the temple, Jesus said, ". . . verily I say unto you, there shall not be left here one stone upon another, that shall not be thrown down" (Matthew 24:2 KJV). "And they asked him, saying, Master, but when shall these things be? and what sign will there be when these things shall come to pass? And Jesus said, Take heed that ye be not deceived: for many shall come in my name, saying, I am Christ; and the time draws near: go ye not therefore after them. But when ye shall hear of wars and commotions, be not terrified: for these things must first come to pass; but the end is not by and by. . . . Nation shall rise against nation, and kingdom against kingdom: And great earthquakes shall be in divers places, and famines, and pestilences; and fearful sights and great signs shall there be from heaven. But before all these, they shall lay their hands on you, and persecute you, delivering you up to the synagogues, and into prisons, being brought before kings and rulers for my name's sake. And it shall turn to you for a testimony. . . . And ye shall be betrayed both by parents, and brethren, and kinsfolks, and friends; and some of you shall they cause to be put to death. And ye shall be hated of all men for my name's sake. . . . And when ye shall see Jerusalem compassed with armies, then know that the desolation thereof is nigh. Then let them which are in Judaea flee to the mountains; and let them which are in the midst of it depart out; and let not them that are in the countries enter thereinto. For these be the days of vengeance, that all things which are written may be fulfilled. But woe unto them that are with child, and to them that give suck, in those days! for there shall be great distress in the land, and wrath upon this people. And they shall fall by the edge of the sword, and shall be led away captive into all nations: and Jerusalem shall be trodden down of the

Gentiles, until the times of the Gentiles be fulfilled" (Luke 21:7-24 KJV). In AD 70, exactly as Jesus foretold, when the Roman armies under Titus sacked Jerusalem, they left not one stone of Herod's temple upon another. More than a million Jews were killed and the remnants were scattered to every nation.

Israel's prophets predicted even the hatred and antisemitism that the Jewish people would be forced to endure. Contrary to popular culture which teaches that the Roman Catholic Crusaders freed the Holy Land for the Jews, the Holy Land was taken for the Catholic Church and many Jews were slaughtered. Pope Urban II, who organized the first crusade, urged the Crusaders to "start upon the road to the Holy Sepulchre to wrest that land from the wicked race and subject it to yourselves."[228] Hordes of volunteers under the banner of the cross massacred Christ's earthly brethren, the Jews all along the route to Jerusalem. The Crusade leader Godfrey of Bouillon vowed to "avenge the blood of Jesus on the Jews, leaving not one alive."[229] Succeeding popes treated Jews with much disdain. They included: Pius the 7th and 8th, Leo the 12th, and Gregory the 16th. "Hitler's abuse of German Jews leading up to World War II uncovered a simmering antisemitism that was . . . worldwide. The ocean liner St. Louis, crammed with 1100 Jewish refugees was turned away from every port in South, Central, and Northern America. Though 700 passengers had valid papers for entering the US, President Roosevelt sent them to perish in Hitler's ovens. Even Switzerland turned fleeing Jews back to their murderers and acted as Hitler's banker, holding billions of dollars for the Nazis in gold and funds stolen from Jewish victims."[230]

As the barren land of Israel continued to mourn, Jews were scattered to every nation. They have been hated, persecuted, and killed like no other people. In 1867, a visiting Mark Twain wrote, "Bethlehem . . . where the angels sang, is untenanted of any living creature . . . Palestine sits in sackcloth and ashes . . . desolate and unlovely."[231] "And I will persecute them with the sword, with the famine, and with the pestilence, and will deliver them to be removed to all the kingdoms of the earth, to be a curse, and an astonishment, and an hissing, and a reproach, among all the nations whither I have driven them" (Jeremiah 29:18 KJV). "And thou shalt become an astonishment, a proverb, and a byword, among all nations" (Deuteronomy 28:37 KJV). Jerusalem has been fought over by every major power in history. The Babylonians held Jerusalem, then the Persians, even Alexander the Great. The Egyptians and Syrians alternately held it until the Romans. Islamic invaders took control to be replaced by the Crusaders. Later, the Islamic Monologues of Egypt possessed it. Then the Ottoman Turkish Empire ruled for about four hundred years. "And they shall fall by the edge of the sword, and shall be led away captive into all nations: and Jerusalem shall be trodden down of the Gentiles, until the times of the Gentiles be fulfilled" (Luke 21:24 KJV). Make no mistake about it, we are in the times of the Gentiles and they are near fulfillment. It is no small thing that the United States, a country founded on the principles of God is the first to recognize the sovereignty of Israel in modern times.

On December 6, 2017, President Donald J. Trump announced what no previous president had officially declared while in office: Jerusalem is the capital of Israel. Against all odds, President Trump announced that the US embassy would be moved from Tel Aviv to Jerusalem, the capital of Israel. On September 15, 2020, Bahrain and the United Arab Emirates (UAE) followed suit and joined the United States in signing the Abraham Accord to "foster mutual understanding, respect, co-existence, and a culture of peace between their societies in the spirit of their common ancestor, Abraham."[232] As such, Bahrain and the UAE also recognize Israel as a sovereign nation and Jerusalem as its capital. They will establish their own embassies in Jerusalem with their own resident ambassadors. At the signing of the Abraham Accord, it was announced that other nations are in the wings and waiting to do the same.

Marking his return to his people by the fulfillment of Scripture, God gathers the people of Israel that have been scattered throughout the world and brings them back to their homeland in the beginning of the end times. After centuries of separation, hundreds of thousands of Jews have returned to their homeland beginning in the late 1800s. Millions more returned after Israel declared independence in 1948. "As a shepherd seeks out his flock in the day that he is among his sheep that are scattered; so, will I seek out my sheep, and will deliver them out of all places where they have been scattered in the cloudy and dark day. And I will bring them out from the people, and gather them from the countries, and will bring them to their own land, and feed them upon the mountains of Israel by the rivers, and in all the inhabited places of the country" (Ezekiel 34:12-13 KJV). God's promises were assured. "From 1945 to 1948, in spite of a cruel British Naval blockade, ten aging ships smuggled about 70,000 holocaust survivors into the promised land." As one of them who made it said, "It was better to risk dangers at sea and the British fleet than to stay in Europe . . . For the first time in years, we had a purpose: to create a Jewish state."[233]

Jewish Agency Chairman, Natan Sharansky oversees the campaign to bring Jews back home and refers to the return to Israel as, "'the 'Gathering of the Exiles'—a movement that saw 27,000 new Jewish immigrants move to Israel last year—with more than 3,600 of them coming from the United States alone. 'For almost 3,000 years we were disconnected, but we were praying for Jerusalem, so it's really the gathering of the exiles—and it continues every day,' Sharansky told CBN News. 'I'm very proud to be head of the organization now, which brought 3.5 million Jews from the creation of the State of Israel and 700,000 from Arab countries; a few hundred thousand Jews from concentration camps from Europe; 1 million from [the] Soviet Union. We reached Ethiopia and brought more than 100,000 Jews, [and also] the Lost Tribes.'"[234] Founded by Rabbi Yechiel Eckstein in 1983, the International Fellowship of Christians and Jews (IFCJ) is another organization dedicated to bringing Jews back to Israel. Even before the words of Ezekiel, the prophet Moses foretold, "That then the Lord thy God will turn thy captivity, and have compassion upon thee, and will return and gather thee from all the nations, whither the Lord thy God hath scattered thee. If any of thine be driven out unto the outmost parts of heaven, from thence will the Lord thy God gather thee, and from thence will he fetch thee: And the Lord thy God will bring thee into the land which thy fathers possessed, and thou shalt possess it; and he will do thee good, and multiply thee above thy fathers" (Deuteronomy 30:3-5 KJV).

Just as it was foretold by the prophet Isaiah, the nation of Israel was established in a single day. On May 14, 1948, the Jews declared independence for Israel as a united and sovereign nation for the first time in 2900 years. That same day, the United States issued a statement recognizing Israel's sovereignty. As if by providence, only hours before, a United Nations mandate expired, ending British control of the Promised Land. Within a twenty-four-hour span of time, foreign control of the land of Israel had formally ceased and Israel had declared its independence—an independence that was acknowledged by other nations. Modern Israel was literally born in a single day. Isaiah said that the birth would take place before there would be labor pains. And that, too, is exactly what happened. A movement known as Zionism began in the 1800s to encourage Jews from around the world to move back to Israel, which at the time was called Palestine. Within hours of the declaration of independence in 1948, Israel was attacked by the surrounding countries of Egypt, Jordan, Syria, Lebanon, Iraq, and Saudi Arabia. As you read Isaiah's prophesy, bear in mind that Israel's status as a sovereign nation was established and reaffirmed during the course of a single day, the nation of Israel was born of a movement called Zionism, and Israel's declaration of independence was not the result of a war, but rather the cause of one. Isaiah prophesied that, "Before she travailed, she brought forth; before her pain came, she was delivered of a man child. Who hath heard such a thing? who hath seen such things? Shall the earth be made to bring forth in one day? or shall a nation be born at once? for as soon as Zion travailed, she brought forth her children" (Isaiah 66:7-8 KJV).

Just as the prophet Isaiah had foretold of how Israel would again become a nation, the prophet Ezekiel predicted when it would happen. Ezekiel said that the Jews were to be punished for 430 years because they had turned away from God. As part of their punishment, the Jews lost control of their homeland to Babylon. Babylon was later conquered by

Cyrus in 539 BC who allowed the Jews to leave Babylon and to return to their homeland. But only a small number returned. According to the Hebrew calendar, the return had taken place some seventy years after Judah lost independence to Babylon.

According to Bible scholar Grant Jeffrey, because most of the exiles chose to stay in Babylon rather than return to the Holy Land, the remaining 360 years of their punishment would be multiplied by seven. The reason for this is explained in Leviticus (Leviticus 26:18, 21, 24 & 28). The book of Leviticus tells us that when God's people do not repent in their punishment, their punishment will be multiplied by seven. By staying in Babylon, most exiles refused to repent. Taking the remaining 360 years of punishment and multiplying by 7, you get 2520 years. But Jeffrey says those years are based on an ancient 360-day lunar calendar. If those years are adjusted to the modern solar calendar, the result is 2484 years. And, there were exactly 2484 years from 536 BC to 1948, the year that Israel regained independence. "Moreover, take thou unto thee an iron pan, and set it for a wall of iron between thee and the city: and set thy face against it, and it shall be besieged, and thou shalt lay siege against it. This shall be a sign to the house of Israel. Lie thou also upon thy left side, and lay the iniquity of the house of Israel upon it: according to the number of the days that thou shalt lie upon it thou shalt bear their iniquity. For I have laid upon thee the years of their iniquity, according to the number of the days, three hundred and ninety days: so shalt thou bear the iniquity of the house of Israel. And when thou hast accomplished them, lie again on thy right side, and thou shalt bear the iniquity of the house of Judah forty days: I have appointed thee each day for a year" (Ezekiel 4:3-6 KJV).

The "Temple Mount, on the summit of Mount Moriah, is the heart of Jerusalem. This thirty-five-acre parcel arouses such explosive passions that it could trigger World War III at any time. This is where Abraham obediently built an altar and bound his son, Isaac, upon it to offer him as a sacrifice to God, but God stopped him and provided a ram in Isaac's place (Genesis 22:9-13). Nine hundred years later, about three thousand years ago, the sacred ground was purchased by King David from Ornan the Jebusite to build there an altar to God (1 Chronicles 21:15-25). And it was there that Solomon built the first temple. The Jewish temple, twice destroyed, is gone. In its place sits the Dome of the Rock, a monument to Islam's moon god, Allah. Israel's capture of East Jerusalem in 1967, and with it, the Temple Mount, seem to contradict Christ's prophesy of Jerusalem being trodden under foot by the Gentiles until his return (Luke 21:24), but incredibly, Israel immediately gave the Temple Mount back to the custodial care of King Hussein of Jordan who turned it over in 1994 to Yasser Arafat and his PLO. Thus, the very heart of Jerusalem remains in Gentile hands and the Gentile nations of the world demand control."[235]

To fully understand where we are in time, in relation to the required building of the foretold third temple that will usher in an end of times of the Gentiles (Luke 21:24), we must also account for the location of the holy ark of God. The ark of the covenant contains every item that is important to the history of the Jews. According to Rabbi Shlomo Goren, "It is the highest state of sanctity that man can have; tablets of the Ten Commandments, the holy pot of manna, and Aaron's budding rod."[236] For the Jews of modern-day Israel, the building of the foretold third temple is hand-in-hand with the possession of the ark of the covenant. In the words of Dr. Gershon Salomon, Director of the Temple Mount Faithful, "... in this country, in this time, changes are happening quickly and I, and you, and every one of us can awake one morning and we shall meet not only the Messiah in this land, in this hill, in this city, the Messiah of the people of Israel, but also, the ark of the covenant because never before in the history of the last two thousand five hundred years we were so close to the place where the ark of the covenant and the altar of God from the wilderness, the menorah of the seven candles, and other vessels from the wilderness which will be in the third temple. Never before, we were so close to them."[237] In the second epistle of Paul the apostle to the Thessalonians, Paul writes, "Let no man deceive you by any means: for that day shall not come, except there comes a falling away first, and that man of sin be revealed, the son of perdition; Who opposes and exalts himself above all that is called God, or that is worshipped; so that he as God sits in the temple of God, shewing himself that he is God" (2 Thessalonians 2:3-4 KJV).

Generations before the birth of the apostle Paul and the Son of God, the prophet Daniel also foretold of the need for a third temple that would be desecrated by the antichrist before the second coming of the Messiah. Daniel foretold, "And he shall confirm the covenant with many for one week: and in the midst of the week, he shall cause the (temple) sacrifice and the oblation to cease, and for the overspreading of abominations he shall make it desolate, even until the consummation, and that determined shall be poured upon the desolate" (Daniel 9:27 KJV). To begin to predict where we are in relation to the building of the third temple, we must first identify how close we are to locating the ark of covenant. The temple cannot exist without the Holy of the Holies and the Holy of the Holies cannot exist without the holy ark of the covenant. The effect of discovering the ark would serve as a catalyst for those organizations seeking to rebuild the Jewish temple. When the tabernacle, and later, the temple was constructed, it was for the purpose of housing the holy ark of the covenant. If the ark were today rediscovered, its presence would demand the building of a temple. There are many theories that speculate on the current location of the ark. Many believe that the ark is hidden in a cave with the remains of Moses on Mount Nebo. According to the Jewish Apocrypha book of 2 Maccabees 2:5-8, before the destruction of the first temple, the prophet Jeremiah carried the ark to Mount Nebo in present-day Jordan. "And when Jeremy came thither, he found a hollow cave, wherein he laid the tabernacle, and the ark, and the altar of incense, and so stopped the door. And some of those that followed him came to mark the way, but they could not find it. Which when Jeremy perceived, he blamed them, saying, 'As for that place, it shall be unknown until the time that God gather His people again together, and receive them unto mercy. Then shall the Lord show them these things, and the glory of the Lord shall appear.'"

Some say that the ark is hidden in the vaults below the Nea Church (New Church of the Virgin Mary or New Church of St. Mary, Mother of

God) that was consecrated by the Emperor Justinian in AD 543. One of the largest churches of the Christian world at the time, the Nea Church has been linked to the Church of the Holy Sepulchre. In approximately AD 540 many of the relics captured when Justinian took possession of Rome, including relics from the AD 70 destruction of the second temple were sent back to Jerusalem for the consecration of the new church, the church which Justinian himself built. Several ark hunters believe that the returned relics included the holy ark of the covenant. Searches for the ark have been undertaken at the Cave of the Columns in Qumran, beneath the Mount of Olives, in the Warren Shaft, in the valley below the Abu-Tor Observatory, and behind the Ein Gedi Cave of the Wild Goats, where David happened upon King Saul near the spring at Ein Gedi. In 1982, author Ron Wyatt claimed that the ark of the covenant was located beneath the Protestant Gordon's Calvary Church. He speculated that criminals were executed on top of the hill and that in the case of Jesus, when the earthquake occurred, blood ran between the cracks and fell upon the mercy seat of the ark of the covenant, beneath the site of the crucifixion. There is, of course, no historical or archaeological evidence for this theory. During the period of the second temple, the ark was absent from the Holy of Holies. The historical writings of the time record that only the top of Mount Moriah protruded within that sacred place and that the high priest poured out his sacrifice on this rock. "Most searches have taken place in Jerusalem based on the belief that the city of Jerusalem continued in sanctity because the presence of God remained at the holy ark and that the ark within the Holy of the Holies would have been tightly guarded, that it could never have been removed very far from its home on the Temple Mount."[238]

By far, the most popular theory in Israel concerning the present-day location of the ark of the covenant is based on the Talmud. Talmud sages discussed the location of the missing ark of the covenant over 1800 years ago. The sages conjectured that because the prophets had already been foretelling of the destruction of the temple for some time, thirty-five years before the first destruction of the Temple of God, King Josiah (Yoshiah) hid the ark in a secret chamber that had been constructed for this purpose. Tradition states that when King Solomon built the temple, he prepared a hidden shaft and room deep beneath the Temple Mount for just such an eventuality (Maimonides, in the Hilchot Beit HaBechirah 4:1). The Jews of Israel today overwhelmingly believe that only by keeping the ark of the covenant at the Holy Place that God himself ordained to be his own (Leviticus 25:23), by having the Holy of Holies in alignment with heaven and keeping the ark of the covenant in alignment with the Holy of Holies and heaven, will God remain with his chosen people, in his chosen land. If this is true, which I tend to believe that it is, God was most certainly with his people in Jerusalem when his Son gave his life for us. "And Jesus cried out again with a loud voice, and yielded up His spirit. Then, behold, the veil of the temple was torn in two from top to bottom; and the earth quaked, and the rocks were split, and the graves were opened; and many bodies of the saints who had fallen asleep were raised; and coming out of the graves after His resurrection, they went into the holy city and appeared to many. So, when the centurion and those with him, who were guarding Jesus, saw the earthquake and the things that had happened, they feared greatly, saying, "Truly this was the Son of God!" (Matthew 27:50-54).

As General Mordechai (Motta) Gur approached the Old City of Jerusalem on June 7, 1967, halfway through the Six-Day War, he announced to his company commanders, "We're sitting right now on the ridge and we're seeing the Old City. Shortly we're going to go into the Old City of Jerusalem, that all generations have dreamed about. We will be the first to enter the Old City . . ." and shortly afterward, "The Temple Mount is in our hands! I repeat, the Temple Mount is in our hands!"[239] General Rabbi Shlomo Goren, chief chaplain of the IDF, sounded the shofar at the Western Wall to signify its liberation. In 1981, a secret excavation was begun deep beneath the Temple Mount at a newly discovered gate within the Western Wall tunnel. Then Askenazi Chief Rabbi Shlomo Goren, assisted by Rabbi Mayer Yehuda Getz, sought the direction of the Holy of Holies, under which they believed was a passageway which led to the ark of the covenant. In a 1993 interview with Dr. Randall Price, Rabbi Mayer Yehuda Getz recalled, "Twelve years ago, it was July of 1981, we started to build a synagogue up above. There was water leaking down. We wanted to see where the water was coming from, so we started digging and we found a big hole. It was twenty-five meters long and thirty meters high and measured about eight meters wide. What a beautiful hole—very old—from the first temple. And from that hole, we found a few tunnels that go in different directions. We took out all the water and mud, but somehow, on the outside, all of this was heard. The news went out to our Arab neighbors. All of them came. Because this was a holy place, I said that we should not shed blood. The government of Israel closed this place and the Arabs came and sealed this wall with a lot of cement and with iron so we could not get in again. Since the government said not to go in, we will not go in because we do not go against the government."[240]

Rabbi Shlomo Goren, former chief rabbi of the armed forces, responsible for all holy places in Israel recalled, "After we entered the Temple Mount, I sent in for a fortnight, fourteen days, a group of engineers . . . and they . . . prepared . . . the measurements throughout the Temple Mount. We were so excited . . . We could enter the Dome of the Rock and investigate beneath the Dome of the Rock everywhere. We . . . decided to start digging beneath the Temple Mount, to the direction, according to my measurements, we have to reach the direction of the Holy of the Holies. And it took us a long time. It was a very hard work. We found chambers with water—half of it was filled with water. We have to take out the water and swamps and so on. It was very hard. We . . . dig a year and a half. It was very secret; nobody outside knew what we were doing inside. And I hoped, if we would have enough time, another year and a half, we would be able to reach the surface of the Holy of the Holiest, beneath the Temple Mount. . . . We are about fifty meters or fifty yards from, in a straight line, the place from the chamber where the Aron Ha-Brit [ark of the covenant] was hidden; but, not in the deepness. In the deep, maybe hundreds of meters. On a specific day, one of the Jubilees, a good friend of mine came up to me, telling me that he knows what we are doing beneath the Temple Mount. So they announced on the radio that we were digging beneath the Temple Mount in order to get the direction of the Holy of the Holies. We are looking for the holy ark. After I did it, the Arabs said they are preparing themselves to open the entrances from, through the Temple Mount, to go down and to prevent our work." According to Dr. Gershon Salomon, Director of Temple Mount Faithful, "Arab demonstrations brought the government to a position of weakness. . . . and they decided to stop the work."[241]

So great is the belief of the Jews in modern-day Jerusalem that the ark of the covenant will be recaptured at any moment that on April 17, 2014, Ateret Cohanim purchased over 10,000 square feet in a building that overlooks the Flowers Gate to the Old City, where he established a Yeshiva (Jewish secondary school), the Crown of Priests Seminary to train men for the temple priesthood. Yeshiva Otzmat Yerushalayim has since partnered with Mechina boys from the Pre-Army Academy of Otzem in Cholot Chalutza. Due to the size of the Yeshiva, class sizes are limited to thirty students.[242] Established by Rabbi Yisrael Ariel in 1987, the long-term aims of the Temple Institute are, "to build the third Jewish temple on the Temple Mount, on the site currently occupied by the Dome of the Rock, and to reinstate animal sacrificial worship. It aspires to reach this goal through the study of temple construction and ritual and through the development of actual temple ritual objects, garments, and building plans suitable for immediate use in the event conditions permit its reconstruction."[243] All but the ark of the covenant and the treasures within the ark that have been touched by the hand of God can be reconstructed. Each ritual object for the temple is researched in the Torah, as well as many other ancient sources, in order to obtain the precise understanding necessary to fabricate authentic objects worthy of housing in the holy temple of God. Vessels are constructed from originally specified materials, such as gold and copper. The objects on display at the Temple Institute include musical instruments for the Levites to play, including a harp and a lyre. There is a gold incense altar, incense chalice, and incense shovel for an incense offering.

The breastplate, the golden crown, and the ephod have been on display at the Temple Institute for nearly a decade.

Awaiting the fulfillment of a prophecy by Jeremiah that foretells of continual burnt offerings in the temple, the Temple Institute also seeks a pure red heifer without blemish (Parah Adumah), which is required for spiritual purification before entering the holy temple of God. The prophet Jeremiah proclaimed, "Behold, the days come, saith the Lord, that I will perform that good thing which I have promised unto the house of Israel and to the house of Judah. In those days and at that time, will I cause the Branch of righteousness to grow up unto David: and he shall execute judgement and righteousness in the land. In those days shall Judah be saved, and Jerusalem shall dwell safely: and this is the name wherewith she shall be called. The Lord our Righteousness. For thus says the Lord: 'David shall never want a man to sit upon the throne of the house of Israel; Neither shall the priests, the Levites, want a man before me to offer burnt offerings, and to kindle meat offerings, and to do sacrifice continually'" (Jeremiah 33:14-18 KJV). God promised, "As the host of heaven cannot be numbered, neither the sand of the sea measured: so, will I multiply the seed of David my servant, and the Levites that minister unto me" (Jeremiah 33:22 KJV). A Jewish philosopher and rabbinic scholar, Maimonides, predicted before his death in 1204 that ". . . the tenth red heifer will be accomplished by the king, the Messiah; may he be revealed speedily, Amen, may it be God's will."[244] Maimonides recounted an ancient tradition that states the tenth red heifer is associated with the messianic era. Does this perhaps mean that the appearance of a red heifer in these waning end times is an indication, a forerunner of the appearance of the Messiah himself? One cannot help but wonder, if there have been no red heifers for the past 2000 years and kosher red heifers that meet biblical specifications (Numbers 19:1-22) have now suddenly begun to appear, is this the era that we will need them?

The Temple Institute is known to have identified two red heifers worthy of sacrifice, one in 1997 and one in 2002. The red heifers and candidates for temple ashes have been kept from yokes and performing work, and are routinely inspected for the growth of non-red hairs, injuries, or blemishes. The red heifers are required to reach full maturity before they can be made a burnt offering. Despite the Temple Institute providing a favorable update of the two red heifers in June of 2020, the red heifers have since been found unworthy and removed from Temple Institute guardianship.[245] Nevertheless, for the first time in 2000 years, perfect red heifers were born. The first part of the Talmud, the Mishnah teaches that up until the destruction of the second temple, ashes had been prepared from a total of only nine red heifers. The very first red heifer was processed by Moshe himself—as the verse states, ". . . have them bring you a red heifer."[246] The second was done by the prophet Ezra in the days of the first temple, and during the entire era of the second temple only seven more heifers were used for ashes. This was enough to provide for the nation's needs for purification throughout all those years.[247]

On "Jerusalem Day," 2009, the Temple Mount & Land of Israel Faithful Movement celebrated what many believe to be the most exciting event to take place in Israel since the destruction of the holy temple in AD 70. "The cornerstone of the third temple, weighing thirteen tons, that the Temple Mount Faithful Movement had prepared to be laid on the Temple Mount and start the process of the building of the third temple, was carried by the Temple Mount and Land of Israel Faithful Movement as they marched from Ammunition Hill to Temple Mount on "Jerusalem Day," 27 Iyar 5769 (21 May 2009). The holy cornerstone was driven from Ammunition Hill to Jaffa Gate and along the western walls of the Old City to the downtown streets of Jerusalem and was presented to the people of Israel and the entire world for the first time since the destruction of the holy temple in the year 70 CE."[248] God's people long for the day that the Lord will rule over all nations from the temple on the hill. As foretold by Isaiah, ". . . And it shall come to pass in the last days, that the mountain of the Lord's house shall be established in the top of the mountains, and shall be exalted above the hills; and all nations shall flow unto it. And many people shall go and say, come ye, and let us go up to the mountain of the Lord, to the house of the God of Jacob; and he will teach us of his ways, and we will walk in his paths: for out of Zion shall go forth the law, and the word of the Lord from Jerusalem. And he shall judge among the nations, and shall rebuke many people: and they shall beat their swords into plowshares, and their spears into pruninghooks: nation shall not lift up sword against nation, neither shall they learn war any more" (Isaiah 2:2-4 KJV).

Prior to Armageddon, the antichrist will confirm a seven-year covenant that will guarantee a false peace between Arab and Jew, promise security to Israel, allow her to rebuild the temple and commence animal sacrifices after more than 1900 years without them. We are awaiting the building of the third temple that will signify the fulfillment of "the times of the Gentiles" and the start of what Jeremiah called, "the time of Jacob's trouble" (Jeremiah 30:7-11 KJV). Temple construction will signify the beginning of the seventieth week of years specified in Daniel 9:27 and prepare the way for the messianic era. It is where we are in relation to the fulfillment of biblical prophecy. Only God knows the day and time when temple construction will begin. We can only look at the facts and take an educated guess. What we do know is that things will happen quickly once temple construction is undertaken and the seventieth week of years begins. "And he (the antichrist) shall confirm the covenant with many for one week: and in the midst of the week, he shall cause the (temple) sacrifice and the oblation to cease, and for the overspreading of abominations he shall make it desolate, even until the consummation, and that determined shall be poured upon the desolate" (Daniel 9:27 KJV). In that day, God ". . . will gather all nations against Jerusalem to battle; and the city shall be taken, and the houses rifled, and the women ravished; and half of the city shall go forth into captivity, and the residue of the people shall not be cut off from the city. Then shall the Lord go forth, and fight against those nations" (Zechariah 14:2-3 KJV). Led by the antichrist, the armies of the world will be brought to Armageddon by Yahweh to punish them for their hatred, persecution, and slaughter of his people, Israel, who themselves will not go unscathed for their unbelief.

Ezekiel declared, "And thou shalt come up against my people of Israel, as a cloud to cover the land; it shall be in the latter days, and I will bring thee against my land, that the heathen may know me, when I shall be sanctified in thee, O Gog, before their eyes. Thus, saith the Lord God; Art thou he of whom I have spoken in old time by my servants the prophets of Israel, which prophesied in those days many years that I would bring thee against them? And it shall come to pass at the same time when Gog shall come against the land of Israel, saith the Lord God, that my fury shall come up in my face. For in my jealousy and in the fire of my wrath have I spoken, surely in that day there shall be a great shaking in the land of Israel; So that the fishes of the sea, and the fowls of the heaven, and the beasts of the field, and all creeping things that creep upon the earth, and all the men that are upon the face of the earth, shall shake at my presence, and the mountains shall be thrown down, and the steep places shall fall, and every wall shall fall to the ground. And I will call for a sword against him throughout all my mountains, saith the Lord God: every man's sword shall be against his brother. And I will plead against him with pestilence and with blood; and I will rain upon him, and upon his bands, and upon the many people that are with him, an overflowing rain, and great hailstones, fire, and brimstone. Thus, will I magnify myself, and sanctify myself; and I will be known in the eyes of many nations, and they shall know that I am the Lord" (Ezekiel 38:16-23 KJV).

Bearing the name of blasphemy, Jeremiah tells us that a seven-headed beast that has ten horns and ten crowns shall rise from the sea. "And the beast which I saw was like unto a leopard, and his feet were as the feet of a bear, and his mouth as the mouth of a lion: and the dragon gave him his power, and his seat, and great authority. And I saw one of his heads as it were wounded to death; and his deadly wound was healed: and all the world wondered after the beast. And they worshipped the dragon which gave power unto the beast: and they worshipped the beast, saying, who is like unto the beast? who is able to make war with him? And there was given unto him a mouth speaking great things and blasphemies; and power was given unto him to continue forty and two months"

(Revelation 13:2-5 KJV). Though we are told by John that the Antichrist shall have ". . . power to give life unto the image of the beast, that the image of the beast should both speak, and cause that as many as would not worship the image of the beast should be killed" (Revelation 13:15 KJV), the prophet Jeremiah brings comfort to God's chosen when he predicts, "Alas! for that day is great, so that none is like it: it is even the time of Jacob's trouble, but he shall be saved out of it. For it shall come to pass in that day, saith the Lord of hosts, that I will break his yoke from off thy neck, and will burst thy bonds, and strangers shall no more serve themselves of him: But they shall serve the Lord their God, and David their king, whom I will raise up unto them. Therefore, fear thou not, O my servant Jacob, saith the Lord; neither be dismayed, O Israel: for, lo, I will save thee from afar, and thy seed from the land of their captivity; and Jacob shall return, and shall be in rest, and be quiet, and none shall make him afraid. For I am with thee, saith the Lord, to save thee: though I make a full end of all nations whither I have scattered thee, yet I will not make a full end of thee: but I will correct thee in measure, and will not leave thee altogether unpunished" (Jeremiah 30:7-11 KJV).

John tells us of how we will know that the end of evil is at hand and warns us of the choices that we must make if we are still alive at that time. "And I saw heaven opened, and behold a white horse; and he that sat upon him was called Faithful and True, and in righteousness he doth judge and make war. His eyes were as a flame of fire, and on his head were many crowns; and he had a name written, that no man knew, but he himself. And he was clothed with a vesture dipped in blood: and his name is called The Word of God. And the armies which were in heaven followed him upon white horses, clothed in fine linen, white and clean. And out of his mouth goeth a sharp sword, that with it he should smite the nations: and he shall rule them with a rod of iron: and he treadeth the winepress of the fierceness and wrath of Almighty God. And he hath on his vesture and on his thigh a name written, King Of Kings, And Lord Of Lords. And I saw an angel standing in the sun; and he cried with a loud voice, saying to all the fowls that fly in the midst of heaven, Come and gather yourselves together unto the supper of the great God; That ye may eat the flesh of kings, and the flesh of captains, and the flesh of mighty men, and the flesh of horses, and of them that sit on them, and the flesh of all men, both free and bond, both small and great. And I saw the beast (antichrist), and the kings of the earth, and their armies, gathered together to make war against him that sat on the horse, and against his army. And the beast was taken, and with him the false prophet that wrought miracles before him, with which he deceived them that had received the mark of the beast, and them that worshipped his image. These both were cast alive into a lake of fire burning with brimstone" (Revelation 19:11-20 KJV).

The prophet Zechariah tells us of the peace that will follow the battle. "In that day there shall be a fountain opened to the house of David and to the inhabitants of Jerusalem for sin and for uncleanness" (Zechariah 13:1 KJV). He tells us of the second coming of Christ. "And his feet shall stand in that day upon the mount of Olives, which is before Jerusalem on the east, and the mount of Olives shall cleave in the midst thereof toward the east and toward the west, and there shall be a very great valley; and half of the mountain shall remove toward the north, and half of it toward the south. And ye shall flee to the valley of the mountains; for the valley of the mountains shall reach unto Azal: yea, ye shall flee, like as ye fled from before the earthquake in the days of Uzziah king of Judah: and the Lord my God shall come, and all the saints with thee. And it shall come to pass in that day, that the light shall not be clear, nor dark: But it shall be one day which shall be known to the Lord, not day, nor night: but it shall come to pass, that at evening time it shall be light. And it shall be in that day, that living waters shall go out from Jerusalem; half of them toward the former sea, and half of them toward the hinder sea: in summer and in winter shall it be. And the Lord shall be king over all the earth: in that day shall there be one Lord, and his name one" (Zechariah 14:4-9 KJV). The curse that was predicted by Hosea, "the children of Israel shall abide many days without a king, and without a prince, and without a sacrifice, and without an image, and without an ephod, and without teraphim" (Hosea 3:4 KJV) shall be ended. The apostle Luke paints a beautiful picture of what is to come when he predicts, "He shall be great, and shall be called the Son of the Highest: and the Lord God shall give unto him the throne of his father David: And he shall reign over the house of Jacob forever; and of his kingdom there shall be no end" (Luke 1:32-33 KJV).

On Pentecost, after the crucifixion, when the apostles had been filled with the Holy Spirit and were speaking in foreign tongues, Peter reminded the residents of Jerusalem and the men of Judea of what the prophet Joel had foretold, "And it shall come to pass in the last days, saith God, I will pour out of my Spirit upon all flesh: and your sons and your daughters shall prophesy, and your young men shall see visions, and your old men shall dream dreams" (Acts 2:17 KJV). Many believe that these days are at hand. On March 25, 1983, Thomas Zimmer, a holy man known as the hermit of Loretto, prophesied in Rome that Donald J. Trump would bring America back to God. A veteran of World War II, Thomas devoted his life to praying for humanity. Each morning, he gathered the news of the day and selected the focus of his prayers for that evening. He attended six to ten masses a day, praying for those he had identified. Indicating an awareness of God's intentions for Donald Trump, in June of 2020, Archbishop Carlo Maria Vigano, the former Apostolic Nuncio to the United States wrote a letter to President Trump. Per the request of the former papal representative, Archbishop Carlo Maria Vigano's letter to President Trump has since been made public. It says in part that, "For the first time, the United States has in you a president who courageously defends the right to life, who is not ashamed to denounce the persecution of Christians throughout the world, who speaks of Jesus Christ and the right of citizens to the freedom of worship. Your participation in the March for Life and more recently, your proclamation of the month of April as the national child abuse prevention month are actions that confirm which side you wish to fight on. And I dare to believe that both of us are on the same side in this battle, albeit with different weapons."[249]

During the pontificate of Pope John Paul II, because it was so long, the Pope had two Holy Years; he had an "extraordinary year" in 1983 to mark the 1950th anniversary of Christ's crucifixion and resurrection, and a "Jubilee Year" in 2000. During a Holy Year, the Vatican Holy Door is opened. When the Holy Year is over, the Vatican Holy Door is again closed until the next Holy Year and sealed internally with mortar and bricks. At that time, pilgrims are invited by the Vatican to donate bricks with inscribed intentions to be used in the sealing up of the Holy Door. The names, intentions, and prayers inscribed on the bricks then receive blessings from the masses and prayers of the Vatican until the next Holy Year, when the Holy Door is again opened. As it turns out, Thomas Zimmer made his prediction on the day that the Vatican was celebrating the end of the extraordinary year. Thomas shared his prediction with a visiting friend and pilgrim to the Holy Land, Dr. Claude Curran, a psychiatrist from Massachusetts. He also told Dr. Curran that he so believed that Donald Trump was chosen to bring America back to God that he had purchased a brick for the sealing of the Vatican Holy Door and had "Donald J. Trump" inscribed on the brick. The "Donald J. Trump" brick remained in the Vatican Holy Door, where it was prayed over for seventeen years, until the Holy Door was again unsealed in the 2000 Jubilee Year. Years later, Dr. Curran shared what the hermit of Loretto had prophesied with Fr Giacomo Capoverde of Road Island. Father Capoverde traveled to Italy and met with Thomas. On February 17, 2017, Father Capoverde uploaded a video to YouTube in which he shared the second-hand story of Dr. Curran's March 25, 1983 encounter with the hermit of Loretto. The video immediately went viral and the rest of the world heard of Thomas's prediction. Thomas Raymond Zimmer died on September 10, 2009, but Dr. Curran and Father Capoverde still live and testify to the prophecy.

The likelihood of billionaire playboy Donald Trump fulfilling a prophecy made in 1983 is greatly bolstered by the fulfillment of another Trump prophesy that was made in 2011. On April 28, 2011, the Spirit of God visited retired firefighter Mark Taylor in his sleep, saying, "I have chosen this man, Donald Trump for such a time as this. For as Benjamin Netanyahu is to Israel, so shall this man be to the United States of America. America will again, stand hand-in-hand with Israel. And the two shall be as one." In 2012, Mark was struggling with PTSD and receiving counseling from a psychiatrist. He confessed to the psychiatrist that he believed an angel was occasionally visiting him in his sleep and that he had been keeping a journal of what the angel had been telling him. Taylor was convinced that Trump would run against Barack Obama and win the White House in 2012. Trump never ran and Taylor just assumed he was crazy. When Donald Trump officially announced that he was running for the office of the president of the United States in June of 2015, Mark shared his dream journal with his psychiatrist who in turn, shared it with his wife. The psychiatrist's wife so believed that the journal was the prophetic Word of God that she started an international prayer chain that prayed for Donald Trump's election in 2016. Sometime prior to the election and in honor of the parties involved in the prophecy, the decision was made to blow the shofar on election day. When Donald Trump was elected, thousands of Israelis that had been participating in the prayer chain sounded their shofars.[250]

Seemingly manifested, "Taylor's prophecy caught fire during the 2016 election with a certain segment of the GOP's evangelical base. Now it's been turned into a new movie. . . . The movie, which was available in theaters for just two days last year, was produced with students and faculty from Jerry Falwell's Liberty University. . . . Despite the controversy over Taylor's prophetic claims, the film has been promoted through outlets like Fox News Radio and Glenn Beck's The Blaze, and embraced by evangelical leaders. . . ."[251] In June of 2019, The Jerusalem Post reported that "Netanyahu has commended the president for having 'changed history' by acknowledging Jerusalem as Israel's capital. He has also applauded Trump for his 'robust defense of Israel's right of self-defense' and for championing Israel at the UN—something few have been brave enough to do."[252] Just as predicted by Mark Taylor, it appears that Israel and the United States now stand hand-in-hand.

If you believe in the Trump prophecies and the prophetic predictions of Joel (Joel 2:28), you must acknowledge that we are at the door to the last days. If you immediately dismiss any possibility of a Trump prophesy, I encourage you to remember that it has nothing to do with Donald

Trump, whether he was a good man or a bad man, whether you liked him or not. God chooses who he will. Lest we forget, few were feared more by Christians than Saul who became the apostle Paul, Christ's apostle to the Gentiles. After his conversion, Paul confessed to Jerusalem (Acts 22:4-5) and King Agrippa, "Many of the saints did I shut up in prison, having received authority from the chief priests; and when they were put to death, I gave my voice against them. And I punished them oft in every synagogue, and compelled them to blaspheme; and being exceedingly mad against them, I persecuted them even unto strange cities" (Acts 26:10-11 KJV). I am reminded of what Joseph told his brothers when he again saw them after they sold him into captivity, "But as for you, ye thought evil against me; but God meant it unto good, to bring to pass, as it is this day, to save much people alive" (Genesis 50:20 KJV).

The Creator God who spoke life into existence is not subject to the laws of time and space. To believe that God or his angels will come to earth in a flying craft from a distant star system is to limit the powers of Almighty God and tantamount to blasphemy. The God of Abraham and Jacob put time in motion and established the end from the beginning (Isaiah 46:10). God's prophets testify to the truth of his Word in the fulfillment of their prophecies. "The heavens declare the glory of God; and the firmament shows His handiwork" (Psalm 19:1). Each answered prayer and godly intercession build the faith for which we must be grateful because, "Through faith we understand that the worlds were framed by the word of God, so that things which are seen were not made of things which do appear" (Hebrews 11:3 KJV). In his epistle to the Romans, the apostle Paul reminds us, ". . . faith cometh by hearing, and hearing by the Word of God" (Romans 10:17 KJV) and ". . . the invisible things of him from the creation of the world are clearly seen, being understood by the things that are made, even his eternal power and Godhead; so that they are without excuse" (Romans 1:20 KJV). The God above all others is all-knowing and omnipresent. He is here; anywhere and everywhere. If he wishes it, he wills it, and by his Word, it is done.

Great and worthy of all praises, God loves and cares for us. Long has he endured our iniquity in the hopes that we might chose to put our pride aside and walk back into his open arms. Who can know or understand the love of a Son who would give his life to save the eternal souls of his Father's creation? How much more must the Father love his Son to look away from the cross as Jesus bore the sins of the world? Praise be to Almighty God that we have been given an eternity in the love of the Father who cleanses us with the blood of the most sacred, blessed Lamb of God. Hosanna in the highest. All glory and honor be to Almighty God, the Son, and the Holy Spirit of God that we invite to reside in our hearts, our minds, and our souls. I pray that we would know and recognize the voice of your Holy Spirit, that we would have the strength to go where you would send us, and that our faith would endure all temptation, for it is not our will, but your will that we chose to embrace. Amen.

12

AWAKENED:
THE KEYS TO THE KINGDOM

I have intentionally listened to no opinions but my own and the influence of the Holy Spirit in the writing of this book. You can be assured that if you've read this book, the beliefs expressed and supported herein are my own. These are my truths as I see them, the facts and evidence that I considered in reaching my conclusions; and ultimately, my understanding.

I have attempted to show that provided explanations should not always be accepted at face value, and that many explanations taught as fact are based on theories that cannot be proven or substantiated by real science. Provided explanations are promoted and explanations that are contrary to the intentions of perceived underlying forces are discriminated against. I found this to be particularly true when referring to anything Christian. This bias is demonstrated by an education system that promotes evolution, carbon dating, and the geologic column as scientific fact, and creation as a fable. The evidence provided herein tells a different story. Using recent scientific discoveries, accepted scientific principles, and the opinions of experts, I have established the premise for accepting that evolution is an unproven theory with no supporting evidence, carbon dating is fraught with significant errors and omissions, and the geologic column was derived to support an established best-guess timeline.

In my efforts to defend the Word of God against provided explanations that are contrary to God, I found myself also questioning modern theories that associate God with ancient aliens. What I discovered was that many of the facts and discoveries unearthed by proponents of the ancient alien theory are indeed remarkable. However, little basis exists for stringing the facts together in the manner promoted to support the intended theory. At the same time, in defense of the Word of God, I found reasonable and satisfactory explanation for the same unearthed facts and discoveries in the Bible that I now offer as a verifiable historic record. By examination of the evidence used to promote concepts of the ancient alien theory, I was able to define what I believe to be the complete and total corruption of mankind that is spoken of in Genesis and draw a comparison to similar corruption that exists in today's world. This corresponds to the chapter on prophecy that pinpoints where we are in relation to the end and the foretold second coming of Christ. I found that secret knowledge of ancient and advanced civilizations has been lost to time or only recently duplicated. Contrary to the alien theory which dictates that technologically advanced ancient civilizations were established by star-traveling extraterrestrials, I was able to establish an argument for attributing these lost technologies to the fallen angels. I presented evidence to show that there are likely star-traveling extraterrestrials visiting our planet and that they have been for a long time. However, contrary to ancient alien theory, I explained why these star-traveling extraterrestrials are absolutely not our gods or agents of our God. As I speculated in chapter 10, they are likely another creation of our God elsewhere in the universe, the descendants of fallen angels, possibly our former taskmasters, but they are not our gods.

It was my desire to create reasonable doubt in the minds of those who have been conditioned to automatically disavow any possibility of God or his creation, to provide confirmation through additional evidence for those who believe in biblical creation, and to show the unwavering truth of the Word of God. Combining Scripture with recent scientific discoveries, I was able to show that dinosaurs likely lived only a few thousand years ago, rather than millions of years ago as we are told. I found substantial evidence to support the existence and intended cover up of the giants and Nephilim spoken of in the Bible. I drew upon the research of noted experts to show that the biblical flood of Noah likely took place when and how it is described in the Bible. Even the animals of Noah's ark are accounted for through clarification of "kind," the area encompassed by the biblical story, and the possibility of other arks. I showed how supposed impossibilities could take place as miracles under known laws of physics and mathematics. I demonstrated that the truth of God's Word is documented in the fulfillment of prophecy. These truths are gathered together as the foundation to support the truth of the Word of God and God's telling of the creation story. Seeking the answers to these age-old questions seems just as relevant today as it was 2000 years ago. Under the guise of personal safety and social responsibility to reduce the spread of COVID-19, social distancing requirements have been imposed and public gatherings of more than six people are now discouraged. Reminiscent of the Roman persecution of the early Christian church, the enforcement of current government policies has resulted in the arrest of many Christian leaders for illegally gathering to conduct church services. Christian church services are now secretly held in dining rooms and basements throughout the United States. The holy eucharist is quietly distributed. Though I firmly believe that the COVID-19 sanctions are only temporary, I also fear that they are just a trial run for worse things to come.

As relevant today as it was when first documented by the scribes, King David, the destroyer of Goliath lamented, "Why do the heathen rage, and the people imagine a vain thing? The kings of the earth set themselves, and the rulers take counsel together, against the Lord, and against his anointed, saying, let us break their bands asunder, and cast away their cords from us." Enraged, David declared, "He that sits in the heavens shall laugh: the Lord shall have them in derision. Then shall he speak unto them in his wrath, and vex them in his sore displeasure. Yet have I set my king upon my holy hill of Zion. I will declare the decree: the Lord hath said unto me, thou art my Son; this day have I begotten thee.

Ask of me, and I shall give thee the heathen for thine inheritance, and the uttermost parts of the earth for thy possession. Thou shalt break them with a rod of iron; thou shalt dash them in pieces like a potter's vessel. Be wise now therefore, O ye kings: be instructed, ye judges of the earth. Serve the Lord with fear, and rejoice with trembling. Kiss the Son, lest he be angry, and ye perish from the way, when his wrath is kindled but a little. Blessed are all they that put their trust in him" (Psalm 2:1-12 KJV).

Just as it was for David and every generation since Adam, with life comes pain, disappointment, condemnation, and loss. In our anguish, we may ask why God would allow bad things to happen to good people. However, simply asking this question assumes that an injustice has been done. This may or may not be true. The world is masked in darkness and plagued with evil. We are instructed, "Put on the whole armor of God, that ye may be able to stand against the wiles of the devil. For we wrestle not against flesh and blood, but against principalities, against powers, against the rulers of the darkness of this world, against spiritual wicked-ness in high places" (Ephesians 6:11-12 KJV). We struggle for under-standing because true evil hides in the darkness and the ways of God are sometimes beyond our ability to comprehend. The Lord said, "For my thoughts are not your thoughts, neither are your ways my ways. . . . For as the heavens are higher than the earth, so are my ways higher than your ways, and my thoughts than your thoughts" (Isaiah 55:8-9 KJV). Though by the grace of God, we may receive correction, we are wise to remember that God is incapable of being unjust. Saint John the Divine tells us that a great voice in heaven will cry out, "Alleluia; Salvation, and glory, and honor, and power, unto the Lord our God: For true and righteous are his judgements" (Revelation 19:1-2 KJV). Rather than asking why bad things happen to good people, we would be wiser to ask, how will my suffering serve the kingdom to further glorify God? Unlike the works of the devil that seek to remain in the darkness, the works of God are done in the light so that all with eyes to see will see. It is better to seek God's purpose than attempt to place blame for what we cannot understand. No bad thing comes from God.

The watchman cried, "My lord, I stand continually upon the watchtower in the daytime, and I am set in my ward whole nights: And, behold, here cometh a chariot of men, with a couple of horsemen. And he answered and said, Babylon is fallen, is fallen; and all the graven images of her gods he hath broken unto the ground" (Isaiah 21:8-9 KJV). God prepares the way for his kingdom on earth, the return of Christ, and the final harvest. Similar to the destruction of Aaron's golden calf (Exodus 32:20), the year 2020 has brought about a relative end to universal faith and trust in the false gods of science, the judicial system, and our government. The corruption of our government has been laid bare by a global socialist agenda that seeks to increase the power and wealth of the elite through financial enslavement and the stripping away of constitutionally guaranteed rights. Special interests supersede the will of the people. Intimidated by threats of riots, our judicial system now selects which cases are worthy of being heard and which have no standing to be heard. Fearing the unknown, voter fraud, ballot manipulations, lies, and corruptions are allowed to stand. If we follow the science on the pandemic, we find that science is most likely the source of the pandemic. The immunologist in charge of advising our leaders on combating COVID-19, Dr. Anthony Fauci is now known to have financed the gain-of-function research that is most likely responsible for the inception of the virus. Emails released under the Freedom of Information Act now show that in January of 2020, Dr. Fauci was aware that the virus was likely genetically engineered in the lab that he funded. Science has no answers and has provided nothing but contradictions. Dr. Fauci has recommended everything from don't wear a mask to wear two masks, even when vaccinated.

Enduring the daily onslaught of a one-sided media that has no room for God, it becomes increasingly difficult to recognize actual truth even when presented. Fortunately, for the first time in history, the entire world, every country in the world is now admitting openly that man does not have all the answers. It appears that our prideful arrogance has finally been broken and we are at last ready to be reconstructed anew. Perhaps we are now open to hear the truth of the gospel and receive Christ as our king. Our idols have been destroyed and our stubbornness replaced with humility. The prophet Isaiah foretold, "And the loftiness of man shall be bowed down, and the haughtiness of men shall be made low: and the Lord alone shall be exalted in that day. And the idols he shall utterly abolish. And they shall go into the holes of the rocks, and into the caves of the earth, for fear of the Lord, and for the glory of his majesty, when he arises to shake terribly the earth" (Isaiah 2:17-19 KJV). Our birthing pains are now subsiding and it is a time for us to rejoice and be happy. Let us embrace the rebirth of a common morality that is strong enough to unite the entire world. The Messiah you are expecting is not coming, the Messiah that is coming is so much better. When Christ returns, we will thank him that we have been blessed with the suffering that brought about his glory. A great and unimaginable goodness is dawning.

Those of us who share a common belief that the Bible is the true Word of God first believed before we searched to know what it was that God wanted of us. To our delight and astonishment, what we found was that God asked very little of us and promised us everything, including the keys to the kingdom and a room in his house. When Jesus knew that his hour was at hand, he reassured the apostles, "Let not your heart be troubled: ye believe in God, believe also in me. In my Father's house are many mansions: if it were not so, I would have told you. I go to prepare a place for you. And if I go and prepare a place for you, I will come again, and receive you unto myself; that where I am, there ye may be also" (John 14:1-3 KJV).

Jesus said, "I am the bread of life: he that cometh to me shall never hunger; and he that believeth on me shall never thirst" (John 6:35 KJV). After nearly a half-century of seeking, I have found the truth that bridges understanding and is so profoundly life changing that I cannot help but share it with those who still search for something yet unknown. If you do not necessarily consider yourself to be saved by the grace of God and the most holy and selfless sacrifice of Jesus; who before you took a breath, suffered a torturous death on your behalf so that you might be saved from the eternal absence of our Father, please bear with me for just a bit longer.

Allow me just one more opportunity to defend the Holy Trinity of God the Father. Though our happiness is fleeting, we are born seeking a purpose and direction that will lead to our self-fulfillment. Knowing full well that life is short, we replace our emptiness with worldly distractions that bring only temporary relief. Drugs no longer bring the euphoric high that they once did, the shot of adrenaline I once experienced when playing the ponies is now replaced by threats of bankruptcy, my promiscuous behavior has resulted in non-specific urethritis (NSU), and the 1968 Opal GT in my driveway now looks silly next to my neighbor's 2021 Porsche 911. In our search, we take many wrong turns and walk to the bottom of many dead ends before finding the path that Jesus has set before us. Jesus told the Samaritan woman, ". . . whosoever drinks of the water that I shall give him shall never thirst; but the water that I shall give him shall be in him a well of water springing up into everlasting life" (John 4:14 KJV). Not unlike Almighty God and my brothers and sisters in Christ, I desire that all would drink of the everlasting waters that bring eternal peace before they perish or time comes to an end.

I pray that those who have lived a lifetime without knowing God would now know him and seek him in every aspect of their lives. I pray that they will see that the rewards are without measure, the cost has been paid, and the burden is light.

The apostle Paul tells us that ". . . he that cometh to God must believe that he is, and that he is a rewarder of them that diligently seek him" (Hebrews 11:6 KJV). Although God himself revealed to Simon Peter that Jesus was the Son of God before the crucifixion (Matthew 16:15-17), it was the resurrection that caused all of the apostles to believe, many unto a torturous death. The Son of God testifies of the Father who sent him and the Father testifies of the Son through the resurrection. In the words of Simon Peter, "Who by him do believe in God, that raised him up from the dead, and gave him glory; that your faith and hope might be in God" (1 Peter 1:21 KJV). Few events are as well attested as the resurrection of Jesus Christ. Not only did many of the apostles see the resurrected Christ together, while gathered in Galilee, but they touched him, spoke to him, ate with him, and drank with him. Christ ministered to them always (Acts 10:39-43). The risen Christ was seen by the chosen multitudes for nearly forty days and witnessed by greater than five hundred disciples who testified to his resurrection. After Christ's ascension, Jesus gave commandments to the apostles that he had chosen through the Holy Spirit of God: "To whom also he shewed himself alive after his passion by many infallible proofs, being seen of them forty days, and speaking of the things pertaining to the kingdom of God: And, being assembled together with them, commanded them that they should not depart from Jerusalem, but wait for the promise of the Father, which, saith he, ye have heard of me. For John truly baptized with water; but ye shall be baptized with the Holy Ghost not many days hence" (Acts 1:3-5 KJV). Paul proclaimed, "For I delivered unto you first of all that which I also received, how that Christ died for our sins according to the scriptures; And that he was buried, and that he rose again the third day according to the scriptures: And that he was seen of Cephas, then of the twelve: After that, he was seen of above five hundred brethren at once; of whom the greater part remain unto this present, but some are fallen asleep. After that, he was seen of James; then of all the apostles. And last of all he was seen of me also, as of one born out of due time" (1 Corinthians 15:3-8 KJV).

According to the gospel of John, Mary Magdalene was the first to see the risen Christ after the resurrection. She didn't recognize him at first and thought that he was a gardener. But when Jesus spoke her name, she immediately knew who he was. The gospel of John gives the most detailed description of what happened on the morning of the resurrection. It says that Mary Magdalene went to the tomb of Christ shortly before dawn and saw that it was open. Thinking that someone had moved the body of Jesus, she ran and told Peter and an unnamed disciple what she had seen. These two men ran to the tomb, found it empty, and left the area. But Mary lingered nearby and began to weep. Eventually she looked into the tomb again and saw two angels, who asked her why she was weeping. She told them that someone had moved Jesus's body and she didn't know where it was. Then suddenly she turned and saw Jesus himself. As told by the apostle John, ". . . she turned herself back, and saw Jesus standing, and knew not that it was Jesus. Jesus saith unto her, Woman, why weepest thou? whom seekest thou? She, supposing him to be the gardener, saith unto him, Sir, if thou have borne him hence, tell me where thou hast laid him, and I will take him away. Jesus saith unto her, Mary" (John 20:14-16 KJV). Mary then turned toward the risen Christ and cried out in Aramaic, "Rabboni!" (Which is to say, teacher.)

It would no doubt be a life-changing experience to witness your friend who you walked with and talked with being brutally murdered, and then brought back to life three days later as prophesied. Suddenly, confirmed by the resurrection, the profound weight of everything that the Lord had said would be understood and known to be true. He was the Son of God and you knew it. Because of Jesus, you believed in the Father who resurrected the Son. However, we today have no eyewitness accounts to build our faith upon. What we do have is the Holy Spirit of God that bears witness to both the Father and Son. When the apostles had all gathered with Jesus, ". . . they asked of him, saying, Lord, wilt thou at this time restore again the kingdom to Israel? And he said unto them, it is not for you to know the times or the seasons, which the Father hath put in his own power. But ye shall receive power, after that the Holy Ghost is come upon you: and ye shall be witnesses unto me both in Jerusalem, and in all Judaea, and in Samaria, and unto the uttermost part of the earth. And when he had spoken these things, while they beheld, he was taken up; and a cloud received him out of their sight" (Acts 1:6-9 KJV). Gathered together after the ascension, Peter reminded the apostles, ". . . he commanded us to preach unto the people, and to testify that it is he which was ordained of God to be the Judge of quick and dead. To him give all the prophets witness, that through his name whosoever believeth in him shall receive remission of sins. While Peter yet spoke these words, the Holy Ghost fell on all them which heard the word" (Acts 10:41-44 KJV). ". . . The place was shaken where they were assembled together; and they were all filled with the Holy Ghost, and they spake the word of God with boldness. . . . And with great power gave the apostles witness of the resurrection of the Lord Jesus: and great grace was upon them all" (Acts 4:31-33 KJV).

When the Holy Spirit of God first fell upon the apostles, ". . . there came a sound from heaven as of a rushing mighty wind, and it filled all the house where they were sitting. And there appeared unto them cloven tongues like as of fire, and it sat upon each of them. And they were all filled with the Holy Ghost, and began to speak with other tongues, as the Spirit gave them utterance. And there were dwelling at Jerusalem Jews, devout men, out of every nation under heaven. Now when this was noised abroad, the multitude came together, and were confounded, because that every man heard them speak in his own language. And they were all amazed and marveled, saying one to another, Behold, are not all these which speak Galilaeans? And how hear we every man in our own tongue, wherein we were born? Parthians, and Medes, and Elamites, and the dwellers in Mesopotamia, and in Judaea, and Cappadocia, in Pontus, and Asia, Phrygia, and Pamphylia, in Egypt, and in the parts of Libya about Cyrene, and strangers of Rome, Jews and proselytes, Cretes and Arabians, we do hear them speak in our tongues the wonderful works of God. And they were all amazed, and were in doubt, saying one to another, What meaneth this? Others mocking said, these men are full of new wine.

"But Peter, standing up with the eleven, lifted up his voice, and said unto them, Ye men of Judaea, and all ye that dwell at Jerusalem, be this known unto you, and hearken to my words: For these are not drunken, as ye suppose, seeing it is but the third hour of the day. But this is that which was spoken by the prophet Joel; And it shall come to pass in the last days, saith God, I will pour out of my Spirit upon all flesh: and your sons and your daughters shall prophesy, and your young men shall see visions, and your old men shall dream dreams: And on my servants and on my handmaidens I will pour out in those days of my Spirit; and they shall prophesy: And I will shew wonders in heaven above, and signs in the earth beneath; blood, and fire, and vapor of smoke: The sun shall be turned into darkness, and the moon into blood, before the great and notable day of the Lord come: And it shall come to pass, that whosoever shall call on the name of the Lord shall be saved" (Acts 2:2-21 KJV).

Be still and listen to the quiet voice that debates within you, the holy voice of the Spirit of God that tells you right from wrong, what you should do, and what you shouldn't. The more you listen to the Spirit of God, the louder the voice will become and the more the Spirit of God will guide you. Listen and sanctify the temple of God that resides within you. Before Stephen, a deacon in the early church was stoned to death, the high priest declared, ". . . the most High dwelleth not in temples made with hands; as saith the prophet, Heaven is my throne, and earth is my footstool: what house will ye build me? saith the Lord: or what is the place of my rest? Hath not my hand made all these things? Ye stiff-necked and uncircumcised in heart and ears, ye do always resist the Holy Ghost: as your fathers did, so do ye" (Acts 7:48-51 KJV). If you ignore the Spirit of God that speaks to your soul, you will eventually no longer hear it. We are instructed, "God that made the world and all things therein, seeing that he is Lord of heaven and earth, dwelleth not in temples made with hands; Neither is he worshipped with men's hands, as though he needed anything, seeing he giveth to all life, and breath, and all things; And hath made of one blood all nations of men for to dwell on all the face of the earth, and hath determined the times before appointed, and the bounds of their habitation; That they should seek the Lord, if haply they might feel after him, and find him, though he be not far from every one of us: For in him we live, and move, and have our being" (Acts 17:24-28 KJV).

Many have been promised the kingdom of God without first receiving water baptism (Luke 23:43, John 3:16, and Acts 16:31). As John the Baptist foretold, "There cometh one mightier than I after me, the latchet of whose shoes I am not worthy to stoop down and unloose. I indeed have baptized you with water: but he shall baptize you with the Holy Ghost" (Mark 1:7-8 KJV). It is my view that water baptism is not something that you have to do to reach the Kingdom of God, but something you should want to do. Always remember that Jesus will introduce you to the Father and he will honor you as you have honored him in your life.

Jesus himself declared, "Whosoever therefore shall be ashamed of me and of my words in this adulterous and sinful generation; of him also shall the Son of man be ashamed, when he cometh in the glory of his Father with the holy angels" (Mark 8:38 KJV). In the gospel of John, we are reminded of the words of Christ, "Verily, verily, I say unto you, He that heareth my word, and believeth on him that sent me, hath everlasting life, and shall not come into condemnation; but is passed from death unto life" (John 5:24). All that is needed to enter the kingdom of God is belief in the Father God and belief in the Son of God who willingly gave his life to purchase you from the eternal bondage of sin. In the first epistle of Paul to the Thessalonians, Paul put it this way, "For if we believe that Jesus died and rose again, even so them also which sleep in Jesus will God bring with him" (1 Thessalonians 4:14 KJV).

Christ himself tells us, ". . . strait is the gate, and narrow is the way, which leadeth unto life, and few there be that find it. Beware of false prophets, which come to you in sheep's clothing, but inwardly they are ravening wolves. Ye shall know them by their fruits. Do men gather grapes of thorns, or figs of thistles? Even so every good tree bringeth forth good fruit; but a corrupt tree bringeth forth evil fruit. A good tree cannot bring forth evil fruit, neither can a corrupt tree bring forth good fruit. Every tree that bringeth not forth good fruit is hewn down, and cast into the fire. Wherefore by their fruits ye shall know them. Not everyone that saith unto me, Lord, Lord, shall enter into the kingdom of heaven; but he that doeth the will of my Father which is in heaven" (Matthew 7:14-21 KJV). Come to the narrow path. Step by faith—the path itself will guide you and Christ will come to meet you. If you now accept the gifts that have been set before you when you were purchased by Christ upon the cross, step boldly next to the Lord, seek him out in all that you do. Humble yourself before the King of Kings and study the Word of God that you may know by faith that he is God. Your faith will grow with each step that you take. You will speak to God and Christ as your friends and they will answer you. Whatsoever is needed will be provided. As you enter the meadow from the forest, all other paths will fade away and you will be home.

Unbind my soul, my Lord. Wash my eyes that I may see the truth of your Word and strengthen my conviction that I may follow the path that you have set before me. I pray that hearts will open to embrace the greatness of the most precious love of our Father. By God's grace, we are free of worldly bondage and given a home in the Father's house where we may spend an eternity without fear, without tears, without pain, and without want. But by the grace of God and the life of his Son, I would remain unworthy of notice. Yet, my God, by your grace, I am loved, I am forgiven, and I am welcomed into your home as I am. Right and wrong have been written into my heart and I am blessed by your Holy Spirit. I have only myself to offer in return for each breath that I am given. You are worthy of all praises. Blessed be the name of God, forever and ever.

Please join me and all who have read this book in the following prayer and first step at the entrance to the narrow path.

Holy Father, God in Heaven who is with me always, I believe you are the Holy of Holies, God above all gods, the Creator and Founder, the beginning and the end.

I believe in your Son, Jesus Christ, who willingly suffered, died a horrendous death for my sins, was buried and rose from the dead to conquer death.

I confess that I am a sinner and I ask for your forgiveness for having offended you. Forgive me of my sins, past, present, and future.

My Lord, save me from worldly bondage and deliver me to the kingdom. I will trust and follow you from this day forward as my Lord and Savior, all the days of my life.

May your Holy Spirit guide my life and give me the knowledge and strength to know and do your will. In the holy and most precious name of Jesus, I pray. Amen.

ENDNOTES

1   Heeren, Fred, *Show Me God* (Day Star Publications, Olathe, KS, 2004), p. 223

2   *Bible Lexicons: Old Testament Hebrew Lexical Dictionary* (Strong's #02328), https://www.studylight.org/lexicons/eng/hebrew/02328. html; *Bible Lexicons: Old Testament Hebrew Lexical Dictionary* (Strong's #02329), https://www.studylight.org/lexicons/eng/hebrew/02329. html; Strong, James, *Strong's Hebrew Dictionary of the Bible* (BN Publishing, 2012), Downloadable Copy of Strong's Hebrew Dictionary, https://www.holybibleinstitute.com/files/STR_HDIC.PDF

3   Wood, Bryant G, "The Discovery of the Sin Cities of Sodom and Gomorrah," *Bible and Spade*, Summer 1999, https://www.galaxie.com/article/bspade12-3-02; https://biblearchaeology.org/research/chronological-categories/patriarchal-era/2364-the-discovery-of-the-sin-cities-of-sodom-and-gomorrah

4   Castro, Joseph, "Found! Hidden Ocean Locked Up Deep in Earth's Mantle," *Live Science*, June 12, 2014, https://www.livescience.com/46292-hidden-ocean-locked-in-earth-mantle.html

5   Castro, Joseph, "Found! Hidden Ocean Locked Up Deep in Earth's Mantle," *Live Science*, June 12, 2014, https://www.livescience.com/46292-hidden-ocean-locked-in-earth-mantle.html; Fellman, Megan, "New evidence for 'oceans' of water deep in Earth: Water

bound in mantle rock alters view of Earth's composition," *Science Daily*, Northwestern University, June 12, 2014, https://www.sciencedaily.com/releases/2014/06/140612142309.htm; Schmandt, Brandon, et al., "Earth's interior. Dehydration melting at the top of the lower mantle," *Science* (PMID: 249260, DOI: 10.1126/science.1253358), June 13, 2014

6   Browne, Malcolm W., "Whale Fossils High In The Andes Show How Mountains Rose From Sea," *New York Times*, Section A, page 22, March 12, 1987, https://www.nytimes.com/1987/03/12/us/whale-fossils-high-in-andes-show-how-mountains-rose-from-sea.html; Lawrence, Matthew, "Whale Fossils High In Andes Show How Mountains Rose From Sea," August 27, 2020, https://www.mattysparadigm.org/whale-fossils-high-in-andes-show-how-mountains-rose-from-sea/

7   Vail, Tom, *Grand Canyon: A Different View* (New Leaf Publishing Group, Master Books, June 1, 2003); "Canyon Ministries—A Different View," uploaded by "FunhogFamily," 2011, https://vimeo.com/24760473; "Grand Canyon Rim Tour with a Different View," Produced by Canyon Ministries, 2017, https://www.bing.com/videos/search?q=Grand+Canyon%3a+A+Different+View+by+Tom+Vail&docid=608004512879302653&mid=0F21E05F0EB67B4E31CB0F21E05F0EB67B4E31CB&view=detail&FORM=VIRE

8   Vail, Tom, *Grand Canyon: A Different View* (2003), p. 96

9   Oliver, Mark, quoting Ian Hodder, "Inside The Mysteries Of Gobekli Tepe, The Oldest Temple In The World," *All That's Interesting*, June 17, 2021, https://allthatsinteresting.com/gobekli-tepe#:~:text=%20"Gobekli%20changes%20everything%2C"%20says%20Ian%20Hodder%2C%20an,out%20of%20pillars%20organized%20into%20great%20stone%20rings., https://www.academia.edu/4681349/Göbekli_Tepe_Changes_Everything

10   Mitchell, Elizabeth, "War and Peace? The Evolutionary History of Human Nature," *Answers in Genesis*, August 1, 2013, https://answers-ingenesis.org/human-evolution/war-or-peace-the-evolutionary-history-of-human-nature/

11   Marusek, James A., *Theory Supporting the Biblical Account of the Great Flood*, Cambridge-Conference Network (Issue 47/2003), www.breadandbutterscience.com/Flood.htm

12   Kalakaua, David, *The Legends and Myths of Hawaii* (Charles E. Tuttle Company, Rutland, VT, 1972 [1888]), p. 37; Barrère, Dorothy B., *The Kumuhonua Legends: A Study of Late 19ᵗʰ Century Hawaiian Stories of Creation and Origins* (Pacific Anthropological Records number 3, Bishop Museum, Honolulu, HI, 1969), pp. 21-22

13   Gaster, Theodor H., *Myth, Legend, and Custom in the Old Testament* (Harper & Row, New York, 1969), pp. 94-95; Kelsen, Hans, *The Principle of Retribution in the Flood and Catastrophe Myths* (Dundes, 1943), p. 128; Frazer, Sir James G, *Folk-Lore in the Old Testament*, vol. 1 (Macmillan & Co., London, 1919), pp. 185-187; Brinton, Daniel G., *The Myths of the New World* (Greenwood Press, New York 1876, 1969), pp. 227-228

14   Holmberg, Uno, *The Mythology of All Races*, v. IV (Marshall Jones Co., Boston 1927), pp. 361-362

15   Gaster, Theodor H., *Myth, Legend, and Custom in the Old Testament* (Harper & Row, New York, 1969), pp. 117-118

16   Frazer, Sir James, *Folk-Lore in the Old Testament*, vol. 1 (Macmillan & Co., London, 1919), pp. 330-331

17   Gaster, Theodor, *Myth, Legend, and Custom in the Old Testament* (Harper & Row, New York, 1969), p. 93

18   Clark, Ella, *Indian Legends of the Pacific Northwest* (University of California Press, 1953), pp. 31-32

19, 20 Choi, Charles, "Earth's Atmospheric Oxygen Levels Continue Long Slide," *Live Science*, September 22, 2016, https://www.livescience.com/56219-earth-atmospheric-oxygen-levels-declining.html

21 Villazon, Luis, "How Does Earth Maintain A Constant Level of Oxygen?" *Science Focus*, 2016, https://www.sciencefocus.com/planet-earth/how-does-earth-maintain-a-constant-level-of-oxygen

22,23 "The Science Wars," *Ancient Aliens*, History Channel, season 12, episode 6, aired on June 2, 2017, executive producer Kevin Burns, https://www.history.com/shows/ancient-aliens/season-12/episode-6

24 Christensen, Kelley, "Detecting cosmic rays from a galaxy far, far away," *ScienceDaily* (Michigan Technological University, September 21, 2017), https://www.sciencedaily.com/releases/2017/09/170921141257.htm

25 Members of the RATE team included soft rock geologist, Steven A. Austin, PhD, geophysicist, John R. Baumgardner, PhD, Hebrew scholar, Steven W. Boyd, PhD, physicist, Eugene F. Chaffin, PhD, physicist, Donald B. DeYoung, PhD, physicist, D. Russell Humphreys, PhD, hard rock geologist, Andrew A. Snelling, PhD, and meteorologist and chairman, Larry Vardiman, PhD, https://www.icr.org/rate/

26 Taylor, et al., "Major Revisions in the Pleistocene Age Assignments for North American Human Skeletons by C-14 Accelerator Mass Spectrometry." *American Antiquity*, Vol. 50, No. 1 (1985), pp. 136-140, https://www.jstor.org/stable/280638

27 "Carbon Dating Flaws," YouTube video, posted by "Truth in Genesis," February 2, 2012, https://www.youtube.com/watch?v=TVuVYnHRuig

28 See Chapter 3, Genesis 1:6-7, 2 Peter 3:3-7, Psalm 148:4

29 "Carbon-14 Measurements in the Atmosphere," April 1, 1965, https://digital.library.unt.edu/ark:/67531/metadc13101/; Zumbrunn, Virgene and Boden, Thomas US, "Carbon-14 Measurements In Atmospheric CO_2 From Northern And Southern Hemisphere Sites, 1962-1993" Department of Energy Contract DE-AC05-96OR22464, Environmental Science Division Publication No. 4582, November 1996, https://cdiac.ess-dive.lbl.gov/epubs/ndp/ndp057/ndp057.htm

30 "The Science Wars," *Ancient Aliens*, History Channel, season 12, episode 6, aired on Jun 2, 2017, executive producer Kevin Burns, https://www.history.com/shows/ancient-aliens/season-12/episode-6

31 Katha, Amar Chitra; Bhagwat, BR; and Dutt, Gayatri Madan, *Mahabharata* (Book 7 of 42), (Amar Chitra Katha, April 22, 2010); Ancient Code Team, "Is Mohenjo-Daro The Ultimate Ancient Astronaut Sanctuary?" *Ancient Code* (2022), https://www.ancient-code.com/is-mohenjo-daro-the-ultimate-ancient-astronaut-sanctuary/; Lowth, Marcus, "*Sodom and Gomorrah, Mohenjo-Daro—Do The Ancient Texts Describe Nuclear Explosions And Weapons*," Me Time For The Mind, February 2016, https://www.metimeforthemind.com/do-ancient-texts-describe-nuclear-explosions-and-weapons.html; Nicolae, Chiriac and Dragomir, Alina, "Ancient Nuclear Explosions? War Between Rama and Atlantis Empire?" *Matrix Disclosure (Science & History News Magazine)*, May 17, 2022, https://matrixdisclosure.com/ancient-nuclear-explosions-rama-atlantis/; Nicolae, Chiriac and Dragomir, Alina, "Nuclear War In Ancient Times—War Between Rama Empire and Atlantis?" *Matrix Disclosure (Science & History News Magazine)*, May 17, 2022, https://matrixdisclosure.com/nuclear-war-ancient-times/

32 Baccarini, Enrico, "Vaimānika Shāstra: Evidence of Nuclear Explosion in Mohenjo Daro?" December 15, 2012, https://www.bibliotecapleyades.net/arqueologia/esp_mohenjo_daro_1.htm

33   Swaenen, Marcel, et al., *Analytical and Bioanalytical Chemistry*, 397
      (7), pp. 2659-2665; Fröhlich, et al., *Meteoritics & Planetary Science*,
      Volume 48, Issue 12, pages 2517–2530, December 2013; Greshake,
      Ansgar, et al. "The non-impact origin of the Libyan Desert Glass
      (LDG)" *The Meteoritical Society*, Volume 53, Issue 3, March 2018;
      www.b14643.de/Sahara/LDG/index.htm Pratesi, Giovanni, et al.,
      "Samples of Libyan Desert Glass were analyzed by X-ray micro-dif-
      fraction technique, Silicate-Silicate liquid immiscibility and graphite
      ribbons in Libyan Desert Glass." *Geochimica et Cosmochimica Acta*
      Volume 66, Issue 5, March 1, 2002, https://www.sciencedirect.
      com/journal/geochimica-et-cosmochimica-acta; Greshake, Ans-
      gar, et al., "Brownish inclusions and dark streaks in Libyan Desert
      Glass," *Meteoritics & Planetary Science Wiley Online Library*, Octo-
      ber 15, 2010, https://onlinelibrary.wiley.com/doi/10.1111/j.1945-
      5100.2010.01283.x#:~:text=Brownish%20Inclusions%20%20
      %20%20%20%20,%20%200.04%20%207%20more%20rows%20;
      Fröhlich, et al., "Libyan Desert Glass: New Field and Fourier
      Transform InfraRed data." *Meteoritics & Planetary Science Wiley
      Online Library*, December 6, 2013, https://onlinelibrary.wiley.com/
      doi/10.1111/j.1945-5100.2010.01283.x#:~:text=Brownish%20
      Inclusions%20%20%20%20%20%20,%20%200.04%20%207%20
      more%20rows%20

34   Reputable and verifiable sources for the biochemical and geochemical
      origins of fossilized radioactive dinosaur bones can be found in the
      following sources: T. Gun-Aazhav, et al., "Investigation of the radio-
      activity of dinosaur bones with a high-resolution gamma spectrom-
      eter" *ATOMIC ENERGY*, Volume 35, Number 2 (1973), https://
      link.springer.com/article/10.1007/BF01127077; Lee, Cin-Ty, "Ura-
      nium, dinosaur bones and agates in the Western Interior Seaway"
      Houston's Rice University Department of Earth Environmental and
      Planetary Sciences article (August 13, 2015, https://earthscience.

rice.edu/2015/08/13/uranium-dinosaur-bones-and-agates-in-the-western-interior-seaway/

35   Wanjek, Christopher, "Explosions in Space May Have Initiated Ancient Extinction on Earth," *NASA*, April 6, 2005, https://www.nasa.gov/vision/universe/starsgalaxies/gammaray_extinction.html

36   Documented in the formal and edited transcript for the NASA Johnson Space Center Oral History Project in which Summer Chick Bergen interviewed Mr. Dawson (November 2000), https://historycollection.jsc.nasa.gov/JSCHistoryPortal/history/oral_histories/DawsonJP/DawsonJP_11-9-00.pdf; https://www.sciencedaily.com/releases/2005/04/050411101721.htm; https://www.nasa.gov/vision/universe/starsgalaxies/gammaray_extinction.html

37   James P. Dawson Oral History, November 9, 2000, https://historycollection.jsc.nasa.gov/JSCHistoryPortal/history/oral_histories/DawsonJP/DawsonJP_11-9-00.pdf; Lunar Receiving Laboratory on JSTOR, https://phys.org/news/2005-04-explosions-space-ancient-extinction-earth.html#:~:text=Explosions%20in%20Space%20May%20Have%20Initiated%20Ancient%20Extinction,by%20a%20star%20explosion%20called%20a%20gamma-ray%20burst

38   Rancitelli and Fisher, "Potassium-Argon Agent of Iron Meteorites," *Science*, vol. 155, 1967, p. 999-1000, https://www.science.org/doi/10.1126/science.155.3765.999

39   Snelling, Andrew, "Excess Argon": The 'Achilles' Heel' of Potassium-Argon and Argon-Argon 'Dating' of Volcanic Rocks," *Impact* #307, January 1999, https://www.icr.org/i/pdf/imp/imp-307.pdf; Craig, William Lane, "Creation Ex Nihilo," *Reasonable Faith*, https://www.reasonablefaith.org/writings/popular-writings/existence-nature-of-god/creation-ex-nihilo-theology-and-science

40   McMurtry, Grady, "Carbon-14 Dating Technique Does Not Work,"
      Creation Worldview Ministries, April 4, 2020, https://www.creation-
      worldview.org/carbon-14-dating-technique-does-not-work; Hov-
      ind, Eric, "Does Carbon Dating Prove The Earth Is Millions Of Years
      Old?," *Creation Today*, 2022, https://creationtoday.org/carbon-
      dating/; Libby, Willard, "Carbon Dating," *Keciro Homeschool*, 2022,
      https://kecirohomeschool.com/carbondating.htm; Chick, Jack,
      "Scientists Admit: Evolution Not Supported By Facts!" *Chick Publica-
      tions*, January/February, 1987, https://www.chick.com/battle-cry/
      article?id=Scientists-Admit-Evolution-Not-Supported-By-Facts!

41   *Science*, vol. 224, 1984, p. 58-61

42   O'Rourke, "Pragmatism versus materialism in stratigraphy," *Ameri-
      can Journal of Science* January, 1976, p. 54, https://www.ajsonline.
      org/content/276/1/47

43   Darwin, Charles, *On the Origin of Species* (John Murray, UK,
      November 24, 1859), (Chapter VI—Difficulties of the Theory)

44   Wagner, Tom, "Darwin vs. the Eye," *Answers In Genesis*, Septem-
      ber 1, 1994, originally published in Creation 16, no 4, p. 10-13
      (September 1994), https://answersingenesis.org/charles-darwin/
      darwin-vs-the-eye/; https://creationstudies.org/Education/dar-
      win_vs_the_eye.html; "How we see [Darwin vs. the Eye]," YouTube
      video, posted by "Health & Origins," November 12, 2018, https://
      www.youtube.com/watch?v=C0RCPmzmC-U&feature=youtu.be

45, 46 Wells, Jonathan, *Icons of Evolution: Science or Myth?* 2000; Wells,
      Jonathan Corrigan, Moon, Sun Myung, *The Unification Church,
      and Artificial Human Intelligent Design*, (April 27, 2014), https://
      jerrykendallisakiller.blogspot.com/2014/04/dr-johnathan-corri-
      gan-wells-ph-d-sun.html

47   "Jonathan Wells Battles Darwin's Zombie Finches," *ID the Future*,
      producer Raymond Bohlin, podcast episode 1582, April 3, 2022,

https://idthefuture.com/1582/; Finly, Darel Rex, *Why Much of What We Teach About Evolution is Wrong* (Regency Press, Washington, DC, January 12, 2002), p. 160; Wells, Jonathan, *Icons of Evolution: Science or Myth?* (Regnery Publications January, 2000); www.abgroupconsultancy.com/icons-of-evolution-science-or-myth-why-much-of-what-we-teach-about-evolution-is-wrong-english.pdf

48   Minnich, Scott and Wells, Jonathan, "Is Antibiotic Resistance Evidence for Darwinian Evolution?" *Discovery Institute*, June 8, 2007, https://www.discovery.org/v/is-antibiotic-resistance-evidence-for-darwinian-evolution/; Coppedge, David F, "Antibiotic Resistance Didn't Evolve; It Was Borrowed," *Creation Evolution Headlines*, June 23, 2017, https://crev.info/2017/06/antibiotic-resistance/; "Antibiotic Resistance and Cancer - Not Evidence for Evolution. Dr. Jonathan Wells.Creation Evidence," YouTube video, posted by "Biblicaltours," November 18, 2020, https://youtu.be/fRfxc6xj65o

49   Wells, Jonathan, *Journal of Unification Studies*, Vol. 15, 2014, pp. 153-155, https://journals.uts.edu/volume-xv-2014/226-comment-by-jonathan-wells

50   Ibid

51   "Biologist Jonathan Wells discusses the failure of Darwinian Evolution (Intelligent Design lecture)," YouTube video, posted by "iReason," October 30, 2021, https://youtu.be/w73NiRdkarw

52   Zimmer, Carl, "Ancestors of Modern Humans Interbred With Extinct Hominins, Study Finds," *The New York Times*, March 17, 2016, https://www.nytimes.com/2016/03/22/science/neanderthals-interbred-with-humans-denisovans.html; Norton, Heather; Scheinfeldt, Laura B; Merriwether, David A; Koki, George; Friedlaender, Jonathan S; Wakefield, Jon; Paabo, Svante; Akey, Joshua M *"Excavating Neandertal and Denisovan DNA from the genomes of*

Melanesian individuals," Science, March 17, 2016, https://www.science.org/doi/10.1126/science.aad9416

53   Associated Press, "Neanderthal 'love child' discovery shows prehistoric interbreeding," *New York Post*, August 22, 2018, https://nypost.com/2018/08/22/neanderthal-love-child-discovery-shows-prehistoric-interbreeding/; Associated Press, "Mom was Neanderthal: Fossil Shows mix of humankind's cousins," *FOX News*, August 22, 2018, https://www.foxnews.com/world/mom-was-neanderthal-fossil-shows-mix-of-humankinds-cousins

54   "Professor Exposes Impossibilities of Evolution," YouTube video, posted by "Delphus G," July 9, 2014, https://youtu.be/xZn7tTdCm6U

55   "Professor Exposes Impossibilities of Evolution," YouTube video, posted by "uwantsun," March 31, 2018, https://youtu.be/qBZQOLQTiJg

56   See also, *The Politically Incorrect Guide to Darwinism and Intelligent Design* by Professor Wells (Regnery, 2007)

57   Ashcraft, Chris, "Evolution, Fraud, and Myths," *Northwest Creation Network*, 2022, https://nwcreation.net/evolutionfraud.html; "The Witness of Fossils: Evolution or the Flood," YouTube video, posted by "*Northwest Creation Network*," October 16 2020, https://www.youtube.com/watch?v=8yB7vb6sRQM&t=1s

58   Skull fragment may not be human, *Knoxville News-Sentinel*, 1983, https://www.evolutionisamyth.com/fossils/orce-man-was-a-donkey-skull/

59   Austin, Steven, "Archaeoraptor: Feathered Dinosaur from National Geographic Doesn't Fly," *Institute for Creation Research*, March 1, 2000, https://www.icr.org/article/archaeoraptor-feathered-dinosaur-from-national-geo/; Czerkas, Stephen, "A Flying Dinosaur?

"IT'S A MISSING LINK between terrestrial dinosaurs and birds that could actually fly," *National Geographic Magazine*, Vol. 196, No. 5, November, 1999, pp. 4-8, https://archive.org/details/november199994

60   "60 Minutes Presents: B-Rex," *60 Minutes*, season 43, episode 14, produced by Shari Finkelstein, Meghan Frank, aired December 26, 2010 on CBS News magazine program, https://www.bing.com/videos/search?q=60+Minutes+Presents%3a+B-Rex&view=detail&mid=00D370C58941822E9BA700D370C58941822E9BA7&FORM=VIRE; "60 Minutes Presents: B-Rex," YouTube video, posted by "CBS News," December 26, 2010, https://youtu.be/yJOQiyLFMNY

61   Service, Robert, "'I don't care what they say about me': Paleontologist stares down critics in her hunt for dinosaur proteins," Science.org (September 13, 2017), https://www.science.org/content/article/i-don-t-care-what-they-say-about-me-paleontologist-stares-down-critics-her-hunt; Yeoman, Barry, "Schweitzer's Dangerous Discovery," *Discover Magazine*, April 26, 2006, https://www.discovermagazine.com/the-sciences/schweitzers-dangerous-discovery

62   Service, Robert, "'I don't care what they say about me': Paleontologist stares down critics in her hunt for dinosaur proteins," Science.org (September 13, 2017), https://www.science.org/content/article/i-don-t-care-what-they-say-about-me-paleontologist-stares-down-critics-her-hunt; Barry Yeoman, "Schweitzer's Dangerous Discovery," *Discover*, April 26, 2006, https://www.discovermagazine.com/the-sciences/schweitzers-dangerous-discovery

63   Conca, James, "Deep Borehole Nuclear Waste Disposal Just Got A Whole Lot More Likely," *Forbes*, June 24, 2019, https://www.forbes.com/sites/jamesconca/2019/06/24/deep-borehole-nuclear-waste-disposal-just-got-a-whole-lot-more-likely/?sh=61109a0667c8

64   DeSousa, Fred, "Bechtel Signs Memorandum of Agreement to Support Safe Disposal of Used Nuclear Fuel," *Bechtel* (June 26, 2019), https://www.bechtel.com/newsroom/releases/2019/07/bechtel-signs-memorandum-of-agreement-to-support-s/

65   Aeck, Zann, "Deep Isolation Announces Memorandum of Agreement with Bechtel," Deep Isolation, Inc. (June 24, 2019), https://www.deepisolation.com/press/deep-isolation-announces-memorandum-of-agreement-with-bechtel/

66   Ibid.

67   Robin W. Winks and Teofilo F. Ruiz, "Medieval Europe and the World: From Late Antiquity to Modernity," Edition 1 (February 17, 2005), pp. 400-1500

68   Fagan, Brian, *The Little Ice Age: How Climate Made History 1300–1850* (Basic Books, December 27, 2001)

69   Keigwin, Lloyd D., *The Little Ice Age and Medieval Warm Period in the Sargasso Sea* (A&E Television Networks, 2005)

70   Keigwin, Lloyd D., "The Little Ice Age and Medieval Warm Period in the Sargasso Sea" (New Series, Vol. 274, No. 5292, pp. 1504-1508), American Association for the Advancement of Science (November 29, 1996), https://www.jstor.org/stable/2892219; https://www2.whoi.edu/staff/lkeigwin/; https://www2.whoi.edu/staff/lkeigwin/publications/

71   Oksana Boyko is a Russian journalist, television host and presenter working for Russia Today (RT). She is the host of *Worlds Apart*, a weekly geopolitical analysis show that tackles the world's most pressing issues through hard-hitting interviews with influential people from across the world.

72   First described in scientific literature by David Eberth, Donald Brinkman, and Vaia Barkas in 2010.

73   Prasad, et al., "Dinosaur Coprolites and the Early Evolution of Grasses and Grazers," *Science Journal* vol. 310, 2005, pp. 1177-1180, https://www.science.org/doi/10.1126/science.1118806

74   Isaacs, Darek, "Dragons or Dinosaurs, Part 1," *Origins: Corner Stone*, 2018, https://www.ctvn.org/wp-content/uploads/2013/04/1405-Dragons-or-Dinosaurs-Part-1.pdf; Woetzel, Dave, "Dragons in History," Genesis Park, 2022, https://www.genesispark.com/exhibits/evidence/historical/dragons/; "Dragons Swallow Up Evolution," *God Said Man Said Ministry*, 2022, http://www.godsaidmansaid.com/topic3.asp?Cat2=262&ItemID=1401

75   Dr. Don Patton's DVDs, *Creation Evidence from South America and Mystery of Acambaro*. https://archive.org/details/CreationEvidenceFromSouthAmerica (2000). Related references: Erle Stanley Gardner, *Host with the Big Hat* (1969); Charles Hapgood, *Mystery in Acambaro* (2000)

76   Woetzel, Dave, "Ancient Dinosaur Depictions," *Genesis Park*, 2022, https://www.genesispark.com/exhibits/evidence/historical/ancient/dinosaur/; Thomas, Brian, "Dragon Art Defies Millions of Years," *Institute for Creation Research*, February 28, 2022, https://www.icr.org/article/dragon-art-defies-millions-of-years; "2. Dinosaurs: The Poster Child of Evolution (Part 1) | Truth Be Told," YouTube video, posted by "World Video Bible School," December 8, 2016, https://www.youtube.com/watch?v=mxbadfE040Q

77   "Record of the Rocks (Dr. Don Patton)," YouTube video, posted by "Michael Bernard," March 2, 2017, https://youtu.be/unLI6XSJmGo

78   Kuban, Glen, "Moab Man—Malachite Man," 2016, http://paleo.cc/paluxy/moab-man.htm; Neyman, Greg, "Creation Science Rebuttal—Answers In Genesis—Moab Man," *Old Earth Ministries*, January 6, 2006, https://oldearth.org/moab_man.htm; Neyman,

Greg, PDF download, "The Moab Man," January 6, 2006, *Old Earth Ministries* https://oldearth.org/print/moab_man.pdf

79   Rose, Mark, "1 Million Fossil Deposits Are Known to Exist World-Wide," *Genesis Alive*, 2018, https://www.genesisalive.com/the-question-of-fossils.html

80   Lyons, Eric, "Have Dinosaur and Human Fossils Been Found Together," *Apologetics Press*, 2019, https://apologeticspress.org/have-dinosaur-and-human-fossils-been-found-together-4664/

81   Evolutionary scientist James Powell, same 2019 *Apologetics Press* article as above, https://apologeticspress.org/have-dinosaur-and-human-fossils-been-found-together-4664/

82   Wise, "The Flood and the fossil record," an informal talk given at the Institute for Creation Research, San Diego (USA) on August 17, 1988; Kurt Wise, "The Nature of the Fossil Record," ICR lecture, Joseph Tan, Good Morning Consulting; Snelling, Andrew, *"Where Are All the Human Fossils?" Creation* 14, No. 1, December 1, 1991, https://answersingenesis.org/fossils/fossil-record/where-are-all-the-human-fossils/

83   Martinez-Friaz, Hochberg, and Rull. 2005. *Naturwissenschaften.* "A review of the contributions of Albert Einstein to Earth Sciences—in commemoration of the World Year of Physics." Accessed April 2023: https://home.ifa.hawaii.edu/users/meech/a740/2006/spring/papers/rull5.pdf

84   "The Hapgood-Einstein Papers." Accessed April 2023: https://www.bibliotecapleyades.net/atlantida_mu/esp_atlantida_9a.htm

85   Jacobsen, Steve and Schmandt, Brandon, "New Evidence for Oceans of Water Deep in the Earth," *Science* (Northwestern University, June 13, 2014), https://www.bnl.gov/newsroom/news.php?a=111648

86   "2017: Nancy Pelosi unwittingly explains 'wrap-up smear' tactic of Democrats." YouTube video, posted by "The News Junkie's

Cartoons," September 6, 2020, https://www.youtube.com/watch?v
=c6wq5LzKLec

87   Library of Congress, image provided by the University of New
      Mexico,   https://chroniclingamerica.loc.gov/lccn/sn84020613/
      1902-01-27/ed-1/seq-4/

88   Morse, John, "The Great Smithsonian Cover-Up: 18 Giant Skeletons
      Discovered in Wisconsin," *The Event Chronicle*, May 5, 2015, https://
      theeventchronicle.com/18-giant-skeletons-discovered-in-wisconsin/;
      Hamilton, Ross, "Ancient America: Holocaust of Giants: The Great
      Smithsonian Cover-Up," *Ancient America*, August 5, 2014, https://
      ancientamerica.com/holocaust-of-giants-the-great-smithsonian
      -cover-up/

89   Vieira, Jim and Newman, Hugh, *Giants on Record: America's Hidden
      History, Secrets in the Mounds and the Smithsonian Files* (Avalon Ris-
      ing Publications, Glastonbury, Somerset, UK, 2015)

90   "Smithsonian Admits to Destruction of Thousands of Giant Human
      Skeletons in Early 1900's," *World News Daily Report*, December 3,
      2014, https://worldnewsdailyreport.com/smithsonian-admits-to-
      destruction-of-thousands-of-giant-human-skeletons-in-early-
      1900s/

91   Library of Congress, image provided by Arizona State Library,
      Archives and Public Records; Phoenix, AZ, https://chronicling-
      america.loc.gov/lccn/sn87062055/1919-07-11/ed-1/seq-11/

92   "A Race of Giants in Old Gaul," *The New York Times*, October 3,
      1892, https://greaterancestors.com/giants-of-antiquity-found-in-
      old-gaul/

93   Vieira, Jim and Newman, Hugh, *Giants on Record: America's Hid-
      den History, Secrets in the Mounds and the Smithsonian Files* p. 458
      (Avalon Rising Publications, Glastonbury, Somerset, UK, 2015)

94   MacIsaac, Tera, "Ancient Race of White Giants Described in Native Legends From Many Tribes," *Ancient Origins*, April 25, 2016, https://www.ancient-origins.net/myths-legends/ancient-race-white-giants-described-native-legends-many-tribes-005774

95   Daniel, Cory, "Giants," *The Phoenix Enigma*, June 1, 2016, https://thephoenixenigma.com/giants-2/

96   MacIsaac, Tera, "Ancient Race of White Giants Described in Native Legends From Many Tribes," *Ancient Origins*, April 25, 2016, https://www.ancient-origins.net/myths-legends/ancient-race-white-giants-described-native-legends-many-tribes-005774

97   The second part of the *Chronicle of Peru* by Cieza de León, Pedro de, Markham, Clements R. (Hakluyt Society, London 1883) http://www.estudiosindianos.org/en/publications/part-one-of-the-chronicle-of-peru-pedro-cieza-de-leon/; https://archive.org/details/partofchronicleperu00ciez

98   Weed, Tim and Aziz Abu, Sarah, "Nov 4, 1922 CE: King Tut's Tomb Discovered," *National Geographic: This Day in Geographic History*, https://www.nationalgeographic.org/thisday/nov4/king-tuts-tomb-discovered/; Weed, Tim and Aziz Abu, Sarah, "King Tut," *National Geographic*, https://www.nationalgeographic.org/encyclopedia/king-tut/

99   Metcalfe, Tom, "King Tut's Dagger Is 'Out of This World,'" *LiveScience*, December 18, 2017, https://www.livescience.com/61214-king-tut-dagger-outer-space.html

100   Williams, Jeff, "Forged by the Gods," *Ancient Aliens*, History Channel, Season 12, Episode 2, aired on May 5, 2017, producer Kevin Burns, https://www.history.com/shows/ancient-aliens/season-12/episode-2

101 Metcalfe, Tom, "King Tut's Dagger Is Out of This World—New study shows that meteorites rather than terrestrial ore were the sources of Bronze-Age iron," *Scientific American*, December 27, 2017, https://www.scientificamerican.com/article/king-tut-rsquo-s-dagger-is-out-of-this-world/

102 Martell, Jason, "Forged by the Gods: Metals of the Gods," *Ancient Aliens*, History Channel, Season 12, Episode 2, aired on May 5, 2017, Executive Producer Kevin Burns, https://www.history.com/shows/ancient-aliens/season-12/episode-2

103 Young, Jonathan, "Forged by the Gods: Metals of the Gods," *Ancient Aliens*, History Channel, Season 12, Episode 2, aired on May 5, 2017, Executive Producer Kevin Burns, https://www.history.com/shows/ancient-aliens/season-12/episode-2

104 Ibid.

105 Williams, Jeff, "Forged by the Gods: The Potential Alloy of Atlantis," *Ancient Aliens*, History Channel, Season 12, Episode 2, aired on May 5, 2017, producer Kevin Burns, https://www.history.com/shows/ancient-aliens/season-12/episode-2

106 Williams, Jeff, "Forged by the Gods: The Potential Alloy of Atlantis," *Ancient Aliens*, History Channel, Season 12, Episode 2, aired on May 5, 2017, producer Kevin Burns, https://www.history.com/shows/ancient-aliens/season-12/episode-2

107 Samans, Carl, *Engineering Metals and their Alloys* (The Macmillan Company, 1949), https://archive.org/details/in.ernet.dli.2015.19384/page/n3/mode/2up

108 Wikipedia, October 23, 2001, "Ayahuasca," modified February 16, 2002, https://en.wikipedia.org/wiki/Ayahuasca

109   Leonard, Jayne and Warwick, Kathy, "What to know about aya-huasca," *Medical News Today*, 2020, https://www.medicalnewsto-day.com/articles/ayahuasca

110   Black, John, "Brain Surgery in Ancient Times," *Ancient Origins*, 2013, https://www.ancient-origins.net/ancient-technology/brain-surgery-ancient-times-00869

111   Ibid

112   Link to free (PDF) download of Edwin Smith Papyrus: https://www.academia.edu/14875954/The_Edwin_Smith_papyrus_a_clinical_reappraisal_of_the_oldest_known_document_on_spinal_injuries; Van Middendorp, Joost; Sanchez, Gonzalo; Burridge, Alwyn, "The Edwin Smith papyrus: a clinical reappraisal of the oldest known document on spinal injuries," *National Library of Medicine - PubMed Central*, August 10, 2010, https://www.ncbi.nlm.nih.gov/pmc/articles/PMC2989268/; Mingren, Wu, "Edwin Smith Papyrus: 3,600-Year-Old Surgical Treatise Reveals Secrets of Ancient Egyptian Medical Knowledge," *Ancient Origins*, April 15, 2019, https://www.ancient-origins.net/artifacts-other-artifacts/edwin-smith-papyrus-0011746

113   Link to free (PDF) download of Ebers Papyrus: https://bxscience.edu/ourpages/auto/2008/11/10/43216077/egypt%20medicine.pdf

114   Gregersen, Eric, senior editor, *Encyclopedia Britannica*, "Mayan Calendar Chronology," https://www.britannica.com/topic/Mayan-calendar

115   Westcott, Lucy, "Evidence of New 'Planet Nine' Discovered in Solar System," *Newsweek*, 2016, https://www.newsweek.com/new-planet-nine-discovered-caltech-417898; Fesenmaier, Kimm, "Planet Nine—Astronomers Find Evidence of a Real Ninth Planet," California Institute of Technology, *SciTech*

Daily, January 21, 2016, https://scitechdaily.com/caltech-researchers-find-evidence-of-a-real-ninth-planet/

116 Osborne, Hannah, "Forget Planet 9—There Is Evidence of a Tenth Planet Lurking at The Edge of The Solar System," *Newsweek*, 2017, https://www.newsweek.com/planet-10-lurking-edge-solar-system-628517

117 Aceves, Ana and Saks, Caitlin, "The Evidence for Planet Nine's Existence," *NOVA—PBS*, June 9, 2019, https://www.pbs.org/wgbh/nova/video/the-evidence-for-planet-nines-existence/

118 Osborne, Hannah, "Forget Planet 9—There Is Evidence of a Tenth Planet Lurking at The Edge of The Solar System," *Newsweek*, June 23, 2017, https://www.newsweek.com/planet-10-lurking-edge-solar-system-628517

119 *George Noory Presents Zecharia Sitchen with Award*, Coast to Coast AM, https://www.coasttocoastam.com/photo/george-presents-zecharia-sitchin-with-award-photo/

120 *The Skeptic's Dictionary*, by John Wiley & Sons, 2010. Link to free (PDF) download of The Skeptic's Dictionary, https://tengteng-bloggie.blogspot.com/2019/01/download-skeptic-dictionary-pdf-free.html

121 Sitchen, Zecharia, *The 12th Planet* (Stein and Day, 1976), *Genesis Revealed* (Avon, 1991), and *The Wars of Gods and Men* (Bear & Company, 1992)

122 Black, Annette; RHyzer; and Dominikus, "Well of Santa Cristina," *Atlas Obscura*, https://www.atlasobscura.com/places/well-of-santa-cristina; Mingren, Wu, "Master Architects of Sardinia: The Sacred Well of Santa Cristina," *Ancient Origins*, January 9, 2011, https://www.ancient-origins.net/ancient-places-europe/well-santa-cristina-0014779; Marras, Chiara, "Santa Cristina

Well: A Mystery of Sardinia," May 25, 2019, https://ecobnb.com/blog/2019/05/santa-cristina-well/

123   Barone, Addam, "Top 4 Most Scandalous Insider Trading Debacles," *Investopedia*, 2019, https://www.investopedia.com/articles/stocks/09/insider-trading.asp

124   Gross, Daniel, "The Truth About Fannie—The real scandal of Fannie Mae," *Slate Business Podcast*, October 7, 2004, https://slate.com/business/2004/10/the-real-scandal-at-fannie-mae.html

125   Paulson, Henry, "Paulson announces conservatorship on Fannie and Freddie," *Hedge Fund Law Blog*, September 7, 2008, https://hedge-fundlawblog.com/tag/henry-paulson

126   Trumbull, Mark, "Subprime scandal: ex-Fannie Mae, Freddie Mac execs accused of fraud," *Christian Science Monitor*, 2011, https://www.csmonitor.com/USA/Justice/2011/1216/Subprime-scandal-ex-Fannie-Mae-Freddie-Mac-execs-accused-of-fraud

127   Segal, Troy, "Enron Scandal: The Fall of a Wall Street Darling," *Investopedia*, 2019, https://www.investopedia.com/updates/enron-scandal-summary/; Troy Segal, "5 Most Publicized Ethics Violations by CEOs," *Investopedia*, January 27, 2021, https://www.investopedia.com/financial-edge/0113/5-most-publicized-ethics-violations-by-ceos.aspx

128   Tucker, Eric and Balsamo, Michael, "Chinese Military Stole Info on Millions of Americans," *The Associated Press*, 2020, https://www.mercurynews.com/2020/02/10/charges-chinese-military-stole-info-on-millions-of-americans/

129   St. John, Allen, "Justice Department Charges Chinese Nationals with Equifax Data Breach," *Consumer Reports*, 2020, https://www.consumerreports.org/data-theft/justice-department-charges-chinese-nationals-in-equifax-data-breach-a6187489106/

130 Schnell, Lindsay, "Five major Catholic leaders taken down by the church sex abuse scandal," *USA Today*, February 26, 2019, https://www.bishop-accountability.org/2019/02/five-major-catholic-leaders-taken-down-by-the-church-sex-abuse-scandal/;   Schnell, Lindsay, "Five major Catholic leaders taken down by the church sex abuse scandal," *The Herald-Mail*, February 26, 2019, https://www.heraldmailmedia.com/story/news/2019/02/26/five-major-catholic-leaders-taken-down-by-the-church-sex-abuse-scandal/116460720/

131 James, Michael and Bacon, John, "'Men of God hid it all': Church protected more than 300 'predator priests' in Pa.," *USA Today*, 2018, https://www.usatoday.com/story/news/2018/08/14/grand-jury-report-pennsylvania-details-abuse-catholic-priests/980687002/

132 Capatides, Christina, "Catholic Church spent $10.6 million to lobby against legislation that would benefit victims of child sex abuse," *CBS NEWS*, 2019, https://www.cbsnews.com/news/catholic-church-scandal-spent-10-million-lobbyists-fight-extension-statutes-of-limitations-child-sex-abuse-vicims/

133 Schnell, Lindsay, "Five major Catholic leaders taken down by the church sex abuse scandal," *USA Today*, February 26, 2019, https://www.bishop-accountability.org/2019/02/five-major-catholic-leaders-taken-down-by-the-church-sex-abuse-scandal/;   Schnell, Lindsay, "Five major Catholic leaders taken down by the church sex abuse scandal," *The Herald-Mail*, February 26, 2019, https://www.heraldmailmedia.com/story/news/2019/02/26/five-major-catholic-leaders-taken-down-by-the-church-sex-abuse-scandal/116460720/

134 Condliffe, Jamie, "It Costs $30 to Make a DIY EpiPen, and Here's the Proof," *MIT Technical Review*, 2016, https://www.technologyreview.com/2016/09/20/157437/it-costs-30-to-make-a-diy-epipen-and-heres-the-proof/

135 Mangan, Dan, "Mylan CEO Heather Bresch says diversification is boosting company after EpiPen controversy," *CNBC Power Lunch Exclusive*, 2017, https://www.cnbc.com/2017/03/03/mylan-ceo-heather-bresch-discusses-epipen-controversy.html

136 "Mylan CEO on EpiPen Drug Price Controversy: 'I Get the Outrage,'" *CBS News*, produced by Ryan Kadro, January 27, 2016, https://www.cbsnews.com/news/epipen-price-hike-controversy-mylan-ceo-heather-bresch-speaks-out/; Weintraub, Arlene, "Mylan CEO Bresch Admits 'Full Responsibility' For EpiPen Price Hikes," *Forbes*, December 1, 2016, https://www.forbes.com/sites/arlene-weintraub/2016/12/01/mylan-ceo-bresch-admits-full-responsi-bility-for-epipen-price-hikes/?sh=763ac604393c

137 Egan, Matt, "EpiPen maker faces revolt over exec's $98 million pay package," *CNN Business*, 2017, https://money.cnn.com/2017/06/13/investing/epipen-mylan-exec-pay-shareholder-revolt/index.html

138 Sutton, Antony, *America's Secret Establishment: An Introduction to the Order of Skull and Bones* (TrineDay LLC, 1983, 1986, 2002); Millegan, Kris , *Fleshing out Skull and Bones* (TrineDay LLC, 2003, 2008, 2011)

139 "Secrets of 'The Lost Symbol,' Inside Dan Brown's thriller," *Dateline NBC*. Episode 1, by Matt Lauer, produced by Ayala, Leonor, et al., aired October 16, 2009 on NBC, https://www.nbcnews.com/id/wbna33280724

140 Estulin, Daniel, *The True Story of the Bilderberg Group* (TrineDay LLC), February 14, 2009; "The True Story Of The BILDERBERG GROUP," YouTube video, posted by "Alux.com," December 23, 2019, https://youtu.be/OF5xL63PyfA

141 Lendman, Stephen, "A Global Research Review of Daniel Estulin's book," *Liberty International*, 2009, https://libertyinternational.

wordpress.com/2020/03/03/the-true-story-of-the-bilderberg-group-and-what-they-may-be-planning-now-a-review-of-daniel-estulins-book-global-research/; Lendman, Stephen, *The True Story Of The Bilderberg Group And What They May Be Planning Now—A Review of Daniel Estulin's book* (May 29, 2017), https://themillenniumreport.com/2017/05/the-true-story-of-the-bilderberg-group/

142   Adler, Margret, *Drawing Down the Moon: Witches, Druids, Goddess-Worshippers, and Other Pagans in America Today* (Penguin Books, 1979), https://archive.org/details/drawingdownmoonw0000adle

143   Howe, Richard, "Modern Witchcraft: It May Not Be What You Think," *Christian Research Institute* (2009), Article ID: JAW188, https://www.equip.org/article/modern-witchcraft/, https://www.equip.org/PDF/JAW188.pdf

144   Carter, Joe, "9 Things You Should Know About Wicca And Modern Witchcraft," *The Gospel Coalition: Current Events*, May 22, 2018, https://www.thegospelcoalition.org/article/9-things-you-should-know-about-wicca-and-modern-witchcraft/

145   Ibid.

146   Morris, Jill Marie, The Sublime & Supernatural podcast, "The Basics of Demonic Oppression & Possession" (2015); Morris, Jill Marie, "Blocking Spiritual Protection," April 19, 2017

147   Erndl, Kathleen, "DEVI: The Goddesses of India" (Aleph Book Company, 2017), https://www.thefreelibrary.com/Devi%3a+Goddesses+of+India.-a054772495

148   Alexander-Christian, Laurie, "Exposing Satanic World Government—Demonic Possession And Slenderman," *Global Watchman News*, June 5, 2014, https://lauriechristian2012.wordpress.com/2014/06/06/demonic-possession-and-slenderman/

149   Howe, Richard, *Modern Witchcraft: It May Not Be What You Think*, Christian Research Institute, Article ID: JAW188 (2009), https://www.equip.org/article/modern-witchcraft/; https://www.equip.org/PDF/JAW188.pdf

150   Fargas, *Treatise on Satanic Worship and Ritual Practice—Volume 1*, (Lulu) Second Edition 2011, https://www.scribd.com/document/241337810/FvFargas-Treatise-on-Satanic-Worship-and-Ritual-Practice-Vol-I

151   Statham, Dominic, "Tools of Satan?," *Creation Ministries International*, 2013, https://chinese.creation.com/Tools-Satan

152   Chain, Ernst Boris, "Social Responsibility and The Scientist in Modern Western Society," (Council of Christians And Jews, Spring 1971); Chain, Ernst Boris, "Social Responsibility and The Scientist in Modern Western Society—A few words on Chain's Waley Cohen Lecture," *Semantic Scholar* (January 7, 2015), https://www.semanticscholar.org/paper/Social-Responsibility-and-the-Scientist-in-Modern-Chain/41dffd6b098809d8d5f247dd766ef466f90ae84f

153   Beyer, Catherine, "Facts and Fallacies of 'Human Sacrifice' in LaVeyan Satanism," *Learn Religions*, 2018, https://www.learnreligions.com/human-sacrifice-facts-in-laveyan-satanism-95977

154   Lavey, Anton Szandor, *The Satanic Bible* (pp. 87-89), Published by Anton Lavey (1969)

155   Wikipedia, "Dahomey," https://en.wikipedia.org/wiki/Dahomey

156   Beyer, Catherine, "An Introduction to the Basic Beliefs of the Vodou (Voodoo) Religion," *Learn Religions*, updated May 2, 2018, https://www.learnreligions.com/vodou-an-introduction-for-beginners-95712

157   Ibid.

158   Ibid.

159 Tarantola, Andrew, "World's Tallest Mobile Crane Is Also World's Strongest," *GIZMODO: Monster Machines,* July 19, 2011, https://www.gizmodo.com.au/2011/07/worlds-tallest-mobile-crane-is-also-worlds-strongest/

160 Holloway, April, "Do the ancient stone walls of Saksaywaman in Peru contain hidden communication?," *Ancient Origins,* updated April 7, 2014, https://www.ancient-origins.net/news-history-archaeology/do-ancient-stone-walls-saksaywaman-peru-contain-hidden-communication-001536

161 See also Judges 6:28 and 2 Chronicles 23:17, 34:4.

162 See also 1 Kings 16:32 and 2 Chronicles 33:3.

163 Exodus 22:20, 34:13, Numbers 33:50-53, and Deuteronomy 7:1-6, 12:1-3, 13:15-16, 20:17.

164 See Joshua 6:21, 8:26, 10:28-40, and 12:7-24.

165 Romey, Kristin, "Exclusive: This could be the world's largest ancient mass child sacrifice," *National Geographic,* April 26, 2018; Ansede, Manuel, "The Incas sacrificed their children as a military strategy," *Materia,* July 29, 2013; Romey, Kristin, "This could be the world's largest ancient mass child sacrifice," *National Geographic,* April 2018

166 Wikipedia, "Human sacrifice in pre-Columbian cultures," https://en.wikipedia.org/wiki/Human_sacrifice_in_pre-Columbian_cultures

167 McEwan, Gordon, *The Incas: New Perspectives* (W. W. Norton & Company, 2008)

168 Childress, David Hatcher, *Ancient Technology in Peru & Bolivia* (Adventures Unlimited Press), November 15, 2012

169 Leon, Pedro de Cieza, *The Discovery and Conquest of Peru (Chronicles of the New World Encounter),* Kindle Edition. Cook, David Noble (Translator), Cook, Alexandra Parma (Translator), (Duke University Press Books, February 11, 1999)

170   Leon, *The Discovery and Conquest of Peru, Chronicles of the New World Encounter*, edited and translated by Cook and Cook (Duke University Press, Durham, 1998); Wikipedia, "Sacsayhuamán," https://en.wikipedia.org/wiki/Sacsayhuamán

171   Wikipedia, "Nan_Madol," https://en.wikipedia.org/wiki/Nan_Madol

172   Wikipedia, "Moai," https://en.wikipedia.org/wiki/Moai

173   Cartwright, Mark, *Ancient History Encyclopedia*, "Teotihuacan," February 17, 2015, https://www.worldhistory.org/Teotihuacan/

174   Shaer, Matthew, "A Secret Tunnel Found in Mexico May Finally Solve the Mysteries of Teotihuacan," *Smithsonian Magazine*, June 2016, https://www.smithsonianmag.com/history/discovery-secret-tunnel-mexico-solve-mysteries-teotihuacan-180959070/

175   Ancient Code Team, "Sacred Alignment: The Constellation of Orion and Ancient Egypt," *Ancient Code*, 2022, https://www.ancient-code.com/sacred-allignment-the-constellation-of-orion-and-ancient-egypt/; Justin (staff writer), "Secrets of the Ancients: Sacred Alignment and the Constellation of Orion," *Stillness in the Storm* (February 16, 2020), https://stillnessinthestorm.com/2020/02/secrets-of-the-ancients-sacred-alignment-and-the-constellation-of-orion/

176   Barbezat, Suzanne, "Maya Culture and Civilization," *ThoughtCo*, January 17, 2019, https://www.thoughtco.com/maya-culture-and-civilization-1588857

177   Minster, Christopher, "The Ancient Maya and Human Sacrifice," *ThoughtCo*, July 14, 2019, https://www.thoughtco.com/the-ancient-maya-and-human-sacrifice-2136173

178   Cartwright, Mark, *Ancient History Encyclopedia*, "Teotihuacan," February 17, 2015, https://www.worldhistory.org/Teotihuacan/

179 Black, Jeremy and Green, Anthony, *Gods, Demons and Symbols of Ancient Mesopotamia: An Illustrated Dictionary* (University of Texas Press, May 1, 1992)

180 Rogers, John, "Origins of the Ancient Astronomical Constellations: The Mesopotamian Traditions," *Journal of the British Astronomical Association* vol.108, pp.9-28, February 1998, https://adsabs.harvard. edu/full/1998JBAA..108....9R;   https://ui.adsabs.harvard.edu/ abs/1998JBAA..108....9R/abstract; Rogers, John, "Origins of the Ancient Constellations: II. The Mediterranean Traditions," *Journal of the British Astronomical Association*, vol.108, no.2, p.79-89 (April 1998), https://ui.adsabs.harvard.edu/abs/1998JBAA..108...79R/ abstract#:~:text=The%20classical%20map%20of%20the%20 sky%2C%20with%20the,in%20Mesopotamia%20in%20a%20 religious%20or%20ritual%20tradition

181 Black, Jeremy and Green, Anthony, *Gods, Demons and Symbols of Ancient Mesopotamia: An Illustrated Dictionary* (University of Texas Press, May 1, 1992)

182 "The Beginning: Those Who From Heaven Came Down To Earth," posted by "Seeker of Knowledge," November 2, 2020, https:// rebirthoftheword.com/those-who-from-heaven-came-down-to-earth/,   https://www.bing.com/videos/search?q=Anunnaki+defi ned+as+those+who+from+heaven+to+earth+came&docid=6 08039946340543487&mid=3DE3088451F0B94D8D6F3DE 3088451F0B94D8D6F&view=detail&FORM=VIRE;   "Sume-rian Anunnaki—reveals alien past," *Unexplained Mysteries,* January 12, 2013, https://coolinterestingstuff.com/sumerian-anunnaki-reveals-alien-past#:~:text=Ancient%20Sumerian%20texts%20 define%20the%20Anunnaki%20as%20"those,extracted%20 from%20the%20Sumerian%20Epic%20of%20Creation%20 %28~6000-8500BC%29

183 Barton, David Watts, "Amaterasu and the Gods of Ancient Japan," *Japanology*, January 24, 2017, https://japanology.org/2017/01/amaterasu-and-the-gods-of-ancient-japan/

184 Ellwood, Robert, "Harvest and Renewal at the Grand Shrine of Ise," JSTOR Journal Article, Vol. 15, Fasc. 3 (Brill, November 1968); Barton, David Watts, "The Grand Shrine At Ise," *Japanology*, April 5, 2017, https://japanology.org/2017/04/the-grand-shrine-at-ise/

185 Callaway, *The Religious System of the Amazulu PART I, UNKU-LUNKULU; OR The Tradition as Existing Among Amazulu and Other Tribes of South Africa, In Their Own Words with A Translation into English and Notes* (Davis and Sons, Juta, and Trubner and Co., 1868), https://books.google.com/books?id=x3yOVtckoJIC&printsec=frontcover&source=gbs_ge_summary_r&cad=0#v=onepage&q&f=false, https://sacred-texts.com/afr/rsa/rsa01.htm

186 Baglin, Douglas and Mullins, Barbara, *Aboriginal Art of Australia* (Shepp Books, January 1, 1988)

187 Author: Walker, Bill; Contributors: Popp, Tom, and Popp, N., *Footprints on Rock* (Metropolitan Local Aboriginal Land Council, Redfern, NSW, 1997)

188 Rothschild, Mike, "Secret Technologies Invented by The Nazis," *Ranker,* May 18, 2020, https://www.ranker.com/list/secret-technologies-invented-by-nazis/mike-rothschild

189 Ibid.

190 Ibid.

191 Ibid.

192 Ibid.

193 Ibid.

194 Ibid.

195-201 *In Search of History—Hitler and The Occult* (History Channel Documentary), A&E, aired 8/30/18, released on DVD 08/19/21; "In Search Of History – Hitler And The Occult (History Channel Documentary)," YouTube video, posted by "Peter David," August 30, 2018, https://youtu.be/SAq3bJUOkGE

202 Salla, Michael, "Bob Lazar, Element 115, Massive Stars & Heavy Metals," *Science & Technology*, February 16, 2019, https://exonews.org/bob-lazar-element-115-massive-stars-heavy-metals/; https://exopolitics.org/bob-lazar-element-115-massive-stars-and-heavy-metals-repost/

203 Wikipedia, "Moscovium," https://en.wikipedia.org/wiki/Moscovium

204 "Element 115," *Ancient Aliens*, History Channel, season 14, episode 3, producer Kevin Burns, aired June 21, 2019, https://www.history.com/shows/ancient-aliens/season-14/episode-80

205, 206 "Congressional Citizen Hearings on UFO Disclosure," YouTube video, posted by "Citizen Hearing on UFO Disclosure," September 3, 2021, https://youtu.be/AdPBanWpQco (Hearings held April 2013); "UFOs – Nuclear Tampering / Part 1," YouTube video, posted by "Citizen Hearing on UFO Disclosure," June 4, 2021, https://youtu.be/UDu3FlK-mI0; "Citizen Hearing On UFO Disclosure (UFOs History Background Part 2) HD 1080p," YouTube video, posted by "ARTISTS FOR DISCLOSURE," May 4, 2021, https://youtu.be/YFvgWdCyTBY; "Steven Greer: Citizen Hearing On Disclosure 2013 HD," posted by "ADGUKNEWS," May 4, 2013, https://youtu.be/SgKMgJKLB5s

207 Friedman also suggested reading *The UFO Experience – A Scientific Inquiry* by Dr. J. Allen Hynek. Chairman of the Astronomy Department at North-Western University; Dr. Hynek had been United States Air Force Consultant to Project Blue Book.

208 Internet Archive Python library 0.9.8, Project Blue Book (January 15, 2016), https://archive.org/details/project-blue-book?&sort=-week&page=2 "Project BLUE BOOK—Unidentified Flying Objects," National Archives: Military Records, September 29, 2020, https://www.archives.gov/research/military/air-force/ufos; MacDonald, David, Director of the Cincinnati-based Mutual UFO Network, MUFON Mutual UFO Network (website) established in 1969, https://mufon.com/ufo-news/; Sheets, Megan, "Declassified report from the CIA's bombshell UFO dossier reveals the meeting where top military officials launched 16-year Project Blue Book study of 'flying saucers' in 1952," *Daily Mail*, January 3, 2021, https://www.dailymail.co.uk/news/article-9142891/Unsealed-CIA-reports-UFOs-reveal-1952-meeting-Project-Blue-Book.html

209 Ciaccia, Chris, "Harry Reid wants hearings on what the military knows about UFOs: 'They would be surprised how the American public would accept it,'" Fox News, June 14, 2019, https://www.foxnews.com/science/harry-reid-hearings-military-ufos

210 Halaschak, Zachary, "'The American people deserve to be informed' Harry Reid says UFO footage 'only scratches the surface,'" *Washington Examiner*, May 21, 2022, https://www.washingtonexaminer.com/news/the-american-people-deserve-to-be-informed-harry-reid-says-ufo-footage-only-scratches-the-surface; Senator Harry Reid, Twitter post, April 27, 2020, 2:16 PM, https://twitter.com/SenatorReid/status/1254836730546384897

211 Phelan, Matthew, "Navy Pilot Who Filmed the 'Tic Tac' UFO Speaks: 'It Wasn't Behaving by the Normal Laws of Physics,'" *New York Intelligencer*, December 19, 2019, https://nymag.com/intelligencer/2019/12/tic-tac-ufo-video-q-and-a-with-navy-pilot-chad-underwood.html

212 "Ancient Aircraft and Atomic War in India," An Ancient Astronaut Archive Production, April 2, 2019, https://ancientastronautarchive.com/2019/04/ancient-aircraft-and-atomic-war-in-india/;

"Flying Machines in Ancient India? The Vedic Vimanas," *Ashtronort*, November 22, 2013, https://ashtronort.wordpress.com/2013/11/22/flying-machines-in-indias-ancient-past/

213 "The Hindu Texts Describe Flying Vimanas And Details Of An Ancient Nuclear War," *Gaia*, October 8, 2021, https://www.gaia.com/article/do-hindu-texts-describing-the-flying-vimanas-also-detail-a-nuclear-war; Baccarini, Enrico and Shāstra, Vaimānika, "Vimanas in Sanskrit Literature," *Vaimanika*, November 3, 2012, https://vaimanika.com/vimanas-in-sanskrit-literature/

214 "Ancient Aircraft and Atomic War in India," An Ancient Astronaut Archive Production, April 2, 2019, https://ancientastronautarchive.com/2019/04/ancient-aircraft-and-atomic-war-in-india/; "Flying Machines in Ancient India? The Vedic Vimanas," *Ashtronort*, November 22, 2013, https://ashtronort.wordpress.com/2013/11/22/flying-machines-in-indias-ancient-past/

215 Whitaker, Phil, "Ancient Indian Flying Saucers," *Exemplore*, April 23, 2020, https://exemplore.com/advanced-ancients/Ancient-Indian-Flying-Saucers; Garcia, Ava, "What Made The Vimana Fly—the Ancient Indian Flying Machine," *The True Defender*, July 11, 2021, https://thetruedefender.com/what-made-the-vimana-fly-the-ancient-indian-flying-machine/

216 "Voices of the Gods," *Ancient Aliens*, History Channel, season 12, episode 11, July 21, 2017, https://www.history.com/shows/ancient-aliens/season-12/episode-11; "Ancient Aliens—Voices of the Gods," October 11, 2020, https://hdclump.com/ancient-aliens-voices-of-the-gods/

217 Fitzpatrick, Colette, "The City of Turin And Its Magical Past," October 23, 2015, https://www.italy-villas.com/to-italy/2015/tourist-attractions/legends/turin-and-magic

218-220 Ryan, Shane, *WESTALL '66 A Suburban UFO Mystery*, Screen Australia Documentary: Endangered Pictures Production presented in association with Fil Victoria, 2010; "UFO

Encounter at Australia High School (Full Documentary)," You-Tube video, posted by "Charan Oblate," 2014, https://youtu.be/5aZPK_6Y1OM; Swancer, Brent, "A Mass UFO Sighting at an Australian High School," *Mysterious Universe*, May 5, 2020, https://mysteriousuniverse.org/2020/05/a-mass-ufo-sighting-at-an-australian-high-school/

221, 222 "Exclusive Interview: Jim Penniston Rendlesham Forest UFO Incident," YouTube video, posted by "Eric Mintel Investigates," October 9, 2019, https://youtu.be/rSquWTS1teM "EXCLUSIVE: new interview with military witness to Rendlesham Forest UFO incidents—Michael Stacy Smith's story," *The Debate*, July 24, 2019, https://thedebate.org/2019/07/24/exclusive-new-interview-with-a-rendlesham-forest-ufo-witness/; Luciano, Joe, "How the Rendlesham Forest Incident binary code message was received, revealed and decoded," *The Rendlesham Forest Incident Official Blog*, April 2022, https://www.therendleshamforestincident.com/2022/04/2010-it-was-revealed-by-jim-penniston.html

223 "Exclusive Interview: Jim Penniston Rendlesham Forest UFO Incident," YouTube video, posted by "Eric Mintel Investigates," October 9, 2019, https://youtu.be/rSquWTS1teM

224 "Britain's X-Files," *UFO Files*, History Channel, season 2, episode 3, aired May 4, 2017, (first aired 2005), https://www.bing.com/videos/search?q=History+Channel%3a+UFO+Files+-+Britain's+X-Files%2c+2012&docid=608002292343785414&mid=091293E610A9ADEEAE39091293E610A9ADEEAE39&view=detail&FORM=VIRE

225 Salla, Michael, "The Admiral Wilson Leaked UFO Document & Corporate Reverse Engineering of Alien Technology," *ExoPolitics.org*, June 15, 2019

PART 1:
https://exopolitics.org/bombshell-document-confirms-navy-admiral-was-denied-access-to-ufo-crash-retrieval-program/;

PART 2:
https://exopolitics.org/navy-admiral-describes-reverse-engineering-program-involving-extraterrestrial-spacecraft/;

PART 3:
https://exonews.org/the-admiral-wilson-leaked-ufo-document-corporate-reverse-engineering-of-alien-technology/

226 Wikipedia, "Cyrus the Great in the Bible," https://en.wikipedia.org/wiki/Cyrus_the_Great_in_the_Bible

227 Hunt, Dave, "Israel, Islam And Armageddon," *The Berean Call, A Ministry of Biblical Discernment*, May 24, 2021, https://www.thebereancall.org/content/israel-islam-and-armageddon-2

228 Halsall, Paul, "Pope Urban II's Speech Calling for the First Crusade," *Christian Broadcast Network* (CBN), December 1997, https://www1.cbn.com/spirituallife/calling-for-the-first-crusade; CFT Team, *"Pope Urban II's 1095 Speech Reveals That Christian Crusaders Were Engaged in a Race War,"* Christians For Truth, November 18, 2018, https://christiansfortruth.com/pope-urban-iis-1095-speech-reveals-that-the-crusaders-were-engaged-in-a-race-war/

229 Hunt, Dave, "O JERUSALEM, JERUSALEM!," *The Berean Call: A Ministry of Biblical Discernment*, September 1, 2000, https://www.thebereancall.org/content/o-jerusalem-jerusalem

230 Ibid.

231 Ibid.

232 US Embassy Beirut, US Embassy in Lebanon, *Abraham Accords Peace Agreement: Treaty of Peace, Diplomatic Relations and*

Full Normalization Between the United Arab Emirates and the State of Israel, September 15, 2020 https://lb.usembassy.gov/abraham-accords-peace-agreement/, https://www.state.gov/wp-content/uploads/2020/09/UAE_Israel-treaty-signed-FINAL-15-Sept-2020-508.pdf#:~:text=The%20Parties%20undertake%20to%20foster%20mutual%20understanding%2C%20respect%2C,youth%2C%20scientific%2C%20and%20other%20exchanges%20between%20their%20peoples

233 Ibid.

234 Haverluck, Michael, "Tens of thousands of Jews returning to Israel," *The Clarion Sound,* 2018, https://www.theclarionsound.com/in-the-news/tens-of-thousands-of-jews-returning-to-israel/ "Tens of thousands of Jews returning to Israel," *End Time Ministries,* April 16, 2018, https://www.endtime.com/prophecy-news/tens-thousands-jews-returning-israel/

235 Price, Randall, "In Search of Temple Treasures," World of the Bible Productions (Harvest House Publishers, October 1, 1994), https://www.worldofthebible.com

236 Ibid.

237 Ibid.

238 Ibid.

239-241 Goren, "The Six-Day War: The Liberation of the Temple Mount and Western Wall," *Jewish Virtual Library,* June 7 1967, https://www.jewishvirtuallibrary.org/the-liberation-of-the-temple-mount-and-western-wall-june-1967, Committee for Accuracy in Middle East Reporting in America (CAMERA): 1967; "1967: Reunification of Jerusalem," *Committee for Accuracy in Middle East Reporting in America,* 2022, http://www.sixdaywar.org/content/ReunificationJerusalem.asp#:~:text=There%20are%20sound%20recordings%20of%20the%20scene%2C%20

as,of%20Jerusalem%2C%20that%20all%20generations%20
have%20dreamed%20about.

242 Beaumont, Peter, "Jewish organization opens religious school
in Palestinian East Jerusalem," *The Guardian*, April 17, 2014,
https://www.theguardian.com/world/2014/apr/17/jewish-east-
jerusalem-ateret-cohanim-yeshiva-palestine

243 Wikipedia, "The Temple Institute," https://en.wikipedia.org/wiki/
The_Temple_Institute; https://templeinstitute.org; Berkowitz,
Adam Eliyahu, *"JERUSALEM PROPHECY OF 'HOUSE OF
PRAYER FOR ALL PEOPLES' FULFILLED WITH MULTI-
FAITH PRAYER,"* ISRAEL365 *News*, May 11, 2016, https://
www.israel365news.com/67469/multi-faith-prayer-fulfills-jerusa-
lems-biblical-destiny-house-prayer-nations-photos/

244 "Rabbi Moses Maimonides (Rambam)," *Jewish Roots*, 2022, http://
jewishroots.net/library/miscellaneous/maimonides.html;   "Red
Heifer—The Red Heifer Sacrifice," *Jewish Roots*, 2022, http://
jewishroots.net/library/end-times/red-heifer.html; "Maimonides,"
Stanford Encyclopedia of Philosophy (Stanford Department of
Philosophy in February 4, 2021), https://plato.stanford.edu/
entries/maimonides/; Berkowitz, Adam Eliyahu, "RED HEIFER
BIRTH, PAVES WAY FOR RENEWED TEMPLE SER-
VICE," ISRAEL365 *News*, September 5, 2018, https://www.israel-
365news.com/113476/temple-institute-certifies-red-heifer/

245 Wikipedia, "The Temple Institute," https://en.wikipedia.org/wiki/
The_Temple_Institute

246, 247 Ariel, Yisrael, "The Oral Tradition: Shedding Light on the
Secrets of the Bible," *Temple Institute*, 2020, https://templein-
stitute.org/red-heifer-the-oral-tradition-shedding-light-on-
the-secrets-of-the-bible/; Ariel, Yisrael, "The Mystery of the
Red Heifer: Divine Promise of Purity," *Temple Institute*, 2020,
https://templeinstitute.org/red-heifer/

248 "The Temple Mount Faithful Movement Held the Most Exciting Event in Israel on "Jerusalem Day" Since the Destruction of the Holy Temple in 70 CE," May 21, 2009, https://templemount-faithful.org/events/jerusalemDay2009-2.php; Salomon, Gershon, "Thirteen Ton Temple Corner Stone to be Presented to the People of Israel," May 16, 2009, https://shamar.org/weblog/thirteen_ton_temple_corner_stone.html

249 "Life SiteNews: 'President Trump will 'lead America back to God,'" YouTube video, posted by "The John-Henry Westen Show," June 30, 2020, https://youtu.be/ZmQOfndQ-Oc

250 Cinedigm Entertainment Corporation DVD: *The Trump Prophecy* (2018); Wikipedia, "The Trump Prophecy," https://en.wikipedia.org/wiki/The_Trump_Prophecy; Brown, Michael, "The Trump reelection prophecy that you never heard about," *The Christian Post*, May 8, 2021, https://www.christianpost.com/voices/the-trump-reelection-prophecy-that-you-never-heard-about.html

251 Sommer, Will, "Politics: God Gave Us Donald, 'Firefighter Prophet' Says in Film," *The Daily Beast*, October 6, 2018, https://www.thedaily-beast.com/god-gave-us-the-donald-firefighter-prophet-says-in-film

252 Evans, Mike, "Donald Trump: Good for Israel," *The Jerusalem Post*, June 23, 2019, https://www.jpost.com/Opinion/Donald-Trump-Good-for-Israel-593416; Evans, Mike, "Israel's Greatest Friend Sits in the White House," *The Jerusalem Post*, (May 29, 2019), https://www.jpost.com/Opinion/Israels-greatest-friend-sits-in-the-White-House-591063